D1074052

(

COLLECTED POEMS

OF

THOMAS HARDY

New York

THE MACMILLAN COMPANY

1926

Printed in the United States of America
By The Cornwall Press

PREFACE

OF the miscellaneous collection of verse that follows, only four pieces have been published, though many were written long ago, and others partly written. In some few cases the verses were turned into prose and printed as such, it having been unanticipated at that time that they might see the light.

Whenever an ancient and legitimate word of the district, for which there was no equivalent in received English, suggested itself as the most natural, nearest, and often only expression of a thought, it has been made use of, on what seemed good grounds.

The pieces are in a large degree dramatic or personative in conception ; and this even where they are not obviously so.

The dates attached to some of the poems do not apply to the rough sketches given in illustration,[1] which have been recently made, and, as may be surmised, are inserted for personal and local reasons rather than for their intrinsic qualities.

T. H.

[1] The early editions were illustrated by the writer.

September 1898.

CONTENTS

WESSEX POEMS AND OTHER VERSES

	PAGE
PREFACE	3
THE TEMPORARY THE ALL	5
AMABEL	6
HAP	7
"IN VISION I ROAMED"	7
AT A BRIDAL	8
POSTPONEMENT	8
A CONFESSION TO A FRIEND IN TROUBLE	9
NEUTRAL TONES	9
SHE	10
HER INITIALS	10
HER DILEMMA	10
REVULSION	11
SHE, TO HIM, I.	11
" " II.	12
" " III.	12
" " IV.	13
DITTY	13
THE SERGEANT'S SONG	15
VALENCIENNES	15
SAN SEBASTIAN	17
THE STRANGER'S SONG	19
THE BURGHERS	20
LEIPZIG	22
THE PEASANT'S CONFESSION	26

		PAGE
THE ALARM		30
HER DEATH AND AFTER		34
THE DANCE AT THE PHŒNIX		38
THE CASTERBRIDGE CAPTAINS . . .		42
A SIGN-SEEKER		43
MY CICELY		45
HER IMMORTALITY		48
THE IVY-WIFE		50
A MEETING WITH DESPAIR		51
UNKNOWING		51
FRIENDS BEYOND		52
TO OUTER NATURE		54
THOUGHTS OF PHENA		55
MIDDLE-AGE ENTHUSIASMS		55
IN A WOOD		56
TO A LADY		57
TO A MOTHERLESS CHILD		58
NATURE'S QUESTIONING		58
THE IMPERCIPIENT		59
AT AN INN		60
THE SLOW NATURE		61
IN A EWELEAZE NEAR WEATHERBURY . .		62
THE BRIDE-NIGHT FIRE		63
HEIRESS AND ARCHITECT		67
THE TWO MEN		68
LINES		71
"I LOOK INTO MY GLASS"		72

POEMS OF THE PAST AND THE PRESENT

PREFACE		75
V.R. 1819–1901		77

WAR POEMS—

EMBARCATION		78
DEPARTURE		78
THE COLONEL'S SOLILOQUY . . .		79
THE GOING OF THE BATTERY . .		80

CONTENTS

	PAGE
AT THE WAR OFFICE	82
A CHRISTMAS GHOST-STORY	82
DRUMMER HODGE	83
A WIFE IN LONDON	83
THE SOULS OF THE SLAIN	84
SONG OF THE SOLDIERS' WIVES AND SWEETHEARTS	87
THE SICK BATTLE-GOD	88

POEMS OF PILGRIMAGE—

GENOA AND THE MEDITERRANEAN	91
SHELLEY'S SKYLARK	92
IN THE OLD THEATRE, FIESOLE	92
ROME: ON THE PALATINE	93
,, BUILDING A NEW STREET IN THE ANCIENT QUARTER	93
,, THE VATICAN: SALA DELLE MUSE	94
,, AT THE PYRAMID OF CESTIUS: NEAR THE GRAVES OF SHELLEY AND KEATS	95
LAUSANNE: IN GIBBON'S OLD GARDEN	96
ZERMATT: TO THE MATTERHORN	96
THE BRIDGE OF LODI	97
ON AN INVITATION TO THE UNITED STATES	99

MISCELLANEOUS POEMS—

THE MOTHER MOURNS	101
"I SAID TO LOVE"	103
A COMMONPLACE DAY	104
AT A LUNAR ECLIPSE	105
THE LACKING SENSE	106
TO LIFE	107
DOOM AND SHE	108
THE PROBLEM	109
THE SUBALTERNS	110
THE SLEEP-WORKER	110
THE BULLFINCHES	111
GOD-FORGOTTEN	112
THE BEDRIDDEN PEASANT TO AN UNKNOWN GOD	113
BY THE EARTH'S CORPSE	114
MUTE OPINION	115

	PAGE
To an Unborn Pauper Child	116
To Flowers from Italy in Winter	117
On a Fine Morning	118
To Lizbie Browne	118
Song of Hope	120
The Well-Beloved	121
Her Reproach	123
The Inconsistent	123
A Broken Appointment	124
"Between us now"	124
"How Great my Grief"	125
"I need not go"	125
The Coquette, and after	126
A Spot	127
Long plighted	128
The Widow betrothed	128
At a Hasty Wedding	130
The Dream-Follower	130
His Immortality	130
The To-be-Forgotten	131
Wives in the Sere	132
The Superseded	133
An August Midnight	134
The Caged Thrush freed and Home again	134
Birds at Winter Nightfall	135
The Puzzled Game-Birds	135
Winter in Durnover Field	136
The Last Chrysanthemum	136
The Darkling Thrush	137
The Comet at Yalbury or Yell'ham	138
Mad Judy	138
A Wasted Illness	139
A Man	140
The Dame of Athelhall	141
The Seasons of her Year	143
The Milkmaid	143
The Levelled Churchyard	144
The Ruined Maid	145

CONTENTS

PAGE

THE RESPECTABLE BURGHER ON "THE HIGHER CRITICISM"   146

ARCHITECTURAL MASKS   147

THE TENANT-FOR-LIFE   147

THE KING'S EXPERIMENT   148

THE TREE: AN OLD MAN'S STORY .   .   149

HER LATE HUSBAND   151

THE SELF-UNSEEING   152

IN TENEBRIS I.   153

    ,,   ,,   II.   154

    ,,   ,,   III. .   .   .   155

THE CHURCH-BUILDER   156

THE LOST PYX: A MEDIÆVAL LEGEND .   .   158

TESS'S LAMENT   161

THE SUPPLANTER: A TALE .   .   .   162

IMITATIONS, ETC.—

SAPPHIC FRAGMENT   166

CATULLUS: XXXI   166

AFTER SCHILLER   167

SONG FROM HEINE   167

FROM VICTOR HUGO   167

CARDINAL BEMBO'S EPITAPH ON RAPHAEL .   168

RETROSPECT—

"I HAVE LIVED WITH SHADES" .   .   .   169

MEMORY AND I   170

ΑΓΝΩΣΤΩι ΘΕΩι   171

TIME'S LAUGHINGSTOCKS AND OTHER VERSES

TIME'S LAUGHINGSTOCKS—

PREFACE   175

THE REVISITATION   177

A TRAMPWOMAN'S TRAGEDY .   .   182

THE TWO ROSALINDS   185

A SUNDAY MORNING TRAGEDY .   .   188

PAGE

THE HOUSE OF HOSPITALITIES . . . 192

BEREFT 192

JOHN AND JANE 193

THE CURATE'S KINDNESS . . . 194

THE FLIRT'S TRAGEDY . . . 195

THE REJECTED MEMBER'S WIFE . . 199

THE FARM-WOMAN'S WINTER . . . 199

AUTUMN IN KING'S HINTOCK PARK . . 200

SHUT OUT THAT MOON 201

REMINISCENCES OF A DANCING MAN . . 201

THE DEAD MAN WALKING 202

MORE LOVE LYRICS—

1967 204

HER DEFINITION 204

THE DIVISION 205

ON THE DEPARTURE PLATFORM . . 205

IN A CATHEDRAL CITY . . . 206

"I SAY I'LL SEEK HER" . . . 207

HER FATHER 207

AT WAKING 208

FOUR FOOTPRINTS 209

IN THE VAULTED WAY 210

THE PHANTOM 210

THE END OF THE EPISODE . . . 211

THE SIGH 211

"IN THE NIGHT SHE CAME" . . . 212

THE CONFORMERS 213

THE DAWN AFTER THE DANCE . . . 214

THE SUN ON THE LETTER . . . 215

THE NIGHT OF THE DANCE . . . 215

MISCONCEPTION 216

THE VOICE OF THE THORN . . . 216

FROM HER IN THE COUNTRY . . 217

HER CONFESSION 218

TO AN IMPERSONATOR OF ROSALIND . 218

TO AN ACTRESS 219

CONTENTS

	PAGE
THE MINUTE BEFORE MEETING	219
HE ABJURES LOVE	220

A SET OF COUNTRY SONGS—

LET ME ENJOY	222
AT CASTERBRIDGE FAIR :	
I. The Ballad Singer . . .	223
II. Former Beauties . . .	223
III. After the Club Dance . .	224
IV. The Market-Girl . . .	224
V. The Inquiry . . .	224
VI. A Wife waits . . .	225
VII. After the Fair . . .	226
THE DARK-EYED GENTLEMAN . . .	227
TO CARREY CLAVEL	227
THE ORPHANED OLD MAID . . .	228
THE SPRING CALL	228
JULIE-JANE	229
NEWS FOR HER MOTHER . . .	230
THE FIDDLER	231
THE HUSBAND'S VIEW	232
ROSE-ANN	233
THE HOMECOMING	234

PIECES OCCASIONAL AND VARIOUS—

A CHURCH ROMANCE	236
THE RASH BRIDE	236
THE DEAD QUIRE	240
THE CHRISTENING	244
A DREAM QUESTION	245
BY THE BARROWS	246
A WIFE AND ANOTHER . . .	246
THE ROMAN ROAD	248
THE VAMPIRINE FAIR	249
THE REMINDER	252
THE RAMBLER	252
NIGHT IN THE OLD HOME . . .	253

                                                    PAGE
After the Last Breath   253
In Childbed   254
The Pine Planters.   255
The Dear   257
One we knew   257
She hears the Storm   258
A Wet Night   259
Before Life and after   .   .   .   260
New Year's Eve   260
God's Education   261
To Sincerity   262
Panthera   262
The Unborn   268
The Man he killed   269
Geographical Knowledge   270
One Ralph Blossom soliloquizes   .   .   271
The Noble Lady's Tale   .   .   .   272
Unrealized   278
Wagtail and Baby   278
Aberdeen : 1905   279
George Meredith, 1828–1909   .   .   .   279
Yell'ham-Wood's Story   .   .   .   280
A Young Man's Epigram on Existence .   .   281

SATIRES OF CIRCUMSTANCE
LYRICS AND REVERIES

LYRICS AND REVERIES—

In Front of the Landscape   .   .   .   285
Channel Firing   287
The Convergence of the Twain.   .   .   288
The Ghost of the Past   .   .   .   290
After the Visit   291
To meet, or otherwise   .   .   .   292
The Difference   292
The Sun on the Bookcase   .   .   .   293
"When I set out for Lyonnesse"   .   .   293

CONTENTS

PAGE

A Thunderstorm in Town 294

The Torn Letter 294

Beyond the Last Lamp 296

The Face at the Casement 297

Lost Love 299

"My Spirit will not haunt the Mound" . . 299

Wessex Heights 300

In Death divided 301

The Place on the Map 302

The Schreckhorn 303

A Singer Asleep 304

A Plaint to Man 306

God's Funeral 307

Spectres that grieve 309

"Ah, are you digging on my Grave?" . . 310

Self-Unconscious 311

The Discovery 313

Tolerance 313

Before and after Summer 314

At Day-Close in November 314

The Year's Awakening 315

Under the Waterfall 315

POEMS OF 1912-13—

The Going 318

Your Last Drive 319

The Walk 320

Rain on a Grave 321

"I found her out there" 322

Without Ceremony 323

Lament 323

The Haunter 324

The Voice 325

His Visitor 326

A Circular 327

A Dream or No 327

After a Journey 328

A Death-Day recalled 329

PAGE

Beeny Cliff 330
At Castle Boterel 330
Places 331
The Phantom Horsewoman 332
The Spell of the Rose 334
St. Launce's revisited 335
Where the Picnic was 336

MISCELLANEOUS PIECES—

The Wistful Lady 337
The Woman in the Rye 338
The Cheval-Glass 338
The Re-Enactment 339
Her Secret 343
"She charged me" 343
The Newcomer's Wife 344
A Conversation at Dawn 344
A King's Soliloquy 350
The Coronation 351
Aquae Sulis 353
Seventy-Four and Twenty 354
The Elopement 354
"I rose up as my Custom is" 355
A Week 356
Had you wept 357
Bereft, she thinks she dreams . . . 358
In the British Museum 358
In the Servants' Quarters 359
The Obliterate Tomb 361
"Regret not me" 365
The Recalcitrants 366
Starlings on the Roof 366
The Moon looks in 367
The Sweet Hussy 368
The Telegram 368
The Moth-Signal 369
Seen by the Waits 370
The Two Soldiers 371

CONTENTS

THE DEATH OF REGRET 371
IN THE DAYS OF CRINOLINE 372
THE ROMAN GRAVEMOUNDS 373
THE WORKBOX 374
THE SACRILEGE 375
THE ABBEY MASON 379
THE JUBILEE OF A MAGAZINE 386
THE SATIN SHOES 387
EXEUNT OMNES 389
A POET 390

SATIRES OF CIRCUMSTANCE—

I. AT TEA 391
II. IN CHURCH 391
III. BY HER AUNT'S GRAVE 392
IV. IN THE ROOM OF THE BRIDE-ELECT . . 392
V. AT A WATERING-PLACE 393
VI. IN THE CEMETERY 393
VII. OUTSIDE THE WINDOW 394
VIII. IN THE STUDY 394
IX. AT THE ALTAR-RAIL 395
X. IN THE NUPTIAL CHAMBER . . . 395
XI. IN THE RESTAURANT 396
XII. AT THE DRAPER'S 396
XIII. ON THE DEATH-BED 397
XIV. OVER THE COFFIN 398
XV. IN THE MOONLIGHT 398

MOMENTS OF VISION AND MISCELLANEOUS VERSES

MOMENTS OF VISION 401
THE VOICE OF THINGS 401
"WHY BE AT PAINS?" 402
"WE SAT AT THE WINDOW" 402
AFTERNOON SERVICE AT MELLSTOCK . . . 403
AT THE WICKET-GATE 403

PAGE

In a Museum 404

Apostrophe to an Old Psalm Tune . . . 404

At the Word "Farewell" 405

First Sight of her and after 406

The Rival 407

Heredity 407

"You were the Sort that Men forget" . . 408

She, I, and They 408

Near Lanivet, 1872 409

Joys of Memory 410

To the Moon 410

Copying Architecture in an Old Minster . . 411

To Shakespeare 412

Quid hic agis? 413

On a Midsummer Eve 415

Timing her 416

Before Knowledge 418

The Blinded Bird 418

"The Wind blew Words" 419

The Faded Face 420

The Riddle 420

The Duel 421

At Mayfair Lodgings 422

To my Father's Violin 423

The Statue of Liberty 424

The Background and the Figure . . . 426

The Change 426

Sitting on the Bridge 428

The Young Churchwarden 429

"I travel as a Phantom now" 429

Lines to a Movement in Mozart's E-flat Symphony 430

"In the Seventies" 430

The Pedigree 431

His Heart. A Woman's Dream . . . 432

Where they lived 434

The Occultation 434

Life laughs onward 435

The Peace-Offering 435

CONTENTS

PAGE

"Something tapped" 436

The Wound 436

A Merrymaking in Question . . . 436

"I said and sang her Excellence" . . 437

A January Night. 1879 438

A Kiss 438

The Announcement 439

The Oxen 439

The Tresses 440

The Photograph 440

On a Heath 441

An Anniversary 441

"By the Runic Stone" 442

The Pink Frock 443

Transformations 443

In her Precincts 444

The Last Signal 444

The House of Silence 445

Great Things 445

The Chimes 446

The Figure in the Scene 447

"Why did I sketch" 447

Conjecture 448

The Blow 449

Love the Monopolist 450

At Middle-Field Gate in February . . 451

The Youth who carried a Light . . 451

The Head above the Fog . . . 452

Overlooking the River Stour . . . 452

The Musical Box 453

On Sturminster Foot-Bridge . . . 454

Royal Sponsors 455

Old Furniture 456

A Thought in Two Moods . . . 457

The Last Performance 457

"You on the Tower" 458

The Interloper 458

Logs on the Hearth 459

PAGE

The Sunshade 460
The Ageing House 461
The Caged Goldfinch 461
At Madame Tussaud's in Victorian Years . . 462
The Ballet 462
The Five Students 463
The Wind's Prophecy 464
During Wind and Rain 465
He prefers her earthly 466
The Dolls 466
Molly Gone 467
A Backward Spring 468
Looking Across 468
At a Seaside Town in 1869 469
The Glimpse 471
The Pedestrian 472
"Who's in the Next Room?" 473
At a Country Fair 474
The Memorial Brass: 186– 474
Her Love-Birds 475
Paying Calls 476
The Upper Birch-Leaves 476
"It never looks like Summer" 477
Everything comes 477
The Man with a Past 478
He fears his Good Fortune 479
He wonders about himself 479
Jubilate 480
He revisits his First School 481
"I thought, my Heart" 481
Fragment 482
Midnight on the Great Western . . . 483
Honeymoon Time at an Inn 484
The Robin 485
"I rose and went to Rou'tor Town" . . . 486
The Nettles 486
In a Waiting-Room 487
The Clock-Winder 488

CONTENTS

	PAGE
OLD EXCURSIONS	489
THE MASKED FACE	490
IN A WHISPERING GALLERY	490
THE SOMETHING THAT SAVED HIM	491
THE ENEMY'S PORTRAIT	492
IMAGININGS	493
ON THE DOORSTEP	494
SIGNS AND TOKENS	494
PATHS OF FORMER TIME	496
THE CLOCK OF THE YEARS	496
AT THE PIANO	497
THE SHADOW ON THE STONE	498
IN THE GARDEN	499
THE TREE AND THE LADY	499
AN UPBRAIDING	500
THE YOUNG GLASS-STAINER	500
LOOKING AT A PICTURE ON AN ANNIVERSARY	501
THE CHOIRMASTER'S BURIAL	502
THE MAN WHO FORGOT	503
WHILE DRAWING IN A CHURCHYARD	504
"FOR LIFE I HAD NEVER CARED GREATLY"	505

POEMS OF WAR AND PATRIOTISM—

"MEN WHO MARCH AWAY" (SONG OF THE SOLDIERS)	506
HIS COUNTRY	507
ENGLAND TO GERMANY IN 1914	508
ON THE BELGIAN EXPATRIATION	508
AN APPEAL TO AMERICA ON BEHALF OF THE BELGIAN DESTITUTE	509
THE PITY OF IT	509
IN TIME OF WARS AND TUMULTS	510
IN TIME OF "THE BREAKING OF NATIONS"	511
CRY OF THE HOMELESS	511
BEFORE MARCHING AND AFTER	512
"OFTEN WHEN WARRING"	513
THEN AND NOW	513
A CALL TO NATIONAL SERVICE	514

The Dead and the Living One . . . 515
A New Year's Eve in War Time . . . 516
"I met a Man" 517
"I looked up from my Writing" . . . 519

FINALE—

The Coming of the End 520
Afterwards 521

LATE LYRICS AND EARLIER

Apology 525
Weathers 533
The Maid of Keinton Mandeville . . . 533
Summer Schemes 534
Epeisodia 535
Faintheart in a Railway Train . . . 536
At Moonrise and Onwards . . . 536
The Garden Seat 537
Barthélémon at Vauxhall 537
"I sometimes think" 538
Jezreel 538
A Jog-trot Pair 539
"The Curtains now are drawn" . . . 540
"According to the Mighty Working" . . 541
"I was not He" 541
The West-of-Wessex Girl 542
Welcome Home 542
Going and Staying 543
Read by Moonlight 543
At a House in Hampstead . . . 544
A Woman's Fancy 545
Her Song 546
A Wet August 547
The Dissemblers 548
To a Lady playing and singing in the Morning . 548
"A Man was drawing near to Me" . . 549

CONTENTS

	PAGE
THE STRANGE HOUSE	549
"AS 'TWERE TO-NIGHT"	551
THE CONTRETEMPS	551
A GENTLEMAN'S EPITAPH ON HIMSELF AND A LADY	553
THE OLD GOWN	554
A NIGHT IN NOVEMBER	555
A DUETTIST TO HER PIANOFORTE	555
"WHERE THREE ROADS JOINED"	556
"AND THERE WAS A GREAT CALM"	557
HAUNTING FINGERS	559
THE WOMAN I MET	560
"IF IT'S EVER SPRING AGAIN"	563
THE TWO HOUSES	563
ON STINSFORD HILL AT MIDNIGHT	565
THE FALLOW DEER AT THE LONELY HOUSE	566
THE SELFSAME SONG	566
THE WANDERER	567
A WIFE COMES BACK	568
A YOUNG MAN'S EXHORTATION	569
AT LULWORTH COVE A CENTURY BACK	570
A BYGONE OCCASION	570
TWO SERENADES	571
THE WEDDING MORNING	572
END OF THE YEAR 1912	573
THE CHIMES PLAY "LIFE'S A BUMPER!"	573
"I WORKED NO WILE TO MEET YOU"	574
AT THE RAILWAY STATION, UPWAY	575
SIDE BY SIDE	575
DREAM OF THE CITY SHOPWOMAN	576
A MAIDEN'S PLEDGE	577
THE CHILD AND THE SAGE	578
MISMET	579
AN AUTUMN RAIN-SCENE	579
MEDITATIONS ON A HOLIDAY	580
AN EXPERIENCE	582
THE BEAUTY	583
THE COLLECTOR CLEANS HIS PICTURE	584
THE WOOD FIRE	585

CONTENTS

PAGE

SAYING GOOD-BYE 586
ON THE TUNE CALLED THE OLD-HUNDRED-AND-FOURTH . 587
THE OPPORTUNITY 587
EVELYN G. OF CHRISTMINSTER 588
THE RIFT 589
VOICES FROM THINGS GROWING IN A CHURCHYARD . 590
ON THE WAY 591
" SHE DID NOT TURN " 592
GROWTH IN MAY 592
THE CHILDREN AND SIR NAMELESS . . . 593
AT THE ROYAL ACADEMY 593
HER TEMPLE 594
A TWO-YEARS' IDYLL 594
BY HENSTRIDGE CROSS AT THE YEAR'S END . . 595
PENANCE 596
" I LOOK IN HER FACE " 597
AFTER THE WAR 597
" IF YOU HAD KNOWN " 598
THE CHAPEL-ORGANIST 598
FETCHING HER 602
" COULD I BUT WILL " 603
SHE REVISITS ALONE THE CHURCH OF HER MARRIAGE . 604
AT THE ENTERING OF THE NEW YEAR . . . 605
THEY WOULD NOT COME 606
AFTER A ROMANTIC DAY 607
THE TWO WIVES 607
" I KNEW A LADY " 608
A HOUSE WITH A HISTORY 608
A PROCESSION OF DEAD DAYS 609
HE FOLLOWS HIMSELF 610
THE SINGING WOMAN 611
WITHOUT, NOT WITHIN HER 612
" O I WON'T LEAD A HOMELY LIFE " . . . 612
IN THE SMALL HOURS 613
THE LITTLE OLD TABLE 613
VAGG HOLLOW 614
THE DREAM IS—WHICH ? 615
THE COUNTRY WEDDING 615

CONTENTS

PAGE

FIRST OR LAST 616

LONELY DAYS 617

"WHAT DID IT MEAN?" 618

AT THE DINNER-TABLE 619

THE MARBLE TABLET 620

THE MASTER AND THE LEAVES 620

LAST WORDS TO A DUMB FRIEND . . . 621

A DRIZZLING EASTER MORNING . . . 623

ON ONE WHO LIVED AND DIED WHERE HE WAS BORN 623

THE SECOND NIGHT 624

SHE WHO SAW NOT 626

THE OLD WORKMAN 626

THE SAILOR'S MOTHER 627

OUTSIDE THE CASEMENT 628

THE PASSER-BY 629

"I WAS THE MIDMOST" 630

A SOUND IN THE NIGHT 630

ON A DISCOVERED CURL OF HAIR . . . 632

AN OLD LIKENESS 633

HER APOTHEOSIS 634

"SACRED TO THE MEMORY" 634

TO A WELL-NAMED DWELLING . . . 635

THE WHIPPER-IN 635

A MILITARY APPOINTMENT 636

THE MILESTONE BY THE RABBIT-BURROW . . 637

THE LAMENT OF THE LOOKING-GLASS . . 638

CROSS-CURRENTS 638

THE OLD NEIGHBOUR AND THE NEW . . 639

THE CHOSEN 640

THE INSCRIPTION 641

THE MARBLE-STREETED TOWN . . . 644

A WOMAN DRIVING 645

A WOMAN'S TRUST 645

BEST TIMES 646

THE CASUAL ACQUAINTANCE . . . 647

INTRA SEPULCHRUM 647

THE WHITEWASHED WALL 648

JUST THE SAME 649

PAGE

The Last Time 650

The Seven Times 650

The Sun's Last Look on the Country Girl . . . 651

In a London Flat 652

Drawing Details in an Old Church 653

Rake-hell Muses 653

The Colour 655

Murmurs in the Gloom 656

Epitaph 657

An Ancient to Ancients 658

After Reading Psalms xxxix, xl, etc. . . . 660

Surview 660

HUMAN SHOWS — FAR PHANTASIES

Waiting Both 665

A Bird-Scene at a Rural Dwelling . . . 665

"Any little Old Song" 666

In a former Resort after many Years . . . 666

A Cathedral Façade at Midnight . . . 666

The Turnip-Hoer 667

The Carrier 670

Lover to Mistress 670

The Monument-Maker 671

Circus-Rider to Ringmaster 672

Last Week in October 673

Come not; yet come! 673

The Later Autumn 674

"Let me" 674

At a Fashionable Dinner 675

Green Slates 676

An East-End Curate 676

At Rushy-Pond 677

Four in the Morning 678

On the Esplanade 679

In St. Paul's a while ago 680

Coming up Oxford Street: Evening . . . 681

A Last Journey 681

CONTENTS

PAGE

SINGING LOVERS 683

THE MONTH'S CALENDAR 683

A SPELLBOUND PALACE 684

WHEN DEAD 685

SINE PROLE 686

TEN YEARS SINCE 686

EVERY ARTEMISIA 687

THE BEST SHE COULD 688

THE GRAVEYARD OF DEAD CREEDS . . . 689

"THERE SEEMED A STRANGENESS" . . . 689

A NIGHT OF QUESTIONINGS 690

XENOPHANES, THE MONIST OF COLOPHON . . 692

LIFE AND DEATH AT SUNRISE 695

NIGHT-TIME IN MID-FALL 695

A SHEEP FAIR 696

SNOW IN THE SUBURBS 697

A LIGHT SNOW-FALL AFTER FROST . . . 698

WINTER NIGHT IN WOODLAND 698

ICE ON THE HIGHWAY 699

MUSIC IN A SNOWY STREET 700

THE FROZEN GREENHOUSE 701

TWO LIPS 702

NO BUYERS 702

ONE WHO MARRIED ABOVE HIM 703

THE NEW TOY 705

QUEEN CAROLINE TO HER GUESTS . . . 705

PLENA TIMORIS 706

THE WEARY WALKER 707

LAST LOVE-WORD 708

NOBODY COMES 708

IN THE STREET 709

THE LAST LEAF 709

AT WYNYARD'S GAP 710

AT SHAG'S HEATH, 1685 716

A SECOND ATTEMPT 718

"FREED THE FRET OF THINKING" . . . 719

THE ABSOLUTE EXPLAINS 720

"SO, TIME" 723

CONTENTS

PAGE

An Inquiry 724

The Faithful Swallow 725

In Sherborne Abbey 725

The Pair he saw pass 726

The Mock Wife 728

The Fight on Durnover Moor . . . 730

Last Look round St. Martin's Fair . . 732

The Caricature 732

A Leader of Fashion 734

Midnight on Beechen 735

The Aërolite 736

The Prospect 737

Genitrix Laesa 737

The Fading Rose 738

When Oats were reaped 739

Louie 739

"She opened the Door" 740

"What's there to tell?" 740

The Harbour Bridge 741

Vagrant's Song 742

Farmer Dunman's Funeral 743

The Sexton at Longpuddle 744

The Harvest-Supper 745

At a Pause in a Country Dance . . . 746

On the Portrait of a Woman about to be Hanged . 747

The Church and the Wedding . . . 748

The Shiver 749

"Not only I" 749

She saw him, she said 750

Once at Swanage 751

The Flower's Tragedy 751

At the Aquatic Sports 752

A Watcher's Regret 752

Horses aboard 753

The History of an Hour 753

The Missed Train 754

Under High-Stoy Hill 754

At the Mill 755

CONTENTS

ALIKE AND UNLIKE 756
THE THING UNPLANNED 756
THE SHEEP-BOY 756
RETTY'S PHASES 757
A POOR MAN AND A LADY 759
AN EXPOSTULATION 760
TO A SEA-CLIFF 761
THE ECHO ELF ANSWERS 762
CYNIC'S EPITAPH 762
A BEAUTY'S SOLILOQUY DURING HER HONEYMOON . 763
DONAGHADEE 764
HE INADVERTENTLY CURES HIS LOVE-PAINS . . 765
THE PEACE PEAL 765
LADY VI 766
A POPULAR PERSONAGE AT HOME . . . 767
INSCRIPTIONS FOR A PEAL OF EIGHT BELLS . . 768
A REFUSAL 769
EPITAPH ON A PESSIMIST 771
THE PROTEAN MAIDEN 771
A WATERING PLACE LADY INVENTORIED . . . 772
THE SEA FIGHT 772
PARADOX 773
THE ROVER COME HOME 773
"KNOWN HAD I" 774
THE PAT OF BUTTER 775
BAGS OF MEAT 775
THE SUNDIAL ON A WET DAY 777
HER HAUNTING GROUND 777
A PARTING SCENE 778
SHORTENING DAYS AT THE HOMESTEAD . . . 778
DAYS TO RECOLLECT 779
TO C. F. H. 780
THE HIGH-SCHOOL LAWN 780
THE FORBIDDEN BANNS 781
THE PAPHIAN BALL 782
ON MARTOCK MOOR 785
THAT MOMENT 786
PREMONITIONS 786

	PAGE
THIS SUMMER AND LAST	787
"NOTHING MATTERS MUCH"	787
IN THE EVENING	788
THE SIX BOARDS	789
BEFORE MY FRIEND ARRIVED	790
COMPASSION: AN ODE	791
"WHY SHE MOVED HOUSE"	792
TRAGEDIAN TO TRAGEDIENNE . . .	792
THE LADY OF FOREBODINGS	793
THE BIRD-CATCHER'S BOY	794
A HURRIED MEETING	796
DISCOURAGEMENT	798
A LEAVING	798
SONG TO AN OLD BURDEN	799
"WHY DO I?"	799
INDEX TO FIRST LINES	801
SUPPLEMENTARY INDEX	815

WESSEX POEMS

AND OTHER VERSES

THE TEMPORARY THE ALL

(SAPPHICS)

Change and chancefulness in my flowering youthtime,
Set me sun by sun near to one unchosen ;
Wrought us fellowlike, and despite divergence,
    Fused us in friendship.

"Cherish him can I while the true one forthcome—
Come the rich fulfiller of my prevision ;
Life is roomy yet, and the odds unbounded."
    So self-communed I.

'Thwart my wistful way did a damsel saunter,
Fair, albeit unformed to be all-eclipsing ;
"Maiden meet," held I, "till arise my forefelt
    Wonder of women."

Long a visioned hermitage deep desiring,
Tenements uncouth I was fain to house in ;
"Let such lodging be for a breath-while," thought I,
    "Soon a more seemly.

"Then high handiwork will I make my life-deed,
Truth and Light outshow ; but the ripe time pending,
Intermissive aim at the thing sufficeth."
    Thus I. . . . But lo, me !

Mistress, friend, place, aims to be bettered straightway,
Bettered not has Fate or my hand's achievement ;
Sole the showings those of my onward earth-track—
    Never transcended !

5

AMABEL

I MARKED her ruined hues,
Her custom-straitened views,
And asked, " Can there indwell
        My Amabel ? "

I looked upon her gown,
Once rose, now earthen brown :
The change was like the knell
        Of Amabel.

Her step's mechanic ways
Had lost the life of May's ;
Her laugh, once sweet in swell,
        Spoilt Amabel.

I mused : " Who sings the strain
I sang ere warmth did wane ?
Who thinks its numbers spell
        His Amabel ? "—

Knowing that, though Love cease,
Love's race shows no decrease ;
All find in dorp or dell
        An Amabel.

—I felt that I could creep
To some housetop, and weep
That Time the tyrant fell
        Ruled Amabel !

I said (the while I sighed
That love like ours had died),
" Fond things I'll no more tell
        To Amabel,

" But leave her to her fate,
And fling across the gate,
' Till the Last Trump, farewell,
        O Amabel ! ' "

1865.

HAP

IF but some vengeful god would call to me
From up the sky, and laugh : " Thou suffering thing,
Know that thy sorrow is my ecstasy,
That thy love's loss is my hate's profiting !"

Then would I bear it, clench myself, and die,
Steeled by the sense of ire unmerited ;
Half-eased in that a Powerfuller than I
Had willed and meted me the tears I shed.

But not so.   How arrives it joy lies slain,
And why unblooms the best hope ever sown ?
—Crass Casualty obstructs the sun and rain,
And dicing Time for gladness casts a moan. . . .
These purblind Doomsters had as readily strown
Blisses about my pilgrimage as pain.

1866.

"IN VISION I ROAMED"

TO ——

IN vision I roamed the flashing Firmament,
So fierce in blazon that the Night waxed wan,
As though with awe at orbs of such ostént ;
And as I thought my spirit ranged on and on

In footless traverse through ghast heights of sky,
To the last chambers of the monstrous Dome,
Where stars the brightest here are lost to the eye :
Then, any spot on our own Earth seemed Home !

And the sick grief that you were far away
Grew pleasant thankfulness that you were near
Who might have been, set on some foreign Sphere,
Less than a Want to me, as day by day
I lived unware, uncaring all that lay
Locked in that Universe taciturn and drear.

1866.

AT A BRIDAL

NATURE'S INDIFFERENCE

WHEN you paced forth, to await maternity,
A dream of other offspring held my mind,
Compounded of us twain as Love designed ;
Rare forms, that corporate now will never be !

Should I, too, wed as slave to Mode's decree,
And each thus found apart, of false desire,
A stolid line, whom no high aims will fire
As had fired ours could ever have mingled we ;

And, grieved that lives so matched should miscompose,
Each mourn the double waste ; and question dare
To the Great Dame whence incarnation flows,
Why those high-purposed children never were :
What will she answer ?   That she does not care
If the race all such sovereign types unknows.

1866.

POSTPONEMENT

SNOW-BOUND in woodland, a mournful word,
Dropt now and then from the bill of a bird,
Reached me on wind-wafts ; and thus I heard,
        Wearily waiting :—

" I planned her a nest in a leafless tree,
But the passers eyed and twitted me,
And said : ' How reckless a bird is he,
        Cheerily mating !'

" Fear-filled, I stayed me till summer-tide,
In lewth of leaves to throne her bride ;
But alas ! her love for me waned and died,
        Wearily waiting.

"Ah, had I been like some I see,
Born to an evergreen nesting-tree,
None had eyed and twitted me,
        Cheerily mating !"
        1866.

A CONFESSION TO A FRIEND IN TROUBLE

YOUR troubles shrink not, though I feel them less
Here, far away, than when I tarried near ;
I even smile old smiles—with listlessness—
Yet smiles they are, not ghastly mockeries mere.

A thought too strange to house within my brain
Haunting its outer precincts I discern :
—*That I will not show zeal again to learn
Your griefs, and, sharing them, renew my pain.* . . .

It goes, like murky bird or buccaneer
That shapes its lawless figure on the main,
And staunchness tends to banish utterly
The unseemly instinct that had lodgment here ;
Yet, comrade old, can bitterer knowledge be
Than that, though banned, such instinct was in me !
    1866.

NEUTRAL TONES

WE stood by a pond that winter day,
And the sun was white, as though chidden of God,
And a few leaves lay on the starving sod ;
        —They had fallen from an ash, and were gray.

Your eyes on me were as eyes that rove
Over tedious riddles of years ago ;
And some words played between us to and fro
        On which lost the more by our love.

The smile on your mouth was the deadest thing
Alive enough to have strength to die ;
And a grin of bitterness swept thereby
        Like an ominous bird a-wing. . . .

Since then, keen lessons that love deceives,
And wrings with wrong, have shaped to me
Your face, and the God-curst sun, and a tree,
        And a pond edged with grayish leaves.
    1867.

SHE

AT HIS FUNERAL

THEY bear him to his resting-place—
In slow procession sweeping by;
I follow at a stranger's space;
His kindred they, his sweetheart I.
Unchanged my gown of garish dye,
Though sable-sad is their attire;
But they stand round with griefless eye,
Whilst my regret consumes like fire!

187-.

HER INITIALS

UPON a poet's page I wrote
Of old two letters of her name;
Part seemed she of the effulgent thought
Whence that high singer's rapture came.
—When now I turn the leaf the same
Immortal light illumes the lay,
But from the letters of her name
The radiance has waned away!

1869.

HER DILEMMA

(IN ——— CHURCH)

THE two were silent in a sunless church,
Whose mildewed walls, uneven paving-stones,
And wasted carvings passed antique research;
And nothing broke the clock's dull monotones.

Leaning against a wormy poppy-head,
So wan and worn that he could scarcely stand,
—For he was soon to die,—he softly said,
"Tell me you love me!"—holding long her hand.

She would have given a world to breathe "yes" truly,
So much his life seemed hanging on her mind,
And hence she lied, her heart persuaded throughly
'Twas worth her soul to be a moment kind.

But the sad need thereof, his nearing death,
So mocked humanity that she shamed to prize
A world conditioned thus, or care for breath
Where Nature such dilemmas could devise.

   1866.

REVULSION

THOUGH I waste watches framing words to fetter
Some unknown spirit to mine in clasp and kiss,
Out of the night there looms a sense 'twere better
To fail obtaining whom one fails to miss.

For winning love we win the risk of losing,
And losing love is as one's life were riven;
It cuts like contumely and keen ill-using
To cede what was superfluously given.

Let me then never feel the fateful thrilling
That devastates the love-worn wooer's frame,
The hot ado of fevered hopes, the chilling
That agonizes disappointed aim!
So may I live no junctive law fulfilling,
And my heart's table bear no woman's name.

   1866.

SHE, TO HIM

I

WHEN you shall see me in the toils of Time,
My lauded beauties carried off from me,
My eyes no longer stars as in their prime,
My name forgot of Maiden Fair and Free;

When, in your being, heart concedes to mind,
And judgment, though you scarce its process know,
Recalls the excellencies I once enshrined,
And you are irked that they have withered so:

Remembering mine the loss is, not the blame,
That Sportsman Time but rears his brood to kill,
Knowing me in my soul the very same—
One who would die to spare you touch of ill !—
Will you not grant to old affection's claim
The hand of friendship down Life's sunless hill ?

1865.

SHE, TO HIM

II

PERHAPS, long hence, when I have passed away,
Some other's feature, accent, thought like mine,
Will carry you back to what I used to say,
And bring some memory of your love's decline.

Then you may pause awhile and think, " Poor jade ! "
And yield a sigh to me—as ample due,
Not as the tittle of a debt unpaid
To one who could resign her all to you—

And thus reflecting, you will never see
That your thin thought, in two small words conveyed,
Was no such fleeting phantom-thought to me,
But the Whole Life wherein my part was played ;
And you amid its fitful masquerade
A Thought—as I in your life seem to be !

1866.

SHE, TO HIM

III

I WILL be faithful to thee ; aye, I will !
And Death shall choose me with a wondering eye
That he did not discern and domicile
One his by right ever since that last Good-bye !

I have no care for friends, or kin, or prime
Of manhood who deal gently with me here ;
Amid the happy people of my time
Who work their love's fulfilment, I appear

Numb as a vane that cankers on its point,
True to the wind that kissed ere canker came :
Despised by souls of Now, who would disjoint
The mind from memory, making Life all aim,

My old dexterities in witchery gone,
And nothing left for Love to look upon.

1866.

SHE, TO HIM

IV

THIS love puts all humanity from me ;
I can but maledict her, pray her dead,
For giving love and getting love of thee—
Feeding a heart that else mine own had fed !

How much I love I know not, life not known,
Save as one unit I would add love by ;
But this I know, my being is but thine own—
Fused from its separateness by ecstasy.

And thus I grasp thy amplitudes, of her
Ungrasped, though helped by nigh-regarding eyes ;
Canst thou then hate me as an envier
Who see unrecked what I so dearly prize ?
Believe me, Lost One, Love is lovelier
The more it shapes its moan in selfish-wise.

1866.

DITTY

(E. L. G.)

BENEATH a knap where flown
        Nestlings play,
Within walls of weathered stone,
        Far away
From the files of formal houses,
By the bough the firstling browses,
Lives a Sweet : no merchants meet
No man barters, no man sells
        Where she dwells.

Upon that fabric fair
 " Here is she ! "
Seems written everywhere
 Unto me.
But to friends and nodding neighbours,
Fellow-wights in lot and labours,
Who descry the times as I,
No such lucid legend tells
 Where she dwells.

Should I lapse to what I was
 Ere we met ;
(Such will not be, but because
 Some forget
Let me feign it)—none would notice
That where she I know by rote is
Spread a strange and withering change,
Like a drying of the wells
 Where she dwells.

To feel I might have kissed—
 Loved as true—
Otherwhere, nor Mine have missed
 My life through,
Had I never wandered near her,
Is a smart severe—severer
In the thought that she is nought,
Even as I, beyond the dells
 Where she dwells.

And Devotion droops her glance
 To recall
What bond-servants of Chance
 We are all.
I but found her in that, going
On my errant path unknowing,
I did not out-skirt the spot
That no spot on earth excels,
 —Where she dwells !

1870.

THE SERGEANT'S SONG
(1803)

WHEN Lawyers strive to heal a breach,
And Parsons practise what they preach;
Then Boney he'll come pouncing down,
And march his men on London town!
    Rollicum-rorum, tol-lol-lorum,
    Rollicum-rorum, tol-lol-lay!

When Justices hold equal scales,
And Rogues are only found in jails;
Then Boney he'll come pouncing down,
And march his men on London town!
    Rollicum-rorum, &c.

When Rich Men find their wealth a curse,
And fill therewith the Poor Man's purse;
Then Boney he'll come pouncing down,
And march his men on London town!
    Rollicum-rorum, &c.

When Husbands with their Wives agree,
And Maids won't wed from modesty;
Then Boney he'll come pouncing down,
And march his men on London town!
    Rollicum-rorum, tol-tol-lorum,
    Rollicum-rorum, tol-lol-lay!
1878.
Published in " The Trumpet-Major" 1880.

VALENCIENNES
(1793)

BY CORP'L TULLIDGE, in " *The Trumpet Major*"

IN MEMORY OF S. C. (PENSIONER).   DIED 184–

WE trenched, we trumpeted and drummed,
And from our mortars tons of iron hummed
    Ath'art the ditch, the month we bombed
      The Town o' Valencieën.

'Twas in the June o' Ninety-dree
(The Duke o' Yark our then Commander been)
The German Legion, Guards, and we
Laid siege to Valencieën.

This was the first time in the war
That French and English spilled each other's gore;
—Few dreamt how far would roll the roar
Begun at Valencieën!

'Twas said that we'd no business there
A-topperèn the French for disagreën;
However, that's not my affair—
We were at Valencieën.

Such snocks and slats, since war began
Never knew raw recruit or veteràn:
Stone-deaf therence went many a man
Who served at Valencieën.

Into the streets, ath'art the sky,
A hundred thousand balls and bombs were fleën;
And harmless townsfolk fell to die
Each hour at Valencieën!

And, sweatèn wi' the bombardiers,
A shell was slent to shards anighst my ears:
—'Twas nigh the end of hopes and fears
For me at Valencieën!

They bore my wownded frame to camp,
And shut my gapèn skull, and washed en cleän,
And jined en wi' a zilver clamp
Thik night at Valencieën.

" We've fetched en back to quick from dead:
But never more on earth while rose is red
Will drum rouse Corpel!" Doctor said
O' me at Valencieën..

Twer true. No voice o' friend or foe
Can reach me now, or any livèn beën;
And little have I power to know
Since then at Valencieën!

I never hear the zummer hums
O' bees ; and don' know when the cuckoo comes ;
But night and day I hear the bombs
     We threw at Valencieën. . . .

As for the Duke o' Yark in war,
There may be volk whose judgment o' en is meän ;
But this I say—he was not far
     From great at Valencieën.

O' wild wet nights, when all seems sad,
My wownds come back, as though new wownds I'd had ;
But yet—at times I'm sort o' glad
     I fout at Valencieën.

Well : Heaven wi' its jasper halls
Is now the on'y Town I care to be in. . . .
     Good Lord, if Nick should bomb the walls
     As we did Valencieën !

1878-1897.

SAN SEBASTIAN

(*August* 1813)

<small>WITH THOUGHTS OF SERGEANT M—— (PENSIONER), WHO DIED 185-</small>

" WHY, Sergeant, stray on the Ivel Way,
As though at home there were spectres rife ?
From first to last 'twas a proud career !
And your sunny years with a gracious wife
     Have brought you a daughter dear.

" I watched her to-day ; a more comely maid,
As she danced in her muslin bowed with blue,
Round a Hintock maypole never gayed."
—"Aye, aye ; I watched her this day, too,
     As it happens," the Sergeant said.

" My daughter is now," he again began,
" Of just such an age as one I knew
When we of the Line, the Forlorn-hope van,
On an August morning—a chosen few—
     Stormed San Sebastian.

" She's a score less three ; so about was *she*—
The maiden I wronged in Peninsular days. . . .
You may prate of your prowess in lusty times,
But as years gnaw inward you blink your bays,
  And see too well your crimes !

" We'd stormed it at night, by the flapping light
Of burning towers, and the mortar's boom :
We'd topped the breach ; but had failed to stay,
For our files were misled by the baffling gloom ;
  And we said we'd storm by day.

" So, out of the trenches, with features set,
On that hot, still morning, in measured pace,
Our column climbed ; climbed higher yet,
Past the fauss'bray, scarp, up the curtain-face,
  And along the parapet.

" From the battered hornwork the cannoneers
Hove crashing balls of iron fire ;
On the shaking gap mount the volunteers
In files, and as they mount expire
  Amid curses, groans, and cheers.

" Five hours did we storm, five hours re-form,
As Death cooled those hot blood pricked on ;
Till our cause was helped by a woe within :
They were blown from the summit we'd leapt upon,
  And madly we entered in.

" On end for plunder, 'mid rain and thunder
That burst with the lull of our cannonade,
We vamped the streets in the stifling air—
Our hunger unsoothed, our thirst unstayed—
  And ransacked the buildings there.

" From the shady vaults of their walls of white
We rolled rich puncheons of Spanish grape,
Till at length, with the fire of the wine alight,
I saw at a doorway a fair fresh shape—
  A woman, a sylph, or sprite.

"Afeard she fled, and with heated head
I pursued to the chamber she called her own ;
—When might is right no qualms deter,
And having her helpless and alone
          I wreaked my will on her.

"She raised her beseeching eyes to me,
And I heard the words of prayer she sent
In her own soft language. . . . Fatefully
I copied those eyes for my punishment
          In begetting the girl you see !

"So, to-day I stand with a God-set brand
Like Cain's, when he wandered from kindred's ken. . . .
I served through the war that made Europe free ;
I wived me in peace-year.   But, hid from men,
          I bear that mark on me.

"Maybe we shape our offspring's guise
From fancy, or we know not what,
And that no deep impression dies,—
For the mother of my child is not
          The mother of her eyes.

"And I nightly stray on the Ivel Way
As though at home there were spectres rife ;
I delight me not in my proud career ;
And 'tis coals of fire that a gracious wife
          Should have brought me a daughter dear !"

THE STRANGER'S SONG

(*As sung by* MR. CHARLES CHARRINGTON *in the play of*
          "*The Three Wayfarers*")

O MY trade it is the rarest one,
                    Simple shepherds all—
          My trade is a sight to see ;
For my customers I tie, and take 'em up on high,
          And waft 'em to a far countree !

My tools are but common ones,
                 Simple shepherds all—
    My tools are no sight to see :
A little hempen string, and a post whereon to swing,
     Are implements enough for me !

To-morrow is my working day,
                 Simple shepherds all—
    To-morrow is a working day for me :
For the farmer's sheep is slain, and the lad who did it ta'en
     And on his soul may God ha' mer-cy !

Printed in " The Three Strangers," 1883.

THE BURGHERS

(17—)

THE sun had wheeled from Grey's to Dammer's Crest,
And still I mused on that Thing imminent :
At length I sought the High-street to the West.

The level flare raked pane and pediment
And my wrecked face, and shaped my nearing friend
Like one of those the Furnace held unshent.

" I've news concerning her," he said.   " Attend.
They fly to-night at the late moon's first gleam :
Watch with thy steel : two righteous thrusts will end

Her shameless visions and his passioned dream.
I'll watch with thee, to testify thy wrong—
To aid, maybe.—Law consecrates the scheme."

I started, and we paced the flags along
Till I replied : " Since it has come to this
I'll do it !   But alone.   I can be strong."

Three hours past Curfew, when the Froom's mild hiss
Reigned sole, undulled by whirr of merchandize,
From Pummery-Tout to where the Gibbet is,

I crossed my pleasaunce hard by Glyd'path Rise,
And stood beneath the wall.   Eleven strokes went,
And to the door they came, contrariwise,

And met in clasp so close I had but bent
My lifted blade on either to have let
Their two souls loose upon the firmament.

But something held my arm. "A moment yet
As pray-time ere you wantons die!" I said;
And then they saw me. Swift her gaze was set

With eye and cry of love illimited
Upon her Heart-king. Never upon me
Had she thrown look of love so thoroughsped! . . .

At once she flung her faint form shieldingly
On his, against the vengeance of my vows;
The which o'erruling, her shape shielded he.

Blanked by such love, I stood as in a drowse,
And the slow moon edged from the upland nigh,
My sad thoughts moving thuswise: "I may house

And I may husband her, yet what am I
But licensed tyrant to this bonded pair?
Says Charity, Do as ye would be done by." . . .

Hurling my iron to the bushes there,
I bade them stay. And, as if brain and breast
Were passive, they walked with me to the stair.

Inside the house none watched; and on we prest
Before a mirror, in whose gleam I read
Her beauty, his,—and mine own mien unblest;

Till at her room I turned. "Madam," I said,
"Have you the wherewithal for this? Pray speak.
Love fills no cupboard. You'll need daily bread."

"We've nothing, sire," she lipped; "and nothing seek.
'Twere base in me to rob my lord unware;
Our hands will earn a pittance week by week."

And next I saw she had piled her raiment rare
Within the garde-robes, and her household purse,
Her jewels, her least lace of personal wear;

And stood in homespun.   Now grown wholly hers,
I handed her the gold, her jewels all,
And him the choicest of her robes diverse.

" Ill take you to the doorway in the wall,
And then adieu," I told them.   "Friends, withdraw."
They did so ; and she went—beyond recall.

And as I paused beneath the arch I saw
Their moonlit figures—slow, as in surprise—
Descend the slope, and vanish on the haw.

" ' Fool,' some will say," I thought.—" But who is wise,
Save God alone, to weigh my reasons why ? "
—" Hast thou struck home ? " came with the boughs' night-sighs.

It was my friend.   " I have struck well.   They fly,
But carry wounds that none can cicatrize."
—" Not mortal ? " said he.   " Lingering—worse," said I.

LEIPZIG

(1813)

SCENE.—*The Master-tradesmen's Parlour at the Old Ship Inn,*
Casterbridge.   Evening.

" OLD Norbert with the flat blue cap—
    A German said to be—
Why let your pipe die on your lap,
    Your eyes blink absently ? "

—" Ah ! . . . Well, I had thought till my cheek was wet
    Of my mother—her voice and mien
When she used to sing and pirouette,
    And tap the tambourine

" To the march that yon street-fiddler plies :
    She told me 'twas the same
She'd heard from the trumpets, when the Allies
    Burst on her home like flame.

"My father was one of the German Hussars,
  My mother of Leipzig ; but he,
Being quartered here, fetched her at close of the wars,
  And a Wessex lad reared me.

'And as I grew up, again and again
  She'd tell, after trilling that air,
Of her youth, and the battles on Leipzig plain
  And of all that was suffered there ! . . .

"—'Twas a time of alarms.   Three Chiefs-at-arms
  Combined them to crush One,
And by numbers' might, for in equal fight
  He stood the matched of none.

"Carl Schwarzenberg was of the plot,
  And Blücher, prompt and prow,
And Jean the Crown-Prince Bernadotte :
  Buonaparte was the foe.

"City and plain had felt his reign
  From the North to the Middle Sea,
And he'd now sat down in the noble town
  Of the King of Saxony.

"October's deep dew its wet gossamer threw
  Upon Leipzig's lawns, leaf-strewn,
Where lately each fair avenue
  Wrought shade for summer noon.

"To westward two dull rivers crept
  Through miles of marsh and slough,
Whereover a streak of whiteness swept—
  The Bridge of Lindenau.

"Hard by, in the City, the One, care-tossed,
  Sat pondering his shrunken power ;
And without the walls the hemming host
  Waxed denser every hour.

"He had speech that night on the morrow's designs
  With his chiefs by the bivouac fire,
While the belt of flames from the enemy's lines
  Flared nigher him yet and nigher.

" Three rockets then from the girdling trine
    Told, ' Ready!' As they rose
Their flashes seemed his Judgment-Sign
    For bleeding Europe's woes.

" 'Twas seen how the French watch-fires that night
    Glowed still and steadily ;
And the Three rejoiced, for they read in the sight
    That the One disdained to flee. . . .

" —Five hundred guns began the affray
    On next day morn at nine ;
Such mad and mangling cannon-play
    Had never torn human line.

" Around the town three battles beat,
    Contracting like a gin ;
As nearer marched the million feet
    Of columns closing in.

" The first battle nighed on the low Southern side ;
    The second by the Western way ;
The nearing of the third on the North was heard ;
    —The French held all at bay.

" Against the first band did the Emperor stand ;
    Against the second stood Ney ;
Marmont against the third gave the order-word :
    —Thus raged it throughout the day.

" Fifty thousand sturdy souls on those trampled plains and knolls,
    Who met the dawn hopefully,
And were lotted their shares in a quarrel not theirs,
    Dropt then in their agony.

" ' O,' the old folks said, ' ye Preachers stern !
    O so-called Christian time !
When will men's swords to ploughshares turn ?
    When come the promised prime ?' . . .

" —The clash of horse and man which that day began,
    Closed not as evening wore ;
And the morrow's armies, rear and van,
    Still mustered more and more.

" From the City towers the Confederate Powers
    Were eyed in glittering lines,
And up from the vast a murmuring passed
    As from a wood of pines.

" ' 'Tis well to cover a feeble skill
    By numbers' might ! ' scoffed He ;
' But give me a third of their strength, I'd fill
    Half Hell with their soldiery ! '

" All that day raged the war they waged,
    And again dumb night held reign,
Save that ever upspread from the dank deathbed
    A miles-wide pant of pain.

" Hard had striven brave Ney, the true Bertrand,
    Victor, and Augereau,
Bold Poniatowski, and Lauriston,
    To stay their overthrow ;

" But, as in the dream of one sick to death
    There comes a narrowing room
That pens him, body and limbs and breath,
    To wait a hideous doom,

" So to Napoleon, in the hush
    That held the town and towers
Through these dire nights, a creeping crush
    Seemed borne in with the hours.

" One road to the rearward, and but one,
    Did fitful Chance allow ;
'Twas where the Pleiss' and Elster run—
    The Bridge of Lindenau.

" The nineteenth dawned.   Down street and Platz
    The wasted French sank back,
Stretching long lines across the Flats
    And on the bridgeway track :

" When there surged on the sky an earthen wave,
    And stones, and men, as though
Some rebel churchyard crew updrave
    Their sepulchres from below.

" To Heaven is blown Bridge Lindenau ;
  Wrecked regiments reel therefrom ;
And rank and file in masses plough
  The sullen Elster-Strom.

" A gulf was Lindenau ; and dead
  Were fifties, hundreds, tens ;
And every current rippled red
  With Marshal's blood and men's.

" The smart Macdonald swam therein,
  And barely won the verge ;
Bold Poniatowski plunged him in
  Never to re-emerge.

" Then stayed the strife.   The remnants wound
  Their Rhineward way pell-mell ;
And thus did Leipzig City sound
  An Empire's passing bell ;

" While in cavalcade, with band and blade,
  Came Marshals, Princes, Kings ;
And the town was theirs. . . . Ay, as simple maid,
  My mother saw these things !

" And whenever those notes in the street begin,
  I recall her, and that far scene,
And her acting of how the Allies marched in,
  And her tap of the tambourine ! "

THE PEASANT'S CONFESSION

" Si le maréchal Grouchy avait été rejoint par l'officier que Napoléon lui
avait expédié la veille à dix heures du soir, toute question eût disparu.   Mais
cet officier n'était point parvenu à sa destination, ainsi que le maréchal n'a
cessé de l'affirmer toute sa vie, et il faut l'en croire, car autrement il n'aurait
eu aucune raison pour hésiter.   Cet officier avait-il été pris ? avait-il passé à
l'ennemi ?   C'est ce qu'on a toujours ignoré."—THIERS, *Histoire de l'Empire.*
" Waterloo."

GOOD Father ! . . . It was eve in middle June,
  And war was waged anew
By great Napoleon, who for years had strewn
  Men's bones all Europe through.

Three nights ere this, with columned corps he'd cross'd
    The Sambre at Charleroi,
To move on Brussels, where the English host
    Dallied in Parc and Bois.

The yestertide we'd heard the gloomy gun
    Growl through the long-sunned day
From Quatre-Bras and Ligny; till the dun
    Twilight suppressed the fray;

Albeit therein—as lated tongues bespoke—
    Brunswick's high heart was drained,
And Prussia's Line and Landwehr, though unbroke,
    Stood cornered and constrained.

And at next noon-time Grouchy slowly passed
    With thirty thousand men:
We hoped thenceforth no army, small or vast,
    Would trouble us again.

My hut lay deeply in a vale recessed,
    And never a soul seemed nigh
When, reassured at length, we went to rest—
    My children, wife, and I.

But what was this that broke our humble ease?
    What noise, above the rain,
Above the dripping of the poplar trees
    That smote along the pane?

—A call of mastery, bidding me arise,
    Compelled me to the door,
At which a horseman stood in martial guise—
    Splashed—sweating from every pore.

Had I seen Grouchy! Yes? What track took he?
    Could I lead thither on?—
Fulfilment would ensure much gold for me,
    Perhaps more gifts anon.

"I bear the Emperor's mandate," then he said,
    "Charging the Marshal straight
To strike between the double host ahead
    Ere they co-operate,

" Engaging Blücher till the Emperor put
      Lord Wellington to flight,
And next the Prussians.   This to set afoot
      Is my emprise to-night."

I joined him in the mist ; but, pausing, sought
      To estimate his say.
Grouchy had made for Wavre ; and yet, on thought,
      I did not lead that way.

I mused : " If Grouchy thus and thus be told,
      The clash comes sheer hereon ;
My farm is stript.   While, as for gifts of gold,
      Money the French have none.

" Grouchy unwarned, moreo'er, the English win,
      And mine is left to me—
They buy, not borrow."—Hence did I begin
      To lead him treacherously.

And as we edged Joidoigne with cautious view
      Dawn pierced the humid air ;
And still I easted with him, though I knew
      Never marched Grouchy there.

Near Ottignies we passed, across the Dyle
      (Lim'lette left far aside),
And thence direct toward Pervez and Noville
      Through green grain, till he cried :

" I doubt thy conduct, man ! no track is here—
      I doubt thy gagèd word ! "
Thereat he scowled on me, and prancing near,
      He pricked me with his sword.

" Nay, Captain, hold ! We skirt, not trace the course
      Of Grouchy," said I then :
" As we go, yonder went he, with his force
      Of thirty thousand men."

—At length noon nighed ; when west, from Saint-John's-Mound,
      A hoarse artillery boomed,
And from Saint-Lambert's upland, chapel-crowned,
      The Prussian squadrons loomed.

Then leaping to the wet wild path we had kept,
    "My mission fails!" he cried;
"Too late for Grouchy now to intercept,
    For, peasant, you have lied!"

He turned to pistol me. I sprang, and drew
    The sabre from his flank,
And 'twixt his nape and shoulder, ere he knew,
    I struck, and dead he sank.

I hid him deep in nodding rye and oat—
    His shroud green stalks and loam;
His requiem the corn-blade's husky note—
    And then I hastened home. . . .

—Two armies writhe in coils of red and blue,
    And brass and iron clang
From Goumont, past the front of Waterloo,
    To Pap'lotte and Smohain.

The Guard Imperial wavered on the height;
    The Emperor's face grew glum;
"I sent," he said, "to Grouchy yesternight,
    And yet he does not come!"

'Twas then, Good Father, that the French espied,
    Streaking the summer land,
The men of Blücher. But the Emperor cried,
    "Grouchy is now at hand!"

And meanwhile Vand'leur, Vivian, Maitland, Kempt,
    Met d'Erlon, Friant, Ney;
But Grouchy—mis-sent, blamed, yet blame-exempt—
    Grouchy was far away.

By even, slain or struck, Michel the strong,
    Bold Travers, Dnop, Delord,
Smart Guyot, Reil-le, l'Heriter, Friant,
    Scattered that champaign o'er.

Fallen likewise wronged Duhesme, and skilled Lobau
    Did that red sunset see;
Colbert, Legros, Blancard! . . . And of the foe
    Picton and Ponsonby;

With Gordon, Canning, Blackman, Ompteda,
    L'Estrange, Delancey, Packe,
Grose, D'Oyly, Stables, Morice, Howard, Hay,
    Von Schwerin, Watzdorf, Boek,

Smith, Phelips, Fuller, Lind, and Battersby,
    And hosts of ranksmen round. . . .
Memorials linger yet to speak to thee
    Of those that bit the ground !

The Guards' last column yielded ; dykes of dead
    Lay between vale and ridge,
As, thinned yet closing, faint yet fierce, they sped
    In packs to Genappe Bridge.

Safe was my stock ; my capple cow unslain ;
    Intact each cock and hen ;
But Grouchy far at Wavre all day had lain,
    And thirty thousand men.

O Saints, had I but lost my earing corn
    And saved the cause once prized !
O Saints, why such false witness had I borne
    When late I'd sympathized ! . . .

So now, being old, my children eye askance
    My slowly dwindling store,
And crave my mite ; till, worn with tarriance,
    I care for life no more.

To Almighty God henceforth I stand confessed,
    And Virgin-Saint Marie ;
O Michael, John, and Holy Ones in rest,
    Entreat the Lord for me !

THE ALARM

(TRADITIONAL)

IN MEMORY OF ONE OF THE WRITER'S FAMILY WHO WAS A
VOLUNTEER DURING THE WAR WITH NAPOLEON

IN a ferny byway
  Near the great South-Wessex Highway,
A homestead raised its breakfast-smoke aloft ;
The dew-damps still lay steamless, for the sun had made no skyway,
    And twilight cloaked the croft.

It was almost past conceiving
　Here, where woodbines hung inweaving,
That quite closely hostile armaments might steer,
Save from seeing in the porchway a fair woman mutely grieving,
　　And a harnessed Volunteer.

　　In haste he'd flown there
　　To his comely wife alone there,
While marching south hard by, to still her fears,
For she soon would be a mother, and few messengers were known
　　there
　　　In these campaigning years.

　　'Twas time to be Good-bying,
　　Since the assembly-hour was nighing
In royal George's town at six that morn ;
And betwixt its wharves and this retreat were ten good miles of
　　hieing
　　　Ere ring of bugle-horn.

　　" I've laid in food, Dear,
　　And broached the spiced and brewed, Dear ;
And if our July hope should antedate,
Let the char-wench mount and gallop by the halterpath and
　　wood, Dear,
　　　And fetch assistance straight.

　　" As for Buonaparte, forget him ;
　　He's not like to land ! But let him,
Those strike with aim who strike for wives and sons !
And the war-boats built to float him ; 'twere but wanted to upset
　　him
　　　A slat from Nelson's guns !

　　" But, to assure thee,
　　And of creeping fears to cure thee,
If he *should* be rumoured anchoring in the Road,
Drive with the nurse to Kingsbere ; and let nothing thence allure
　　thee
　　　Till we have him safe-bestowed.

　　" Now, to turn to marching matters :—
　　I've my knapsack, firelock, spatters,

Crossbelts, priming-horn, stock, bay'net, blackball, clay,
Pouch, magazine, and flint-box that at every quick-step clatters ;—
My heart, Dear ; that must stay ! "

—With breathings broken
Farewell was kissed unspoken,
And they parted there as morning stroked the panes ;
And the Volunteer went on, and turned, and twirled his glove for
token,
And took the coastward lanes.

When above He'th Hills he found him,
He saw, on gazing round him,
The Barrow-Beacon burning—burning low,
As if, perhaps, enkindled ever since he'd homeward bound him ;
And it meant : Expect the Foe !

Leaving the byway,
He entered on the highway,
Where were cars and chariots, faring fast inland ;
" He's anchored, Soldier ! " shouted some : " God save thee,
marching thy way,
Th'lt front him on the strand ! "

He slowed ; he stopped ; he paltered
Awhile with self, and faltered,
" Why courting misadventure shoreward roam ?
To Molly, surely ! Seek the woods with her till times have
altered ;
Charity favours home.

" Else, my denying
He'd come, she'll read as lying—
Think the Barrow-Beacon must have met my eyes—
That my words were not unwareness, but deceit of her, while
vying
In deeds that jeopardize.

" At home is stocked provision,
And to-night, without suspicion,
We might bear it with us to a covert near ;
Such sin, to save a childing wife, would earn it Christ's remission,
Though none forgive it here ! "

While he stood thinking,
A little bird, perched drinking
Among the crowfoot tufts the river bore,
Was tangled in their stringy arms and fluttered, almost sinking
Near him, upon the moor.

He stepped in, reached, and seized it,
And, preening, had released it
But that a thought of Holy Writ occurred,
And Signs Divine ere battle, till it seemed him Heaven had
pleased it
As guide to send the bird.

"O Lord, direct me ! . . .
Doth Duty now expect me
To march a-coast, or guard my weak ones near ?
Give this bird a flight according, that I thence learn to elect me
The southward or the rear."

He loosed his clasp ; when, rising,
The bird—as if surmising—
Bore due to southward, crossing by the Froom,
And Durnover Great Field and Fort, the soldier clear advising—
Prompted he deemed by Whom.

Then on he panted
By grim Mai-Don, and slanted
Up the steep Ridge-way, hearkening between whiles ;
Till nearing coast and harbour he beheld the shore-line planted
With Foot and Horse for miles.

Mistrusting not the omen,
He gained the beach, where Yeomen
Militia, Fencibles and Pikemen bold,
With Regulars in thousands, were enmassed to meet the Foemen,
Whose fleet had not yet shoaled.

Captain and Colonel,
Sere Generals, Ensigns vernal,
Were there ; of neighbour-natives, Michel, Smith,
Meggs, Bingham, Gambier, Cunningham, to face the said
nocturnal
Swoop on their land and kith.

But Buonaparte still tarried :
His project had miscarried ;
At the last hour, equipped for victory,
The fleet had paused ; his subtle combinations had been parried
      By British strategy.

Homeward returning
Anon, no beacons burning,
No alarms, the Volunteer, in modest bliss,
Te Deum sang with wife and friends : "We praise Thee, Lord,
      discerning
      That Thou hast helped in this !"

HER DEATH AND AFTER

THE summons was urgent : and forth I went—
By the way of the Western Wall, so drear
On that winter night, and sought a gate,
      Where one, by Fate,
      Lay dying that I held dear.

And there, as I paused by her tenement,
And the trees shed on me their rime and hoar,
I thought of the man who had left her lone—
      Him who made her his own
      When I loved her, long before.

The rooms within had the piteous shine
That home-things wear when there's aught amiss ;
From the stairway floated the rise and fall
      Of an infant's call,
      Whose birth had brought her to this.

Her life was the price she would pay for that whine—
For a child by the man she did not love.
"But let that rest for ever," I said,
      And bent my tread
      To the bedchamber above.

She took my hand in her thin white own,
And smiled her thanks—though nigh too weak—
And made them a sign to leave us there,
      Then faltered, ere
      She could bring herself to speak.

"Just to see you—before I go—he'll condone
Such a natural thing now my time's not much—
When Death is so near it hustles hence
    All passioned sense
   Between woman and man as such!

"My husband is absent. As heretofore
The City detains him. But, in truth,
He has not been kind. . . . I will speak no blame,
    But—the child is lame;
   O, I pray she may reach his ruth!

"Forgive past days—I can say no more—
Maybe had we wed you would now repine! . . .
But I treated you ill. I was punished. Farewell!
    —Truth shall I tell?
   Would the child were yours and mine!

"As a wife I was true. But, such my unease
That, could I insert a deed back in Time,
I'd make her yours, to secure your care;
    And the scandal bear,
   And the penalty for the crime!"

—When I had left, and the swinging trees
Rang above me, as lauding her candid say,
Another was I. Her words were enough:
    Came smooth, came rough,
   I felt I could live my day.

Next night she died; and her obsequies
In the Field of Tombs where the earthworks frowned
Had her husband's heed. His tendance spent,
    I often went
   And pondered by her mound.

All that year and the next year whiled,
And I still went thitherward in the gloam;
But the Town forgot her and her nook,
    And her husband took
   Another Love to his home.

And the rumour flew that the lame lone child
Whom she wished for its safety child of mine,
Was treated ill when offspring came
    Of the new-made dame,
    And marked a more vigorous line.

A smarter grief within me wrought
Than even at loss of her so dear
That the being whose soul my soul suffused
    Had a child ill-used,
    While I dared not interfere !

One eve as I stood at my spot of thought
In the white-stoned Garth, brooding thus her wrong,
Her husband neared ; and to shun his nod
    By her hallowed sod
    I went from the tombs among

To the Cirque of the Gladiators which faced——
That haggard mark of Imperial Rome,
Whose Pagan echoes mock the chime
    Of our Christian time
    From its hollows of chalk and loam.

The sun's gold touch was scarce displaced
From the vast Arena where men once bled,
When her husband followed ; bowed ; half-passed
    With lip upcast ;
    Then halting sullenly said :

' It is noised that you visit my first wife's tomb.
Now, I gave her an honoured name to bear
While living, when dead.   So I've claim to ask
    By what right you task
    My patience by vigiling there ?

" There's decency even in death, I assume ;
Preserve it, sir, and keep away ;
For the mother of my first-born you
    Show mind undue !
    —Sir, I've nothing more to say."

A desperate stroke discerned I then—
God pardon—or pardon not—the lie ;
She had sighed that she wished (lest the child should pine
      Of slights) 'twere mine,
   So I said : " But the father I.

" That you thought it yours is the way of men ;
But I won her troth long ere your day :
You learnt how, in dying, she summoned me ?
      'Twas in fealty.
   —Sir, I've nothing more to say,

" Save that, if you'll hand me my little maid,
I'll take her, and rear her, and spare you toil.
Think it more than a friendly act none can ;
      I'm a lonely man,
   While you've a large pot to boil.

" If not, and you'll put it to ball or blade—
To-night, to-morrow night, anywhen—
I'll meet you here. . . . But think of it,
      And in season fit
   Let me hear from you again."

—Well, I went away, hoping ; but nought I heard
Of my stroke for the child, till there greeted me
A little voice that one day came
      To my window-frame
   And babbled innocently :

" My father who's not my own, sends word
I'm to stay here, sir, where I belong ! "
Next a writing came : " Since the child was the fruit
      Of your lawless suit,
   Pray take her, to right a wrong."

And I did.   And I gave the child my love,
And the child loved me, and estranged us none.
But compunctions loomed ; for I'd harmed the dead
      By what I said
   For the good of the living one.

—Yet though, God wot, I am sinner enough,
And unworthy the woman who drew me so,
Perhaps this wrong for her darling's good
    She forgives, or would,
  If only she could know!

THE DANCE AT THE PHŒNIX

To Jenny came a gentle youth
  From inland leazes lone,
His love was fresh as apple-blooth
  By Parrett, Yeo, or Tone.
And duly he entreated her
To be his tender minister,
    And take him for her own.

Now Jenny's life had hardly been
  A life of modesty;
And few in Casterbridge had seen
  More loves of sorts than she
From scarcely sixteen years above;
Among them sundry troopers of
    The King's-Own Cavalry.

But each with charger, sword, and gun,
  Had bluffed the Biscay wave;
And Jenny prized her rural one
  For all the love he gave.
She vowed to be, if they were wed,
His honest wife in heart and head
    From bride-ale hour to grave.

Wedded they were. Her husband's trust
  In Jenny knew no bound,
And Jenny kept her pure and just,
  Till even malice found
No sin or sign of ill to be
In one who walked so decently
    The duteous helpmate's round.

Two sons were born, and bloomed to men,
    And roamed, and were as not :
Alone was Jenny left again
    As ere her mind had sought
A solace in domestic joys,
And ere the vanished pair of boys
    Were sent to sun her cot.

She numbered near on sixty years,
    And passed as elderly,
When, on a day, with flushing fears,
    She learnt from shouts of glee,
And shine of swords, and thump of drum,
Her early loves from war had come,
    The King's-Own Cavalry.

She turned aside, and bowed her head
    Anigh Saint Peter's door ;
" Alas for chastened thoughts ! " she said ;
    " I'm faded now, and hoar,
And yet those notes—they thrill me through,
And those gay forms move me anew
    As they moved me of yore ! " . . .

'Twas Christmas, and the Phœnix Inn
    Was lit with tapers tall,
For thirty of the trooper men
    Had vowed to give a ball
As " Theirs " had done ('twas handed down)
When lying in the selfsame town
    Ere Buonaparté's fall.

That night the throbbing " Soldier's Joy,"
    The measured tread and sway
" Of " Fancy-Lad " and " Maiden Coy,"
    Reached Jenny as she lay
Beside her spouse ; till springtide blood
Seemed scouring through her like a flood
    That whisked the years away.

She rose, arrayed, and decked her head
    Where the bleached hairs grew thin ;
Upon her cap two bows of red
    She fixed with hasty pin ;

Unheard descending to the street
  She trod the flags with tune-led feet,
    And stood before the Inn.

Save for the dancers', not a sound
    Disturbed the icy air;
No watchman on his midnight round
    Or traveller was there;
But over All-Saints', high and bright,
Pulsed to the music Sirius white,
    The Wain by Bullstake Square.

She knocked, but found her further stride
    Checked by a sergeant tall:
"Gay Granny, whence come you?" he cried:
    "This is a private ball."
—"No one has more right here than me!
Ere you were born, man," answered she,
    "I knew the regiment all!"

"Take not the lady's visit ill!"
    The steward said; "for see,
We lack sufficient partners still,
    So, prithee, let her be!"
They seized and whirled her mid the maze,
And Jenny felt as in the days
    Of her immodesty.

Hour chased each hour, and night advanced;
    She sped as shod with wings;
Each time and every time she danced—
    Reels, jigs, poussettes, and flings:
They cheered her as she soared and swooped,
(She had learnt ere art in dancing drooped
    From hops to slothful swings).

The favourite Quick-step "Speed the Plough"—
    (Cross hands, cast off, and wheel)—
"The Triumph," "Sylph," "The Row-dow-dow,"
    Famed "Major Malley's Reel,"
"The Duke of York's," "The Fairy Dance,"
"The Bridge of Lodi" (brought from France),
    She beat out, toe and heel.

The " Fall of Paris " clanged its close,
    And Peter's chime went four,
When Jenny, bosom-beating, rose
    To seek her silent door.
They tiptoed in escorting her,
Lest stroke of heel or clink of spur
    Should break her goodman's snore.

The fire that lately burnt fell slack
    When lone at last was she ;
Her nine-and-fifty years came back ;
    She sank upon her knee
Beside the durn, and like a dart
A something arrowed through her heart
    In shoots of agony.

Their footsteps died as she leant there,
    Lit by the morning star
Hanging above the moorland, where
    The aged elm-rows are ;
As overnight, from Pummery Ridge
To Maembury Ring and Standfast Bridge
    No life stirred, near or far.

Though inner mischief worked amain,
    She reached her husband's side ;
Where, toil-weary, as he had lain
    Beneath the patchwork pied
When forthward yestereve she crept,
And as unwitting, still he slept
    Who did in her confide.

A tear sprang as she turned and viewed
    His features free from guile ;
She kissed him long, as when, just wooed,
    She chose his domicile.
She felt she would give more than life
To be the single-hearted wife
    That she had been erstwhile. . . ,

Time wore to six.   Her husband rose
    And struck the steel and stone ;
He glanced at Jenny, whose repose
    Seemed deeper than his own.

With dumb dismay, on closer sight,
He gathered sense that in the night,
    Or morn, her soul had flown.

When told that some too mighty strain
    For one so many-yeared
Had burst her bosom's master-vein,
    His doubts remained unstirred.
His Jenny had not left his side
Betwixt the eve and morning-tide :
    —The King's said not a word.

Well ! times are not as times were then,
    Nor fair ones half so free ;
And truly they were martial men,
    The King's-Own Cavalry.
And when they went from Casterbridge
And vanished over Mellstock Ridge,
    'Twas saddest morn to see.

THE CASTERBRIDGE CAPTAINS

(KHYBER PASS, 1842)

A TRADITION OF J. B. L——, T. G. B——, AND J. L——

THREE captains went to Indian wars,
    And only one returned :
Their mate of yore, he singly wore
    The laurels all had earned.

At home he sought the ancient aisle
    Wherein, untrumped of fame,
The three had sat in pupilage,
    And each had carved his name.

The names, rough-hewn, of equal size,
    Stood on the panel still ;
Unequal since.—" 'Twas theirs to aim,
    Mine was it to fulfil ! "

—"Who saves his life shall lose it, friends!"
    Outspake the preacher then,
Unweeting he his listener, who
    Looked at the names again.

That he had come and they had been stayed
    Was but the chance of war:
Another chance, and they had been here,
    And he had lain afar.

Yet saw he something in the lives
    Of those who had ceased to live
That sphered them with a majesty
    Which living failed to give.

Transcendent triumph in return
    No longer lit his brain;
Transcendence rayed the distant urn
    Where slept the fallen twain.

A SIGN-SEEKER

I MARK the months in liveries dank and dry,
    The noontides many-shaped and hued;
    I see the nightfall shades subtrude,
And hear the monotonous hours clang negligently by.

I view the evening bonfires of the sun
    On hills where morning rains have hissed;
    The eyeless countenance of the mist
Pallidly rising when the summer droughts are done.

I have seen the lightning-blade, the leaping star,
    The cauldrons of the sea in storm,
    Have felt the earthquake's lifting arm,
And trodden where abysmal fires and snow-cones are.

I learn to prophesy the hid eclipse,
    The coming of eccentric orbs;
    To mete the dust the sky absorbs,
To weigh the sun, and fix the hour each planet dips.

I witness fellow earth-men surge and strive ;
    Assemblies meet, and throb, and part ;
    Death's sudden finger, sorrow's smart ;
—All the vast various moils that mean a world alive.

But that I fain would wot of shuns my sense—
    Those sights of which old prophets tell,
    Those signs the general word so well
As vouchsafed their unheed, denied my long suspense.

In graveyard green, where his pale dust lies pent
    To glimpse a phantom parent, friend,
    Wearing his smile, and " Not the end ! "
Outbreathing softly : that were blest enlightenment ;

Or, if a dead Love's lips, whom dreams reveal
    When midnight imps of King Decay
    Delve sly to solve me back to clay,
Should leave some print to prove her spirit-kisses real ;

Or, when Earth's Frail lie bleeding of her Strong,
    If some Recorder, as in Writ,
    Near to the weary scene should flit
And drop one plume as pledge that Heaven inscrolls the wrong

—There are who, rapt to heights of trancelike trust,
    These tokens claim to feel and see,
    Read radiant hints of times to be—
Of heart to heart returning after dust to dust.

Such scope is granted not to lives like mine . . .
    I have lain in dead men's beds, have walked
    The tombs of those with whom I had talked,
Called many a gone and goodly one to shape a sign,

And panted for response.   But none replies ;
    No warnings loom, nor whisperings
    To open out my limitings,
And Nescience mutely muses : When a man falls he lies.

MY CICELY

(17—)

"ALIVE?"—And I leapt in my wonder,
    Was faint of my joyance,
And grasses and grove shone in garments
    Of glory to me.

"She lives, in a plenteous well-being,
    To-day as aforehand ;
The dead bore the name—though a rare one—
    The name that bore she."

She lived . . . I, afar in the city
    Of frenzy-led factions,
Had squandered green years and maturer
    In bowing the knee

To Baals illusive and specious,
    Till chance had there voiced me
That one I loved vainly in nonage
    Had ceased her to be.

The passion the planets had scowled on,
    And change had let dwindle,
Her death-rumour smartly relifted
    To full apogee.

I mounted a steed in the dawning
    With acheful remembrance,
And made for the ancient West Highway
    To far Exonb'ry.

Passing heaths, and the House of Long Sieging,
    I neared the thin steeple
That tops the fair fane of Poore's olden
    Episcopal see ;

And, changing anew my blown bearer,
    I traversed the downland
Whereon the bleak hill-graves of Chieftains
    Bulge barren of tree ;

And still sadly onward I followed
    That Highway the Icen,
Which trails its pale riband down Wessex
    By lynchet and lea.

Along through the Stour-bordered Forum,
    Where Legions had wayfared,
And where the slow river-face glasses
    Its green canopy,

And by Weatherbury Castle, and thencefrom
    Through Casterbridge held I
Still on, to entomb her my mindsight
    Saw stretched pallidly.

No highwayman's trot blew the night-wind
    To me so life-weary,
But only the creak of a gibbet
    Or waggoner's jee.

Triple-ramparted Maidon gloomed grayly
    Above me from southward,
And north the hill-fortress of Eggar
    And square Pummerie.

The Nine-Pillared Cromlech, the Bride-streams,
    The Axe, and the Otter
I passed, to the gate of the city
    Where Exe scents the sea ;

Till, spent, in the graveacre pausing,
    I learnt 'twas not *my* Love
To whom Mother Church had just murmured
    A last lullaby.

—"Then, where dwells the Canon's kinswoman,
    My friend of aforetime ?"
I asked, to disguise my heart-heavings
    And new ecstasy.

" She wedded."—" Ah !"—" Wedded beneath her—
    She keeps the stage-hostel
Ten miles hence, beside the great Highway—
    The famed Lions-Three.

"Her spouse was her lackey—no option
  'Twixt wedlock and worse things ;
A lapse over-sad for a lady
  Of her pedigree ! "

I shuddered, said nothing, and wandered
  To shades of green laurel :
More ghastly than death were these tidings
  Of life's irony !

For, on my ride down I had halted
  Awhile at the Lions,
And her—her whose name had once opened
  My heart as a key—

I'd looked on, unknowing, and witnessed
  Her jests with the tapsters,
Her liquor-fired face, her thick accents
  In naming her fee.

"O God, why this seeming derision !
  I cried in my anguish :
"O once Loved, O fair Unforgotten—
  That Thing—meant it thee !

"Inurned and at peace, lost but sainted,
  Were grief I could compass ;
Depraved—'tis for Christ's poor dependent
  A cruel decree ! "

I backed on the Highway ; but passed not
  The hostel. Within there
Too mocking to Love's re-expression
  Was Time's repartee !

Uptracking where Legions had wayfared
  By cromlechs unstoried,
And lynchets, and sepultured Chieftains,
  In self-colloquy,

A feeling stirred in me and strengthened
  That *she* was not my Love,
But she of the garth, who lay rapt in
  Her long reverie.

And thence till to-day I persuade me
    That this was the true one;
That Death stole intact her young dearness
    And innocency.

Frail-witted, illuded they call me;
    I may be.   Far better
To dream than to own the debasement
    Of sweet Cicely.

Moreover I rate it unseemly
    To hold that kind Heaven
Could work such device—to her ruin
    And my misery.

So, lest I disturb my choice vision,
    I shun the West Highway,
Even now, when the knaps ring with rhythms
    From blackbird and bee;

And feel that with slumber half-conscious
    She rests in the church-hay,
Her spirit unsoiled as in youth-time
    When lovers were we.

HER IMMORTALITY

Upon a noon I pilgrimed through
    A pasture, mile by mile,
Unto the place where last I saw
    My dead Love's living smile.

And sorrowing I lay me down
    Upon the heated sod:
It seemed as if my body pressed
    The very ground she trod.

I lay, and thought; and in a trance
    She came and stood thereby—
The same, even to the marvellous ray
    That used to light her eye.

" You draw me, and I come to you,
  My faithful one," she said,
In voice that had the moving tone
  It bore ere she was wed.

" Seven years have circled since I died :
  Few now remember me ;
My husband clasps another bride .
  My children's love has she.

" My brethren, sisters, and my friends
  Care not to meet my sprite :
Who prized me most I did not know
  Till I passed down from sight."

I said : " My days are lonely here ;
  I need thy smile alway :
I'll use this night my ball or blade,
  And join thee ere the day."

A tremor stirred her tender lips,
  Which parted to dissuade :
" That cannot be, O friend," she cried ;
  " Think, I am but a Shade !

" A Shade but in its mindful ones
  Has immortality ;
By living, me you keep alive,
  By dying you slay me.

" In you resides my single power
  Of sweet continuance here ;
On your fidelity I count
  Through many a coming year.'

—I started through me at her plight,
  So suddenly confessed :
Dismissing late distaste for life,
  I craved its bleak unrest.

" I will not die, my One of all !—
  To lengthen out thy days
I'll guard me from minutest harms
  That may invest my ways ! "

She smiled and went.   Since then she comes
    Oft when her birth-moon climbs,
Or at the seasons' ingresses,
    Or anniversary times ;

But grows my grief.   When I surcease,
    Through whom alone lives she,
Her spirit ends its living lease,
    Never again to be !

THE IVY-WIFE

I LONGED to love a full-boughed beech
    And be as high as he :
I stretched an arm within his reach,
    And signalled unity.
But with his drip he forced a breach,
    And tried to poison me.

I gave the grasp of partnership
    To one of other race—
A plane : he barked him strip by strip
    From upper bough to base ;
And me therewith ; for gone my grip,
    My arms could not enlace.

In new affection next I strove
    To coll an ash I saw,
And he in trust received my love ;
    Till with my soft green claw
I cramped and bound him as I wove . . .
    Such was my love : ha-ha !

By this I gained his strength and height
    Without his rivalry.
But in my triumph I lost sight
    Of afterhaps.   Soon he,
Being bark-bound, flagged, snapped, fell outright,
    And in his fall felled me !

A MEETING WITH DESPAIR

As evening shaped I found me on a moor
    Sight shunned to entertain :
The black lean land, of featureless contour,
    Was like a tract in pain.

"This scene, like my own life," I said, "is one
    Where many glooms abide ;
Toned by its fortune to a deadly dun—
    Lightless on every side."

I glanced aloft and halted, pleasure-caught
    To see the contrast there :
The ray-lit clouds gleamed glory ; and I thought,
    "There's solace everywhere !"

Then bitter self-reproaches as I stood
    I dealt me silently
As one perverse, misrepresenting Good
    In graceless mutiny.

Against the horizon's dim-discernèd wheel
    A form rose, strange of mould :
That he was hideous, hopeless, I could feel
    Rather than could behold.

"'Tis a dead spot, where even the light lies spent
    To darkness !" croaked the Thing.
"Not if you look aloft !" said I, intent
    On my new reasoning.

"Yea—but await awhile !" he cried.   "Ho-ho !—
    Now look aloft and see !"
I looked.   There, too, sat night : Heaven's radiant show
    Had gone that heartened me.

UNKNOWING

When, soul in soul reflected,
    We breathed an æthered air,
When we neglected
    All things elsewhere,

And left the friendly friendless
To keep our love aglow,
We deemed it endless . . .
—We did not know !

When panting passion-goaded,
We planned to hie away,
But, unforeboded,
All the long day
The storm so pierced and pattered
That none could up and go,
Our lives seemed shattered . . .
—We did not know !

When I found you helpless lying,
And you waived my long misprise,
And swore me, dying,
In phantom-guise
To wing to me when grieving,
And touch away my woe,
We kissed, believing . . .
—We did not know !

But though, your powers outreckoning,
You tarry dead and dumb,
Or scorn my beckoning,
And will not come :
And I say, " Why thus inanely
Brood on her memory so !"
I say it vainly—
I feel and know !

FRIENDS BEYOND

WILLIAM DEWY, Tranter Reuben, Farmer Ledlow late at plough,
Robert's kin, and John's, and Ned's,
And the Squire, and Lady Susan, lie in Mellstock churchyard
now !

" Gone," I call them, gone for good, that group of local hearts
and heads ;
Yet at mothy curfew-tide,
And at midnight when the noon-heat breathes it back from walls
and leads,

They've a way of whispering to me—fellow-wight who yet abide—
    In the muted, measured note
Of a ripple under archways, or a lone cave's stillicide :

"We have triumphed : this achievement turns the bane to
    antidote,
    Unsuccesses to success,
Many thought-worn eves and morrows to a morrow free of
    thought.

"No more need we corn and clothing, feel of old terrestial stress ;
    Chill detraction stirs no sigh ;
Fear of death has even bygone us : death gave all that we
    possess."

W. D.—"Ye mid burn the old bass-viol that I set such value
    by."

Squire.—"You may hold the manse in fee,
    You may wed my spouse, may let my children's memory of
    me die."

Lady S.—"You may have my rich brocades, my laces ; take each
    household key ;
    Ransack coffer, desk, bureau ;
    Quiz the few poor treasures hid there, con the letters kept by
    me."

Far.—"Ye mid zell my favourite heifer, ye mid let the charlock
    grow,
    Foul the grinterns, give up thrift."

Far. Wife.—"If ye break my best blue china, children, I shan't
    care or ho."

All.—"We've no wish to hear the tidings, how the people's
    fortunes shift ;
    What your daily doings are ;
Who are wedded, born, divided ; if your lives beat slow or swift.

"Curious not the least are we if our intents you make or mar,
    If you quire to our old tune,
If the City stage still passes, if the weirs still roar afar."

—Thus, with very gods' composure, freed those crosses late
    and soon
    Which, in life, the Trine allow
(Why, none witteth), and ignoring all that haps beneath the moon,

William Dewy, Tranter Reuben, Farmer Ledlow late at plough,
    Robert's kin, and John's, and Ned's,
And the Squire, and Lady Susan, murmur mildly to me now.

TO OUTER NATURE

Show thee as I thought thee
When I early sought thee,
    Omen-scouting,
    All undoubting
Love alone had wrought thee—

Wrought thee for my pleasure,
Planned thee as a measure
    For expounding
    And resounding
Glad things that men treasure.

O for but a moment
Of that old endowment—
    Light to gaily
    See thy daily
Iris-hued embowment!

But such re-adorning
Time forbids with scorning—
    Makes me see things
    Cease to be things
They were in my morning.

Fad'st thou, glow-forsaken,
Darkness-overtaken!
    Thy first sweetness,
    Radiance, meetness,
None shall re-awaken.

Why not sempiternal
Thou and I? Our vernal
    Brightness keeping,
    Time outleaping;
Passed the hodiernal!

THOUGHTS OF PHENA

AT NEWS OF HER DEATH

NOT a line of her writing have I,
　　Not a thread of her hair,
No mark of her late time as dame in her dwelling, whereby
　　　I may picture her there ;
　　And in vain do I urge my unsight
　　　To conceive my lost prize
At her close, whom I knew when her dreams were upbrimming
　　　　　with light,
　　　And with laughter her eyes.

　　What scenes spread around her last days,
　　　Sad, shining, or dim ?
Did her gifts and compassions enray and enarch her sweet ways
　　　With an aureate nimb ?
　　Or did life-light decline from her years,
　　　And mischances control
Her full day-star ; unease, or regret, or forebodings, or fears
　　　Disennoble her soul ?

　　Thus I do but the phantom retain
　　　Of the maiden of yore
As my relic ; yet haply the best of her—fined in my brain
　　　It may be the more
　　That no line of her writing have I,
　　　Nor a thread of her hair,
No mark of her late time as dame in her dwelling, whereby
　　　I may picture her there.

March 1890.

MIDDLE-AGE ENTHUSIASMS

TO M. H.

　　WE passed where flag and flower
　　Signalled a jocund throng ;
　　We said : " Go to, the hour
　　Is apt !"—and joined the song ;
　　And, kindling, laughed at life and care,
　　Although we knew no laugh lay there.

We walked where shy birds stood
　　Watching us, wonder-dumb ;
　　Their friendship met our mood ;
　　We cried : " We'll often come :
We'll come morn, noon, eve, everywhen ! "
—We doubted we should come again.

We joyed to see strange sheens
　　Leap from quaint leaves in shade ;
　　A secret light of greens
　　They'd for their pleasure made.
We said : " We'll set such sorts as these ! "
—We knew with night the wish would cease.

" So sweet the place," we said,
　　" Its tacit tales so dear,
　　Our thoughts, when breath has sped,
　　Will meet and mingle here ! " . . . .
" Words ! " mused we.　" Passed the mortal door.
Our thoughts will reach this nook no more."

IN A WOOD

From " The Woodlanders "

PALE beech and pine so blue,
　　Set in one clay,
　　Bough to bough cannot you
　　Live out your day ?
When the rains skim and skip,
Why mar sweet comradeship,
Blighting with poison-drip
　　Neighbourly spray ?

Heart-halt and spirit-lame,
　　City-opprest,
　　Unto this wood I came
　　As to a nest ;
Dreaming that sylvan peace
Offered the harrowed ease—
Nature a soft release
　　From men's unrest.

But, having entered in,
　　Great growths and small
Show them to men akin——
　　Combatants all !
Sycamore shoulders oak,
Bines the slim sapling yoke,
Ivy-spun halters choke
　　Elms stout and tall.

Touches from ash, O wych,
　　Sting you like scorn !
You, too, brave hollies, twitch
　　Sidelong from thorn.
Even the rank poplars bear
Lothly a rival's air,
Cankering in black despair
　　If overborne.

Since, then, no grace I find
　　Taught me of trees,
Turn I back to my kind,
　　Worthy as these.
There at least smiles abound,
There discourse trills around,
There, now and then, are found
　　Life-loyalties.

1887 : 1896.

TO A LADY

OFFENDED BY A BOOK OF THE WRITER'S

Now that my page is exiled,—doomed, maybe,
Never to press thy cosy cushions more,
Or wake thy ready Yeas as heretofore,
Or stir thy gentle vows of faith in me :

Knowing thy natural receptivity,
I figure that, as flambeaux banish eve,
My sombre image, warped by insidious heave
Of those less forthright, must lose place in thee.

So be it.   I have borne such.   Let thy dreams
Of me and mine diminish day by day,
And yield their space to shine of smugger things ;
Till I shape to thee but in fitful gleams,
And then in far and feeble visitings,
And then surcease.   Truth will be truth alway.

TO A MOTHERLESS CHILD

AH, child, thou art but half thy darling mother's ;
        Hers couldst thou wholly be,
My light in thee would outglow all in others ;
        She would relive to me.
But niggard Nature's trick of birth
        Bars, lest she overjoy,
Renewal of the loved on earth
        Save with alloy.

The Dame has no regard, alas, my maiden,
        For love and loss like mine—
No sympathy with mindsight memory-laden ;
        Only with fickle eyne.
To her mechanic artistry
        My dreams are all unknown,
And why I wish that thou couldst be
        But One's alone !

NATURE'S QUESTIONING

WHEN I look forth at dawning, pool,
        Field, flock, and lonely tree,
        All seem to gaze at me
Like chastened children sitting silent in a school ;

Their faces dulled, constrained, and worn,
        As though the master's ways
        Through the long teaching days
Had cowed them till their early zest was overborne.

Upon them stirs in lippings mere
    (As if once clear in call,
    But now scarce breathed at all)—
" We wonder, ever wonder, why we find us here !

  " Has some Vast Imbecility,
    Mighty to build and blend,
    But impotent to tend,
Framed us in jest, and left us now to hazardry ?

  " Or come we of an Automaton
    Unconscious of our pains ? . . .
    Or are we live remains
Of Godhead dying downwards, brain and eye now gone ?

  " Or is it that some high Plan betides,
    As yet not understood,
    Of Evil stormed by Good,
We the Forlorn Hope over which Achievement strides ? "

Thus things around.   No answerer I. . .
    Meanwhile the winds, and rains,
    And Earth's old glooms and pains
Are still the same, and Life and Death are neighbours nigh.

THE IMPERCIPIENT

(AT A CATHEDRAL SERVICE)

THAT with this bright believing band
    I have no claim to be,
That faiths by which my comrades stand
    Seem fantasies to me,
And mirage-mists their Shining Land,
    Is a strange destiny.

Why thus my soul should be consigned
    To infelicity,
Why always I must feel as blind
    To sights my brethren see,
Why joys they've found I cannot find,
    Abides a mystery.

Since heart of mine knows not that ease
    Which they know ; since it be
That He who breathes All's Well to these
    Breathes no All's-Well to me,
My lack might move their sympathies
    And Christian charity !

I am like a gazer who should mark
    An inland company
Standing upfingered, with, " Hark ! hark !
    The glorious distant sea ! "
And feel, " Alas, 'tis but yon dark
    And wind-swept pine to me ! "

Yet I would bear my shortcomings
    With meet tranquillity,
But for the charge that blessed things
    I'd liefer not have be.
O, doth a bird deprived of wings
    Go earth-bound wilfully !

.   .   .   .

Enough.   As yet disquiet clings
    About us.   Rest shall we.

AT AN INN

WHEN we as strangers sought
    Their catering care,
Veiled smiles bespoke their thought
    Of what we were.
They warmed as they opined
    Us more than friends—
That we had all resigned
    For love's dear ends.

And that swift sympathy
    With living love
Which quicks the world—maybe
    The spheres above,
Made them our ministers,
    Moved them to say,
" Ah, God, that bliss like theirs
    Would flush our day ! "

And we were left alone
    As Love's own pair;
Yet never the love-light shone
    Between us there!
But that which chilled the breath
    Of afternoon,
And palsied unto death
    The pane-fly's tune.

The kiss their zeal foretold,
    And now deemed come,
Came not: within his hold
    Love lingered numb.
Why cast he on our port
    A bloom not ours?
Why shaped us for his sport
    In after-hours?

As we seemed we were not
    That day afar,
And now we seem not what
    We aching are.
O severing sea and land,
    O laws of men,
Ere death, once let us stand
    As we stood then!

THE SLOW NATURE

(AN INCIDENT OF FROOM VALLEY)

"THY husband—poor, poor Heart!—is dead—
    Dead, out by Moreford Rise;
A bull escaped the barton-shed,
    Gored him, and there he lies!"

—"Ha, ha—go away! 'Tis a tale, methink,
    Thou joker Kit!" laughed she.
"I've known thee many a year, Kit Twink,
    And ever hast thou fooled me!"

—" But, Mistress Damon—I can swear
  Thy goodman John is dead !
And soon th'lt hear their feet who bear
  His body to his bed."

So unwontedly sad was the merry man's face—
  That face which had long deceived—
That she gazed and gazed ; and then could trace
  The truth there ; and she believed.

She laid a hand on the dresser-ledge,
  And scanned far Egdon-side ;
And stood ; and you heard the wind-swept sedge
  And the rippling Froom ; till she cried ·

" O my chamber's untidied, unmade my bed.
  Though the day has begun to wear !
' What a slovenly hussif !' it will be said,
  When they all go up my stair ! "

She disappeared ; and the joker stood
  Depressed by his neighbour's doom,
And amazed that a wife struck to widowhood
  Thought first of her unkempt room.

But a fortnight thence she could take no food,
  And she pined in a slow decay ;
While Kit soon lost his mournful mood
  And laughed in his ancient way.

 1894.

IN A EWELEAZE NEAR WEATHERBURY

THE years have gathered grayly
  Since I danced upon this leaze
With one who kindled gaily
  Love's fitful ecstasies !
But despite the term as teacher,
  I remain what I was then
In each essential feature
  Of the fantasies of men.

Yet I note the little chisel
　Of never-napping Time
Defacing wan and grizzel
　The blazon of my prime.
When at night he thinks me sleeping
　I feel him boring sly
Within my bones, and heaping
　Quaintest pains for by-and-by.

Still, I'd go the world with Beauty,
　I would laugh with her and sing,
I would shun divinest duty
　To resume her worshipping.
But she'd scorn my brave endeavour,
　She would not balm the breeze
By murmuring " Thine for ever ! "
　As she did upon this leaze.

1890.

THE BRIDE-NIGHT FIRE

(A WESSEX TRADITION)

THEY had long met o' Zundays—her true love and she—
　And at junketings, maypoles, and flings ;
But she bode wi' a thirtover [1] uncle, and he
Swore by noon and by night that her goodman should be
Naibour Sweatley—a wight often weak at the knee
　From taking o' sommat more cheerful than tea—
　Who tranted,[2] and moved people's things.

She cried, " O pray pity me ! "   Nought would he hear ;
　Then with wild rainy eyes she obeyed.
She chid when her Love was for clinking off wi' her :
The pa'son was told, as the season drew near,
To throw over pu'pit the names of the pair
　As fitting one flesh to be made.

The wedding-day dawned and the morning drew on ;
　The couple stood bridegroom and bride ;
The evening was passed, and when midnight had gone
The feasters horned,[3] " God save the King," and anon
　The pair took their homealong [4] ride.

---

[1] *thirtover*, cross.   [2] *tranted*, traded as carrier.
[3] *horned*, sang loudly.   [4] *homealong*, homeward.

The lover Tim Tankens mourned heart-sick and leer [1]
  To be thus of his darling deprived :
He roamed in the dark ath'art field, mound, and mere,
And, a'most without knowing it, found himself near
The house of the tranter, and now of his Dear,
  Where the lantern-light showed 'em arrived.

The bride sought her chamber so calm and so pale
  That a Northern had thought her resigned ;
But to eyes that had seen her in tidetimes [2] of weal,
Like the white cloud o' smoke, the red battlefield's vail,
  That look spak' of havoc behind.

The bridegroom yet laitered a beaker to drain,
  Then reeled to the linhay [3] for more,
When the candle-snoff kindled some chaff from his grain—
Flames spread, and red vlankers [4] wi' might and wi' main
  Around beams, thatch, and chimley-tun [5] roar.

Young Tim away yond, rafted [6] up by the light,
  Through brimbles and underwood tears,
Till he comes to the orchet, when crooping [7] from sight
In the lewth [8] of a codlin-tree, bivering [9] wi' fright,
Wi' on'y her night-rail to cover her plight,
  His lonesome young Barbree appears.

Her cwold little figure half-naked he views
  Played about by the frolicsome breeze,
Her light-tripping totties,[10] her ten little tooes,
All bare and besprinkled wi' Fall's [11] chilly dews,
While her great gallied [12] eyes through her hair hanging loose
  Shone as stars through a tardle [13] o' trees.

She eyed him ; and, as when a weir-hatch is drawn,
  Her tears, penned by terror afore,
With a rushing of sobs in a shower were strawn,
Till her power to pour 'em seemed wasted and gone
  From the heft [14] o' misfortune she bore.

---

1 *leer*, empty-stomached.   2 *tidetimes*, holidays.
3 *linhay*, lean-to building.   4 *vlankers*, fire-flakes.
5 *chimley-tun*, chimney-stack.   6 *rafted*, roused.
7 *crooping*, squatting down.   8 *lewth*, shelter.
9 *bivering*. with chattering teeth   10 *totties*, feet.
11 *Fall*, autumn.   12 *gallied*. frightened.
13 *tardle*. entanglement.   14 *heft*, weight.

"O Tim, my *own* Tim I must call 'ee—I will!
    All the world has turned round on me so!
Can you help her who loved 'ee, though acting so ill?
Can you pity her misery—feel for her still?
When worse than her body so quivering and chill
    Is her heart in its winter o' woe!

"I think I mid [1] almost ha' borne it," she said,
    "Had my griefs one by one come to hand;
But O, to be slave to thik husbird,[2] for bread,
And then, upon top o' that, driven to wed,
And then, upon top o' that, burnt out o' bed,
    Is more than my nater can stand!"

Like a lion 'ithin' en Tim's spirit outsprung—
    (Tim had a great soul when his feelings were wrung)—
    "Feel for 'ee, dear Barbree?" he cried;
And his warm working-jacket then straightway he flung
Round about her, and horsed her by jerks, till she clung
Like a chiel on a gipsy, her figure uphung
    By the sleeves that he tightly had tied.

Over piggeries, and mixens,[3] and apples, and hay,
    They lumpered [4] straight into the night;
And finding ere long where a halter-path [5] lay,
Sighted Tim's house by dawn, on'y seen on their way
By a naibour or two who were up wi' the day,
    But who gathered no clue to the sight.

Then tender Tim Tankens he searched here and there
    For some garment to clothe her fair skin;
But though he had breeches and waistcoats to spare,
He had nothing quite seemly for Barbree to wear,
Who, half shrammed [6] to death, stood and cried on a chair
    At the caddle [7] she found herself in.

There was one thing to do, and that one thing he did,
    He lent her some clothes of his own,

---

[1] *mid*, might.
[2] *thik husbird*, that rascal.
[3] *mixens*, manure-heaps.
[4] *lumpered* stumbled.
[5] *halter-path*, bridle-path.
[6] *shrammed*, numbed.
[7] *caddle*, quandary.

And she took 'em perforce ; and while swiftly she slid
Them upon her Tim turned to the winder, as bid,
Thinking, " O that the picter my duty keeps hid
　　To the sight o' my eyes mid [1] be shown ! "

In the tallet [2] he stowed her ; there huddied [3] she lay,
　　Shortening sleeves, legs, and tails to her limbs ;
But most o' the time in a mortal bad way,
Well knowing that there'd be the divel to pay
If 'twere found that, instead o' the element's prey,
　　She was living in lodgings at Tim's.

" Where's the tranter ? " said men and boys ; " where can
　　　　he be ? "
　　" Where's the tranter ? " said Barbree alone.
" Where on e'th is the tranter ? " said everybod-y :
They sifted the dust of his perished roof-tree,
　　And all they could find was a bone.

Then the uncle cried, " Lord, pray have mercy on me ! "
　　And in terror began to repent.
But before 'twas complete, and till sure she was free,
Barbree drew up her loft-ladder, tight turned her key—
Tim bringing up breakfast and dinner and tea—
　　Till the news of her hiding got vent.

Then followed the custom-kept rout, shout, and flare
Of a skimmity-ride [4] through the naibourhood, ere
　　Folk had proof o' wold [5] Sweatley's decay.
Whereupon decent people all stood in a stare,
Saying Tim and his lodger should risk it, and pair :
So he took her to church. An' some laughing lads there
Cried to Tim, " After Sweatley ! " She said, " I declare
　　I stand as a maiden to-day ! "

　　　　　Written 1866 ; *printed* 1875.

1 *mid*, might.　　　　　　　　2 *tallet*, loft.
3 *huddied*, hidden.　　　　　4 *skimmity-ride*, satirical procession with effigies.
　　　　　　　　　　　　　　　5 *wold*, old.

HEIRESS AND ARCHITECT

FOR A. W. BLOMFIELD

SHE sought the Studios, beckoning to her side
An arch-designer, for she planned to build.
He was of wise contrivance, deeply skilled
In every intervolve of high and wide—
      Well fit to be her guide.

    "Whatever it be,"
    Responded he,
With cold, clear voice, and cold, clear view,
"In true accord with prudent fashionings
For such vicissitudes as living brings,
And thwarting not the law of stable things,
      That will I do."

"Shape me," she said, "high halls with tracery
And open ogive-work, that scent and hue
Of buds, and travelling bees, may come in through,
The note of birds, and singings of the sea,
      For these are much to me."

    "An idle whim!"
    Broke forth from him
Whom nought could warm to gallantries:
"Cede all these buds and birds, the zephyr's call,
And scents, and hues, and things that falter all,
And choose as best the close and surly wall,
      For winters freeze."

"Then frame," she cried, "wide fronts of crystal glass,
That I may show my laughter and my light—
Light like the sun's by day, the stars' by night—
Till rival heart-queens, envying, wail, 'Alas,
      Her glory!' as they pass."

    "O maid misled!"
    He sternly said
Whose facile foresight pierced her dire;
"Where shall abide the soul when, sick of glee,
It shrinks, and hides, and prays no eye may see?
Those house them best who house for secrecy,
      For you will tire."

"A little chamber, then, with swan and dove
Ranged thickly, and engrailed with rare device
Of reds and purples, for a Paradise
Wherein my Love may greet me, I my Love,
    When he shall know thereof?"

      "This, too, is ill,"
      He answered still,
The man who swayed her like a shade.
"An hour will come when sight of such sweet nook
Would bring a bitterness too sharp to brook,
When brighter eyes have won away his look ;
    For you will fade."

Then said she faintly : "O, contrive some way—
Some narrow winding turret, quite mine own,
To reach a loft where I may grieve alone !
It is a slight thing ; hence do not, I pray,
    This last dear fancy slay !"

      "Such winding ways
      Fit not your days,"
Said he, the man of measuring eye ;
"I must even fashion as the rule declares,
To wit : Give space (since life ends unawares)
To hale a coffined corpse adown the stairs ;
    For you will die."

1867.   8 ADELPHI TERRACE.

THE TWO MEN

THERE were two youths of equal age,
Wit, station, strength, and parentage ;
They studied at the selfsame schools,
And shaped their thoughts by common rules.

One pondered on the life of man,
His hopes, his ending, and began
To rate the Market's sordid war
As something scarce worth living for

" I'll brace to higher aims," said he,
" I'll further Truth and Purity;
Thereby to mend the mortal lot
And sweeten sorrow.   Thrive I not,

" Winning their hearts, my kind will give
Enough that I may lowly live,
And house my Love in some dim dell,
For pleasing them and theirs so well."

Idly attired, with features wan,
In secret swift he laboured on :
Such press of power had brought much gold
Applied to things of meaner mould.

Sometimes he wished his aims had been
To gather gains like other men ;
Then thanked his God he'd traced his track
Too far for wish to drag him back.

He looked down from his loft one day
To where his slighted garden lay ;
Nettles and hemlock hid each lawn,
And every flower was starved and gone.

He fainted in his heart, whereon
He rose, and sought his plighted one,
Resolved to loose her bond withal,
Lest she should perish in his fall.

He met her with a careless air,
As though he'd ceased to find her fair,
And said : " True love is dust to me ;
I cannot kiss : I tire of thee ! "

(That she might scorn him was he fain,
To put her sooner out of pain ;
For angered love breathes quick and dies,
When famished love long-lingering lies.)

Once done, his soul was so betossed,
It found no more the force it lost :
Hope was his only drink and food,
And hope extinct, decay ensued.

And, living long so closely penned,
He had not kept a single friend ;
He dwindled thin as phantoms be,
And drooped to death in poverty. . . .

Meantime his schoolmate had gone out
To join the fortune-finding rout ;
He liked the winnings of the mart,
But wearied of the working part.

He turned to seek a privy lair,
Neglecting note of garb and hair,
And day by day reclined and thought
How he might live by doing nought.

"I plan a valued scheme" he said
To some. "But lend me of your bread,
And when the vast result looms nigh,
In profit you shall stand as I."

Yet they took counsel to restrain
Their kindness till they saw the gain ;
And, since his substance now had run,
He rose to do what might be done.

He went unto his Love by night,
And said : "My Love, I faint in fight :
Deserving as thou dost a crown,
My cares shall never drag thee down."

(He had descried a maid whose line
Would hand her on much corn and wine,
And held her far in worth above
One who could only pray and love.)

But this Fair read him ; whence he failed
To do the deed so blithely hailed ;
He saw his projects wholly marred,
And gloom and want oppressed him hard ;

Till, living to so mean an end,
Whereby he'd lost his every friend,
He perished in the pauper sty
Where his old mate lay dying nigh.

And moralists, reflecting, said,
As " dust to dust " anon was read
And echoed from each coffin-lid,
" These men were like in all they did."
    1866.

LINES

Spoken by Miss ADA REHAN *at the Lyceum Theatre, July* 23,
*1890, at a performance on behalf of Lady Jeune's Holiday
Fund for City Children.*

BEFORE we part to alien thoughts and aims,
Permit the one brief word the occasion claims :
—When mumming and grave motives are allied,
Perhaps an Epilogue is justified.

Our under-purpose has, in truth, to-day
Commanded most our musings ; least the play :
A purpose futile but for your good-will
Swiftly responsive to the cry of ill :
A purpose all too limited !— to aid
Frail human flowerets, sicklied by the shade,
In winning some short spell of upland breeze,
Or strengthening sunlight on the level leas.

Who has not marked, where the full cheek should be,
Incipient lines of lank flaccidity,
Lymphatic pallor where the pink should glow,
And where the throb of transport, pulses low ?—
Most tragical of shapes from Pole to Line,
O wondering child, unwitting Time's design,
Why should Man add to Nature's quandary,
And worsen ill by thus immuring thee ?
—That races do despite unto their own,
That Might supernal do indeed condone
Wrongs individual for the general ease,
Instance the proof in victims such as these.

Launched into thoroughfares too thronged before,
Mothered by those whose protest is " No more ! "

Vitalized without option : who shall say
That did Life hang on choosing—Yea or Nay—
They had not scorned it with such penalty,
And nothingness implored of Destiny ?

And yet behind the horizon smile serene
The down, the cornland, and the stretching green—
Space—the child's heaven : scenes which at least ensure
Some palliative for ill they cannot cure.

Dear friends—now moved by this poor show of ours
To make your own long joy in buds and bowers
For one brief while the joy of infant eyes,
Changing their urban murk to paradise—
You have our thanks !—may your reward include
More than our thanks, far more : their gratitude.

SAVILE CLUB, *Midnight, July* 1890.

"I LOOK INTO MY GLASS"

I LOOK into my glass,
And view my wasting skin,
And say, "Would God it came to pass
My heart had shrunk as thin !"

For then, I, undistrest
By hearts grown cold to me,
Could lonely wait my endless rest
With equanimity.

But Time, to make me grieve,
Part steals, lets part abide ;
And shakes this fragile frame at eve
With throbbings of noontide.

POEMS OF
THE PAST AND THE PRESENT

PREFACE

HEREWITH I tender my thanks to the editors and proprietors of the *Times*, the *Morning Post*, the *Daily Chronicle*, the *Westminster Gazette*, *Literature*, the *Graphic*, *Cornhill*, *Sphere*, and other papers, for permission to reprint from their pages such of the following pieces of verse as have already been published.

Of the subject-matter of this volume—even that which is in other than narrative form—much is dramatic or impersonative even where not explicitly so. Moreover, that portion which may be regarded as individual comprises a series of feelings and fancies written down in widely differing moods and circumstances, and at various dates. It will probably be found, therefore, to possess little cohesion of thought or harmony of colouring. I do not greatly regret this. Unadjusted impressions have their value, and the road to a true philosophy of life seems to lie in humbly recording diverse readings of its phenomena as they are forced upon us by chance and change.

T.H.

August 1901.

V.R. 1819–1901

A REVERIE

THE mightiest moments pass uncalendared,
    And when the Absolute
In backward Time pronounced the deedful word
    Whereby all life is stirred :
"Let one be born and throned whose mould shall constitute
The norm of every royal-reckoned attribute,"
    No mortal knew or heard.

    But in due days the purposed Life outshone—
      Serene, sagacious, free ;
    Her waxing seasons bloomed with deeds well done,
      And the world's heart was won . . .
Yet may the deed of hers most bright in eyes to be
Lie hid from ours—as in the All-One's thought lay she—
      Till ripening years have run.

SUNDAY NIGHT,
   27th January 1901.

77

WAR POEMS

EMBARCATION

(Southampton Docks: October 1899)

HERE, where Vespasian's legions struck the sands,
And Cerdic with his Saxons entered in,
And Henry's army leapt afloat to win
Convincing triumphs over neighbour lands,

Vaster battalions press for further strands,
To argue in the selfsame bloody mode
Which this late age of thought, and pact, and code,
Still fails to mend.—Now deckward tramp the bands,

Yellow as autumn leaves, alive as spring;
And as each host draws out upon the sea
Beyond which lies the tragical To-be,
None dubious of the cause, none murmuring,

Wives, sisters, parents, wave white hands and smile,
As if they knew not that they weep the while.

DEPARTURE

(Southampton Docks: October 1899)

WHILE the far farewell music thins and fails,
And the broad bottoms rip the bearing brine—
All smalling slowly to the gray sea-line—
And each significant red smoke-shaft pales,

Keen sense of severance everywhere prevails,
Which shapes the late long tramp of mounting men
To seeming words that ask and ask again :
" How long, O striving Teutons, Slavs, and Gaels

Must your wroth reasonings trade on lives like these,
That are as puppets in a playing hand ?—
When shall the saner softer polities
Whereof we dream, have sway in each proud land
And patriotism, grown Godlike, scorn to stand
Bondslave to realms, but circle earth and seas ? "

THE COLONEL'S SOLILOQUY

(Southampton Docks : October 1899)

" THE quay recedes.   Hurrah ! Ahead we go ! . . .
It's true I've been accustomed now to home,
And joints get rusty, and one's limbs may grow
      More fit to rest than roam.

" But I can stand as yet fair stress and strain ;
There's not a little steel beneath the rust ;
My years mount somewhat, but here's to't again !
      And if I fall, I must.

" God knows that for myself I have scanty care ;
Past scrimmages have proved as much to all ;
In Eastern lands and South I have had my share
      Both of the blade and ball.

" And where those villains ripped me in the flitch
With their old iron in my early time,
I'm apt at change of wind to feel a twitch,
      Or at a change of clime.

"And what my mirror shows me in the morning
Has more of blotch and wrinkle than of bloom ;
My eyes, too, heretofore all glasses scorning,
    Have just a touch of rheum. . . .

"Now sounds 'The Girl I've left behind me,'—Ah,
The years, the ardours, wakened by that tune !
Time was when, with the crowd's farewell 'Hurrah !'
    'Twould lift me to the moon.

"But now it's late to leave behind me one
Who if, poor soul, her man goes underground,
Will not recover as she might have done
    In days when hopes abound.

"She's waving from the wharfside, palely grieving,
As down we draw. . . . Her tears make little show,
Yet now she suffers more than at my leaving
    Some twenty years ago !

"I pray those left at home will care for her ;
I shall come back ; I have before ; though when
The Girl you leave behind you is a grandmother,
    Things may not be as then."

THE GOING OF THE BATTERY

WIVES' LAMENT

(*November* 2, 1899)

I

O IT was sad enough, weak enough, mad enough—
Light in their loving as soldiers can be—
First to risk choosing them, leave alone losing them
Now, in far battle, beyond the South Sea ! . . .

II

—Rain came down drenchingly ; but we unblenchingly
Trudged on beside them through mirk and through mire,
They stepping steadily—only too readily !—
Scarce as if stepping brought parting-time nigher.

III

Great guns were gleaming there, living things seeming there,
Cloaked in their tar-cloths, upmouthed to the night ;
Wheels wet and yellow from axle to felloe,
Throats blank of sound, but prophetic to sight.

IV

Gas-glimmers drearily, blearily, eerily
Lit our pale faces outstretched for one kiss,
While we stood prest to them, with a last quest to them
Not to court perils that honour could miss.

V

Sharp were those sighs of ours, blinded these eyes of ours,
When at last moved away under the arch
All we loved.   Aid for them each woman prayed for them,
Treading back slowly the track of their march.

VI

Some one said : " Nevermore will they come : evermore
Are they now lost to us." O it was wrong !
Though may be hard their ways, some Hand will guard their
     ways,
Bear them through safely, in brief time or long.

VII

—Yet, voices haunting us, daunting us, taunting us,
Hint in the night-time when life beats are low
Other and graver things. . . . Hold we to braver things,
Wait we, in trust, what Time's fulness shall show.

AT THE WAR OFFICE, LONDON

(Affixing the Lists of Killed and Wounded : December 1899)

I

LAST year I called this world of gaingivings
The darkest thinkable, and questioned sadly
If my own land could heave its pulse less gladly,
So charged it seemed with circumstance that brings
        The tragedy of things.

II

Yet at that censured time no heart was rent
Or feature blanched of parent, wife, or daughter
By hourly posted sheets of scheduled slaughter ;
Death waited Nature's wont ; Peace smiled unshent
        From Ind to Occident.

A CHRISTMAS GHOST-STORY

SOUTH of the Line, inland from far Durban,
A mouldering soldier lies—your countryman.
Awry and doubled up are his gray bones,
And on the breeze his puzzled phantom moans
Nightly to clear Canopus : " I would know
By whom and when the All-Earth-gladdening Law
Of Peace, brought in by that Man Crucified,
Was ruled to be inept, and set aside ?
And what of logic or of truth appears
In tacking 'Anno Domini' to the years?
Near twenty-hundred liveried thus have hied,
But tarries yet the Cause for which He died."

Christmas-eve 1899.

DRUMMER HODGE

I

THEY throw in Drummer Hodge, to rest
    Uncoffined—just as found :
His landmark is a kopje-crest
    That breaks the veldt around ;
And foreign constellations west
    Each night above his mound.

II

Young Hodge the Drummer never knew—
    Fresh from his Wessex home—
The meaning of the broad Karoo,
    The Bush, the dusty loam,
And why uprose to nightly view
    Strange stars amid the gloam.

III

Yet portion of that unknown plain
    Will Hodge for ever be ;
His homely Northern breast and brain
    Grow to some Southern tree,
And strange-eyed constellations reign
    His stars eternally.

A WIFE IN LONDON

(*December* 1899)

I

SHE sits in the tawny vapour
    That the Thames-side lanes have uprolled,
    Behind whose webby fold on fold
Like a waning taper
    The street-lamp glimmers cold.

A messenger's knock cracks smartly,
    Flashed news is in her hand
    Of meaning it dazes to understand
Though shaped so shortly :
    He—has fallen—in the far South Land. . . .

II

'Tis the morrow ; the fog hangs thicker,
  The postman nears and goes :
    A letter is brought whose lines disclose
  By the firelight flicker
    His hand, whom the worm now knows :

Fresh—firm—penned in highest feather—
  Page-full of his hoped return,
    And of home-planned jaunts by brake and burn
  In the summer weather,
    And of new love that they would learn.

THE SOULS OF THE SLAIN

I

The thick lids of Night closed upon me
  Alone at the Bill
    Of the Isle by the Race [1]—
Many-caverned, bald, wrinkled of face—
And with darkness and silence the spirit was on me
  To brood and be still.

II

No wind fanned the flats of the ocean,
  Or promontory sides,
    Or the ooze by the strand,
    Or the bent-bearded slope of the land,
Whose base took its rest amid everlong motion
  Of criss-crossing tides.

III

Soon from out of the Southward seemed nearing
  A whirr, as of wings
    Waved by mighty-vanned flies,
    Or by night-moths of measureless size,
And in softness and smoothness weil-nigh beyond hearing
  Of corporal things.

[1] The "Race" is the turbulent sea-area off the Bill of Portland, where contrary tides meet.

IV

And they bore to the bluff, and alighted—
A dim-discerned train
Of sprites without mould,
Frameless souls none might touch or might hold—
On the ledge by the turreted lantern, far-sighted
By men of the main.

V

And I heard them say "Home!" and I knew them
For souls of the felled
On the earth's nether bord
Under Capricorn, whither they'd warred,
And I neared in my awe, and gave heedfulness to them
With breathings inheld.

VI

Then, it seemed, there approached from the northward
A senior soul-flame
Of the like filmy hue:
And he met them and spake: "Is it you,
O my men?" Said they, "Aye! We bear homeward and hearthward
To feast on our fame!"

VII

"I've flown there before you," he said then:
"Your households are well;
But—your kin linger less
On your glory and war-mightiness
Than on dearer things."—"Dearer?" cried these from the dead then,
"Of what do they tell?"

VIII

"Some mothers muse sadly, and murmur
Your doings as boys—
Recall the quaint ways
Of your babyhood's innocent days.
Some pray that, ere dying, your faith had grown firmer,
And higher your joys.

IX

"A father broods : ' Would I had set him
        To some humble trade,
        And so slacked his high fire,
And his passionate martial desire ;
And told him no stories to woo him and whet him
        To this dire crusade ! ' "

X

"And, General, how hold out our sweethearts,
        Sworn loyal as doves ? "
        —" Many mourn ; many think
It is not unattractive to prink
Them in sables for heroes.   Some fickle and fleet hearts
        Have found them new loves."

XI

"And our wives ? " quoth another resignedly,
        " Dwell they on our deeds ? "
        —" Deeds of home ; that live yet
Fresh as new—deeds of fondness or fret ;
Ancient words that were kindly expressed or unkindly,
        These, these have their heeds."

XII

—" Alas ! then it seems that our glory
        Weighs less in their thought
        Than our old homely acts,
And the long-ago commonplace facts
Of our lives—held by us as scarce part of our story,
        And rated as nought ! "

XIII

Then bitterly some : " Was it wise now
        To raise the tomb-door
        For such knowledge ?   Away ! "
But the rest : " Fame we prized till to-day ;
Yet that hearts keep us green for old kindness we prize now
        A thousand times more ! "

XIV

Thus speaking, the trooped apparitions
      Began to disband
      And resolve them in two :
Those whose record was lovely and true
Bore to northward for home : those of bitter traditions
      Again left the land,

XV

And, towering to seaward in legions,
      They paused at a spot
      Overbending the Race—
That engulphing, ghast, sinister place—
Whither headlong they plunged, to the fathomless regions
      Of myriads forgot.

XVI

And the spirits of those who were homing
      Passed on, rushingly,
      Like the Pentecost Wind ;
And the whirr of their wayfaring thinned
And surceased on the sky, and but left in the gloaming
      Sea-mutterings and me.

December 1899.

SONG OF THE SOLDIERS' WIVES AND
SWEETHEARTS

I

At last ! In sight of home again,
      Of home again ;
No more to range and roam again
      As at that bygone time ?
No more to go away from us
      And stay from us ?—
Dawn, hold not long the day from us,
      But quicken it to prime !

II

Now all the town shall ring to them,
        Shall ring to them,
And we who love them cling to them
        And clasp them joyfully ;
And cry, " O much we'll do for you
        Anew for you,
Dear Loves !—aye, draw and hew for you,
        Come back from oversea."

III

Some told us we should meet no more,
        Yea, meet no more !—
Should wait, and wish, but greet no more
        Your faces round our fires ;
That, in a while, uncharily
        And drearily
Men gave their lives—even wearily,
        Like those whom living tires.

IV

And now you are nearing home again,
        Dears, home again ;
No more, may be, to roam again
        As at that bygone time,
Which took you far away from us
        To stay from us ;
Dawn, hold not long the day from us,
        But quicken it to prime !

THE SICK BATTLE-GOD

I

IN days when men found joy in war,
A God of Battles sped each mortal jar ;
    The peoples pledged him heart and hand,
    From Israel's land to isles afar.

II

His crimson form, with clang and chime,
Flashed on each murk and murderous meeting-time,
And kings invoked, for rape and raid,
His fearsome aid in rune and rhyme.

III

On bruise and blood-hole, scar and seam,
On blade and bolt, he flung his fulgid beam:
His haloes rayed the very gore,
And corpses wore his glory-gleam.

IV

Often an early King or Queen,
And storied hero onward, caught his sheen;
'Twas glimpsed by Wolfe, by Ney anon,
And Nelson on his blue demesne.

V

But new light spread.   That god's gold nimb
And blazon have waned dimmer and more dim;
Even his flushed form begins to fade,
Till but a shade is left of him.

VI

That modern meditation broke
His spell, that penmen's pleadings dealt a stroke,
Say some; and some that crimes too dire
Did much to mire his crimson cloak.

VII

Yea, seeds of crescent sympathy
Were sown by those more excellent than he,
Long known, though long contemned till then—
The gods of men in amity.

VIII

Souls have grown seers, and thought outbrings
The mournful many-sidedness of things
With foes as friends, enfeebling ires
And fury-fires by gaingivings!

IX

He rarely gladdens champions now ;
They do and dare, but tensely—pale of brow ;
    And would they fain uplift the arm
    Of that weak form they know not how.

X

Yet wars arise, though zest grows cold ;
Wherefore, at times, as if in ancient mould
    He looms, bepatched with paint and lath ;
    But never hath he seemed the old !

XI

Let men rejoice, let men deplore,
The lurid Deity of heretofore
    Succumbs to one of saner nod ;
    The Battle-god is god no more.

POEMS OF PILGRIMAGE

GENOA AND THE MEDITERRANEAN

(*March* 1887)

O EPIC-FAMED, god-haunted Central Sea,
Heave careless of the deep wrong done to thee
When from Torino's track I saw thy face first flash on me.

And multimarbled Genova the Proud,
Gleam all unconscious how, wide-lipped, up-browed,
I first beheld thee clad—not as the Beauty but the Dowd.

Out from a deep-delved way my vision lit
On housebacks pink, green, ochreous—where a slit
Shoreward 'twixt row and row revealed the classic blue through it.

And thereacross waved fishwives' high-hung smocks,
Chrome kerchiefs, scarlet hose, darned underfrocks ;
Often since when my dreams of thee, O Queen, that frippery
        mocks :

Whereat I grieve, Superba ! . . . Afterhours
Within Palazzo Doria's orange bowers
Went far to mend these marrings of thy soul-subliming powers.

But, Queen, such squalid undress none should see,
Those dream-endangering eyewounds no more be
Where lovers first behold thy form in pilgrimage to thee.

SHELLEY'S SKYLARK

(The neighbourhood of Leghorn : March 1887)

SOMEWHERE afield here something lies
In Earth's oblivious eyeless trust
That moved a poet to prophecies—
A pinch of unseen, unguarded dust :

The dust of the lark that Shelley heard,
And made immortal through times to be ;—
Though it only lived like another bird,
And knew not its immortality :

Lived its meek life ; then, one day, fell—
A little ball of feather and bone ;
And how it perished, when piped farewell,
And where it wastes, are alike unknown.

Maybe it rests in the loam I view,
Maybe it throbs in a myrtle's green,
Maybe it sleeps in the coming hue
Of a grape on the slopes of yon inland scene.

Go find it, faeries, go and find
That tiny pinch of priceless dust,
And bring a casket silver-lined,
And framed of gold that gems encrust ;

And we will lay it safe therein,
And consecrate it to endless time ;
For it inspired a bard to win
Ecstatic heights in thought and rhyme.

IN THE OLD THEATRE, FIESOLE

(April 1887)

I TRACED the Circus whose gray stones incline
Where Rome and dim Etruria interjoin,
Till came a child who showed an ancient coin
That bore the image of a Constantine.

She lightly passed ; nor did she once opine
How, better than all books, she had raised for me
In swift perspective Europe's history
Through the vast years of Cæsar's sceptred line.

For in my distant plot of English loam
'Twas but to delve, and straightway there to find
Coins of like impress.   As with one half blind
Whom common simples cure, her act flashed home
In that mute moment to my opened mind
The power, the pride, the reach of perished Rome.

ROME: ON THE PALATINE

(*April* 1887)

WE walked where Victor Jove was shrined awhile,
And passed to Livia's rich red mural show,
Whence, thridding cave and Criptoportico,
We gained Caligula's dissolving pile.

And each ranked ruin tended to beguile
The outer sense, and shape itself as though
It wore its marble gleams, its pristine glow
Of scenic frieze and pompous peristyle.

When lo, swift hands, on strings nigh overhead,
Began to melodize a waltz by Strauss :
It stirred me as I stood, in Cæsar's house,
Raised the old routs Imperial lyres had led,

And blended pulsing life with lives long done,
Till Time seemed fiction, Past and Present one.

ROME

BUILDING A NEW STREET IN THE ANCIENT QUARTER

(*April* 1887)

THESE umbered cliffs and gnarls of masonry
Outskeleton Time's central city, Rome ;
Whereof each arch, entablature, and dome
Lies bare in all its gaunt anatomy.

And cracking frieze and rotten metope
Express, as though they were an open tome
Top-lined with caustic monitory gnome;
"Dunces, Learn here to spell Humanity!"

And yet within these ruins' very shade
The singing workmen shape and set and join
Their frail new mansion's stuccoed cove and quoin
With no apparent sense that years abrade,
Though each rent wall their feeble works invade
Once shamed all such in power of pier and groin.

ROME

THE VATICAN: SALA DELLE MUSE

(1887)

I SAT in the Muses' Hall at the mid of the day,
And it seemed to grow still, and the people to pass away,
And the chiselled shapes to combine in a haze of sun,
Till beside a Carrara column there gleamed forth One.

She looked not this nor that of those beings divine,
But each and the whole—an essence of all the Nine;
With tentative foot she neared to my halting-place,
A pensive smile on her sweet, small, marvellous face.

"Regarded so long, we render thee sad?" said she.
"Not you," sighed I, "but my own inconstancy!
I worship each and each; in the morning one,
And then, alas! another at sink of sun.

"To-day my soul clasps Form; but where is my troth
Of yesternight with Tune: can one cleave to both?"
—"Be not perturbed," said she.   "Though apart in fame,
As I and my sisters are one, those, too, are the same."

—"But my love goes further—to Story, and Dance, and Hymn,
The lover of all in a sun-sweep is fool to whim—
Is swayed like a river-weed as the ripples run!"
—"Nay, wooer, thou sway'st not.   These are but phases of one;

"And that one is I ; and I am projected from thee,
One that out of thy brain and heart thou causest to be—
Extern to thee nothing.   Grieve not, nor thyself becall,
Woo where thou wilt ; and rejoice thou canst love at all ! "

ROME

AT THE PYRAMID OF CESTIUS NEAR THE
GRAVES OF SHELLEY AND KEATS

(1887)

Who, then, was Cestius,
  And what is he to me ?—
Amid thick thoughts and memories multitudinous
  One thought alone brings he.

I can recall no word
  Of anything he did ;
For me he is a man who died and was interred
  To leave a pyramid

Whose purpose was exprest
  Not with its first design,
Nor till, far down in Time, beside it found their rest
  Two countrymen of mine.

Cestius in life, maybe,
  Slew, breathed out threatening ;
I know not.   This I know : in death all silently
  He does a finer thing,

In beckoning pilgrim feet
  With marble finger high
To where, by shadowy wall and history-haunted street,
  Those matchless singers lie. . . .

—Say, then, he lived and died
  That stones which bear his name
Should mark, through Time, where two immortal Shades abide ;
  It is an ample fame.

LAUSANNE

IN GIBBON'S OLD GARDEN: 11-12 P.M.

June 27, 1897

(*The 110th anniversary of the completion of the "Decline and Fall" at the same hour and place*)

A SPIRIT seems to pass,
Formal in pose, but grave withal and grand:
He contemplates a volume in his hand,
And far lamps fleck him through the thin acacias.

Anon the book is closed,
With "It is finished!" And at the alley's end
He turns, and when on me his glances bend
As from the Past comes speech—small, muted, yet composed.

"How fares the Truth now?—Ill?
—Do pens but slily further her advance?
May one not speed her but in phrase askance?
Do scribes aver the Comic to be Reverend still?

"Still rule those minds on earth
At whom sage Milton's wormwood words were hurled:
'*Truth like a bastard comes into the world
Never without ill-fame to him who gives her birth*'?"

ZERMATT

TO THE MATTERHORN

(*June-July* 1897)

THIRTY-TWO years since, up against the sun,
Seven shapes, thin atomies to lower sight,
Labouringly leapt and gained thy gabled height,
And four lives paid for what the seven had won.

They were the first by whom the deed was done,
And when I look at thee, my mind takes flight
To that day's tragic feat of manly might,
As though, till then, of history thou hadst none.

Yet ages ere men topped thee, late and soon
Thou didst behold the planets lift and lower ;
Saw'st, maybe, Joshua's pausing sun and moon,
And the betokening sky when Cæsar's power
Approached its bloody end ; yea, even that Noon
When darkness filled the earth till the ninth hour.

THE BRIDGE OF LODI[1]

(*Spring* 1887)

I

When of tender mind and body,
　　I was moved by minstrelsy,
And that air " The Bridge of Lodi "
　　Brought a strange delight to me.

II

In the battle-breathing jingle
　　Of its forward-footing tune
I could see the armies mingle,
　　And the columns crushed and hewn

III

On that far-famed spot by Lodi
　　Where Napoleon clove his way
To his fame, when like a god he
　　Bent the nations to his sway.

IV

Hence the tune came capering to me
　　While I traced the Rhone and Po ;
Nor could Milan's Marvel woo me
　　From the spot englamoured so.

V

And to-day, sunlit and smiling,
　　Here I stand upon the scene,
With its saffron walls, dun tiling,
　　And its meads of maiden green,

Pronounce " Loddy. '

VI

Even as when the trackway thundered
    With the charge of grenadiers,
And the blood of forty hundred
    Splashed its parapets and piers. . . .

VII

Any ancient crone I'd toady
    Like a lass in young-eyed prime,
Could she tell some tale of Lodi
    At that moving mighty time.

VIII

So, I ask the wives of Lodi
    For traditions of that day;
But, alas! not anybody
    Seems to know of such a fray.

IX

And they heed but transitory
    Marketings in cheese and meat,
Till I judge that Lodi's story
    Is extinct in Lodi's street.

X

Yet while here and there they thrid them
    In their zest to sell and buy,
Let me sit me down amid them
    And behold those thousands die. . .

XI

—Not a creature cares in Lodi
    How Napoleon swept each arch,
Or where up and downward trod he,
    Or for his outmatching march!

XII

So that wherefore should I be here,
    Watching Adda lip the lea,
When the whole romance to see here
    Is the dream I bring with me?

XIII

And why sing " The Bridge of Lodi "
    As I sit thereon and swing,
When none shows by smile or nod he
    Guesses why or what I sing ? . . .

XIV

Since all Lodi, low and head ones,
    Seem to pass that story by,
It may be the Lodi-bred ones
    Rate it truly, and not I.

XV

Once engrossing Bridge of Lodi,
    Is thy claim to glory gone ?
Must I pipe a palinody,
    Or be silent thereupon ?

XVI

And if here, from strand to steeple,
    Be no stone to fame the fight,
Must I say the Lodi people
    Are but viewing war aright ? . . .

XVII

Nay ; I'll sing " The Bridge of Lodi "—
    That long-loved, romantic thing,
Though none show by smile or nod he
    Guesses why and what I sing !

ON AN INVITATION TO THE UNITED STATES

I

My ardours for emprize nigh lost
Since Life has bared its bones to me,
I shrink to seek a modern coast
Whose riper times have yet to be ;
Where the new regions claim them free
From that long drip of human tears
Which peoples old in tragedy
Have left upon the centuried years.

II

For, wonning in these ancient lands,
Enchased and lettered as a tomb,
And scored with prints of perished hands,
And chronicled with dates of doom,
Though my own Being bear no bloom
I trace the lives such scenes enshrine,
Give past exemplars present room,
And their experience count as mine.

MISCELLANEOUS POEMS

THE MOTHER MOURNS

When mid-autumn's moan shook the night-time,
    And sedges were horny,
And summer's green wonderwork faltered
    On leaze and in lane,

I fared Yell'ham-Firs way, where dimly
    Came wheeling around me
Those phantoms obscure and insistent
    That shadows unchain.

Till airs from the needle-thicks brought me
    A low lamentation,
As though from a tree-god disheartened,
    Perplexed, or in pain.

And, heeding, it awed me to gather
    That Nature herself there
Was breathing in aëry accents,
    With dirge-like refrain,

Weary plaint that Mankind, in these late days,
    Had grieved her by holding
Her ancient high fame of perfection
    In doubt and disdain. . . .

—"I had not proposed me a Creature
    (She soughed) so excelling
All else of my kingdom in compass
    And brightness of brain

101

" As to read my defects with a god-glance,
        Uncover each vestige
Of old inadvertence, annunciate
        Each flaw and each stain !

" My purpose went not to develop
        Such insight in Earthland ;
Such potent appraisements affront me,
        And sadden my reign !

" Why loosened I olden control here
        To mechanize skywards,
Undeeming great scope could outshape in
        A globe of such grain ?

" Man's mountings of mindsight I checked not,
        Till range of his vision
Now tops my intent, and finds blemish
        Throughout my domain.

" He holds as inept his own soul-shell—
        My deftest achievement—
Contemns me for fitful inventions
        Ill-timed and inane :

" No more sees my sun as a Sanct-shape,
        My moon as the Night-queen,
My stars as august and sublime ones
        That influences rain :

" Reckons gross and ignoble my teaching,
        Immoral my story,
My love-lights a lure that my species
        May gather and gain.

" ' Give me,' he has said, ' but the matter
        And means the gods lot her,
My brain could evolve a creation
        More seemly, more sane.'

—" If ever a naughtiness seized me
        To woo adulation
From creatures more keen than those crude ones
        That first formed my train—

" If inly a moment I murmured,
    ' The simple praise sweetly,
But sweetlier the sage '—and did rashly
    Man's vision unrein,

" I rue it ! . . . His guileless forerunners,
    Whose brains I could blandish,
To measure the deeps of my mysteries
    Applied them in vain.

" From them my waste aimings and futile
    I subtly could cover ;
' Every best thing,' said they, ' to best purpose
    Her powers preordain.'—

" No more such ! . . . My species are dwindling,
    My forests grow barren,
My popinjays fail from their tappings,
    My larks from their strain.

" My leopardine beauties are rarer,
    My tusky ones vanish,
My children have aped mine own slaughters
    To quicken my wane.

" Let me grow, then, but mildews and mandrakes,
    And slimy distortions,
Let nevermore things good and lovely
    To me appertain ;

" For Reason is rank in my temples,
    And Vision unruly,
And chivalrous laud of my cunning
    Is heard not again ! "

"I SAID TO LOVE"

I SAID to Love,
" It is not now as in old days
When men adored thee and thy ways
    All else above ;
Named thee the Boy, the Bright, the One
Who spread a heaven beneath the sun,"
    I said to Love.

I said to him,
" We now know more of thee than then ;
We were but weak in judgment when,
    With hearts abrim,
We clamoured thee that thou would'st please
Inflict on us thine agonies,"
    I said to him.

I said to Love,
" Thou art not young, thou art not fair,
No elfin darts, no cherub air,
    Nor swan, nor dove
Are thine ; but features pitiless,
And iron daggers of distress,"
    I said to Love.

    " Depart then, Love ! . . .
—Man's race shall perish, threatenest thou,
Without thy kindling coupling-vow ?
The age to come the man of now
    Know nothing of ?—
We fear not such a threat from thee ;
We are too old in apathy !
Mankind shall cease.—So let it be,"
    I said to Love.

A COMMONPLACE DAY

THE day is turning ghost,
And scuttles from the kalendar in fits and furtively,
    To join the anonymous host
Of those that throng oblivion ; ceding his place, maybe,
    To one of like degree.

I part the fire-gnawed logs,
Rake forth the embers, spoil the busy flames, and lay the ends
    Upon the shining dogs ;
Further and further from the nooks the twilight's stride extends,
    And beamless black impends.

Nothing of tiniest worth
Have I wrought, pondered, planned ; no one thing asking blame
    or praise,
    Since the pale corpse-like birth
Of this diurnal unit, bearing blanks in all its rays—
    Dullest of dull-hued Days !

    Wanly upon the panes
The rain slides, as have slid since morn my colourless thoughts ;
    and yet
    Here, while Day's presence wanes,
And over him the sepulchre-lid is slowly lowered and set,
    He wakens my regret.

    Regret—though nothing dear
That I wot of, was toward in the wide world at his prime,
    Or bloomed elsewhere than here,
To die with his decease, and leave a memory sweet, sublime,
    Or mark him out in Time. . . .

    —Yet, maybe, in some soul,
In some spot undiscerned on sea or land, some impulse rose,
    Or some intent upstole
Of that enkindling ardency from whose maturer glows
    The world's amendment flows ;

    But which, benumbed at birth
By momentary chance or wile, has missed its hope to be
    Embodied on the earth ;
And undervoicings of this loss to man's futurity
    May wake regret in me.

AT A LUNAR ECLIPSE

Thy shadow, Earth, from Pole to Central Sea,
Now steals along upon the Moon's meek shine
In even monochrome and curving line
Of imperturbable serenity.

How shall I link such sun-cast symmetry
With the torn troubled form I know as thine,
That profile, placid as a brow divine,
With continents of moil and misery ?

And can immense Mortality but throw
So small a shade, and Heaven's high human scheme
Be hemmed within the coasts yon arc implies?

Is such the stellar gauge of earthly show,
Nation at war with nation, brains that teem,
Heroes, and women fairer than the skies?

THE LACKING SENSE

SCENE.—*A sad-coloured landscape, Waddon Vale*

I

"O TIME, whence comes the Mother's moody look amid her
      labours,
As of one who all unwittingly has wounded where she loves?
   Why weaves she not her world-webs to according lutes and
      tabors,
With nevermore this too remorseful air upon her face,
         As of angel fallen from grace?"

II

—"Her look is but her story: construe not its symbols keenly:
   In her wonderworks yea surely has she wounded where she
      loves.
The sense of ills misdealt for blisses blanks the mien most queenly,
   Self-smitings kill self-joys; and everywhere beneath the sun
         Such deeds her hands have done."

III

—"And how explains thy Ancient Mind her crimes upon her
      creatures,
   These fallings from her fair beginnings, woundings where she
      loves,
Into her would-be perfect motions, modes, effects, and features
   Admitting cramps, black humours, wan decay, and baleful
      blights,
         Distress into delights?"

IV

—"Ah! knowest thou not her secret yet, her vainly veiled deficience,
    Whence it comes that all unwittingly she wounds the lives she loves?
That sightless are those orbs of hers?—which bar to her omniscience
    Brings those fearful unfulfilments, that red ravage through her zones
        Whereat all creation groans.

V

"She whispers it in each pathetic strenuous slow endeavour,
    When in mothering she unwittingly sets wounds on what she loves;
Yet her primal doom pursues her, faultful, fatal is she ever;
    Though so deft and nigh to vision is her facile finger-touch
        That the seers marvel much.

VI

"Deal, then, her groping skill no scorn, no note of malediction;
    Not long on thee will press the hand that hurts the lives it loves;
And while she plods dead-reckoning on, in darkness of affliction,
    Assist her where thy creaturely dependence can or may,
        For thou art of her clay."

TO LIFE

O LIFE with the sad seared face,
    I weary of seeing thee,
And thy draggled cloak, and thy hobbling pace,
    And thy too-forced pleasantry!

I know what thou would'st tell
    Of Death, Time, Destiny—
I have known it long, and know, too, well
    What it all means for me.

But canst thou not array
    Thyself in rare disguise,
And feign like truth, for one mad day,
    That Earth is Paradise?

I'll tune me to the mood,
   And mumm with thee till eve;
And maybe what as interlude
   I feign, I shall believe!

DOOM AND SHE

I

THERE dwells a mighty pair—
   Slow, statuesque, intense—
   Amid the vague Immense:
None can their chronicle declare,
   Nor why they be, nor whence.

II

Mother of all things made,
   Matchless in artistry,
   Unlit with sight is she.—
And though her ever well-obeyed
   Vacant of feeling he.

III

The Matron mildly asks—
   A throb in every word—
   " Our clay-made creatures, lord,
How fare they in their mortal tasks
   Upon Earth's bounded bord?

IV

" The fate of those I bear,
   Dear lord, pray turn and view,
   And notify me true;
Shapings that eyelessly I dare
   Maybe I would undo.

V

" Sometimes from lairs of life
   Methinks I catch a groan,
   Or multitudinous moan,
As though I had schemed a world of strife,
   Working by touch alone."

VI

"World-weaver!" he replies,
"I scan all thy domain ;
But since nor joy nor pain
It lies in me to recognize,
Thy questionings are vain.

VII

"World-weaver! what *is* Grief?
And what are Right, and Wrong,
And Feeling, that belong
To creatures all who owe thee fief?
Why is Weak worse than Strong?" . . .

VIII

—Unanswered, curious, meek,
She broods in sad surmise. . . .
—Some say they have heard her sighs
On Alpine height or Polar peak
When the night tempests rise.

THE PROBLEM

SHALL we conceal the Case, or tell it—
We who believe the evidence?
Here and there the watch-towers knell it
With a sullen significance,
Heard of the few who hearken intently and carry an eagerly
upstrained sense.

Hearts that are happiest hold not by it ;
Better we let, then, the old view reign :
Since there is peace in that, why decry it ?
Since there is comfort, why disdain?
Note not the pigment so long as the painting determines
humanity's joy and pain.

THE SUBALTERNS

I

"POOR wanderer," said the leaden sky,
  "I fain would lighten thee,
But there are laws in force on high
  Which say it must not be."

II

—"I would not freeze thee, shorn one," cried
  The North, "knew I but how
To warm my breath, to slack my stride;
  But I am ruled as thou."

III

—"To-morrow I attack thee, wight,"
  Said Sickness. "Yet I swear
I bear thy little ark no spite,
  But am bid enter there."

IV

—"Come hither, Son," I heard Death say;
  "I did not will a grave
Should end thy pilgrimage to-day,
  But I, too, am a slave!"

V

We smiled upon each other then,
  And life to me had less
Of that fell look it wore ere when
  They owned their passiveness.

THE SLEEP-WORKER

WHEN wilt thou wake, O Mother, wake and see—
As one who, held in trance, has laboured long
By vacant rote and prepossession strong—
The coils that thou hast wrought unwittingly;

Wherein have place, unrealized by thee,
Fair growths, foul cankers, right enmeshed with wrong,
Strange orchestras of victim-shriek and song,
And curious blends of ache and ecstasy?—

Should that morn come, and show thy opened eyes
All that Life's palpitating tissues feel,
How wilt thou bear thyself in thy surprise?—

Wilt thou destroy, in one wild shock of shame,
Thy whole high heaving firmamental frame,
Or patiently adjust, amend, and heal?

THE BULLFINCHES

BROTHER Bulleys, let us sing
From the dawn till evening!—
For we know not that we go not
    When to-day's pale pinions fold
    Where they be that sang of old.

When I flew to Blackmoor Vale,
    Whence the green-gowned faeries hail,
Roosting near them I could hear them
    Speak of queenly Nature's ways,
    Means, and moods,—well known to fays.

All we creatures, nigh and far
    (Said they there), the Mother's are;
Yet she never shows endeavour
    To protect from warrings wild
    Bird or beast she calls her child.

Busy in her handsome house
    Known as Space, she falls a-drowse;
Yet, in seeming, works on dreaming,
    While beneath her groping hands
    Fiends make havoc in her bands.

How her hussif'ry succeeds
    She unknows or she unheeds,
All things making for Death's taking!
    —So the green-gowned faeries say
    Living over Blackmoor way.

Come then, brethren, let us sing,
From the dawn till evening !—
For we know not that we go not
When the day's pale pinions fold
Where those be that sang of old.

GOD-FORGOTTEN

I TOWERED far, and lo ! I stood within
The presence of the Lord Most High,
Sent thither by the sons of Earth, to win
    Some answer to their cry.

—" The Earth, sayest thou ? The Human race ?
By Me created ? Sad its lot ?
Nay : I have no remembrance of such place :
    Such world I fashioned not."—

—" O Lord, forgive me when I say
Thou spakest the word that made it all."—
" The Earth of men—let me bethink me. . . . Yea !
    I dimly do recall

" Some tiny sphere I built long back
(Mid millions of such shapes of mine)
So named . . . It perished, surely—not a wrack
    Remaining, or a sign ?

" It lost my interest from the first,
My aims therefor succeeding ill ;
Haply it died of doing as it durst ? "—
    " Lord, it existeth still."—

" Dark, then, its life ! For not a cry
Of aught it bears do I now hear ;
Of its own act the threads were snapt whereby
    Its plaints had reached mine ear.

" It used to ask for gifts of good,
Till came its severance, self-entailed,
When sudden silence on that side ensued,
    And has till now prevailed.

"All other orbs have kept in touch ;
  Their voicings reach me speedily :
Thy people took upon them overmuch
      In sundering them from me !

"And it is strange—though sad enough—
  Earth's race should think that one whose call
Frames, daily, shining spheres of flawless stuff
      Must heed their tainted ball ! . . .

"But sayest it is by pangs distraught,
  And strife, and silent suffering ?—
Sore grieved am I that injury should be wrought
      Even on so poor a thing !

"Thou shouldst have learnt that *Not to Mend*
  For Me could mean but *Not to Know* :
Hence, Messengers ! and straightway put an end
      To what men undergo." . .

Homing at dawn, I thought to see
  One of the Messengers standing by.
—Oh, childish thought ! . . . Yet often it comes to me
      When trouble hovers nigh.

THE BEDRIDDEN PEASANT

TO AN UNKNOWING GOD

MUCH wonder I—here long low-laid—
  That this dead wall should be
Betwixt the Maker and the made,
  Between Thyself and me !

For, say one puts a child to nurse,
  He eyes it now and then
To know if better it is, or worse,
  And if it mourn, and when.

But Thou, Lord, giv'st us men our day
  In helpless bondage thus
To Time and Chance, and seem'st straightway
  To think no more of us !

That some disaster cleft Thy scheme
    And tore us wide apart,
So that no cry can cross, I deem ;
    For Thou art mild of heart,

And wouldst not shape and shut us in
    Where voice can not be heard :
Plainly Thou meant'st that we should win
    Thy succour by a word.

Might but Thy sense flash down the skies
    Like man's from clime to clime,
Thou wouldst not let me agonize
    Through my remaining time ;

But, seeing how much Thy creatures bear—
    Lame, starved, or maimed, or blind—
Wouldst heal the ills with quickest care
    Of me and all my kind.

Then, since Thou mak'st not these things be,
    But these things dost not know,
I'll praise Thee as were shown to me
    The mercies Thou wouldst show !

BY THE EARTH'S CORPSE

I

"O Lord, why grievest Thou ?—
    Since Life has ceased to be
Upon this globe, now cold
    As lunar land and sea,
And humankind, and fowl, and fur
    Are gone eternally,
All is the same to Thee as ere
    They knew mortality."

II

"O Time," replied the Lord,
    "Thou readest me ill, I ween ;
Were all *the same*, I should not grieve
    At that late earthly scene,

Now blestly past—though planned by me
    With interest close and keen !—
Nay, nay : things now are *not* the same
    As they have earlier been.

III

"Written indelibly
    On my eternal mind
Are all the wrongs endured
    By Earth's poor patient kind,
Which my too oft unconscious hand
    Let enter undesigned.
No god can cancel deeds foredone,
    Or thy old coils unwind !

IV

"As when, in Noë's days,
    I whelmed the plains with sea,
So at this last, when flesh
    And herb but fossils be,
And, all extinct, their piteous dust
    Revolves obliviously,
That I made Earth, and life, and man,
    It still repenteth me !"

MUTE OPINION

I

I TRAVERSED a dominion
Whose spokesmen spake out strong
Their purpose and opinion
Through pulpit, press, and song.
I scarce had means to note there
A large-eyed few, and dumb,
Who thought not as those thought there
That stirred the heat and hum.

II

When, grown a Shade, beholding
That land in lifetime trode,
To learn if its unfolding
Fulfilled its clamoured code,
I saw, in web unbroken,
Its history outwrought
Not as the loud had spoken,
But as the mute had thought.

TO AN UNBORN PAUPER CHILD

I

BREATHE not, hid Heart : cease silently,
And though thy birth-hour beckons thee,
Sleep the long sleep :
The Doomsters heap
Travails and teens around us here,
And Time-wraiths turn our songsingings to fear.

II

Hark, how the peoples surge and sigh,
And laughters fail, and greetings die :
Hopes dwindle ; yea,
Faiths waste away,
Affections and enthusiasms numb ;
Thou canst not mend these things if thou dost come.

III

Had I the ear of wombèd souls
Ere their terrestrial chart unrolls,
And thou wert free
To cease, or be,
Then would I tell thee all I know,
And put it to thee : Wilt thou take Life so ?

IV

Vain vow ! No hint of mine may hence
To theeward fly : to thy locked sense
Explain none can
Life's pending plan :
Thou wilt thy ignorant entry make
Though skies spout fire and blood and nations quake.

V

Fain would I, dear, find some shut plot
Of earth's wide wold for thee, where not
    One tear, one qualm,
    Should break the calm.
But I am weak as thou and bare ;
No man can change the common lot to rare.

VI

Must come and bide. And such are we—
Unreasoning, sanguine, visionary—
    That I can hope
    Health, love, friends, scope
In full for thee ; can dream thou wilt find
Joys seldom yet attained by humankind !

TO FLOWERS FROM ITALY IN WINTER

Sunned in the South, and here to-day ;
    —If all organic things
Be sentient, Flowers, as some men say,
    What are your ponderings ?

How can you stay, nor vanish quite
    From this bleak spot of thorn,
And birch, and fir, and frozen white
    Expanse of the forlorn ?

Frail luckless exiles hither brought !
    Your dust will not regain
Old sunny haunts of Classic thought
    When you shall waste and wane ;

But mix with alien earth, be lit
    With frigid Boreal flame,
And not a sign remain in it
    To tell man whence you came.

ON A FINE MORNING

I

WHENCE comes Solace ?—Not from seeing
What is doing, suffering, being,
Not from noting Life's conditions,
Nor from heeding Time's monitions ;
    But in cleaving to the Dream,
    And in gazing at the gleam
    Whereby gray things golden seem.

II

Thus do I this heyday, holding
Shadows but as lights unfolding,
As no specious show this moment
With its iris-hued embowment ;
    But as nothing other than
    Part of a benignant plan ;
    Proof that earth was made for man.

February 1899.

TO LIZBIE BROWNE

I

DEAR Lizbie Browne,
Where are you now?
In sun, in rain ?—
Or is your brow
Past joy, past pain,
Dear Lizbie Browne ?

II

Sweet Lizbie Browne
How you could smile,
How you could sing !—
How archly wile
In glance-giving,
Sweet Lizbie Browne !

III

And, Lizbie Browne,
Who else had hair
Bay-red as yours,
Or flesh so fair
Bred out of doors,
Sweet Lizbie Browne?

IV

When, Lizbie Browne,
You had just begun
To be endeared
By stealth to one,
You disappeared
My Lizbie Browne!

V

Ay, Lizbie Browne,
So swift your life,
And mine so slow,
You were a wife
Ere I could show
Love, Lizbie Browne.

VI

Still, Lizbie Browne,
You won, they said,
The best of men
When you were wed. . . .
Where went you then,
O Lizbie Browne?

VII

Dear Lizbie Browne,
I should have thought,
"Girls ripen fast,"
And coaxed and caught
You ere you passed,
Dear Lizbie Browne!

VIII

But, Lizbie Browne,
I let you slip;
Shaped not a sign;
Touched never your lip
With lip of mine,
Lost Lizbie Browne!

IX

So, Lizbie Browne,
When on a day
Men speak of me
As not, you'll say,
"And who was he?"—
Yes, Lizbie Browne!

SONG OF HOPE

O SWEET To-morrow!—
After to-day
There will away
This sense of sorrow.
Then let us borrow
Hope, for a gleaming
Soon will be streaming,
Dimmed by no gray—
No gray!

While the winds wing us
Sighs from The Gone,
Nearer to dawn
Minute-beats bring us;
When there will sing us
Larks, of a glory
Waiting our story
Further anon—
Anon!

Doff the black token,
    Don the red shoon,
        Right and retune
Viol-strings broken :
Null the words spoken
In speeches of rueing,
The night cloud is hueing,
        To-morrow shines soon—
            Shines soon !

THE WELL-BELOVED

I WENT by star and planet shine
    Towards the dear one's home
At Kingsbere, there to make her mine
    When the next sun upclomb.

I edged the ancient hill and wood
    Beside the Ikling Way,
Nigh where the Pagan temple stood
    In the world's earlier day.

And as I quick and quicker walked
    On gravel and on green,
I sang to sky, and tree, or talked
    Of her I called my queen.

—" O faultless is her dainty form,
    And luminous her mind ;
She is the God-created norm
    Of perfect womankind !"

A shape whereon one star-blink gleamed
    Slid softly by my side,
A woman's ; and her motion seemed
    The motion of my bride.

And yet methought she'd drawn erstwhile
    Out from the ancient leaze,
Where once were pile and peristyle
    For men's idolatries.

—"O maiden lithe and lone, what may
    Thy name and lineage be
Who so resémblest by this ray
    My darling?—Art thou she?"

The Shape: "Thy bride remains within
    Her father's grange and grove."
—"Thou speakest rightly," I broke in,
    "Thou art not she I love."

—"Nay: though thy bride remains inside
    Her father's walls," said she,
"The one most dear is with thee here,
    For thou dost love but me."

Then I: "But she, my only choice,
    Is now at Kingsbere Grove?"
Again her soft mysterious voice ·
    "I am thy only Love."

Thus still she vouched, and still I said,
    "O sprite, that cannot be!" . . .
It was as if my bosom bled,
    So much she troubled me.

The sprite resumed: "Thou hast transferred
    To her dull form awhile
My beauty, fame, and deed, and word,
    My gestures and my smile.

"O fatuous man, this truth infer,
    Brides are not what they seem;
Thou lovest what thou dreamest her;
    I am thy very dream!"

—"O then," I answered miserably,
    Speaking as scarce I knew,
"My loved one, I must wed with thee
    If what thou sayest be true!"

She, proudly, thinning in the gloom:
    "Though, since troth-plight began,
I have ever stood as bride to groom,
    I wed no mortal man!"

Thereat she vanished by the lane
    Adjoining Kingsbere town,
Near where, men say, once stood the Fane
    To Venus, on the Down.

—When I arrived and met my bride
    Her look was pinched and thin,
As if her soul had shrunk and died,
    And left a waste within.

HER REPROACH

CON the dead page as 'twere live love : press on.
Cold wisdom's words will ease thy track for thee ;
Aye, go ; cast off sweet ways, and leave me wan
To biting blasts that are intent on me.

But if thy object Fame's far summits be,
Whose inclines many a skeleton overlies
That missed both dream and substance, stop and see
How absence wears these cheeks and dims these eyes !

It surely is far sweeter and more wise
To water love, than toil to leave anon
A name whose glory-gleam will but advise
Invidious minds to eclipse it with their own,

And over which the kindliest will but stay
A moment ; musing, " He, too, had his day ! "

WESTBOURNE PARK VILLAS, 1867.

THE INCONSISTENT

I SAY, " She was as good as fair ! "
    When standing by her mound ;
" Such passing sweetness," I declare,
    " No longer treads the ground."
I say, " What living Love can catch
    Her bloom and bonhomie,
And what in recent maidens match
    Her olden warmth to me ! "

—There stands within yon vestry-nook
Where bonded lovers sign,
Her name upon a faded book
With one that is not mine.
To him she breathed the tender vow
She once had breathed to me,
But yet I say, " O Love, even now
Would I had died for thee ! "

A BROKEN APPOINTMENT

You did not come,
And marching Time drew on, and wore me numb.—
Yet less for loss of your dear presence there
Than that I thus found lacking in your make
That high compassion which can overbear
Reluctance for pure lovingkindness' sake
Grieved I, when, as the hope-hour stroked its sum,
You did not come.

You love not me,
And love alone can lend you loyalty ;
—I know and knew it.   But, unto the store
Of human deeds divine in all but name,
Was it not worth a little hour or more
To add yet this : Once you, a woman, came
To soothe a time-torn man ; even though it be
You love not me ?

"BETWEEN US NOW"

Between us now and here—
Two thrown together
Who are not wont to wear
Life's flushest feather—
Who see the scenes slide past,
The daytimes dimming fast,
Let there be truth at last,
Even if despair.

So thoroughly and long
    Have you now known me,
So real in faith and strong
    Have I now shown me,
That nothing needs disguise
Further in any wise,
Or asks or justifies
    A guarded tongue.

Face unto face, then, say,
    Eyes my own meeting,
Is your heart far away,
    Or with mine beating?
When false things are brought low,
And swift things have grown slow,
Feigning like froth shall go,
    Faith be for aye.

"HOW GREAT MY GRIEF"

(TRIOLET)

How great my grief, my joys how few,
Since first it was my fate to know thee!
—Have the slow years not brought to view
How great my grief, my joys how few,
Nor memory shaped old times anew,
    Nor loving-kindness helped to show thee
How great my grief, my joys how few,
    Since first it was my fate to know thee?

"I NEED NOT GO"

I NEED not go
Through sleet and snow
To where I know
She waits for me;
She will tarry me there
Till I find it fair,
And have time to spare
From company.

When I've overgot
The world somewhat,
When things cost not
Such stress and strain,
Is soon enough
By cypress sough
To tell my Love
I am come again.

And if some day,
When none cries nay,
I still delay
To seek her side,
(Though ample measure
Of fitting leisure
Await my pleasure)
She will not chide.

What—not upbraid me
That I delayed me,
Nor ask what stayed me
So long?   Ah, no!—
New cares may claim me,
New loves inflame me,
She will not blame me,
But suffer it so.

THE COQUETTE, AND AFTER

(TRIOLETS)

I

For long the cruel wish I knew
That your free heart should ache for me
While mine should bear no ache for you;
For long—the cruel wish!—I knew
How men can feel, and craved to view
My triumph—fated not to be
For long! . . . The cruel wish I knew
That your free heart should ache for me!

II

At last one pays the penalty—
The woman—women always do.
My farce, I found, was tragedy
At last!—One pays the penalty
With interest when one, fancy-free,
Learns love, learns shame. . . . Of sinners two
At last *one* pays the penalty—
The woman—women always do!

A SPOT

In years defaced and lost,
Two sat here, transport-tossed,
Lit by a living love
The wilted world knew nothing of:
    Scared momently
    By gaingivings,
    Then hoping things
    That could not be. . . .

Of love and us no trace
Abides upon the place;
The sun and shadows wheel,
Season and season sereward steal;
    Foul days and fair
    Here, too, prevail,
    And gust and gale
    As everywhere.

But lonely shepherd souls
Who bask amid these knolls
May catch a faery sound
On sleepy noontides from the ground:
    "O not again
    Till Earth outwears
    Shall love like theirs
    Suffuse this glen!"

LONG PLIGHTED

Is it worth while, dear, now,
To call for bells, and sally forth arrayed
For marriage-rites—discussed, descried, delayed
    So many years?

Is it worth while, dear, now,
To stir desire for old fond purposings,
By feints that Time still serves for dallyings,
    Though quittance nears?

Is it worth while, dear, when
The day being so far spent, so low the sun,
The undone thing will soon be as the done,
    And smiles as tears?

Is it worth while, dear, when
Our cheeks are worn, our early brown is gray;
When, meet or part we, none says yea or nay,
    Or heeds, or cares?

Is it worth while, dear, since
We still can climb old Yell'ham's wooded mounds
Together, as each season steals its rounds
    And disappears?

Is it worth while, dear, since
As mates in Mellstock churchyard we can lie,
Till the last crash of all things low and high
    Shall end the spheres?

THE WIDOW BETROTHED

I PASSED the lodge and avenue
    To her fair tenement,
And sunset on her window-panes
    Reflected our intent.

The creeper on the gable nigh
    Was fired to more than red,
And when I came to halt thereby
    "Bright as my joy!" I said.

Of late days it had been her aim
    To meet me in the hall;
Now at my footsteps no one came,
    And no one to my call.

Again I knocked, and tardily
    An inner tread was heard,
And I was shown her presence then
    With a mere answering word.

She met me, and but barely took
    My proffered warm embrace;
Preoccupation weighed her look,
    And hardened her sweet face.

"To-morrow—could you—would you call?
    Abridge your present stay?
My child is ill—my one, my all!—
    And can't be left to-day."

And then she turns, and gives commands
    As I were out of sound,
Or were no more to her and hers
    Than any neighbour round. . . . .

—As maid I loved her; but one came
    And pleased, and coaxed, and wooed.
And when in time he wedded her
    I deemed her gone for good.

He won, I lost her; and my loss
    I bore I know not how;
But I do think I suffered then
    Less wretchedness than now.

For Time, in taking him, unclosed
    An unexpected door
Of bliss for me, which grew to seem
    Far surer than before.

Yet in my haste I overlooked
    When secondly I sued
That then, as not at first, she had learnt
    The call of motherhood. . . .

Her word is steadfast, and I know
    How firmly pledged are we:
But a new love-claim shares her since
    She smiled as maid on me!

AT A HASTY WEDDING

(TRIOLET)

IF hours be years the twain are blest,
For now they solace swift desire
By bonds of every bond the best,
If hours be years. The twain are blest
Do eastern stars slope never west,
Nor pallid ashes follow fire:
If hours be years the twain are blest,
For now they solace swift desire.

THE DREAM-FOLLOWER

A DREAM of mine flew over the mead
    To the halls where my old Love reigns;
And it drew me on to follow its lead:
    And I stood at her window-panes;

And I saw but a thing of flesh and bone
    Speeding on to its cleft in the clay;
And my dream was scared, and expired on a moan,
    And I whitely hastened away.

HIS IMMORTALITY

I

I SAW a dead man's finer part
Shining within each faithful heart
Of those bereft. Then said I: "This must be
    His immortality."

II

I looked there as the seasons wore,
And still his soul continuously bore
A life in theirs.   But less its shine excelled
Than when I first beheld.

III

His fellow-yearsmen passed, and then
In later hearts I looked for him again ;
And found him—shrunk, alas ! into a thin
And spectral mannikin.

IV

Lastly I ask—now old and chill—
If aught of him remain unperished still ;
And find, in me alone, a feeble spark,
Dying amid the dark.

February 1899.

THE TO-BE-FORGOTTEN

I

I HEARD a small sad sound,
And stood awhile among the tombs around :
"Wherefore, old friends," said I, "are you distrest,
Now, screened from life's unrest ?"

II

—"O not at being here ;
But that our future second death is near ;
When, with the living, memory of us numbs,
And blank oblivion comes !

III

"These, our sped ancestry,
Lie here embraced by deeper death than we ;
Nor shape nor thought of theirs can you descry
With keenest backward eye.

IV

"They count as quite forgot;
They are as men who have existed not;
Theirs is a loss past loss of fitful breath;
     It is the second death.

V

"We here, as yet, each day
Are blest with dear recall; as yet, can say
We hold in some soul loved continuance
     Of shape and voice and glance.

VI

"But what has been will be—
First memory, then oblivion's swallowing sea;
Like men foregone, shall we merge into those
     Whose story no one knows.

VII

"For which of us could hope
To show in life that world-awakening scope
Granted the few whose memory none lets die,
     But all men magnify?

VIII

"We were but Fortune's sport;
Things true, things lovely, things of good report
We neither shunned nor sought . . . We see our bourn
     And seeing it we mourn."

WIVES IN THE SERE

I

NEVER a careworn wife but shows,
     If a joy suffuse her,
Something beautiful to those
     Patient to peruse her,
Some one charm the world unknows
     Precious to a muser,
Haply what, ere years were foes,
     Moved her mate to choose her.

II

But, be it a hint of rose
    That an instant hues her,
Or some early light or pose
    Wherewith thought renews her—
Seen by him at full, ere woes
    Practised to abuse her—
Sparely comes it, swiftly goes,
    Time again subdues her.

THE SUPERSEDED

I

As newer comers crowd the fore,
    We drop behind.
—We who have laboured long and sore
    Times out of mind,
And keen are yet, must not regret
    To drop behind.

II

Yet there are some of us who grieve
    To go behind ;
Staunch, strenuous souls who scarce believe
    Their fires declined,
And know none spares, remembers, cares
    Who go behind.

III

'Tis not that we have unforetold
    The drop behind ;
We feel the new must oust the old
    In every kind ;
But yet we think, must we, must *we*,
    Too, drop behind ?

AN AUGUST MIDNIGHT

I

A SHADED lamp and a waving blind,
And the beat of a clock from a distant floor:
On this scene enter—winged, horned, and spined—
A longlegs, a moth, and a dumbledore;
While 'mid my page there idly stands
A sleepy fly, that rubs its hands . . .

II

Thus meet we five, in this still place,
At this point of time, at this point in space.
—My guests besmear my new-penned line,
Or bang at the lamp and fall supine.
"God's humblest, they!" I muse.   Yet why?
They know Earth-secrets that know not I.

MAX GATE, 1899.

THE CAGED THRUSH FREED AND HOME AGAIN

(VILLANELLE)

"MEN know but little more than we,
Who count us least of things terrene,
How happy days are made to be!

"Of such strange tidings what think ye,
O birds in brown that peck and preen?
Men know but little more than we!

"When I was borne from yonder tree
In bonds to them, I hoped to glean
How happy days are made to be,

"And want and wailing turned to glee;
Alas, despite their mighty mien
Men know but little more than we!

"They cannot change the Frost's decree,
They cannot keep the skies serene ;
How happy days are made to be

"Eludes great Man's sagacity
No less than ours, O tribes in treen !
Men know but little more than we
How happy days are made to be."

BIRDS AT WINTER NIGHTFALL

(TRIOLET)

AROUND the house the flakes fly faster,
And all the berries now are gone
From holly and cotonea-aster
Around the house. The flakes fly !—faster
Shutting indoors that crumb-outcaster
We used to see upon the lawn
Around the house. The flakes fly faster,
And all the berries now are gone !

MAX GATE.

THE PUZZLED GAME-BIRDS

(TRIOLET)

THEY are not those who used to feed us
When we were young—they cannot be—
These shapes that now bereave and bleed us?
They are not those who used to feed us,
For did we then cry, they would heed us.
—If hearts can house such treachery
They are not those who used to feed us
When we were young—they cannot be !

WINTER IN DURNOVER FIELD

Scene.—A wide stretch of fallow ground recently sown with wheat, and frozen to iron hardness. Three large birds walking about thereon, and wistfully eyeing the surface. Wind keen from north-east: sky a dull grey.

(TRIOLET)

Rook.—Throughout the field I find no grain ;
    The cruel frost encrusts the cornland !
Starling.—Aye : patient pecking now is vain
    Throughout the field, I find . . .
Rook.—   No grain !
Pigeon.—Nor will be, comrade, till it rain,
    Or genial thawings loose the lorn land
    Throughout the field.
Rook.—   I find no grain :
    The cruel frost encrusts the cornland !

THE LAST CHRYSANTHEMUM

Why should this flower delay so long
    To show its tremulous plumes ?
Now is the time of plaintive robin-song,
    When flowers are in their tombs.

Through the slow summer, when the sun
    Called to each frond and whorl
That all he could for flowers was being done,
    Why did it not uncurl ?

It must have felt that fervid call
    Although it took no heed,
Waking but now, when leaves like corpses fall,
    And saps all retrocede.

Too late its beauty, lonely thing,
    The season's shine is spent,
Nothing remains for it but shivering
    In tempests turbulent.

Had it a reason for delay,
    Dreaming in witlessness
That for a bloom so delicately gay
    Winter would stay its stress ?

—I talk as if the thing were born
    With sense to work its mind;
Yet it is but one mask of many worn
    By the Great Face behind.

THE DARKLING THRUSH

I LEANT upon a coppice gate
    When Frost was spectre-gray,
And Winter's dregs made desolate
    The weakening eye of day.
The tangled bine-stems scored the sky
    Like strings of broken lyres,
And all mankind that haunted nigh
    Had sought their household fires.

The land's sharp features seemed to be
    The Century's corpse outleant,
His crypt the cloudy canopy,
    The wind his death-lament.
The ancient pulse of germ and birth
    Was shrunken hard and dry,
And every spirit upon earth
    Seemed fervourless as I.

At once a voice arose among
    The bleak twigs overhead
In a full-hearted evensong
    Of joy illimited;
An aged thrush, frail, gaunt, and small,
    In blast-beruffled plume,
Had chosen thus to fling his soul
    Upon the growing gloom.

So little cause for carolings
    Of such ecstatic sound
Was written on terrestrial things
    Afar or nigh around,
That I could think there trembled through
    His happy good-night air
Some blessed Hope, whereof he knew
    And I was unaware.

December 1900.

THE COMET AT YELL'HAM

I

IT bends far over Yell'ham Plain,
   And we, from Yell'ham Height,
Stand and regard its fiery train,
   So soon to swim from sight.

II

It will return long years hence, when
   As now its strange swift shine
Will fall on Yell'ham ; but not then
   On that sweet form of thine.

MAD JUDY

WHEN the hamlet hailed a birth
   Judy used to cry :
When she heard our christening mirth
   She would kneel and sigh.
She was crazed, we knew, and we
Humoured her infirmity.

When the daughters and the sons
   Gathered them to wed,
And we like-intending ones
   Danced till dawn was red,
She would rock and mutter, " More
Comers to this stony shore ! "

When old Headsman Death laid hands
   On a babe or twain,
She would feast, and by her brands
   Sing her songs again.
What she liked we let her do,
Judy was insane, we knew.

A WASTED ILLNESS

THROUGH vaults of pain,
Enribbed and wrought with groins of ghastliness,
I passed, and garish spectres moved my brain
    To dire distress.

And hammerings,
And quakes, and shoots, and stifling hotness, blent
With webby waxing things and waning things
    As on I went.

"Where lies the end
To this foul way?" I asked with weakening breath.
Thereon ahead I saw a door extend—
    The door to Death.

It loomed more clear:
"At last!" I cried. "The all-delivering door!"
And then, I knew not how, it grew less near
    Than theretofore.

And back slid I
Along the galleries by which I came,
And tediously the day returned, and sky,
    And life—the same.

And all was well:
Old circumstance resumed its former show,
And on my head the dews of comfort fell
    As ere my woe.

I roam anew,
Scarce conscious of my late distress. . . . And yet
Those backward steps to strength I cannot view
    Without regret.

For that dire train
Of waxing shapes and waning, passed before,
And those grim chambers, must be ranged again
    To reach that door.

A MAN

(IN MEMORY OF H. OF M.)

I

In Casterbridge there stood a noble pile,
Wrought with pilaster, bay, and balustrade
In tactful times when shrewd Eliza swayed.—
    On burgher, squire, and clown
It smiled the long street down for near a mile.

II

But evil days beset that domicile ;
The stately beauties of its roof and wall
Passed into sordid hands.   Condemned to fall
    Were cornice, quoin, and cove,
And all that art had wove in antique style.

III

Among the hired dismantlers entered there
One till the moment of his task untold.
When charged therewith he gazed, and answered bold :
    " Be needy I or no,
I will not help lay low a house so fair !

IV

" Hunger is hard.   But since the terms be such—
No wage, or labour stained with the disgrace
Of wrecking what our age cannot replace
    To save its tasteless soul—
I'll do without your dole.   Life is not much ! "

V

Dismissed with sneers he backed his tools and went,
And wandered workless ; for it seemed unwise
To close with one who dared to criticize
    And carp on points of taste :
Rude men should work where placed, and be content.

VI

Years whiled.   He aged, sank, sickened ; and was not :
And it was said, "A man intractable
And curst is gone."   None sighed to hear his knell,
      None sought his churchyard-place ;
His name, his rugged face, were soon forgot.

VII

The stones of that fair hall lie far and wide,
And but a few recall its ancient mould ;
Yet when I pass the spot I long to hold
      As truth what fancy saith :
"His protest lives where deathless things abide !"

THE DAME OF ATHELHALL

I

"DEAR !   Shall I see thy face," she said,
      "In one brief hour ?
And away with thee from a loveless bed
To a far-off sun, to a vine-wrapt bower,
And be thine own unseparated,
      And challenge the world's white glower ? "

II

She quickened her feet, and met him where
      They had predesigned :
And they clasped, and mounted, and cleft the air
Upon whirling wheels ; till the will to bind
Her life with his made the moments there
      Efface the years behind.

III

Miles slid, and the port uprose to view
      As they sped on ;
When slipping its bond the bracelet flew
From her fondled arm.   Replaced anon,
Its cameo of the abjured one drew
      Her musings thereupon.

IV

The gaud with his image once had been
        A gift from him :
And so it was that its carving keen
Refurbished memories wearing dim,
Which set in her soul a twinge of teen,
        And a tear on her lashes' brim.

V

" I may not go ! " she at length outspake,
        " Thoughts call me back—
I would still lose all for your dear, true sake ;
My heart is thine, friend !   But my track
Home, home to Athelhall I must take
        To hinder household wrack ! "

VI

He was wroth.   And they parted, weak and wan ;
        And he left the shore ;
His ship diminished, was low, was gone ;
And she heard in the waves as the daytide wore,
And read in the leer of the sun that shone,
        That they parted for evermore.

VII

She homed as she came, at the dip of eve
        On Athel Coomb
Regaining the Hall she had sworn to leave.
The house was soundless as a tomb,
And she stole to her chamber, there to grieve
        Lone, kneeling, in the gloom.

VIII

From the lawn without rose her husband's voice
        To one his friend :
" Another her Love, another my choice,
Her going is good.   Our conditions mend ;
In a change of mates we shall both rejoice ;
        I hoped that it thus might end !

IX

"A quick divorce ; she will make him hers,
          And I wed mine.
So Time rights all things in long, long years—
Or rather she, by her bold design !
I admire a woman no balk deters :
          She has blessed my life, in fine.

X

" I shall build new rooms for my new true bride,
          Let the bygone be :
By now, no doubt, she has crossed the tide
With the man to her mind.   Far happier she
In some warm vineland by his side
          Than ever she was with me."

THE SEASONS OF HER YEAR

I

WINTER is white on turf and tree,
          And birds are fled ;
But summer songsters pipe to me,
          And petals spread,
For what I dreamt of secretly
          His lips have said !

II

O 'tis a fine May morn, they say,
          And blooms have blown ;
But wild and wintry is my day,
          My song-birds moan ;
For he who vowed leaves me to pay
          Alone—alone !

THE MILKMAID

UNDER a daisied bank
There stands a rich red ruminating cow,
          And hard against her flank
A cotton-hooded milkmaid bends her brow.

The flowery river-ooze
Upheaves and falls ; the milk purrs in the pail ;
Few pilgrims but would choose
The peace of such a life in such a vale.

The maid breathes words—to vent,
It seems, her sense of Nature's scenery,
Of whose life, sentiment,
And essence, very part itself is she.

She bends a glance of pain,
And, at a moment, lets escape a tear ;
Is it that passing train,
Whose alien whirr offends her country ear ?—

Nay ! Phyllis does not dwell
On visual and familiar things like these ;
What moves her is the spell
Of inner themes and inner poetries :

Could but by Sunday morn
Her gay new gown come, meads might dry to dun,
Trains shriek till ears were torn,
If Fred would not prefer that Other One.

THE LEVELLED CHURCHYARD

" O PASSENGER, pray list and catch
        Our sighs and piteous groans,
Half stifled in this jumbled patch
        Of wrenched memorial stones !

" We late-lamented, resting here,
        Are mixed to human jam,
And each to each exclaims in fear,
        ' I know not which I am ! '

" The wicked people have annexed
        The verses on the good ;
A roaring drunkard sports the text
        Teetotal Tommy should !

"Where we are huddled none can trace,
    And if our names remain,
They pave some path or porch or place
    Where we have never lain!

"Here's not a modest maiden elf
    But dreads the final Trumpet,
Lest half of her should rise herself,
    And half some sturdy strumpet!

"From restorations of Thy fane,
    From smoothings of Thy sward,
From zealous Churchmen's pick and plane
    Deliver us O Lord!   Amen!"

1882.

THE RUINED MAID

"O 'MELIA, my dear, this does everything crown!
Who could have supposed I should meet you in Town?
And whence such fair garments, such prosperi-ty?"—
"O didn't you know I'd been ruined?"   said she.

—"You left us in tatters, without shoes or socks,
Tired of digging potatoes, and spudding up docks;
And now you've gay bracelets and bright feathers three!"—
"Yes: that's how we dress when we're ruined," said she.

—"At home in the barton you said 'thee' and 'thou,'
And 'thik oon,' and 'theäs oon,' and 't'other'; but now
Your talking quite fits 'ee for high compa-ny!"—
"Some polish is gained with one's ruin," said she.

—"Your hands were like paws then, your face blue and bleak
But now I'm bewitched by your delicate cheek,
And your little gloves fit as on any la-dy!"—
"We never do work when we're ruined," said she.

—"You used to call home-life a hag-ridden dream,
And you'd sigh, and you'd sock; but at present you seem
To know not of megrims or melancho-ly!"—
"True.   One's pretty lively when ruined," said she.

—" I wish I had feathers, a fine sweeping gown,
And a delicate face, and could strut about Town ! "—
" My dear—a raw country girl, such as you be,
Cannot quite expect that.   You ain't ruined," said she.

WESTBOURNE PARK VILLAS, 1866.

THE RESPECTABLE BURGHER

ON " THE HIGHER CRITICISM "

SINCE Reverend Doctors now declare
That clerks and people must prepare
To doubt if Adam ever were ;
To hold the flood a local scare ;
To argue, though the stolid stare,
That everything had happened ere
The prophets to its happening sware ;
That David was no giant-slayer,
Nor one to call a God-obeyer
In certain details we could spare,
But rather was a debonair
Shrewd bandit, skilled as banjo-player :
That Solomon sang the fleshly Fair,
And gave the Church no thought whate'er ,
That Esther with her royal wear,
And Mordecai, the son of Jair,
And Joshua's triumphs, Job's despair,
And Balaam's ass's bitter blare ;
Nebuchadnezzar's furnace-flare,
And Daniel and the den affair,
And other stories rich and rare,
Were writ to make old doctrine wear
Something of a romantic air :
That the Nain widow's only heir,
And Lazarus with cadaverous glare
(As done in oils by Piombo's care)
Did not return from Sheol's lair :
That Jael set a fiendish snare,
That Pontius Pilate acted square,

That never a sword cut Malchus' ear ;
And (but for shame I must forbear)
That ⸺ ⸺ did not reappear ! . . .
—Since thus they hint, nor turn a hair,
All churchgoing will I forswear,
And sit on Sundays in my chair,
And read that moderate man Voltaire.

ARCHITECTURAL MASKS

I

THERE is a house with ivied walls,
And mullioned windows worn and old,
And the long dwellers in those halls
Have souls that know but sordid calls,
    And daily dote on gold.

II

In blazing brick and plated show
Not far away a " villa " gleams,
And here a family few may know,
With book and pencil, viol and bow,
    Lead inner lives of dreams.

III

The philosophic passers say,
" See that old mansion mossed and fair,
Poetic souls therein are they :
And O that gaudy box !   Away,
    You vulgar people there."

THE TENANT-FOR-LIFE

THE sun said, watching my watering-pot :
  " Some morn you'll pass away ;
These flowers and plants I parch up hot—
    Who'll water them that day ?

" Those banks and beds whose shape your eye
    Has planned in line so true,
New hands will change, unreasoning why
    Such shape seemed best to you.

" Within your house will strangers sit,
    And wonder how first it came ;
They'll talk of their schemes for improving it,
    And will not mention your name.

" They'll care not how, or when, or at what
    You sighed, laughed, suffered here,
Though you feel more in an hour of the spot
    Than they will feel in a year.

" As I look on at you here, now,
    Shall I look on at these ;
But as to our old times, avow
    No knowledge—hold my peace ! . . .

" O friend, it matters not, I say ;
    Bethink ye, I have shined
On nobler ones than you, and they
    Are dead men out of mind ! "

THE KING'S EXPERIMENT

It was a wet wan hour in spring,
And Nature met King Doom beside a lane,
Wherein Hodge tramped, all blithely ballading
    The Mother's smiling reign.

" Why warbles he that skies are fair
And coombs alight," she cried, " and fallows gay,
When I have placed no sunshine in the air
    Or glow on earth to-day ? "

" 'Tis in the comedy of things
That such should be," returned the one of Doom ;
" Charge now the scene with brightest blazonings,
    And he shall call them gloom."

She gave the word : the sunbeams broke,
All Froomside shone, the hedgebirds raised a strain ;
And later Hodge, upon the midday stroke,
     Returned along the lane,

Low murmuring : " O this bitter scene,
And thrice accurst horizon hung with gloom !
How deadly like this sky, these fields, these treen,
     To trappings of the tomb ! "

The Beldame then : " The fool and blind !
Such mad perverseness who may apprehend ? "—
" Nay ; there's no madness in it ; thou shalt find
     Thy law there," said her friend.

" When Hodge went forth 'twas to his Love,
To make her, ere this eve, his wedded prize,
And Earth, despite the heaviness above,
     Was bright as Paradise.

" But I sent on my messenger,
With cunning arrows poisonous and keen,
To take forthwith her laughing life from her,
     And dull her little een,

" And white her cheek, and still her breath,
Ere her too buoyant Hodge had reached her side ;
So, when he came, he clasped her but in death,
     And never as his bride.

" And there's the humour, as I said ;
Thy dreary dawn he saw as gleaming gold,
And in thy glistening green and radiant red
     Funereal gloom and cold."

THE TREE

AN OLD MAN'S STORY

I

ITS roots are bristling in the air
Like some mad Earth-god's spiny hair ;
The loud south-wester's swell and yell
Smote it at midnight, and it fell.
     Thus ends the tree
     Where Some One sat with me.

II

Its boughs, which none but darers trod,
A child may step on from the sod,
And twigs that earliest met the dawn
Are lit the last upon the lawn.
Cart off the tree
Beneath whose trunk sat we!

III

Yes, there we sat: she cooed content,
And bats ringed round, and daylight went;
The gnarl, our seat, is wrenched and sunk,
Prone that queer pocket in the trunk
Where lay the key
To her pale mystery.

IV

"Years back, within this pocket-hole
I found, my Love, a hurried scrawl
Meant not for me," at length said I;
"I glanced thereat, and let it lie:
The words were three—
'Beloved, I agree.'

V

"Who placed it here; to what request
It gave assent, I never guessed.
Some prayer of some hot heart, no doubt,
To some coy maiden hereabout,
Just as, maybe,
With you, Sweet Heart, and me."

VI

She waited, till with quickened breath
She spoke, as one who banisheth
Reserves that lovecraft heeds so well,
To ease some mighty wish to tell:
"'Twas I," said she,
"Who wrote thus clinchingly.

VII

" My lover's wife—aye, wife—knew nought
Of what we felt, and bore, and thought. . . .
He'd said : ' *I wed with thee or die :*
She stands between, 'tis true.   But why ?
          Do thou agree,
          And—she shall cease to be.'

VIII

" How I held back, how love supreme
Involved me madly in his scheme
Why should I say ? . . . I wrote assent
(You found it hid) to his intent. . . .
          She—*died.* . . . But he
          Came not to wed with me.

IX

" O shrink not, Love !—Had these eyes seen
But once thine own, such had not been !
But we were strangers. . . . Thus the plot
Cleared passion's path.—Why came he not
          To wed with me ? . . .
          He wived the gibbet-tree."

X

—Under that oak of heretofore
Sat Sweetheart mine with me no more :
By many a Fiord, and Strom, and Fleuve
Have I since wandered. . . . Soon, for love,
          Distraught went she—
          'Twas said for love of me.

HER LATE HUSBAND

(KING'S HINTOCK, 182–)

" No—not where I shall make my own ;
          But dig his grave just by
The woman's with the initialed stone—
          As near as he can lie—
After whose death he seemed to ail,
          Though none considered why.

" And when I also claim a nook,
    And your feet tread me in,
Bestow me, in my maiden name,
    Among my kith and kin,
That strangers gazing may not dream
    I did a husband win."

" Widow, your wish shall be obeyed :
    Though, thought I, certainly
You'd lay him where your folk are laid,
    And your grave, too, will be,
As custom hath it ; you to right,
    And on the left hand he."

" Aye, sexton ; such the Hintock rule,
    And none has said it nay ;
But now you find a native here
    Eschews that ancient way . . .
And it may be, some Christmas night,
    When angels walk, they'll say :

" ' O strange interment !   Civilized lands
    Afford few types thereof ;
Here is a man who takes his rest
    Beside his very Love,
Beside the one who was his wife
    In our sight up above !' "

THE SELF-UNSEEING

HERE is the ancient floor,
    Footworn and hollowed and thin,
Here was the former door
    Where the dead feet walked in.

She sat here in her chair,
    Smiling into the fire ;
He who played stood there,
    Bowing it higher and higher.

Childlike, I danced in a dream ;
    Blessings emblazoned that day ;
Everything glowed with a gleam ;
    Yet we were looking away !

IN TENEBRIS

I

" Percussus sum sicut foenum, et aruit cor meum."—Ps. ci.

WINTERTIME nighs;
But my bereavement-pain
It cannot bring again:
    Twice no one dies.

Flower-petals flee;
But, since it once hath been,
No more that severing scene
    Can harrow me.

Birds faint in dread:
I shall not lose old strength
In the lone frost's black length:
    Strength long since fled!

Leaves freeze to dun;
But friends can not turn cold
This season as of old
    For him with none.

Tempests may scath;
But love can not make smart
Again this year his heart
    Who no heart hath.

Black is night's cope;
But death will not appal
One who, past doubtings all,
    Waits in unhope.

IN TENEBRIS

II

" Considerabam ad dexteram, et videbam ; et non erat qui cognosceret me. . . . Non est qui requirat animam meam."—Ps. cxli.

WHEN the clouds' swoln bosoms echo back the shouts of the
  many and strong
That things are all as they best may be, save a few to be right
  ere long,
And my eyes have not the vision in them to discern what to
  these is so clear,
The blot seems straightway in me alone ; one better he were not
  here.

The stout upstanders say, All's well with us : ruers have nought
  to rue !
And what the potent say so oft, can it fail to be somewhat true ?
Breezily go they, breezily come ; their dust smokes around their
  career,
Till I think I am one born out of due time, who has no calling
  here.

Their dawns bring lusty joys, it seems ; their evenings all that is
  sweet ;
Our times are blessed times, they cry : Life shapes it as is most
  meet,
And nothing is much the matter ; there are many smiles to a
  tear ;
Then what is the matter is I, I say.   Why should such an one
  be here ? . . .

Let him in whose ears the low-voiced Best is killed by the
  clash of the First,
Who holds that if way to the Better there be, it exacts a full look
  at the Worst,
Who feels that delight is a delicate growth cramped by crooked-
  ness, custom, and fear,
Get him up and be gone as one shaped awry ; he disturbs the
  order here.

1895–96.

IN TENEBRIS

III

'Heu mihi, quia incolatus meus prolongatus est !   Habitavi cum habitantibus
    Cedar ; multum incola fuit anima mea."—*Ps.* cxix.

There have been times when I well might have passed and the
    ending have come—
Points in my path when the dark might have stolen on me,
    artless, unrueing—
Ere I had learnt that the world was a welter of futile doing :
Such had been times when I well might have passed, and the
    ending have come !

Say, on the noon when the half-sunny hours told that April was
    nigh,
And I upgathered and cast forth the snow from the crocus-
    border,
Fashioned and furbished the soil into a summer-seeming order,
Glowing in gladsome faith that I quickened the year thereby.

Or on that loneliest of eves when afar and benighted we stood,
She who upheld me and I, in the midmost of Egdon together,
Confident I in her watching and ward through the blackening
    heather,
Deeming her matchless in might and with measureless scope
    endued.

Or on that winter-wild night when, reclined by the chimney-nook
    quoin,
Slowly a drowse overgat me, the smallest and feeblest of folk
    there,
Weak from my baptism of pain ; when at times and anon I
    awoke there—
Heard of a world wheeling on, with no listing or longing to join.

Even then ! while unweeting that vision could vex or that know-
    ledge could numb,
That sweets to the mouth in the belly are bitter, and tart, and
    untoward,
Then, on some dim-coloured scene should my briefly raised
    curtain have lowered,
Then might the Voice that is law have said " Cease ! " and the
    ending have come.

1896.

THE CHURCH-BUILDER

I

THE church flings forth a battled shade
  Over the moon-blanched sward;
The church; my gift; whereto I paid
  My all in hand and hoard;
    Lavished my gains
    With stintless pains
  To glorify the Lord.

II

I squared the broad foundations in
  Of ashlared masonry;
I moulded mullions thick and thin,
  Hewed fillet and ogee:
    I circleted
    Each sculptured head
  With nimb and canopy.

III

I called in many a craftsmaster
  To fix emblazoned glass,
To figure Cross and Sepulchre
  On dossal, boss, and brass.
    My gold all spent,
    My jewels went
  To gem the cups of Mass.

IV

I borrowed deep to carve the screen
  And raise the ivoried Rood;
I parted with my small demesne
  To make my owings good.
    Heir-looms unpriced
    I sacrificed,
  Until debt-free I stood.

V

So closed the task.   " Deathless the Creed
   Here substanced ! " said my soul :
" I heard me bidden to this deed,
   And straight obeyed the call.
      Illume this fane,
      That not in vain
   I build it, Lord of all ! "

VI

But, as it chanced me, then and there
   Did dire misfortunes burst ;
My home went waste for lack of care,
   My sons rebelled and curst ;
      Till I confessed
      That aims the best
   Were looking like the worst.

VII

Enkindled by my votive work
   No burning faith I find ;
The deeper thinkers sneer and smirk,
   And give my toil no mind ;
      From nod and wink
      I read they think
   That I am fool and blind.

VIII

My gift to God seems futile, quite ;
   The world moves as erstwhile ;
And powerful Wrong on feeble Right
   Tramples in olden style.
      My faith burns down,
      I see no crown ;
   But Cares, and Griefs, and Guile.

IX

So now, the remedy ?   Yea, this :
   I gently swing the door
Here, of my fane—no soul to wis—
   And cross the patterned floor
      To the rood-screen
      That stands between
   The nave and inner chore.

X

The rich red windows dim the moon,
　　But little light need I ;
I mount the prie-dieu, lately hewn
　　From woods of rarest dye ;
　　　　Then from below
　　　　My garment, so,
　　I draw this cord, and tie

XI

One end thereof around the beam
　　Midway 'twixt Cross and truss :
I noose the nethermost extreme,
　　And in ten seconds thus
　　　　I journey hence—
　　　　To that land whence
　　No rumour reaches us.

XII

Well : Here at morn they'll light on one
　　Dangling in mockery
Of what he spent his substance on
　　Blindly and uselessly ! . . .
　　　　" He might," they'll say,
　　　　" Have built, some way,
　　A cheaper gallows-tree ! "

THE LOST PYX

A MEDIÆVAL LEGEND [1]

SOME say the spot is banned : that the pillar Cross-and-Hand
　　Attests to a deed of hell ;
But of else than of bale is the mystic tale
　　That ancient Vale-folk tell.

[1] On a lonely table-land above the Vale of Blackmore, between High-Stoy and Bubb-Down hills, and commanding in clear weather views that extend from the English to the Bristol Channel, stands a pillar, apparently mediæval, called Cross-and-Hand, or Christ-in-Hand. One tradition of its origin is mentioned in *Tess of the d'Urbervilles* ; another, more detailed, preserves the story here given.

Ere Cernel's Abbey ceased hereabout there dwelt a priest,
 (In later life sub-prior
Of the brotherhood there, whose bones are now bare
 In the field that was Cernel choir).

One night in his cell at the foot of yon dell
 The priest heard a frequent cry :
" Go, father, in haste to the cot on the waste,
 And shrive a man waiting to die."

Said the priest in a shout to the caller without,
 " The night howls, the tree-trunks bow ;
One may barely by day track so rugged a way,
 And can I then do so now ? "

No further word from the dark was heard,
 And the priest moved never a limb ;
And he slept and dreamed ; till a Visage seemed
 To frown from Heaven at him.

In a sweat he arose ; and the storm shrieked shrill,
 And smote as in savage joy ;
While High-Stoy trees twanged to Bubb-Down Hill,
 And Bubb-Down to High-Stoy.

There seemed not a holy thing in hail,
 Nor shape of light or love,
From the Abbey north of Blackmore Vale
 To the Abbey south thereof.

Yet he plodded thence through the dark immense,
 And with many a stumbling stride
Through copse and briar climbed nigh and nigher
 To the cot and the sick man's side.

When he would have unslung the Vessels uphung
 To his arm in the steep ascent,
He made loud moan : the Pyx was gone
 Of the Blessed Sacrament.

Then in dolorous dread he beat his head :
 " No earthly prize or pelf
Is the thing I've lost in tempest tossed,
 But the Body of Christ Himself ! "

He thought of the Visage his dream revealed,
    And turned towards whence he came,
Hands groping the ground along foot-track and field,
    And head in a heat of shame.

Till here on the hill, betwixt vill and vill,
    He noted a clear straight ray
Stretching down from the sky to a spot hard by,
    Which shone with the light of day.

And gathered around the illumined ground
    Were common beasts and rare,
All kneeling at gaze, and in pause profound
    Attent on an object there.

'Twas the Pyx, unharmed 'mid the circling rows
    Of Blackmore's hairy throng,
Whereof were oxen, sheep, and does,
    And hares from the brakes among;

And badgers grey, and conies keen,
    And squirrels of the tree,
And many a member seldom seen
    Of Nature's family.

The ireful winds that scoured and swept
    Through coppice, clump, and dell,
Within that holy circle slept
    Calm as in hermit's cell.

Then the priest bent likewise to the sod
    And thanked the Lord of Love,
And Blessed Mary, Mother of God,
    And all the saints above.

And turning straight with his priceless freight,
    He reached the dying one,
Whose passing sprite had been stayed for the rite
    Without which bliss hath none.

And when by grace the priest won place,
    And served the Abbey well,
He reared this stone to mark where shone
    That midnight miracle.

TESS'S LAMENT

I

I WOULD that folk forgot me quite,
            Forgot me quite!
I would that I could shrink from sight,
      And no more see the sun.
Would it were time to say farewell,
To claim my nook, to need my knell,
Time for them all to stand and tell
      Of my day's work as done.

II

Ah! dairy where I lived so long,
            I lived so long;
Where I would rise up staunch and strong,
      And lie down hopefully.
'Twas there within the chimney-seat
He watched me to the clock's slow beat—
Loved me, and learnt to call me Sweet,
      And whispered words to me.

III

And now he's gone; and now he's gone; . . .
            And now he's gone!
The flowers we potted perhaps are thrown
      To rot upon the farm.
And where we had our supper-fire
May now grow nettle, dock, and briar,
And all the place be mould and mire
      So cozy once and warm.

IV

And it was I who did it all,
            Who did it all;
'Twas I who made the blow to fall
      On him who thought no guile.
Well, it is finished—past, and he
Has left me to my misery,
And I must take my Cross on me
      For wronging him awhile.

V

How gay we looked that day we wed,
         That day we wed !
" May joy be with ye ! " they all said
         A-standing by the durn.
I wonder what they say o'us now,
And if they know my lot ; and how
She feels who milks my favourite cow,
         And takes my place at churn !

VI

It wears me out to think of it,
         To think of it ;
I cannot bear my fate as writ,
         I'd have my life unbe ;
Would turn my memory to a blot,
Make every relic of me rot,
My doings be as they were not,
         And gone all trace of me !

THE SUPPLANTER

A TALE

I

HE bends his travel-tarnished feet
         To where she wastes in clay :
From day-dawn until eve he fares
         Along the wintry way ;
From day-dawn until eve he bears
         A wreath of blooms and bay.

II

" Are these the gravestone shapes that meet
         My forward-straining view ?
Or forms that cross a window-blind
         In circle, knot, and queue :
Gay forms, that cross and whirl and wind
         To music throbbing through ? "—

III

"The Keeper of the Field of Tombs
    Dwells by its gateway-pier;
He celebrates with feast and dance
    His daughter's twentieth year:
He celebrates with wine of France
    The birthday of his dear."——

IV

"The gates are shut when evening glooms:
    Lay down your wreath, sad wight;
To-morrow is a time more fit
    For placing flowers aright:
The morning is the time for it;
    Come, wake with us to-night!"——

V

He drops his wreath, and enters in,
    And sits, and shares their cheer.——
"I fain would foot with you, young man,
    Before all others here;
I fain would foot it for a span
    With such a cavalier!"

VI

She coaxes, clasps, nor fails to win
    His first-unwilling hand:
The merry music strikes its staves,
    The dancers quickly band;
And with the Damsel of the Graves
    He duly takes his stand.

VII

"You dance divinely, stranger swain,
    Such grace I've never known.
O longer stay! Breathe not adieu
    And leave me here alone!
O longer stay: to her be true
    Whose heart is all your own!"——

VIII

"I mark a phantom through the pane,
      That beckons in despair,
Its mouth all drawn with heavy moan—
      Her to whom once I sware!"—
"Nay; 'tis the lately carven stone
      Of some strange girl laid there!"—

IX

"I see white flowers upon the floor
      Betrodden to a clot;
My wreath were they?"—"Nay; love me much,
      Swear you'll forget me not!
'Twas but a wreath!   Full many such
      Are brought here and forgot."

.   .   .   .   .

X

The watches of the night grow hoar,
      He wakens with the sun;
"Now could I kill thee here!" he says,
      "For winning me from one
Who ever in her living days
      Was pure as cloistered nun!"

XI

She cowers; and, rising, roves he then
      Afar for many a mile,
For evermore to be apart
      From her who could beguile
His senses by her burning heart,
      And win his love awhile.

XII

A year beholds him wend again
      To her who wastes in clay;
From day-dawn until eve he fares
      Along the wintry way,
From day-dawn until eve repairs
      Towards her mound to pray.

XIII

And there he sets him to fulfil
    His frustrate first intent :
And lay upon her bed, at last,
    The offering earlier meant :
When, on his stooping figure, ghast
    And haggard eyes are bent.

XIV

" O surely for a little while
    You can be kind to me .
For do you love her, do you hate,
    She knows not—cares not she :
Only the living feel the weight
    Of loveless misery !

XV

" I own my sin ; I've paid its cost,
    Being outcast, shamed, and bare :
I give you daily my whole heart,
    Your child my tender care,
I pour you prayers ; this life apart
    Is more than I can bear ! "

XVI

He turns—unpitying, passion-tossed ;
    " I know you not ! " he cries,
" Nor know your child.   I knew this maid,
    But she's in Paradise ! "
And he has vanished in the shade
    From her beseeching eyes.

IMITATIONS, ETC.

SAPPHIC FRAGMENT

"Thou shalt be—Nothing."—OMAR KHAYYÁM.
"Tombless, with no remembrance."—W. SHAKESPEARE.

DEAD shalt thou lie; and nought
　　Be told of thee or thought,
For thou hast plucked not of the Muses' tree:
　　And even in Hades' halls
　　Amidst thy fellow-thralls
No friendly shade thy shade shall company!

CATULLUS: XXXI

(After passing Sirmione, April 1887)

SIRMIO, thou dearest dear of strands
That Neptune strokes in lake and sea,
With what high joy from stranger lands
Doth thy old friend set foot on thee!
Yea, barely seems it true to me
That no Bithynia holds me now,
But calmly and assuringly
Around me stretchest homely Thou.

Is there a scene more sweet than when
Our clinging cares are undercast,
And, worn by alien moils and men,
The long untrodden sill repassed,
We press the pined for couch at last,
And find a full repayment there?
Then hail, sweet Sirmio; thou that wast,
And art, mine own unrivalled Fair!

166

AFTER SCHILLER

KNIGHT, a true sister-love
This heart retains;
Ask me no other love,
That way lie pains!

Calm must I view thee come,
Calm see thee go;
Tale-telling tears of thine
I must not know!

SONG FROM HEINE

I SCANNED her picture, dreaming,
Till each dear line and hue
Was imaged, to my seeming,
As if it lived anew.

Her lips began to borrow
Their former wondrous smile;
Her fair eyes, faint with sorrow,
Grew sparkling as erstwhile.

Such tears as often ran not
Ran then, my love, for thee;
And O, believe I cannot
That thou art lost to me!

FROM VICTOR HUGO

CHILD, were I king, I'd yield my royal rule,
My chariot, sceptre, vassal-service due,
My crown, my porphyry-basined waters cool,
My fleets, whereto the sea is but a pool,
For a glance from you!

Love, were I God, the earth and its heaving airs,
   Angels, the demons abject under me,
Vast chaos with its teeming womby lairs,
Time, space, all would I give—aye, upper spheres,
   For a kiss from thee !

CARDINAL BEMBO'S EPITAPH ON RAPHAEL

HERE'S one in whom Nature feared—faint at such vying—
Eclipse while he lived, and decease at his dying.

RETROSPECT

"I HAVE LIVED WITH SHADES"

I

I HAVE lived with Shades so long,
And talked to them so oft,
Since forth from cot and croft
I went mankind among,
    That sometimes they
    In their dim style
    Will pause awhile
    To hear my say ;

II

And take me by the hand,
And lead me through their rooms
In the To-be, where Dooms
Half-wove and shapeless stand :
    And show from there
    The dwindled dust
    And rot and rust
    Of things that were.

III

" Now turn," they said to me
One day : " Look whence we came,
And signify his name
Who gazes thence at thee."—
    —" Nor name nor race
    Know I, or can,"
    I said, " Of man
    So commonplace.

IV

"He moves me not at all;
I note no ray or jot
Of rareness in his lot,
Or star exceptional.
    Into the dim
    Dead throngs around
    He'll sink, nor sound
    Be left of him.

V

"Yet," said they, "his frail speech,
Hath accents pitched like thine—
Thy mould and his define
A likeness each to each—
    But go! Deep pain
    Alas, would be
    His name to thee,
    And told in vain!"

February 2, 1899.

MEMORY AND I

"O MEMORY, where is now my youth,
Who used to say that life was truth?"

"I saw him in a crumbled cot
    Beneath a tottering tree;
That he as phantom lingers there
    Is only known to me."

"O Memory, where is now my joy,
Who lived with me in sweet employ?"

"I saw him in gaunt gardens lone,
    Where laughter used to be;
That he as phantom wanders there
    Is known to none but me."

"O Memory, where is now my hope,
Who charged with deeds my skill and scope?'

" I saw her in a tomb of tomes,
    Where dreams are wont to be;
That she as spectre haunteth there
    Is only known to me."

"O Memory, where is now my faith,
One time a champion, now a wraith?"

" I saw her in a ravaged aisle,
    Bowed down on bended knee;
That her poor ghost outflickers there
    Is known to none but me."

"O Memory, where is now my love,
That rayed me as a god above?"

" I saw her in an ageing shape
    Where beauty used to be;
That her fond phantom lingers there
    Is only known to me."

'ΑΓΝΩΣΤΩι ΘΕΩι.

LONG have I framed weak phantasies of Thee,
        O Willer masked and dumb!
        Who makest Life become,—
As though by labouring all-unknowingly,
        Like one whom reveries numb.

How much of consciousness informs Thy will,
        Thy biddings, as if blind,
        Of death-inducing kind,
Nought shows to us ephemeral ones who fill
        But moments in Thy mind.

Perhaps Thy ancient rote-restricted ways
    Thy ripening rule transcends ;
    That listless effort tends
To grow percipient with advance of days,
    And with percipience mends.

For, in unwonted purlieus, far and nigh,
    At whiles or short or long,
    May be discerned a wrong
Dying as of self-slaughter ; whereat I
    Would raise my voice in song.

TIME'S LAUGHINGSTOCKS

PREFACE

In collecting the following poems I have to thank the editors and proprietors of the periodicals in which certain of them have appeared for permission to reclaim them.

Now that the miscellany is brought together, some lack of concord in pieces written at widely severed dates, and in contrasting moods and circumstances, will be obvious enough. This I cannot help, but the sense of disconnection, particularly in respect of those lyrics penned in the first person, will be immaterial when it is borne in mind that they are to be regarded, in the main, as dramatic monologues by different characters.

As a whole they will, I hope, take the reader forward, even if not far, rather than backward. I should add that some lines in the early-dated poems have been rewritten, though they have been left substantially unchanged.

T. H.

September 1909.

   Stronger,

THE REVISITATION

As I lay awake at night-time
In an ancient country barrack known to ancient cannoneers,
And recalled the hopes that heralded each seeming brave and
      bright time
   Of my primal purple years,

Much it haunted me that, nigh there,
I had borne my bitterest loss—when One who went, came not again;
In a joyless hour of discord, in a joyless-hued July there—
   A July just such as then.

And as thus I brooded longer,
With my faint eyes on the feeble square of wan-lit window frame,
A quick conviction sprung within me, grew, and grew yet stronger,
   That the month-night was the same,

Too, as that which saw her leave me
On the rugged ridge of Waterstone, the peewits plaining round;
And a lapsing twenty years had ruled that—as it were to
      grieve me—
   I should near the once-loved ground.

Though but now a war-worn stranger
Chance had quartered here, I rose up and descended to the yard.
All was soundless, save the troopers' horses tossing at the manger,
   And the sentry keeping guard.

Through the gateway I betook me
Down the High Street and beyond the lamps, across the battered
      bridge,
Till the country darkness clasped me and the friendly shine
      forsook me,
   And I bore towards the Ridge,

177

With a dim unowned emotion
Saying softly : " Small my reason, now at midnight, to be here . . . .
Yet a sleepless swain of fifty with a brief romantic notion
    May retrace a track so dear."

    Thus I walked with thoughts half-uttered
Up the lane I knew so well, the grey, gaunt, lonely Lane of Slyre ;
And at whiles behind me, far at sea, a sullen thunder muttered
    As I mounted high and higher.

    Till, the upper roadway quitting,
I adventured on the open drouthy downland thinly grassed,
While the spry white scuts of conies flashed before me, earthward
    flitting,
    And an arid wind went past.

    Round about me bulged the barrows
As before, in antique silence—immemorial funeral piles—
Where the sleek herds trampled daily the remains of flint-tipt arrows
    Mid the thyme and chamomiles ;

    And the Sarsen stone there, dateless,
On whose breast we had sat and told the zephyrs many a
    tender vow,
Held the heat of yester sun, as sank thereon one fated mateless
    From those far fond hours till now.

    Maybe flustered by my presence
Rose the peewits, just as all those years back, wailing soft
    and loud,
And revealing their pale pinions like a fitful phosphorescence
    Up against the cope of cloud,

    Where their dolesome exclamations
Seemed the voicings of the self-same throats I had heard when
    life was green,
Though since that day uncounted frail forgotten generations
    Of their kind had flecked the scene.—

    And so, living long and longer
In a past that lived no more, my eyes discerned there, suddenly,
That a figure broke the skyline—first in vague contour, then
    stronger,
    And was crossing near to me.

Some long-missed familiar gesture,
Something wonted, struck me in the figure's pause to list and
    heed,
Till I fancied from its handling of its loosely wrapping vesture
    That it might be She indeed.

'Twas not reasonless : below there
In the vale, had been her home ; the nook might hold her
    even yet,
And the downlands were her father's fief ; she still might come
    and go there ;—
    So I rose, and said, "Agnette!"

With a little leap, half-frightened,
She withdrew some steps ; then letting intuition smother fear
In a place so long-accustomed, and as one whom thought
    enlightened,
    She replied : "What—*that* voice ?—here !"

"Yes, Agnette !—And did the occasion
Of our marching hither make you think I *might* walk where
    we two—"
"O, I often come," she murmured with a moment's coy evasion,
    "('Tis not far),—and —think of you."

Then I took her hand, and led her
To the ancient people's stone whereon I had sat. There now
    sat we ;
And together talked, until the first reluctant shyness fled her,
    And she spoke confidingly.

"It is *just* as ere we parted !"
Said she, brimming high with joy.—"And when, then, came you
    here, and why ?"
"—Dear, I could not sleep for thinking of our trystings when
    twin-hearted."
    She responded, "Nor could I.

"There are few things I would rather
Than be wandering at this spirit-hour—lone-lived, my kindred
    dead—
On this wold of well-known feature I inherit from my father :
    Night or day, I have no dread . . . . .

"O I wonder, wonder whether
Any heartstring bore a signal-thrill between us twain or no ?—
Some such influence can, at times, they say, draw severed soul
    together."
I said, " Dear, we'll dream it so."

Each one's hand the other's grasping,
And a mutual forgiveness won, we sank to silent thought,
A large content in us that seemed our rended lives reclasping,
    And contracting years to nought.

Till I, maybe overweary
From the lateness, and a wayfaring so full of strain and stress
For one no longer buoyant, to a peak so steep and eery,
    Sank to slow unconsciousness . . . .

How long I slept I knew not,
But the brief warm summer night had slid when, to my swift
    surprise,
A red upedging sun, of glory chambered mortals view not,
    Was blazing on my eyes,

From the Milton Woods to Dole-Hill
All the spacious landscape lighting, and around about my feet
Flinging tall thin tapering shadows from the meanest mound
    and mole-hill,
    And on trails the ewes had beat.

She was sitting still beside me,
Dozing likewise ; and I turned to her, to take her hanging hand
When, the more regarding, that which like a spectre shook
    and tried me
    In her image then I scanned ;

That which Time's transforming chisel
Had been tooling night and day for twenty years, and tooled
    too well,
In its rendering of crease where curve was, where was raven
    grizzle—
    Pits, where peonies once did dwell.

She had wakened, and perceiving
(I surmise) my sigh and shock, my quite involuntary dismay,
Up she started, and—her wasted figure all throughout it heaving—
    Said, "Ah, yes : I am *thus* by day !

"Can you really wince and wonder
That the sunlight should reveal you such a thing of skin and bone,
As if unaware a Death's-head must of need lie not far under
     Flesh whose years out-count your own ?

     "Yes : that movement was a warning
Of the worth of man's devotion !—Yes, Sir, I am *old*," said she,
"And the thing which should increase love turns it quickly into
          scorning—
     And your new-won heart from me !"

     Then she went, ere I could call her,
With the too proud temper ruling that had parted us before,
And I saw her form descend the slopes, and smaller grow
          and smaller,
     Till I caught its course no more . . . .

     True ; I might have dogged her downward ;
—But it *may* be (though I know not) that this trick on us of Time
Disconcerted and confused me.—Soon I bent my footsteps
          townward,
     Like to one who had watched a crime.

     Well I knew my native weakness,
Well I know it still.   I cherished her reproach like physic-wine,
For I saw in that emaciate shape of bitterness and bleakness
     A nobler soul than mine.

     Did I not return, then, ever ?—
Did we meet again ? — mend all ? — Alas, what greyhead
          perseveres !—
Soon I got the Route elsewhither.— Since that hour I have seen
          her never :
     Love is lame at fifty years.

A TRAMPWOMAN'S TRAGEDY

(182–)

I

FROM Wynyard's Gap the livelong day,
    The livelong day,
We beat afoot the northward way
    We had travelled times before.
The sun-blaze burning on our backs,
Our shoulders sticking to our packs,
By fosseway, fields, and turnpike tracks
    We skirted sad Sedge-Moor.

II

Full twenty miles we jaunted on,
    We jaunted on,—
My fancy-man, and jeering John,
    And Mother Lee, and I.
And, as the sun drew down to west,
We climbed the toilsome Poldon crest,
And saw, of landskip sights the best,
    The inn that beamed thereby.

III

For months we had padded side by side,
    Ay, side by side
Through the Great Forest, Blackmoor wide,
    And where the Parret ran.
We'd faced the gusts on Mendip ridge,
Had crossed the Yeo unhelped by bridge,
Been stung by every Marshwood midge,
    I and my fancy-man.

IV

Lone inns we loved, my man and I,
    My man and I ;
"King's Stag," "Windwhistle" high and dry,
    "The Horse" on Hintock Green,

The cosy house at Wynyard's Gap,
"The Hut" renowned on Bredy Knap,
And many another wayside tap
    Where folk might sit unseen.

V

Now as we trudged—O deadly day,
    O deadly day !—
I teased my fancy-man in play
    And wanton idleness.
I walked alongside jeering John,
I laid his hand my waist upon ;
I would not bend my glances on
    My lover's dark distress.

VI

Thus Poldon top at last we won,
    At last we won,
And gained the inn at sink of sun
    Far-famed as " Marshal's Elm."
Beneath us figured tor and lea,
From Mendip to the western sea—
I doubt if finer sight there be
    Within this royal realm.

VII

Inside the settle all a-row—
    All four a-row
We sat, I next to John, to show
    That he had wooed and won.
And then he took me on his knee,
And swore it was his turn to be
My favoured mate, and Mother Lee
    Passed to my former one.

VIII

Then in a voice I had never heard,
    I had never heard,
My only Love to me : " One word,
    My lady, if you please !

Whose is the child you are like to bear?—
His? After all my months o' care?"
God knows 'twas not! But, O despair!
    I nodded—still to tease.

IX

Then up he sprung, and with his knife—
    And with his knife
He let out jeering Johnny's life,
    Yes; there, at set of sun.
The slant ray through the window nigh
Gilded John's blood and glazing eye,
Ere scarcely Mother Lee and I
    Knew that the deed was done.

X

The taverns tell the gloomy tale,
    The gloomy tale,
How that at Ivel-chester jail
    My Love, my sweetheart swung;
Though stained till now by no misdeed
Save one horse ta'en in time o' need;
(Blue Jimmy stole right many a steed
    Ere his last fling he flung.)

XI

Thereaft I walked the world alone,
    Alone, alone!
On his death-day I gave my groan
    And dropt his dead-born child.
'Twas nigh the jail, beneath a tree,
None tending me; for Mother Lee
Had died at Glaston, leaving me
    Unfriended on the wild.

XII

And in the night as I lay weak,
    As I lay weak,
The leaves a-falling on my cheek,
    The red moon low declined—

The ghost of him I'd die to kiss
Rose up and said: "Ah, tell me this!
Was the child mine, or was it his?
      Speak, that I rest may find!"

XIII

O doubt not but I told him then,
      I told him then,
That I had kept me from all men
      Since we joined lips and swore.
Whereat he smiled, and thinned away
As the wind stirred to call up day . . .
—'Tis past! And here alone I stray
      Haunting the Western Moor.

NOTES.—"Windwhistle" (Stanza IV.). The highness and dryness of
Windwhistle Inn was impressed upon the writer two or three years ago,
when, after climbing on a hot afternoon to the beautiful spot near which it
stands and entering the inn for tea, he was informed by the landlady that
none could be had, unless he would fetch water from a valley half a mile off,
the house containing not a drop, owing to its situation. However, a tantaliz-
ing row of full barrels behind her back testified to a wetness of a certain sort,
which was not at that time desired.

"Marshal's Elm" (Stanza VI.), so picturesquely situated, is no longer an
inn, though the house, or part of it, still remains. It used to exhibit a fine
old swinging sign.

"Blue Jimmy" (Stanza X.) was a notorious horse-stealer of Wessex in
those days, who appropriated more than a hundred horses before he was
caught, among others one belonging to a neighbour of the writer's grand-
father. He was hanged at the now demolished Ivel-chester or Ilchester
jail above mentioned—that building formerly of so many sinister associations
in the minds of the local peasantry, and the continual haunt of fever, which
at last led to its condemnation. Its site is now an innocent-looking green
meadow.

April 1902.

THE TWO ROSALINDS

I

THE dubious daylight ended,
And I walked the Town alone, unminding whither bound and
      why,
As from each gaunt street and gaping square a mist of light
      ascended
      And dispersed upon the sky.

II

Files of evanescent faces
Passed each other without heeding, in their travail, teen, or joy,
Some in void unvisioned listlessness inwrought with pallid traces
    Of keen penury's annoy.

III

Nebulous flames in crystal cages
Leered as if with discontent at city movement, murk, and grime,
And as waiting some procession of great ghosts from bygone ages
    To exalt the ignoble time.

IV

In a colonnade high-lighted,
By a thoroughfare where stern utilitarian traffic dinned,
On a red and white emblazonment of players and parts, I sighted
    The name of "Rosalind,"

V

And her famous mates of "Arden,"
Who observed no stricter customs than "the seasons' difference"
    bade,
Who lived with running brooks for books in Nature's wildwood
    garden,
    And called idleness their trade . . .

VI

Now the poster stirred an ember
Still remaining from my ardours of some forty years before,
When the self-same portal on an eve it thrilled me to remember
    A like announcement bore ;

VII

And expectantly I had entered,
And had first beheld in human mould a Rosalind woo and plead,
On whose transcendent figuring my speedy soul had centred
    As it had been she indeed . . . .

VIII

So ; all other plans discarding,
I resolved on entrance, bent on seeing what I once had seen,

nd approached the gangway of my earlier knowledge, dis-
    regarding
    The tract of time between.

IX

    " The words, sir ? " cried a creature
Iovering mid the shine and shade as 'twixt the live world and
    the tomb ;
But the well-known numbers needed not for me a text or teacher
    To revive and re-illume.

X

    Then the play. . . . But how unfitted
Was *this* Rosalind !—a mammet quite to me, in memories nurst,
And with chilling disappointment soon I sought the street I had
    quitted,
    To re-ponder on the first.

XI

    The hag still hawked,—I met her
ust without the colonnade. " So you don't like her, sir ? " said
    she.
" Ah—*I* was once that Rosalind !—I acted her—none better—
    Yes—in eighteen sixty-three.

XII

    " Thus I won Orlando to me
n my then triumphant days when I had charm and maidenhood,
Now some forty years ago.—I used to say, *Come woo me, woo*
    me ! "
    And she struck the attitude.

XIII

    It was when I had gone there nightly ;
And the voice—through raucous now—was yet the old one.—
    Clear as noon
My Rosalind was here . . . . Thereon the band withinside
    lightly
    Beat up a merry tune.

A SUNDAY MORNING TRAGEDY

(*circa* 186–)

I BORE a daughter flower-fair,
    In Pydel Vale, alas for me ;
I joyed to mother one so rare,
    But dead and gone I now would be.

Men looked and loved her as she grew,
    And she was won, alas for me ;
She told me nothing, but I knew,
    And saw that sorrow was to be.

I knew that one had made her thrall,
    A thrall to him, alas for me ;
And then, at last, she told me all,
    And wondered what her end would be.

She owned that she had loved too well,
    Had loved too well, unhappy she,
And bore a secret time would tell,
    Though in her shroud she'd sooner be.

I plodded to her sweetheart's door
    In Pydel Vale, alas for me :
I pleaded with him, pleaded sore,
    To save her from her misery.

He frowned, and swore he could not wed,
    Seven times he swore it could not be ;
" Poverty's worse than shame," he said,
    Till all my hope went out of me.

" I've packed my traps to sail the main "—
    Roughly he spake, alas did he—
" Wessex beholds me not again,
    'Tis worse than any jail would be ! "

—There was a shepherd whom I knew,
    A subtle man, alas for me :

I sought him all the pastures through,
Though better I had ceased to be.

I traced him by his lantern light,
And gave him hint, alas for me,
Of how she found her in the plight
That is so scorned in Christendie.

" Is there an herb. . . . ? " I asked.   " Or none ? "
Yes, thus I asked him desperately.
"—There is," he said ; " a certain one. . . ."
Would he had sworn that none knew he !

" To-morrow I will walk your way,"
He hinted low, alas for me.—
Fieldwards I gazed throughout next day ;
Now fields I never more would see !

The sunset-shine, as curfew strook,
As curfew strook beyond the lea,
Lit his white smock and gleaming crook,
While slowly he drew near to me.

He pulled from underneath his smock
The herb I sought, my curse to be—
" At times I use it in my flock,"
He said, and hope waxed strong in me.

"'Tis meant to balk ill-motherings "—
(Ill-motherings !   Why should they be ?)—
" If not, would God have sent such things ? "
So spoke the shepherd unto me.

That night I watched the poppling brew,
With bended back and hand on knee :
I stirred it till the dawnlight grew,
And the wind whiffled wailfully.

" This scandal shall be slain," said I,
" That lours upon her innocency :
I'll give all whispering tongues the lie ; "—
But worse than whispers was to be.

"Here's physic for untimely fruit,"
I said to her, alas for me,
Early that morn in fond salute ;
And in my grave I now would be.

—Next Sunday came, with sweet church chimes
In Pydel Vale, alas for me :
I went into her room betimes ;
No more may such a Sunday be !

"Mother, instead of rescue nigh,"
She faintly breathed, alas for me,
"I feel as I were like to die,
And underground soon, soon should be."

From church that noon the people walked
In twos and threes, alas for me,
Showed their new raiment—smiled and talked,
Though sackcloth-clad I longed to be.

Came to my door her lover's friends,
And cheerly cried, alas for me,
"Right glad are we he makes amends,
For never a sweeter bride can be."

My mouth dried, as 'twere scorched within,
Dried at their words, alas for me :
More and more neighbours crowded in,
(O why should mothers ever be !)

"Ha-ha !   Such well-kept news !" laughed they,
Yes—so they laughed, alas for me.
"Whose banns were called in church to-day ?"—
Christ, how I wished my soul could flee !

"Where is she ?   O the stealthy miss,"
Still bantered they, alas for me,
"To keep a wedding close as this . . . ."
Ay, Fortune worked thus wantonly !

"But you are pale—you did not know ?"
They archly asked, alas for me,

I stammered, " Yes—some days—ago,"
While coffined clay I wished to be.

"'Twas done to please her, we surmise?"
(They spoke quite lightly in their glee)
" Done by him as a fond surprise?"
I thought their words would madden me.

Her lover entered.   " Where's my bird?—
My bird—my flower—my picotee?
First time of asking, soon the third!"
Ah, in my grave I well may be.

To me he whispered : " Since your call—"
So spoke he then, alas for me—
" I've felt for her, and righted all."
—I think of it to agony.

" She's faint to-day—tired—nothing more—"
Thus did I lie, alas for me. . . .
I called her at her chamber door
As one who scarce had strength to be.

No voice replied.   I went within—
O women ! scourged the worst are we. . . .
I shrieked.   The others hastened in
And saw the stroke there dealt on me.

There she lay—silent, breathless, dead,
Stone dead she lay—wronged, sinless she !—
Ghost-white the cheeks once rosy-red :
Death had took her.   Death took not me.

I kissed her colding face and hair,
I kissed her corpse—the bride to be !—
My punishment I cannot bear,
But pray God *not* to pity me.

January 1904.

THE HOUSE OF HOSPITALITIES

HERE we broached the Christmas barrel,
  Pushed up the charred log-ends ;
Here we sang the Christmas carol,
  And called in friends.

Time has tired me since we met here
  When the folk now dead were young,
Since the viands were outset here
  And quaint songs sung.

And the worm has bored the viol
  That used to lead the tune,
Rust eaten out the dial
  That struck night's noon.

Now no Christmas brings in neighbours,
  And the New Year comes unlit ;
Where we sang the mole now labours,
  And spiders knit.

Yet at midnight if here walking,
  When the moon sheets wall and tree,
I see forms of old time talking,
  Who smile on me.

BEREFT

IN the black winter morning
No light will be struck near my eyes
While the clock in the stairway is warning
For five, when he used to rise.
          Leave the door unbarred,
          The clock unwound.
          Make my lone bed hard—
          Would 'twere underground !

When the summer dawns clearly,
And the appletree-tops seem alight,

Who will undraw the curtain and cheerly
Call out that the morning is bright ?

When I tarry at market
No form will cross Durnover Lea
In the gathering darkness, to hark at
Grey's Bridge for the pit-pat o' me.

When the supper crock's steaming,
And the time is the time of his tread,
I shall sit by the fire and wait dreaming
In a silence as of the dead.
Leave the door unbarred,
The clock unwound,
Make my lone bed hard—
Would 'twere underground !

1901.

JOHN AND JANE

I

HE sees the world as a boisterous place
Where all things bear a laughing face,
And humorous scenes go hourly on,
  Does John.

II

They find the world a pleasant place
Where all is ecstasy and grace,
Where a light has risen that cannot wane,
  Do John and Jane.

III

They see as a palace their cottage-place,
Containing a pearl of the human race,
A hero, maybe, hereafter styled,
  Do John and Jane with a baby-child.

IV

They rate the world as a gruesome place,
Where fair looks fade to a skull's grimace,—
As a pilgrimage they would fain get done—
  Do John and Jane with their worthless son.

THE CURATE'S KINDNESS

A WORKHOUSE IRONY

I

I THOUGHT they'd be strangers aroun' me,
    But she's to be there!
Let me jump out o' waggon and go back and drown me
    At Pummery or Ten-Hatches Weir.

II

I thought : "Well, I've come to the Union—
    The workhouse at last—
After honest hard work all the week, and Communion
    O' Zundays, these fifty years past.

III

"'Tis hard ; but," I thought, "never mind it :
    There's gain in the end :
And when I get used to the place I shall find it
    A home, and may find there a friend.

IV

"Life there will be better than t'other,
    For peace is assured.
The men in one wing and their wives in another
    Is strictly the rule of the Board."

V

Just then one young Pa'son arriving
    Steps up out of breath
To the side o' the waggon wherein we were driving
    To Union ; and calls out and saith :

VI

"Old folks, that harsh order is altered,
    Be not sick of heart !
The Guardians they poohed and they pished and they paltered
    When urged not to keep you apart."

VII

"'It is wrong,' I maintained, 'to divide them,
  Near forty years wed.'
'Very well, sir. We promise, then, they shall abide them
  In one wing together,' they said."

VIII

Then I sank—knew 'twas quite a foredone thing
  That misery should be
To the end! . . . To get freed of her there was the one thing
  Had made the change welcome to me.

IX

To go there was ending but badly ;
  'Twas shame and 'twas pain ;
"But anyhow," thought I, "thereby I shall gladly
  Get free of this forty years' chain."

X

I thought they'd be strangers aroun' me,
  But she's to be there !
Let me jump out o' waggon and go back and drown me
  At Pummery or Ten-Hatches Weir.

THE FLIRT'S TRAGEDY

(17—)

HERE alone by the logs in my chamber,
  Deserted, decrepit—
Spent flames limning ghosts on the wainscot
  Of friends I once knew—

My drama and hers begins weirdly
  Its dumb re-enactment,
Each scene, sigh, and circumstance passing
  In spectral review.

—Wealth was mine beyond wish when I met her—
    The pride of the lowland—
Embowered in Tintinhull Valley
    By laurel and yew ;

And love lit my soul, notwithstanding
    My features' ill favour,
Too obvious beside her perfections
    Of line and of hue.

But it pleased her to play on my passion,
    And whet me to pleadings
That won from her mirthful negations
    And scornings undue.

Then I fled her disdains and derisions
    To cities of pleasure,
And made me the crony of idlers
    In every purlieu.

Of those who lent ear to my story,
    A needy Adonis
Gave hint how to grizzle her garden
    From roses to rue,

Could his price but be paid for so purging
    My scorner of scornings :
Thus tempted, the lust to avenge me
    Germed inly and grew.

I clothed him in sumptuous apparel,
    Consigned to him coursers,
Meet equipage, liveried attendants
    In full retinue.

So dowered, with letters of credit
    He wayfared to England,
And spied out the manor she goddessed,
    And handy thereto,

Set to hire him a tenantless mansion
    As coign-stone of vantage
For testing what gross adulation
    Of beauty could do.

He laboured through mornings and evens,
    On new moons and sabbaths,
By wiles to enmesh her attention
    In park, path, and pew ;

And having afar played upon her,
    Advanced his lines nearer,
And boldly outleaping conventions,
    Bent briskly to woo.

His gay godlike face, his rare seeming
    Anon worked to win her,
And later, at noontides and night-tides
    They held rendezvous.

His tarriance full spent, he departed
    And met me in Venice,
And lines from her told that my jilter
    Was stooping to sue.

Not long could be further concealment,
    She pled to him humbly :
" By our love and our sin, O protect me ;
    I fly unto you ! "

A mighty remorse overgat me,
    I heard her low anguish,
And there in the gloom of the *calle*
    My steel ran him through.

A swift push engulphed his hot carrion
    Within the canal there—
That still street of waters dividing
    The city in two.

—I wandered awhile all unable
    To smother my torment,
My brain racked by yells as from Tophet
    Of Satan's whole crew.

A month of unrest brought me hovering
    At home in her precincts,
To whose hiding-hole local story
    Afforded a clue.

Exposed, and expelled by her people,
    Afar off in London
I found her alone, in a sombre
    And soul-stifling mew.

Still burning to make reparation
    I pleaded to wive her,
And father her child, and thus faintly
    My mischief undo.

She yielded, and spells of calm weather
    Succeeded the tempest ;
And one sprung of him stood as scion
    Of my bone and thew. . . .

But Time unveils sorrows and secrets,
    And so it befell now :
By inches the curtain was twitched at,
    And slowly undrew.

As we lay, she and I, in the night-time,
    We heard the boy moaning :
" O misery mine ! My false father
    Has murdered my true ! "

She gasped : yea, she heard ; understood it.
    Next day the child fled us ;
And nevermore sighted was even
    A print of his shoe.

Thenceforward she shunned me, and languished ;
    Till one day the park-pool
Embraced her fair form, and extinguished
    Her eyes' living blue.

—So ; ask not what blast may account for
    This aspect of pallor,
These bones that just prison within them
    Life's poor residue ;

But pass by, and leave unregarded
    A Cain to his suffering,
For vengeance too dark on the woman
    Whose lover he slew.

THE REJECTED MEMBER'S WIFE

WE shall see her no more
                    On the balcony,
Smiling, while hurt, at the roar
                    As of surging sea
From the stormy sturdy band
                    Who have doomed her lord's cause,
Though she waves her little hand
                    As it were applause.

Here will be candidates yet,
                    And candidates' wives,
Fervid with zeal to set
                    Their ideals on our lives:
Here will come market-men
                    On the market-days,
Here will clash now and then
                    More such party assays.

And the balcony will fill
                    When such times are renewed,
And the throng in the street will thrill
                    With to-day's mettled mood;
But she will no more stand
                    In the sunshine there,
With that wave of her white-gloved hand,
                    And that chestnut hair.

        January 1906.

THE FARM-WOMAN'S WINTER

I

IF seasons all were summers,
    And leaves would never fall,
And hopping casement-comers
    Were foodless not at all,
And fragile folk might be here
    That white winds bid depart;
Then one I used to see here
    Would warm my wasted heart!

II

One frail, who, bravely tilling
  Long hours in gripping gusts,
Was mastered by their chilling,
  And now his ploughshare rusts.
So savage winter catches
  The breath of limber things,
And what I love he snatches,
  And what I love not, brings.

AUTUMN IN KING'S HINTOCK PARK

HERE by the baring bough
  Raking up leaves,
Often I ponder how
  Springtime deceives,—
I, an old woman now,
  Raking up leaves.

Here in the avenue
  Raking up leaves,
Lords' ladies pass in view,
  Until one heaves
Sighs at life's russet hue,
  Raking up leaves!

Just as my shape you see
  Raking up leaves,
I saw, when fresh and free,
  Those memory weaves
Into grey ghosts by me,
  Raking up leaves.

Yet, Dear, though one may sigh,
  Raking up leaves,
New leaves will dance on high—
  Earth never grieves!—
Will not, when missed am I
  Raking up leaves.

1901.

SHUT OUT THAT MOON

CLOSE up the casement, draw the blind,
    Shut out that stealing moon,
She wears too much the guise she wore
    Before our lutes were strewn
With years-deep dust, and names we read
    On a white stone were hewn.

Step not out on the dew-dashed lawn
    To view the Lady's Chair,
Immense Orion's glittering form,
    The Less and Greater Bear :
Stay in ; to such sights we were drawn
    When faded ones were fair.

Brush not the bough for midnight scents
    That come forth lingeringly,
And wake the same sweet sentiments
    They breathed to you and me
When living seemed a laugh, and love
    All it was said to be.

Within the common lamp-lit room
    Prison my eyes and thought ;
Let dingy details crudely loom,
    Mechanic speech be wrought :
Too fragrant was Life's early bloom,
    Too tart the fruit it brought !

    1904.

REMINISCENCES OF A DANCING MAN

I

WHO now remembers Almack's balls—
    Willis's sometime named—
In those two smooth-floored upper halls
    For faded ones so famed ?
Where as we trod to trilling sound
The fancied phantoms stood around,

Or joined us in the maze,
Of the powdered Dears from Georgian years
Whose dust lay in sightless sealed-up biers,
    The fairest of former days.

II

Who now remembers gay Cremorne,
    And all its jaunty jills,
And those wild whirling figures born
    Of Jullien's grand quadrilles?
With hats on head and morning coats
There footed to his prancing notes
    Our partner-girls and we;
And the gas-jets winked, and the lustres clinked,
And the platform throbbed as with arms enlinked
    We moved to the minstrelsy.

III

Who now recalls those crowded rooms
    Of old yclept "The Argyle,"
Where to the deep Drum-polka's booms
    We hopped in standard style?
Whither have danced those damsels now!
Is Death the partner who doth moue
    Their wormy chaps and bare?
Do their spectres spin like sparks within
The smoky halls of the Prince of Sin
    To a thunderous Jullien air?

THE DEAD MAN WALKING

THEY hail me as one living,
    But don't they know
That I have died of late years,
    Untombed although?

I am but a shape that stands here,
    A pulseless mould,
A pale past picture, screening
    Ashes gone cold.

Not at a minute's warning,
    Not in a loud hour,
For me ceased Time's enchantments
    In hall and bower.

There was no tragic transit,
    No catch of breath,
When silent seasons inched me
    On to this death. . .

—A Troubadour-youth I rambled
    With Life for lyre,
The beats of being raging
    In me like fire.

But when I practised eyeing
    The goal of men,
It iced me, and I perished
    A little then.

When passed my friend, my kinsfolk,
    Through the Last Door,
And left me standing bleakly,
    I died yet more ;

And when my Love's heart kindled
    In hate of me,
Wherefore I knew not, died I
    One more degree.

And if when I died fully
    I cannot say,
And changed into the corpse-thing
    I am to-day ;

Yet is it that, though whiling
    The time somehow
In walking, talking, smiling,
    I live not now.

MORE LOVE LYRICS

1967

IN five-score summers!   All new eyes,
New minds, new modes, new fools, new wise;
New woes to weep, new joys to prize;

With nothing left of me and you
In that live century's vivid view
Beyond a pinch of dust or two;

A century which, if not sublime,
Will show, I doubt not, at its prime,
A scope above this blinkered time.

—Yet what to me how far above?
For I would only ask thereof
That thy worm should be my worm, Love!

16 WESTBOURNE PARK VILLAS, 1867.

HER DEFINITION

I LINGERED through the night to break of day,
Nor once did sleep extend a wing to me,
Intently busied with a vast array
Of epithets that should outfigure thee.

Full-featured terms—all fitless—hastened by,
And this sole speech remained: "That maiden mine!"—
Debarred from due description then did I
Perceive the indefinite phrase could yet define.

As common chests encasing wares of price
Are borne with tenderness through halls of state,
For what they cover, so the poor device
Of homely wording I could tolerate,
Knowing its unadornment held as freight
The sweetest image outside Paradise.

W. P. V., Summer : 1866.

THE DIVISION

RAIN on the windows, creaking doors,
    With blasts that besom the green,
And I am here, and you are there,
    And a hundred miles between !

O were it but the weather, Dear,
    O were it but the miles
That summed up all our severance,
    There might be room for smiles.

But that thwart thing betwixt us twain,
    Which nothing cleaves or clears,
Is more than distance, Dear, or rain,
    And longer than the years !

189-.

ON THE DEPARTURE PLATFORM

WE kissed at the barrier ; and passing through
She left me, and moment by moment got
Smaller and smaller, until to my view
    She was but a spot ;

A wee white spot of muslin fluff
That down the diminishing platform bore
Through hustling crowds of gentle and rough
    To the carriage door.

Under the lamplight's fitful glowers,
Behind dark groups from far and near,
Whose interests were apart from ours,
    She would disappear,

Then show again, till I ceased to see
That flexible form, that nebulous white;
And she who was more than my life to me
    Had vanished quite. . . .

We have penned new plans since that fair fond day,
And in season she will appear again—
Perhaps in the same soft white array—
    But never as then!

—" And why, young man, must eternally fly
A joy you'll repeat, if you love her well?"
—O friend, nought happens twice thus; why,
    I cannot tell!

IN A CATHEDRAL CITY

THESE people have not heard your name;
No loungers in this placid place
Have helped to bruit your beauty's fame.

The grey Cathedral, towards whose face
Bend eyes untold, has met not yours;
Your shade has never swept its base,

Your form has never darked its doors,
Nor have your faultless feet once thrown
A pensive pit-pat on its floors.

Along the street to maids well known
Blithe lovers hum their tender airs,
But in your praise voice not a tone. . . .

—Since nought bespeaks you here, or bears,
As I, your imprint through and through,
Here might I rest, till my heart shares
The spot's unconsciousness of you!

SALISBURY.

"I SAY I'LL SEEK HER"

I SAY, " I'll seek her side
    Ere hindrance interposes ; "
    But eve in midnight closes,
And here I still abide.

When darkness wears I see
    Her sad eyes in a vision ;
    They ask, " What indecision
Detains you, Love, from me ?—

" The creaking hinge is oiled,
    I have unbarred the backway,
    But you tread not the trackway ;
And shall the thing be spoiled ?

" Far cockcrows echo shrill,
    The shadows are abating,
    And I am waiting, waiting ;
But O, you tarry still ! "

HER FATHER

I MET her, as we had privily planned,
Where passing feet beat busily :
She whispered : " Father is at hand !
    He wished to walk with me."

His presence as he joined us there
Banished our words of warmth away ;
We felt, with cloudings of despair,
    What Love must lose that day.

Her crimson lips remained unkissed,
Our fingers kept no tender hold,
His lack of feeling made the tryst
    Embarrassed, stiff, and cold.

A cynic ghost then rose and said,
" But is his love for her so small
That, nigh to yours, it may be read
        As of no worth at all ?

" You love her for her pink and white ;
But what when their fresh splendours close ?
His love will last her in despite
        Of Time, and wrack, and foes."

WEYMOUTH.

AT WAKING

WHEN night was lifting,
And dawn had crept under its shade,
    Amid cold clouds drifting
Dead-white as a corpse outlaid,
        With a sudden scare
        I seemed to behold
        My Love in bare
        Hard lines unfold.

    Yea, in a moment,
An insight that would not die
    Killed her old endowment
Of charm that had capped all nigh,
        Which vanished to none
        Like the gilt of a cloud,
        And showed her but one
        Of the common crowd.

    She seemed but a sample
Of earth's poor average kind,
    Lit up by no ample
Enrichments of mien or mind.
        I covered my eyes
        As to cover the thought,
        And unrecognize
        What the morn had taught.

O vision appalling
When the one believed-in thing
  Is seen falling, falling,
With all to which hope can cling.
    Off: it is not true;
    For it cannot be
    That the prize I drew
    Is a blank to me!

WEYMOUTH, 1869.

FOUR FOOTPRINTS

HERE are the tracks upon the sand
Where stood last evening she and I—
Pressed heart to heart and hand to hand;
The morning sun has baked them dry.

I kissed her wet face—wet with rain,
For arid grief had burnt up tears,
While reached us as in sleeping pain
The distant gurgling of the weirs.

"I have married him—yes; feel that ring;
'Tis a week ago that he put it on. . . .
A dutiful daughter does this thing,
And resignation succeeds anon!

"But that I body and soul was yours
Ere he'd possession, he'll never know.
He's a confident man. 'The husband scores,'
He says, 'in the long run' . . . Now, Dear, go!"

I went. And to-day I pass the spot;
It is only a smart the more to endure;
And she whom I held is as though she were not,
For they have resumed their honeymoon tour.

IN THE VAULTED WAY

In the vaulted way, where the passage turned
To the shadowy corner that none could see,
You paused for our parting,—plaintively ;
Though overnight had come words that burned
My fond frail happiness out of me.

And then I kissed you,—despite my thought
That our spell must end when reflection came
On what you had deemed me, whose one long aim
Had been to serve you ; that what I sought
Lay not in a heart that could breathe such blame.

But yet I kissed you ; whereon you again
As of old kissed me.   Why, why was it so ?
Do you cleave to me after that light-tongued blow ?
If you scorned me at eventide, how love then ?
The thing is dark, Dear.   I do not know.

THE PHANTOM

That was once her casement,
    And the taper nigh,
Shining from within there
    Beckoned, " Here am I ! "

Now, as then, I see her
    Moving at the pane ;
Ah ; 'tis but her phantom
    Borne within my brain !—

Foremost in my vision
    Everywhere goes she ;
Change dissolves the landscapes,
    She abides with me.

Shape so sweet and shy, Dear,
    Who can say thee nay ?
Never once do I, Dear,
    Wish thy ghost away.

THE END OF THE EPISODE

INDULGE no more may we
In this sweet-bitter pastime :
The love-light shines the last time
    Between you, Dear, and me.

There shall remain no trace
Of what so closely tied us,
And blank as ere love eyed us
    Will be our meeting-place.

The flowers and thymy air,
Will they now miss our coming ?
The dumbles thin their humming
    To find we haunt not there ?

Though fervent was our vow,
Though ruddily ran our pleasure,
Bliss has fulfilled its measure,
    And sees its sentence now.

Ache deep ; but make no moans :
Smile out ; but stilly suffer :
The paths of love are rougher
    Than thoroughfares of stones.

THE SIGH

LITTLE head against my shoulder,
Shy at first, then somewhat bolder,
    And up-eyed ;
Till she, with a timid quaver,
Yielded to the kiss I gave her ;
    But, she sighed.

That there mingled with her feeling
Some sad thought she was concealing
    It implied.
—Not that she had ceased to love me,
None on earth she set above me ;
    But she sighed.

She could not disguise a passion,
Dread, or doubt, in weakest fashion
        If she tried :
Nothing seemed to hold us sundered,
Hearts were victors ; so I wondered
        Why she sighed.

Afterwards I knew her throughly,
And she loved me staunchly, truly,
        Till she died ;
But she never made confession
Why, at that first sweet concession,
        She had sighed.

It was in our May, remember ;
And though now I near November,
        And abide
Till my appointed change, unfretting,
Sometimes I sit half regretting
        That she sighed.

"IN THE NIGHT SHE CAME"

I TOLD her when I left one day
That whatsoever weight of care
Might strain our love, Time's mere assault
        Would work no changes there.
And in the night she came to me,
        Toothless, and wan, and old,
With leaden concaves round her eyes,
        And wrinkles manifold.

I tremblingly exclaimed to her,
" O wherefore do you ghost me thus !
I have said that dull defacing Time
        Will bring no dreads to us."
" And is that true of *you* ? " she cried
        In voice of troubled tune.
I faltered : " Well . . . I did not think
        You would test me quite so soon ! "

She vanished with a curious smile,
Which told me, plainlier than by word,
That my staunch pledge could scarce beguile
    The fear she had averred.
Her doubts then wrought their shape in me,
    And when next day I paid
My due caress, we seemed to be
    Divided by some shade.

THE CONFORMERS

YES ; we'll wed, my little fay,
    And you shall write you mine,
And in a villa chastely gray
    We'll house, and sleep, and dine.
    But those night-screened, divine,
    Stolen trysts of heretofore,
We of choice ecstasies and fine
        Shall know no more.

The formal faced cohue
    Will then no more upbraid
With smiting smiles and whisperings two
    Who have thrown less loves in shade.
    We shall no more evade
    The searching light of the sun,
Our game of passion will be played,
        Our dreaming done.

We shall not go in stealth
    To rendezvous unknown,
But friends will ask me of your health,
    And you about my own.
    When we abide alone,
    No leapings each to each,
But syllables in frigid tone
        Of household speech.

When down to dust we glide
    Men will not say askance,
As now : "How all the country side
    Rings with their mad romance ! "

But as they graveward glance
Remark : " In them we lose
A worthy pair, who helped advance
Sound parish views."

THE DAWN AFTER THE DANCE

HERE is your parents' dwelling with its curtained windows telling
Of no thought of us within it or of our arrival here ;
Their slumbers have been normal after one day more of formal
Matrimonial commonplace and household life's mechanic gear.

I would be candid willingly, but dawn draws on so chillingly
As to render further cheerlessness intolerable now,
So I will not stand endeavouring to declare a day for severing,
But will clasp you just as always—just the olden love avow.

Through serene and surly weather we have walked the ways
together,
And this long night's dance this year's end eve now finishes the
spell ;
Yet we dreamt us but beginning a sweet sempiternal spinning
Of a cord we have spun to breaking—too intemperately, too well.

Yes ; last night we danced I know, Dear, as we did that year
ago, Dear,
When a new strange bond between our days was formed, and
felt, and heard ;
Would that dancing were the worst thing from the latest to the
first thing
That the faded year can charge us with ; but what avails a word

That which makes man's love the lighter and the woman's burn
no brighter
Came to pass with us inevitably while slipped the shortening
year. . . .
And there stands your father's dwelling with its blind bleak
windows telling
That the vows of man and maid are frail as filmy gossamere.

WEYMOUTH, 1869.

THE SUN ON THE LETTER

I DREW the letter out, while gleamed
The sloping sun from under a roof
Of cloud whose verge rose visibly.

The burning ball flung rays that seemed
Stretched like a warp without a woof
Across the levels of the lea

To where I stood, and where they beamed
As brightly on the page of proof
That she had shown her false to me

As if it had shown her true—had teemed
With passionate thought for my behoof
Expressed with their own ardency!

THE NIGHT OF THE DANCE

THE cold moon hangs to the sky by its horn,
    And centres its gaze on me;
The stars, like eyes in reverie,
Their westering as for a while forborne,
    Quiz downward curiously.

Old Robert draws the backbrand in,
    The green logs steam and spit;
The half-awakened sparrows flit
From the riddled thatch; and owls begin
    To whoo from the gable-slit.

Yes; far and nigh things seem to know
    Sweet scenes are impending here;
That all is prepared; that the hour is near
For welcomes, fellowships, and flow
    Of sally, song, and cheer;

That spigots are pulled and viols strung;
    That soon will arise the sound
Of measures trod to tunes renowned;
That She will return in Love's low tongue
    My vows as we wheel around.

MISCONCEPTION

I BUSIED myself to find a sure
        Snug hermitage
That should preserve my Love secure
        From the world's rage ;
Where no unseemly saturnals,
        Or strident traffic-roars,
Or hum of intervolved cabals
        Should echo at her doors.

I laboured that the diurnal spin
        Of vanities
Should not contrive to suck her in
        By dark degrees,
And cunningly operate to blur
        Sweet teachings I had begun ;
And then I went full-heart to her
        To expound the glad deeds done.

She looked at me, and said thereto
        With a pitying smile,
" And *this* is what has busied you
        So long a while ?
O poor exhausted one, I see
        You have worn you old and thin
For naught ! Those moils you fear for me
        I find most pleasure in ! "

THE VOICE OF THE THORN

I

WHEN the thorn on the down
Quivers naked and cold,
And the mid-aged and old
Pace the path there to town,
In these words dry and drear
It seems to them sighing :
" O winter is trying
To sojourners here ! "

II

When it stands fully tressed
On a hot summer day,
And the ewes there astray
Find its shade a sweet rest,
By the breath of the breeze
It inquires of each farer:
"Who would not be sharer
Of shadow with these?"

III

But by day or by night,
And in winter or summer,
Should I be the comer
Along that lone height,
In its voicing to me
Only one speech is spoken:
"Here once was nigh broken
A heart, and by thee."

FROM HER IN THE COUNTRY

I THOUGHT and thought of thy crass clanging town
To folly, till convinced such dreams were ill,
I held my heart in bond, and tethered down
Fancy to where I was, by force of will.

I said: How beautiful are these flowers, this wood,
One little bud is far more sweet to me
Than all man's urban shows; and then I stood
Urging new zest for bird, and bush, and tree;

And strove to feel my nature brought it forth
Of instinct, or no rural maid was I;
But it was vain; for I could not see worth
Enough around to charm a midge or fly,

And mused again on city din and sin,
Longing to madness I might move therein!

16 W. P. V., 1866.

HER CONFESSION

As some bland soul, to whom a debtor says
" I'll now repay the amount I owe to you,"
In inward gladness feigns forgetfulness
That such a payment ever was his due

(His long thought notwithstanding), so did I
At our last meeting waive your proffered kiss
With quick divergent talk of scenery nigh,
By such suspension to enhance my bliss.

And as his looks in consternation fall
When, gathering that the debt is lightly deemed,
The debtor makes as not to pay at all,
So faltered I, when your intention seemed

Converted by my false uneagerness
To putting off for ever the caress.

W. P. V., 1865–67.

TO AN IMPERSONATOR OF ROSALIND

DID he who drew her in the years ago—
Till now conceived creator of her grace—
With telescopic sight high natures know,
Discern remote in Time's untravelled space

Your soft sweet mien, your gestures, as do we,
And with a copyist's hand but set them down,
Glowing yet more to dream our ecstasy
When his Original should be forthshown ?

For, kindled by that animated eye,
Whereto all fairnesses about thee brim,
And by thy tender tones, what wight can fly
The wild conviction welling up in him

That he at length beholds woo, parley, plead,
The "very, very Rosalind" indeed !

8 ADELPHI TERRACE, 21st April 1867.

TO AN ACTRESS

I READ your name when you were strange to me,
Where it stood blazoned bold with many more;
I passed it vacantly, and did not see
Any great glory in the shape it wore.

O cruelty, the insight barred me then!
Why did I not possess me with its sound,
And in its cadence catch and catch again
Your nature's essence floating therearound?

Could *that* man be this I, unknowing you,
When now the knowing you is all of me,
And the old world of then is now a new,
And purpose no more what it used to be—
A thing of formal journeywork, but due
To springs that then were sealed up utterly?

        1867.

THE MINUTE BEFORE MEETING

THE grey gaunt days dividing us in twain
Seemed hopeless hills my strength must faint to climb,
But they are gone; and now I would detain
The few clock-beats that part us; rein back Time,

And live in close expectance never closed
In change for far expectance closed at last,
So harshly has expectance been imposed
On my long need while these slow blank months passed.

And knowing that what is now about to be
Will all *have been* in O, so short a space!
I read beyond it my despondency
When more dividing months shall take its place,
Thereby denying to this hour of grace
A full-up measure of felicity.

        1871.

HE ABJURES LOVE

AT last I put off love,
    For twice ten years
The daysman of my thought,
    And hope, and doing ;
Being ashamed thereof,
    And faint of fears
And desolations, wrought
    In his pursuing,

Since first in youthtime those
    Disquietings
That heart-enslavement brings
    To hale and hoary,
Became my housefellows,
    And, fool and blind,
I turned from kith and kind
    To give him glory.

I was as children be
    Who have no care ;
I did not shrink or sigh,
    I did not sicken ;
But lo, Love beckoned me.
    And I was bare,
And poor, and starved, and dry,
    And fever-stricken.

Too many times ablaze
    With fatuous fires,
Enkindled by his wiles
    To new embraces,
Did I, by wilful ways
    And baseless ires,
Return the anxious smiles
    Of friendly faces.

No more will now rate I
    The common rare,

The midnight drizzle dew,
  The gray hour golden,
The wind a yearning cry,
  The faulty fair,
Things dreamt, of comelier hue
  Than things beholden ! . . .

—I speak as one who plumbs
  Life's dim profound,
One who at length can sound
  Clear views and certain.
But—after love what comes ?
  A scene that lours,
A few sad vacant hours,
  And then, the Curtain.

1883.

A SET OF COUNTRY SONGS

LET ME ENJOY

(MINOR KEY)

I

LET me enjoy the earth no less
Because the all-enacting Might
That fashioned forth its loveliness
Had other aims than my delight.

II

About my path there flits a Fair,
Who throws me not a word or sign;
I'll charm me with her ignoring air,
And laud the lips not meant for mine.

III

From manuscripts of moving song
Inspired by scenes and dreams unknown,
I'll pour out raptures that belong
To others, as they were my own.

IV

And some day hence, towards Paradise
And all its blest—if such should be—
I will lift glad, afar-off eyes,
Though it contain no place for me.

AT CASTERBRIDGE FAIR

I

THE BALLAD-SINGER

SING, Ballad-singer, raise a hearty tune;
Make me forget that there was ever a one
I walked with in the meek light of the moon
    When the day's work was done.

Rhyme, Ballad-rhymer, start a country song;
Make me forget that she whom I loved well
Swore she would love me dearly, love me long,
    Then—what I cannot tell!

Sing, Ballad-singer, from your little book;
Make me forget those heart-breaks, achings, fears;
Make me forget her name, her sweet sweet look—
    Make me forget her tears.

II

FORMER BEAUTIES

THESE market-dames, mid-aged, with lips thin-drawn,
    And tissues sere,
Are they the ones we loved in years agone,
    And courted here?

Are these the muslined pink young things to whom
    We vowed and swore
In nooks on summer Sundays by the Froom,
    Or Budmouth shore?

Do they remember those gay tunes we trod
    Clasped on the green;
Aye; trod till moonlight set on the beaten sod
    A satin sheen?

They must forget, forget! They cannot know
    What once they were,
Or memory would transfigure them, and show
    Them always fair.

III

AFTER THE CLUB-DANCE

BLACK'ON frowns east on Maidon,
    And westward to the sea,
But on neither is his frown laden
    With scorn, as his frown on me!

At dawn my heart grew heavy,
    I could not sip the wine,
I left the jocund bevy
    And that young man o' mine.

The roadside elms pass by me,—
    Why do I sink with shame
When the birds a-perch there eye me?
    They, too, have done the same!

IV

THE MARKET-GIRL

NOBODY took any notice of her as she stood on the causey kerb,
All eager to sell her honey and apples and bunches of garden herb
And if she had offered to give her wares and herself with them
    too that day,
I doubt if a soul would have cared to take a bargain so choice away.

But chancing to trace her sunburnt grace that morning as I
    passed nigh,
I went and I said "Poor maidy dear!—and will none of the
    people buy?"
And so it began; and soon we knew what the end of it all
    must be,
And I found that though no others had bid, a prize had been
    won by me.

V

THE INQUIRY

AND are ye one of Hermitage—
    Of Hermitage, by Ivel Road,
And do ye know, in Hermitage
    A thatch-roofed house where sengreens grow?

And does John Waywood live there still—
He of the name that there abode
When father hurdled on the hill
    Some fifteen years ago?

Does he now speak o' Patty Beech,
The Patty Beech he used to—see,
Or ask at all if Patty Beech
Is known or heard of out this way?
—Ask ever if she's living yet,
And where her present home may be,
And how she bears life's fag and fret
    After so long a day?

In years agone at Hermitage
This faded face was counted fair,
None fairer; and at Hermitage
We swore to wed when he should thrive.
But never a chance had he or I,
And waiting made his wish outwear,
And Time, that dooms man's love to die,
    Preserves a maid's alive.

VI

A WIFE WAITS

WILL's at the dance in the Club-room below,
    Where the tall liquor-cups foam;
I on the pavement up here by the Bow,
    Wait, wait, to steady him home.

Will and his partner are treading a tune,
    Loving companions they be;
Willy, before we were married in June,
    Said he loved no one but me;

Said he would let his old pleasures all go
    Ever to live with his Dear.
Will's at the dance in the Club-room below,
    Shivering I wait for him here.

NOTE.—" The Bow" (line 3). The old name for the curved corner by the cross-streets in the middle of Casterbridge.

VII

AFTER THE FAIR

THE singers are gone from the Cornmarket-place
    With their broadsheets of rhymes,
The street rings no longer in treble and bass
    With their skits on the times,
And the Cross, lately thronged, is a dim naked space
    That but echoes the stammering chimes.

From Clock-corner steps, as each quarter ding-dongs,
    Away the folk roam
By the " Hart " and Grey's Bridge into byways and " drongs,
    Or across the ridged loam ;
The younger ones shrilling the lately heard songs,
    The old saying, " Would we were home."

The shy-seeming maiden so mute in the fair
    Now rattles and talks,
And that one who looked the most swaggering there
    Grows sad as she walks,
And she who seemed eaten by cankering care
    In statuesque sturdiness stalks.

And midnight clears High Street of all but the ghosts
    Of its buried burghees,
From the latest far back to those old Roman hosts
    Whose remains one yet sees,
Who loved, laughed, and fought, hailed their friends, drank
        their toasts
    At their meeting-times here, just as these !

    1902.

NOTE.—" The Chimes " (line 6) will be listened for in vain here at midnight now, having been abolished some years ago.

THE DARK-EYED GENTLEMAN

I

I PITCHED my day's leazings in Crimmercrock Lane,
To tie up my garter and jog on again,
When a dear dark-eyed gentleman passed there and said,
In a way that made all o' me colour rose-red,
        "What do I see—
        O pretty knee!"
And he came and he tied up my garter for me.

II

'Twixt sunset and moonrise it was, I can mind:
Ah, 'tis easy to lose what we nevermore find!—
Of the dear stranger's home, of his name, I knew nought,
But I soon knew his nature and all that it brought.
        Then bitterly
        Sobbed I that he
Should ever have tied up my garter for me!

III

Yet now I've beside me a fine lissom lad,
And my slip's nigh forgot, and my days are not sad;
My own dearest joy is he, comrade, and friend,
He it is who safe-guards me, on him I depend;
        No sorrow brings he,
        And thankful I be
That his daddy once tied up my garter for me!

NOTE—"Leazings" (line 1), bundle of gleaned corn.

TO CARREY CLAVEL

You turn your back, you turn your back,
        And never your face to me,
Alone you take your homeward track,
        And scorn my company.

What will you do when Charley's seen
    Dewbeating down this way?
—You'll turn your back as now, you mean?
    Nay, Carrey Clavel, nay!

You'll see none's looking; put your lip
    Up like a tulip, so;
And he will coll you, bend, and sip:
    Yes, Carrey, yes; I know!

THE ORPHANED OLD MAID

I WANTED to marry, but father said, "No—
'Tis weakness in women to give themselves so;
If you care for your freedom you'll listen to me,
Make a spouse in your pocket, and let the men be."

I spake on't again and again: father cried,
"Why—if you go husbanding, where shall I bide?
For never a home's for me elsewhere than here!"
And I yielded; for father had ever been dear.

But now father's gone, and I feel growing old,
And I'm lonely and poor in this house on the wold,
And my sweetheart that was found a partner elsewhere,
And nobody flings me a thought or a care.

THE SPRING CALL

DOWN Wessex way, when spring's a-shine,
    The blackbird's "pret-ty de-urr!"
In Wessex accents marked as mine
    Is heard afar and near.

He flutes it strong, as if in song
    No R's of feebler tone
Than his appear in "pretty dear,"
    Have blackbirds ever known.

Yet they pipe "prattie deerh!" I glean,
    Beneath a Scottish sky,

And "pehty de-aw!" amid the treen
    Of Middlesex or nigh.

While some folk say—perhaps in play—
    Who know the Irish isle,
'Tis "purrity dare!" in treeland there
    When songsters would beguile.

Well: I'll say what the listening birds
    Say, hearing "pret-ty de-urr!"—
However strangers sound such words,
    That's how we sound them here.

Yes, in this clime at pairing time,
    As soon as eyes can see her
At dawn of day, the proper way
    To call is "pret-ty de-urr!"

JULIE-JANE

Sing; how 'a would sing!
    How 'a would raise the tune
When we rode in the waggon from harvesting
    By the light o' the moon!

Dance; how 'a would dance!
    If a fiddlestring did but sound
She would hold out her coats, give a slanting glance,
    And go round and round.

Laugh; how 'a would laugh!
    Her peony lips would part
As if none such a place for a lover to quaff
    At the deeps of a heart.

Julie, O girl of joy,
    Soon, soon that lover he came.
Ah, yes; and gave thee a baby-boy,
    But never his name. . . .

—Tolling for her, as you guess;
    And the baby too. . . . 'Tis well.
You knew her in maidhood likewise?—Yes,
    That's her burial bell.

" I suppose," with a laugh, she said,
  " I should blush that I'm not a wife ;
But how can it matter, so soon to be dead,
    What one does in life ! "

When we sat making the mourning
  By her death-bed side, said she,
" Dears, how can you keep from your lovers, adorning
    In honour of me ! "

Bubbling and brightsome eyed !
  But now—O never again.
She chose her bearers before she died
    From her fancy-men.

NOTE.—It is, or was, a common custom in Wessex, and probably other
country places, to prepare the mourning beside the death-bed, the dying
person sometimes assisting, who also selects his or her bearers on such
occasions.
" Coats " (line 7), old name for petticoats.

NEWS FOR HER MOTHER

I

ONE mile more is
Where your door is,
    Mother mine !—
Harvest's coming,
Mills are strumming,
    Apples fine,
And the cider made to-year will be as wine.

II

Yet, not viewing
What's a-doing
    Here around
Is it thrills me,
And so fills me
    That I bound
Like a ball or leaf or lamb along the ground.

III

Tremble not now
At your lot now,
        Silly soul!
Hosts have sped them
Quick to wed them,
        Great and small,
Since the first two sighing half-hearts made a whole.

IV

Yet I wonder,
Will it sunder
        Her from me?
Will she guess that
I said "Yes,"—that
        His I'd be,
Ere I thought she might not see him as I see!

V

Old brown gable,
Granary, stable,
        Here you are!
O my mother,
Can another
        Ever bar
Mine from thy heart, make thy nearness seem afar?

THE FIDDLER

THE fiddler knows what's brewing
        To the lilt of his lyric wiles:
The fiddler knows what rueing
        Will come of this night's smiles!

He sees couples join them for dancing,
        And afterwards joining for life,
He sees them pay high for their prancing
        By a welter of wedded strife.

He twangs : " Music hails from the devil,
　　　Though vaunted to come from heaven,
For it makes people do at a revel
　　　What multiplies sins by seven.

" There's many a heart now mangled,
　　　And waiting its time to go,
Whose tendrils were first entangled
　　　By my sweet viol and bow ! "

THE HUSBAND'S VIEW

" CAN anything avail
Beldame, for my hid grief ?—
Listen : I'll tell the tale,
It may bring faint relief !—

" I came where I was not known,
In hope to flee my sin ;
And walking forth alone
A young man said, ' Good e'en,'

" In gentle voice and true
He asked to marry me ;
' You only—only you
Fulfil my dream ! ' said he.

" We married o' Monday morn,
In the month of hay and flowers ;
My cares were nigh forsworn,
And perfect love was ours.

" But ere the days are long
Untimely fruit will show ;
My Love keeps up his song,
Undreaming it is so.

" And I awake in the night,
And think of months gone by,
And of that cause of flight
Hidden from my Love's eye.

" Discovery borders near,
And then ! . . . But something stirred ?—
My husband—he is here !
Heaven—has he overheard ? "—

"Yes ; I have heard, sweet Nan ;
I have known it all the time.
I am not a particular man ;
Misfortunes are no crime :

"And what with our serious need
Of sons for soldiering,
That accident, indeed,
To maids, is a useful thing ! "

ROSE-ANN

WHY didn't you say you was promised, Rose-Ann
    Why didn't you name it to me,
Ere ever you tempted me hither, Rose-Ann,
    So often, so wearifully ?

O why did you let me be near 'ee, Rose-Ann,
    Talking things about wedlock so free,
And never by nod or by whisper, Rose-Ann,
    Give a hint that it wasn't to be ?

Down home I was raising a flock of stock ewes,
    Cocks and hens, and wee chickens by scores,
And lavendered linen all ready to use,
    A-dreaming that they would be yours.

Mother said : "She's a sport-making maiden, my son";
    And a pretty sharp quarrel had we ;
O why do you prove by this wrong you have done
    That I saw not what mother could see ?

Never once did you say you was promised, Rose-Ann,
    Never once did I dream it to be ;
And it cuts to the heart to be treated, Rose-Ann,
    As you in your scorning treat me !

THE HOMECOMING

GRUFFLY growled the wind on Toller downland broad and bare
And lonesome was the house, and dark; and few came there.

" Now don't ye rub your eyes so red; we're home and have no
    cares ;
Here's a skimmer-cake for supper, peckled onions, and some
    pears ;
I've got a little keg o' summat strong, too, under stairs :
—What, slight your husband's victuals ?   Other brides can tackle
    theirs ! "

The wind of winter mooed and mouthed their chimney like a horn
And round the house and past the house 'twas leafless and lorn.

" But my dear and tender poppet, then, how came ye to agree
In Ivel church this morning ?   Sure, there-right you married
    me ! "
—" Hoo-hoo !—I don't know—I forgot how strange and far
    'twould be,
An' I wish I was at home again with dear daddee ! "

Gruffly growled the wind on Toller downland broad and bare,
And lonesome was the house and dark; and few came there.

" I didn't think such furniture as this was all you'd own,
And great black beams for ceiling, and a floor o' wretched stone,
And nasty pewter platters, horrid forks of steel and bone,
And a monstrous crock in chimney.   'Twas to me quite unbe-
    known ! "

Rattle rattle went the door ; down flapped a cloud of smoke,
As shifting north the wicked wind assayed a smarter stroke.

" Now sit ye by the fire, poppet ; put yourself at ease :
And keep your little thumb out of your mouth, dear, please !
And I'll sing to 'ee a pretty song of lovely flowers and bees,
And happy lovers taking walks within a grove o' trees."

Gruffly growled the wind on Toller Down, so bleak and bare,
And lonesome was the house, and dark; and few came there.

Now, don't ye gnaw your handkercher; 'twill hurt your little
   tongue,
d if you do feel spitish, 'tis because ye are over young;
t you'll be getting older, like us all, ere very long,
d you'll see me as I am—a man who never did 'ee wrong."

raight from Whit'sheet Hill to Benvill Lane the blusters pass,
itting hedges, milestones, handposts, trees, and tufts of grass.

Well, had I only known, my dear, that this was how you'd be,
 have married her of riper years that was so fond of me.
t since I can't, I've half a mind to run away to sea,
d leave 'ee to go barefoot to your d—d daddee!"

one wall and down the other—past each window-pane—
ance the gusts, and then away down Crimmercrock's long lane.

—I—don't know what to say to't, since your wife I've vowed
   to be;
d as 'tis done, I s'pose here I must bide—poor me!
e—as you are ki-ki-kind, I'll try to live along with 'ee,
hough I'd fain have stayed at home with dear daddee!"

uffly growled the wind on Toller Down, so bleak and bare,
d lonesome was the house and dark; and few came there.

hat's right, my Heart! And though on haunted Toller Down
   we be,
d the wind swears things in chimley, we'll to supper merrily!
don't ye tap your shoe so pettish-like; but smile at me,
d ye'll soon forget to sock and sigh for dear daddee!"

December 1901.

PIECES OCCASIONAL AND VARIOUS

A CHURCH ROMANCE

(Mellstock: circa 1835)

SHE turned in the high pew, until her sight
Swept the west gallery, and caught its row
Of music-men with viol, book, and bow
Against the sinking sad tower-window light.

She turned again; and in her pride's despite
One strenuous viol's inspirer seemed to throw
A message from his string to her below,
Which said: "I claim thee as my own forthright!"

Thus their hearts' bond began, in due time signed.
And long years thence, when Age had scared Romance,
At some old attitude of his or glance
That gallery-scene would break upon her mind,
With him as minstrel, ardent, young, and trim,
Bowing "New Sabbath" or "Mount Ephraim."

THE RASH BRIDE

AN EXPERIENCE OF THE MELLSTOCK QUIRE

I

WE Christmas-carolled down the Vale, and up the Vale, a
round the Vale,
We played and sang that night as we were yearly wont to do—
A carol in a minor key, a carol in the major D,
Then at each house: "Good wishes: many Christmas joys
you!"

II

ext, to the widow's John and I and all the rest drew on.
    And I
iscerned that John could hardly hold the tongue of him for joy.
he widow was a sweet young thing whom John was bent on
    marrying,
nd quiring at her casement seemed romantic to the boy.

III

She'll make reply, I trust," said he, "to our salute? She
    must!" said he,
And then I will accost her gently—much to her surprise!—
or knowing not I am with you here, when I speak up and call
    her dear
tenderness will fill her voice, a bashfulness her eyes."

IV

o, by her window-square we stood; ay, with our lanterns there
    we stood,
nd he along with us,—not singing, waiting for a sign;
nd when we'd quired her carols three a light was lit and out
    looked she,
shawl about her bedgown, and her colour red as wine.

V

nd sweetly then she bowed her thanks, and smiled, and spoke
    aloud her thanks;
hen lo, behind her back there, in the room, a man appeared.
knew him—one from Woolcomb way—Giles Swetman—honest
    as the day,
at eager, hasty; and I felt that some strange trouble neared.

VI

How comes he there? . . . Suppose," said we, "she's wed of
    late! Who knows?" said we.
—" She married yester-morning—only mother yet has known
he secret o't!" shrilled one small boy. "But now I've told, let's
    wish 'em joy!"
heavy fall aroused us: John had gone down like a stone.

VII

We rushed to him and caught him round, and lifted him, an
    brought him round,
When, hearing something wrong had happened, oped th
    window she :
·" Has one of you fallen ill ? " she asked, " by these night labou
    overtasked ? "
None answered. That she'd done poor John a cruel tur
    felt we.

VIII

Till up spoke Michael : " Fie, young dame ! You've broke yo
    promise, sly young dame,
By forming this new tie, young dame, and jilting John so true,
Who trudged to-night to sing to 'ee because he thought he'
    bring to 'ee
Good wishes as your coming spouse. May ye such trifling rue !

IX

Her man had said no word at all ; but being behind had hear
    it all,
And now cried : " Neighbours, on my soul I knew not 'tw
    like this ! "
And then to her : " If I had known you'd had in tow not m
    alone,
No wife should you have been of mine. It is a dear boug
    bliss ! "

X

She changed death-white, and heaved a cry : we'd never hea
    so grieved a cry
As came from her at this from him : heartbroken quite seem
    she ;
And suddenly, as we looked on, she turned, and rushed ; a
    she was gone,
Whither, her husband, following after, knew not ; nor knew we

XI

We searched till dawn about the house ; within the house, wit
    out the house,
We searched among the laurel boughs that grew beneath t
    wall,

nd then among the crocks and things, and stores for winter
    junketings,
n linhay, loft, and dairy; but we found her not at all.

XII

hen John rushed in: "O friends," he said, "hear this, this,
    this!" and bends his head:
I've—searched round by the—*well*, and find the cover open
    wide!
am fearful that—I can't say what . . . Bring lanterns, and
    some cords to knot."
We did so, and we went and stood the deep dark hole beside.

XIII

nd then they, ropes in hand, and I—ay, John, and all the band,
    and I
et down a lantern to the depths—some hundred feet and more;
t glimmered like a fog-dimmed star; and there, beside its light,
    afar,
White drapery floated, and we knew the meaning that it bore.

XIV

he rest is naught. . . . We buried her o' Sunday. Neighbours
    carried her;
and Swetman—he who'd married her—now miserablest of men,
Walked mourning first; and then walked John; just quivering,
    but composed anon;
and we the quire formed round the grave, as was the custom
    then.

XV

Our old bass player, as I recall—his white hair blown—but why
    recall!—
His viol upstrapped, bent figure—doomed to follow her full
    soon—
stood bowing, pale and tremulous; and next to him the rest
    of us. . . .
We sang the Ninetieth Psalm to her—set to Saint Stephen's
    tune.

THE DEAD QUIRE

I

BESIDE the Mead of Memories,
　　Where Church-way mounts to Moaning Hill,
　　The sad man sighed his phantasies :
　　　　He seems to sigh them still.

II

"'Twas the Birth-tide Eve, and the hamleteers
　　Made merry with ancient Mellstock zest,
　　But the Mellstock quire of former years
　　　　Had entered into rest.

III

"Old Dewy lay by the gaunt yew tree,
　　And Reuben and Michael a pace behind,
　　And Bowman with his family
　　　　By the wall that the ivies bind.

IV

"The singers had followed one by one,
　　Treble, and tenor, and thorough-bass ;
　　And the worm that wasteth had begun
　　　　To mine their mouldering place.

V

"For two-score years, ere Christ-day light,
　　Mellstock had throbbed to strains from these :
　　But now there echoed on the night
　　　　No Christmas harmonies.

VI

"Three meadows off, at a dormered inn,
　　The youth had gathered in high carouse,
　　And, ranged on settles, some therein
　　　　Had drunk them to a drowse.

VII

"Loud, lively, reckless, some had grown,
Each dandling on his jigging knee
Eliza, Dolly, Nance, or Joan—
    Livers in levity.

VIII

"The taper flames and hearthfire shine
Grew smoke-hazed to a lurid light,
And songs on subjects not divine
    Were warbled forth that night.

IX

"Yet many were sons and grandsons here
Of those who, on such eves gone by,
At that still hour had throated clear
    Their anthems to the sky.

X

"The clock belled midnight; and ere long
One shouted, 'Now 'tis Christmas morn;
Here's to our women old and young,
    And to John Barleycorn!'

XI

"They drink the toast and shout again:
The pewter-ware rings back the boom,
And for a breath-while follows then
    A silence in the room.

XII

"When nigh without, as in old days,
The ancient quire of voice and string
Seemed singing words of prayer and praise
    As they had used to sing:

XIII

"*While shepherds watch'd their flocks by night,*—
Thus swells the long familiar sound

In many a quaint symphonic flight—
    To, *Glory shone around.*

XIV

"The sons defined their fathers' tones,
The widow his whom she had wed,
And others in the minor moans
    The viols of the dead.

XV

"Something supernal has the sound
As verse by verse the strain proceeds,
And stilly staring on the ground
    Each roysterer holds and heeds.

XVI

"Towards its chorded closing bar
Plaintively, thinly, waned the hymn,
Yet lingered, like the notes afar
    Of banded seraphim.

XVII

"With brows abashed, and reverent tread,
The hearkeners sought the tavern door:
But nothing, save wan moonlight, spread
    The empty highway o'er.

XVIII

"While on their hearing fixed and tense
The aerial music seemed to sink,
As it were gently moving thence
    Along the river brink.

XIX

"Then did the Quick pursue the Dead
By crystal Froom that crinkles there;
And still the viewless quire ahead
    Voiced the old holy air.

XX

" By Bank-walk wicket, brightly bleached,
It passed, and 'twixt the hedges twain,
Dogged by the living ; till it reached
          The bottom of Church Lane.

XXI

" There, at the turning, it was heard
Drawing to where the churchyard lay :
But when they followed thitherward
          It smalled, and died away.

XXII

" Each headstone of the quire, each mound,
Confronted them beneath the moon ;
But no more floated therearound
          That ancient Birth-night tune.

XXIII

" There Dewy lay by the gaunt yew tree,
There Reuben and Michael, a pace behind,
And Bowman with his family
          By the wall that the ivies bind. . . .

XXIV

" As from a dream each sobered son
Awoke, and musing reached his door :
'Twas said that of them all, not one
          Sat in a tavern more."

XXV

—The sad man ceased ; and ceased to heed
His listener, and crossed the leaze
From Moaning Hill towards the mead—
          The Mead of Memories.

1897.

THE CHRISTENING

WHOSE child is this they bring
    Into the aisle ?—
At so superb a thing
The congregation smile
And turn their heads awhile.

Its eyes are blue and bright,
    Its cheeks like rose ;
Its simple robes unite
Whitest of calicoes
With lawn, and satin bows.

A pride in the human race
    At this paragon
Of mortals, lights each face
While the old rite goes on ;
But ah, they are shocked anon.

What girl is she who peeps
    From the gallery stair,
Smiles palely, redly weeps,
With feverish furtive air
As though not fitly there ?

"I am the baby's mother ;
    This gem of the race
The decent fain would smother,
And for my deep disgrace
I am bidden to leave the place."

"Where is the baby's father ?"—
    "In the woods afar.
He says there is none he'd rather
Meet under moon or star
Than me, of all that are.

"To clasp me in lovelike weather,
    Wish fixing when,
He says : To be together
At will, just now and then,
Makes him the blest of men ;

" But chained and doomed for life
　　　To slovening
As vulgar man and wife,
He says, is another thing :
Yea : sweet Love's sepulchring ! "

　1904.

A DREAM QUESTION

" It shall be dark unto you, that ye shall not divine."
　　　　　　　　　　　　　　　Micah iii. 6.

I ASKED the Lord : " Sire, is this true
Which hosts of theologians hold,
That when we creatures censure you
For shaping griefs and ails untold
(Deeming them punishments undue)
You rage, as Moses wrote of old ?

When we exclaim : ' Beneficent
He is not, for he orders pain,
Or, if so, not omnipotent :
To a mere child the thing is plain ! '
Those who profess to represent
You, cry out : ' Impious and profane ! ' "

He : " Save me from my friends, who deem
That I care what my creatures say !
Mouth as you list : sneer, rail, blaspheme,
O manikin, the livelong day,
Not one grief-groan or pleasure-gleam
Will you increase or take away.

" Why things are thus, whoso derides,
May well remain my secret still . . . .
A fourth dimension, say the guides,
To matter is conceivable.
Think some such mystery resides
Within the ethic of my will."

BY THE BARROWS

Not far from Mellstock—so tradition saith—
Where barrows, bulging as they bosoms were
Of Multimammia stretched supinely there,
Catch night and noon the tempest's wanton breath,

A battle, desperate doubtless unto death,
Was one time fought.   The outlook, lone and bare,
The towering hawk and passing raven share,
And all the upland round is called "The He'th."

Here once a woman, in our modern age,
Fought singlehandedly to shield a child—
One not her own—from a man's senseless rage.
And to my mind no patriots' bones there piled
So consecrate the silence as her deed
Of stoic and devoted self-unheed.

A WIFE AND ANOTHER

"War ends, and he's returning
        Early ; yea,
The evening next to-morrow's !"—
        —This I say
To her, whom I suspiciously survey,

Holding my husband's letter
        To her view.—
She glanced at it but lightly,
        And I knew
That one from him that day had reached her too.

There was no time for scruple ;
        Secretly
I filched her missive, conned it,
        Learnt that he
Would lodge with her ere he came home to me.

To reach the port before her,
        And, unscanned,
There wait to intercept them
        Soon I planned :
That, in her stead, *I* might before him stand.

So purposed, so effected ;
        At the inn
Assigned, I found her hidden :—
        O that sin
Should bear what she bore when I entered in !

Her heavy lids grew laden
        With despairs,
Her lips made soundless movements
        Unawares,
While I peered at the chamber hired as theirs.

And as beside its doorway,
        Deadly hued,
One inside, one withoutside
        We two stood,
He came—my husband—as she knew he would.

No pleasurable triumph
        Was that sight !
The ghastly disappointment
        Broke them quite.
What love was theirs, to move them with such might !

" Madam, forgive me ! " said she,
        Sorrow bent,
" A child—I soon shall bear him. . . .
        Yes—I meant
To tell you—that he won me ere he went."

Then, as it were, within me
        Something snapped,
As if my soul had largened :
        Conscience-capped,
I saw myself the snarer—them the trapped.

" My hate dies, and I promise,
        Grace-beguiled,"

I said, "to care for you, be
            Reconciled ;
And cherish, and take interest in the child."

Without more words I pressed him
            Through the door
Within which she stood, powerless
            To say more,
And closed it on them, and downstairward bore.

"He joins his wife—my sister,"
            I, below,
Remarked in going—lightly—
            Even as though
All had come right, and we had arranged it so. . . .

As I, my road retracing,
            Left them free,
The night alone embracing
            Childless me,
I held I had not stirred God wrothfully.

THE ROMAN ROAD

THE Roman Road runs straight and bare
As the pale parting-line in hair
Across the heath.   And thoughtful men
Contrast its days of Now and Then,
And delve, and measure, and compare ;

Visioning on the vacant air
Helmed legionaries, who proudly rear
The Eagle, as they pace again
                    The Roman Road.

But no tall brass-helmed legionnaire
Haunts it for me.   Uprises there
A mother's form upon my ken,
Guiding my infant steps, as when
We walked that ancient thoroughfare,
                    The Roman Road.

THE VAMPIRINE FAIR

GILBERT had sailed to India's shore,
  And I was all alone :
My lord came in at my open door
  And said, " O fairest one ! "

He leant upon the slant bureau,
  And sighed, " I am sick for thee ! "
" My Lord," said I, " pray speak not so,
  Since wedded wife I be."

Leaning upon the slant bureau,
  Bitter his next words came :
" So much I know ; and likewise know
  My love burns on the same !

" But since you thrust my love away,
  And since it knows no cure,
I must live out as best I may
  The ache that I endure."

When Michaelmas browned the nether Coomb,
  And Wingreen Hill above,
And made the hollyhocks rags of bloom,
  My lord grew ill of love.

My lord grew ill with love for me ;
  Gilbert was far from port ;
And—so it was—that time did see
  Me housed at Manor Court.

About the bowers of Manor Court
  The primrose pushed its head
When, on a day at last, report
  Arrived of him I had wed.

" Gilbert, my Lord, is homeward bound,
  His sloop is drawing near,
What shall I do when I am found
  Not in his house but here ? "

"O I will heal the injuries
  I've done to him and thee.
I'll give him means to live at ease
  Afar from Shastonb'ry."

When Gilbert came we both took thought:
  "Since comfort and good cheer,"
Said he, "So readily are bought,
  He's welcome to thee, Dear."

So when my lord flung liberally
  His gold in Gilbert's hands,
I coaxed and got my brothers three
  Made stewards of his lands.

And then I coaxed him to install
  My other kith and kin,
With aim to benefit them all
  Before his love ran thin.

And next I craved to be possessed
  Of plate and jewels rare.
He groaned: "You give me, Love, no rest,
  Take all the law will spare!"

And so in course of years my wealth
  Became a goodly hoard,
My steward brethren, too, by stealth
  Had each a fortune stored.

Thereafter in the gloom he'd walk,
  And by and by began
To say aloud in absent talk,
  "I am a ruined man!—

"I hardly could have thought," he said,
  "When first I looked on thee,
That one so soft, so rosy red,
  Could thus have beggared me!"

Seeing his fair estates in pawn,
  And him in such decline,
I knew that his domain had gone
  To lift up me and mine.

Next month upon a Sunday morn
    A gunshot sounded nigh :
By his own hand my lordly born
    Had doomed himself to die.

"Live, my dear Lord, and much of thine
    Shall be restored to thee !"
He smiled, and said 'twixt word and sign,
    "Alas—that cannot be !"

And while I searched his cabinet
    For letters, keys, or will,
'Twas touching that his gaze was set
    With love upon me still.

And when I burnt each document
    Before his dying eyes,
'Twas sweet that he did not resent
    My fear of compromise.

The steeple-cock gleamed golden when
    I watched his spirit go :
And I became repentant then
    That I had wrecked him so.

Three weeks at least had come and gone,
    With many a saddened word,
Before I wrote to Gilbert on
    The stroke that so had stirred.

And having worn a mournful gown,
    I joined, in decent while,
My husband at a dashing town
    To live in dashing style.

Yet though I now enjoy my fling,
    And dine and dance and drive,
I'd give my prettiest emerald ring
    To see my lord alive.

And when the meet on hunting-days
    Is near his churchyard home,
I leave my bantering beaux to place
    A flower upon his tomb ;

And sometimes say : " Perhaps too late
    The saints in Heaven deplore
That tender time when, moved by Fate,
    He darked my cottage door."

THE REMINDER

WHILE I watch the Christmas blaze
Paint the room with ruddy rays,
Something makes my vision glide
To the frosty scene outside.

There, to reach a rotting berry,
Toils a thrush,—constrained to very
Dregs of food by sharp distress,
Taking such with thankfulness.

Why, O starving bird, when I
One day's joy would justify,
And put misery out of view,
Do you make me notice you !

THE RAMBLER

I DO not see the hills around,
Nor mark the tints the copses wear ;
I do not note the grassy ground
And constellated daisies there.

I hear not the contralto note
Of cuckoos hid on either hand,
The whirr that shakes the nighthawk's throat
When eve's brown awning hoods the land.

Some say each songster, tree, and mead—
All eloquent of love divine—
Receives their constant careful heed :
Such keen appraisement is not mine.

The tones around me that I hear,
The aspects, meanings, shapes I see,
Are those far back ones missed when near,
And now perceived too late by me!

NIGHT IN THE OLD HOME

WHEN the wasting embers redden the chimney-breast,
And Life's bare pathway looms like a desert track to me,
And from hall and parlour the living have gone to their rest,
My perished people who housed them here come back to me.

They come and seat them around in their mouldy places,
Now and then bending towards me a glance of wistfulness,
A strange upbraiding smile upon all their faces,
And in the bearing of each a passive tristfulness.

"Do you uphold me, lingering and languishing here,
A pale late plant of your once strong stock?" I say to them;
"A thinker of crooked thoughts upon Life in the sere,
And on That which consigns men to night after showing the day
        to them?"

"—O let be the Wherefore! We fevered our years not thus:
Take of Life what it grants, without question!" they answer me
        seemingly.
"Enjoy, suffer, wait: spread the table here freely like us,
And, satisfied, placid, unfretting, watch Time away beamingly!"

AFTER THE LAST BREATH

(J. H. 1813–1904)

THERE'S no more to be done, or feared, or hoped;
None now need watch, speak low, and list, and tire;
No irksome crease outsmoothed, no pillow sloped
        Does she require.

Blankly we gaze. We are free to go or stay;
Our morrow's anxious plans have missed their aim;
Whether we leave to-night or wait till day
        Counts as the same.

The lettered vessels of medicaments
Seem asking wherefore we have set them here ;
Each palliative its silly face presents
    As useless gear.

And yet we feel that something savours well ;
We note a numb relief withheld before ;
Our well-beloved is prisoner in the cell
    Ot Time no more.

We see by littles now the deft achievement
Whereby she has escaped the Wrongers all,
In view of which our momentary bereavement
    Outshapes but small.

    1904.

IN CHILDBED

    In the middle of the night
Mother's spirit came and spoke to me,
    Looking weariful and white—
As 'twere untimely news she broke to me.

    " O my daughter, joyed are you
To own the weetless child you mother there ;
    ' Men may search the wide world through,'
You think, ' nor find so fair another there ! '

    " Dear, this midnight time unwombs
Thousands just as rare and beautiful ;
    Thousands whom High Heaven foredooms
To be as bright, as good, as dutiful.

    " Source of ecstatic hopes and fears
And innocent maternal vanity,
    Your fond exploit but shapes for tears
New thoroughfares in sad humanity.

    " Yet as you dream, so dreamt I
When Life stretched forth its morning ray to me ;
    Other views for by and by ! " . . . .
Such strange things did mother say to me.

THE PINE PLANTERS

(MARTY SOUTH'S REVERIE)

I

WE work here together
    In blast and breeze ;
He fills the earth in,
    I hold the trees.

He does not notice
    That what I do
Keeps me from moving
    And chills me through.

He has seen one fairer
    I feel by his eye,
Which skims me as though
    I were not by.

And since she passed here
    He scarce has known
But that the woodland
    Holds him alone.

I have worked here with him
    Since morning shine,
He busy with his thoughts
    And I with mine.

I have helped him so many,
    So many days,
But never win any
    Small word of praise !

Shall I not sigh to him
    That I work on
Glad to be nigh to him
    Though hope is gone ?

Nay, though he never
    Knew love like mine,
I'll bear it ever
    And make no sign!

II

From the bundle at hand here
    I take each tree,
And set it to stand, here
    Always to be;
When, in a second,
    As if from fear
Of Life unreckoned
    Beginning here,
It starts a sighing
    Through day and night,
Though while there lying
    'Twas voiceless quite.

It will sigh in the morning,
    Will sigh at noon,
At the winter's warning,
    In wafts of June;
Grieving that never
    Kind Fate decreed
It should for ever
    Remain a seed,
And shun the welter
    Of things without,
Unneeding shelter
    From storm and drought.

Thus, all unknowing
    For whom or what
We set it growing
    In this bleak spot,
It still will grieve here
    Throughout its time,
Unable to leave here,
    Or change its clime:

Or tell the story
Of us to-day
When, halt and hoary,
We pass away.

THE DEAR

I PLODDED to Fairmile Hill-top, where
　　A maiden one fain would guard
From every hazard and every care
　　Advanced on the roadside sward.

I wondered how succeeding suns
　　Would shape her wayfarings,
And wished some Power might take such ones
　　Under Its warding wings.

The busy breeze came up the hill
　　And smartened her cheek to red,
And frizzled her hair to a haze.　With a will
　　"Good-morning, my Dear!" I said.

She glanced from me to the far-off gray,
　　And, with proud severity,
"Good-morning to you—though I may say
　　I am not *your* Dear," quoth she:

"For I am the Dear of one not here—
　　One far from his native land!"—
And she passed me by; and I did not try
　　To make her understand.

　　　1901.

ONE WE KNEW

(M. H. 1772–1857)

SHE told how they used to form for the country dances—
　　"The Triumph," "The New-rigged Ship"—
To the light of the guttering wax in the panelled manses,
　　And in cots to the blink of a dip.

VOL. I　　　　　　　　　　　　　　　　　　K

She spoke of the wild "poussetting" and "allemanding"
    On carpet, on oak, and on sod ;
And the two long rows of ladies and gentlemen standing,
    And the figures the couples trod.

She showed us the spot where the maypole was yearly planted,
    And where the bandsmen stood
While breeched and kerchiefed partners whirled, and panted
    To choose each other for good.

She told of that far-back day when they learnt astounded
    Of the death of the King of France :
Of the Terror ; and then of Bonaparte's unbounded
    Ambition and arrogance.

Of how his threats woke warlike preparations
    Along the southern strand,
And how each night brought tremors and trepidations
    Lest morning should see him land.

She said she had often heard the gibbet creaking
    As it swayed in the lightning flash,
Had caught from the neighbouring town a small child's shrieking
    At the cart-tail under the lash. . . .

With cap-framed face and long gaze into the embers—
    We seated around her knees—
She would dwell on such dead themes, not as one who remembers,
    But rather as one who sees.

She seemed one left behind of a band gone distant
    So far that no tongue could hail :
Past things retold were to her as things existent,
    Things present but as a tale.

May 20, 1902.

SHE HEARS THE STORM

THERE was a time in former years—
    While my roof-tree was his—
When I should have been distressed by fears
    At such a night as this !

I should have murmured anxiously,
 "The pricking rain strikes cold;
His road is bare of hedge or tree,
 And he is getting old."

But now the fitful chimney-roar,
 The drone of Thorncombe trees,
The Froom in flood upon the moor,
 The mud of Mellstock Leaze,

The candle slanting sooty wick'd,
 The thuds upon the thatch,
The eaves-drops on the window flicked,
 The clacking garden-hatch,

And what they mean to wayfarers,
 I scarcely heed or mind;
He has won that storm-tight roof of hers
 Which Earth grants all her kind.

A WET NIGHT

I PACE along, the rain-shafts riddling me,
Mile after mile out by the moorland way,
And up the hill, and through the ewe-leaze gray
Into the lane, and round the corner tree;

Where, as my clothing clams me, mire-bestarred,
And the enfeebled light dies out of day,
Leaving the liquid shades to reign, I say,
"This is a hardship to be calendared!"

Yet sires of mine now perished and forgot,
When worse beset, ere roads were shapen here,
And night and storm were foes indeed to fear,
Times numberless have trudged across this spot
In sturdy muteness on their strenuous lot,
And taking all such toils as trifles mere.

BEFORE LIFE AND AFTER

A TIME there was—as one may guess
And as, indeed, earth's testimonies tell—
Before the birth of consciousness,
    When all went well.

None suffered sickness, love, or loss,
None knew regret, starved hope, or heart-burnings;
None cared whatever crash or cross
    Brought wrack to things.

If something ceased, no tongue bewailed,
If something winced and waned, no heart was wrung;
If brightness dimmed, and dark prevailed,
    No sense was stung.

But the disease of feeling germed,
And primal rightness took the tinct of wrong;
Ere nescience shall be reaffirmed
    How long, how long?

NEW YEAR'S EVE

"I HAVE finished another year," said God,
    "In grey, green, white, and brown;
I have strewn the leaf upon the sod,
Sealed up the worm within the clod,
    And let the last sun down."

"And what's the good of it?" I said,
    "What reasons made you call
From formless void this earth we tread,
When nine-and-ninety can be read
    Why nought should be at all?

"Yea, Sire; why shaped you us, 'who in
    This tabernacle groan'—
If ever a joy be found herein,
Such joy no man had wished to win
    If he had never known!"

Then he : " My labours—logicless—
    You may explain ; not I :
Sense-sealed I have wrought, without a guess
That I evolved a Consciousness
    To ask for reasons why.

" Strange that ephemeral creatures who
    By my own ordering are,
Should see the shortness of my view,
Use ethic tests I never knew,
    Or made provision for ! "

He sank to raptness as of yore,
    And opening New Year's Day
Wove it by rote as theretofore,
And went on working evermore
    In his unweeting way.

1906.

GOD'S EDUCATION

I SAW him steal the light away
    That haunted in her eye :
It went so gently none could say
More than that it was there one day
    And missing by-and-by.

I watched her longer, and he stole
    Her lily tincts and rose ;
All her young sprightliness of soul
Next fell beneath his cold control,
    And disappeared like those.

I asked : " Why do you serve her so ?
    Do you, for some glad day,
Hoard these her sweets—? "   He said, " O no,
They charm not me ; I bid Time throw
    Them carelessly away."

Said I : " We call that cruelty—
    We, your poor mortal kind."

He mused.   " The thought is new to me.
Forsooth, though I men's master be,
Theirs is the teaching mind ! "

TO SINCERITY

O SWEET sincerity !—
Where modern methods be
What scope for thine and thee ?

Life may be sad past saying,
Its greens for ever graying,
Its faiths to dust decaying ;

And youth may have foreknown it,
And riper seasons shown it,
But custom cries : " Disown it :

" Say ye rejoice, though grieving,
Believe, while unbelieving,
Behold, without perceiving ! "

—Yet, would men look at true things,
And unilluded view things,
And count to bear undue things,

The real might mend the seeming,
Facts better their foredeeming,
And Life its disesteeming.

February 1899.

PANTHERA

(For other forms of this legend—first met with in the second century— se
    Origen contra Celsum ; the Talmud ; Sepher Toldoth Jeschu ; quote
    fragments of lost Apocryphal gospels ; Strauss, Haeckel ; etc.)

YEA, as I sit here, crutched, and cricked, and bent,
I think of Panthera, who underwent
Much from insidious aches in his decline ;
But his aches were not radical like mine ;

They were the twinges of old wounds—the feel
Of the hand he had lost, shorn by barbarian steel,
Which came back, so he said, at a change in the air,
Fingers and all, as if it still were there.
My pains are otherwise : upclosing cramps
And stiffened tendons from this country's damps,
Where Panthera was never commandant.—
The Fates sent him by way of the Levant.

He had been blithe in his young manhood's time,
And as centurion carried well his prime.
In Ethiop, Araby, climes fair and fell,
He had seen service and had borne him well.
Nought shook him then : he was serene as brave ;
Yet later knew some shocks, and would grow grave
When pondering them ; shocks less of corporal kind
Than phantom-like, that disarranged his mind ;
And it was in the way of warning me
(By much his junior) against levity
That he recounted them ; and one in chief
Panthera loved to set in bold relief.

This was a tragedy of his Eastern days,
Personal in touch—though I have sometimes thought
That touch a possible delusion—wrought
Of half-conviction carried to a craze—
His mind at last being stressed by ails and age :—
Yet his good faith thereon I well could wage.

I had said it long had been a wish with me
That I might leave a scion—some small tree
As channel for my sap, if not my name—
Ay, offspring even of no legitimate claim,
In whose advance I secretly could joy.
Thereat he warmed.

                    "Cancel such wishes, boy !
A son may be a comfort or a curse,
A seer, a doer, a coward, a fool ; yea, worse—
A criminal. . . . That I could testify !" . . .
"Panthera has no guilty son !" cried I
All unbelieving. "Friend, you do not know,"
He darkly dropt : "True, I've none now to show,
For *the law took him.* Ay, in sooth, Jove shaped it so !"

"This noon is not unlike," he again began,
"The noon these pricking memories print on me—
Yea, that day, when the sun grew copper-red,
And I served in Judæa . . . 'Twas a date
Of rest for arms.   The *Pax Romana* ruled,
To the chagrin of frontier legionaries!
Palestine was annexed—though sullen yet,—
I, being in age some two-score years and ten,
And having the garrison in Jerusalem
Part in my hands as acting officer
Under the Governor.   A tedious time
I found it, of routine, amid a folk
Restless, contentless, and irascible.—
Quelling some riot, sentrying court and hall,
Sending men forth on public meeting-days
To maintain order, were my duties there.

"Then came a morn in spring, and the cheerful sun
Whitened the city and the hills around,
And every mountain-road that clambered them,
Tincturing the greyness of the olives warm,
And the rank cacti round the valley's sides.
The day was one whereon death-penalties
Were put in force, and here and there were set
The soldiery for order, as I said,
Since one of the condemned had raised some heat,
And crowds surged passionately to see him slain.
I, mounted on a Cappadocian horse,
With some half-company of auxiliaries,
Had captained the procession through the streets
When it came streaming from the judgment-hall
After the verdicts of the Governor.
It drew to the great gate of the northern way
That bears towards Damascus; and to a knoll
Upon the common, just beyond the walls—
Whence could be swept a wide horizon round
Over the housetops to the remotest heights.
Here was the public execution-ground
For city crimes, called then and doubtless now
Golgotha, Kranion, or Calvaria.

"The usual dooms were duly meted out;
Some three or four were stript, transfixed, and nailed,

And no great stir occurred.   A day of wont
It was to me, so far, and would have slid
Clean from my memory at its squalid close
But for an incident that followed these.

    "Among the tag-rag rabble of either sex
That hung around the wretches as they writhed,
Till thrust back by our spears, one held my eye—
A weeping woman, whose strained countenance,
Sharpened against a looming livid cloud,
Was mocked by the crude rays of afternoon—
The mother of one of those who suffered there
I had heard her called when spoken roughly to
By my ranged men for pressing forward so.
It stole upon me hers was a face I knew ;
Yet when, or how, I had known it, for a while
Eluded me.   And then at once it came.

    "Some thirty years or more before that noon
I was sub-captain of a company
Drawn from the legion of Calabria,
That marched up from Judæa north to Tyre.
We had pierced the old flat country of Jezreel,
The great Esdraelon Plain and fighting-floor
Of Jew with Canaanite, and with the host
Of Pharaoh-Necho, king of Egypt, met
While crossing there to strike the Assyrian pride.
We left behind Gilboa ; passed by Nain ;
Till bulging Tabor rose, embossed to the top
With arbute, terabinth, and locust growths.

    "Encumbering me were sundry sick, so fallen
Through drinking from a swamp beside the way ;
But we pressed on, till, bearing over a ridge,
We dipt into a world of·pleasantness—
A vale, the fairest I had gazed upon—
Which lapped a village on its furthest slopes
Called Nazareth, brimmed round by uplands nigh.
In the midst thereof a fountain bubbled, where,
Lime-dry from marching, our glad halt we made
To rest our sick ones, and refresh us all.

    "Here a day onward, towards the eventide,
Our men were piping to a Pyrrhic dance

Trod by their comrades, when the young women came
To fill their pitchers, as their custom was.
I proffered help to one—a slim girl, coy
Even as a fawn, meek, and as innocent.
Her long blue gown, the string of silver coins
That hung down by her banded beautiful hair,
Symboled in full immaculate modesty.

　"Well, I was young, and hot, and readily stirred
To quick desire.　'Twas tedious timing out
The convalescence of the soldiery;
And I beguiled the long and empty days
By blissful yieldance to her sweet allure,
Who had no arts, but what out-arted all,
The tremulous tender charm of trustfulness.
We met, and met, and under the winking stars
That passed which peoples earth—true union, yea,
To the pure eye of her simplicity.

　"Meanwhile the sick found health; and we pricked on
I made her no rash promise of return,
As some do use; I was sincere in that;
I said we sundered never to meet again—
And yet I spoke untruth unknowingly!—
For meet again we did.　Now, guess you aught?
The weeping mother on Calvaria
Was she I had known—albeit that time and tears
Had wasted rudely her once flowerlike form,
And her soft eyes, now swollen with sorrowing.

　"Though I betrayed some qualms, she marked me not;
And I was scarce of mood to comrade her
And close the silence of so wide a time
To claim a malefactor as my son—
(For so I guessed him).　And inquiry made
Brought rumour how at Nazareth long before
An old man wedded her for pity's sake
On finding she had grown pregnant, none knew how,
Cared for her child, and loved her till he died.

　"Well; there it ended; save that then I learnt
That he—the man whose ardent blood was mine—
Had waked sedition long among the Jews,

And hurled insulting parlance at their god,
Whose temple bulked upon the adjoining hill,
Vowing that he would raze it, that himself
Was god as great as he whom they adored,
And by descent, moreover, was their king;
With sundry other incitements to misrule.

"The impalements done, and done the soldiers' game
Of raffling for the clothes, a legionary,
Longinus, pierced the young man with his lance
At signs from me, moved by his agonies
Through naysaying the drug they had offered him.
It brought the end.   And when he had breathed his last
The woman went.   I saw her never again. . . .
Now glares my moody meaning on you, friend?—
That when you talk of offspring as sheer joy
So trustingly, you blink contingencies.
Fors Fortuna!   He who goes fathering
Gives frightful hostages to hazardry!"

Thus Panthera's tale.   'Twas one he seldom told,
But yet it got abroad.   He would unfold,
At other times, a story of less gloom,
Though his was not a heart where jests had room.
He would regret discovery of the truth
Was made too late to influence to ruth
The Procurator who had condemned his son—
Or rather him so deemed.   For there was none
To prove that Panthera erred not: and indeed,
When vagueness of identity I would plead,
Panther himself would sometimes own as much—
Yet lothly.   But, assuming fact was such,
That the said woman did not recognize
Her lover's face, is matter for surprise.
However, there's his tale, fantasy or otherwise.

Thereafter shone not men of Panthera's kind:
The indolent heads at home were ill-inclined
To press campaigning that would hoist the star
Of their lieutenants valorous afar.
Jealousies kept him irked abroad, controlled
And stinted by an Empire no more bold.

Yet in some actions southward he had share—
In Mauretania and Numidia; there
With eagle eye, and sword and steed and spur,
Quelling uprisings promptly.   Some small stir
In Parthia next engaged him, until maimed,
As I have said; and cynic Time proclaimed
His noble spirit broken.   What a waste
Of such a Roman!—one in youth-time graced
With indescribable charm, so I have heard,
Yea, magnetism impossible to word
When faltering as I saw him.   What a fame,
O Son of Saturn, had adorned his name,
Might the Three so have urged Thee!—Hour by hour
His own disorders hampered Panthera's power
To brood upon the fate of those he had known,
Even of that one he always called his own—
Either in morbid dream or memory. . . .
He died at no great age, untroublously,
An exit rare for ardent soldiers such as he.

THE UNBORN

I ROSE at night, and visited
      The Cave of the Unborn:
And crowding shapes surrounded me
For tidings of the life to be,
Who long had prayed the silent Head
      To haste its advent morn.

Their eyes were lit with artless trust,
      Hope thrilled their every tone;
"A scene the loveliest, is it not?
A pure delight, a beauty-spot
Where all is gentle, true and just,
      And darkness is unknown?"

My heart was anguished for their sake,
      I could not frame a word;
And they descried my sunken face,
And seemed to read therein, and trace

The news that pity would not break,
     Nor truth leave unaverred.

And as I silently retired
     I turned and watched them still,
And they came helter-skelter out,
Driven forward like a rabble rout
Into the world they had so desired,
     By the all-immanent Will.

1905.

THE MAN HE KILLED

    " HAD he and I but met
      By some old ancient inn,
We should have sat us down to wet
      Right many a nipperkin !

    " But ranged as infantry,
      And staring face to face,
I shot at him as he at me,
      And killed him in his place.

    " I shot him dead because—
      Because he was my foe,
Just so : my foe of course he was ;
      That's clear enough ; although

    " He thought he'd 'list, perhaps,
      Off-hand like—just as I—
Was out of work—had sold his traps—
      No other reason why.

    " Yes ; quaint and curious war is !
      You shoot a fellow down
You'd treat if met where any bar is,
      Or help to half-a-crown."

    1902.

GEOGRAPHICAL KNOWLEDGE

(A MEMORY OF CHRISTIANA C——)

WHERE Blackmoor was, the road that led
        To Bath, she could not show,
Nor point the sky that overspread
        Towns ten miles off or so.

But that Calcutta stood this way,
        Cape Horn there figured fell,
That here was Boston, here Bombay,
        She could declare full well.

Less known to her the track athwart
        Froom Mead or Yell'ham Wood
Than how to make some Austral port
        In seas of surly mood.

She saw the glint of Guinea's shore
        Behind the plum-tree nigh,
Heard old unruly Biscay's roar
        In the weir's purl hard by. . . .

" My son's a sailor, and he knows
        All seas and many lands,
And when he's home he points and shows
        Each country where it stands.

" He's now just there—by Gib's high rock—
        And when he gets, you see,
To Portsmouth here, behind the clock,
        Then he'll come back to me ! "

ONE RALPH BLOSSOM SOLILOQUIZES

("It being deposed that vij women who were mayds before he knew them
have been brought upon the towne [rates?] by the fornicacions of one
Ralph Blossom, Mr. Maior inquired why he should not contribute xiv
pence weekly toward their mayntenance. But it being shewn that the
sayd R. B. was dying of a purple feaver, no order was made."—
Budmouth Borough Minutes: 16—.)

WHEN I am in hell or some such place,
A-groaning over my sorry case,
What will those seven women say to me
Who, when I coaxed them, answered "Aye" to me?

"I did not understand your sign!"
Will be the words of Caroline;
While Jane will cry, "If I'd had proof of you,
I should have learnt to hold aloof of you!"

"I won't reproach: it was to be!"
Will dryly murmur Cicely;
And Rosa: "I feel no hostility,
For I must own I lent facility."

Lizzy says: "Sharp was my regret,
And sometimes it is now! But yet
I joy that, though it brought notoriousness,
I knew Love once and all its gloriousness!"

Says Patience: "Why are we apart?
Small harm did you, my poor Sweet Heart!
A manchild born, now tall and beautiful,
Was worth the ache of days undutiful."

And Anne cries: "O the time was fair,
So wherefore should you burn down there?
There is a deed under the sun, my Love,
And that was ours. What's done is done, my Love.
These trumpets here in Heaven are dumb to me
With you away. Dear, come, O come to me!"

THE NOBLE LADY'S TALE

(circa 1790)

I

"WE moved with pensive paces,
            I and he,
And bent our faded faces
            Wistfully,
For something troubled him, and troubled me.

    "The lanthorn feebly lightened
            Our grey hall,
    Where ancient brands had brightened
            Hearth and wall,
And shapes long vanished whither vanish all.

    "'O why, Love, nightly, daily,
            I had said,
    'Dost sigh, and smile so palely,
            As if shed
Were all Life's blossoms, all its dear things dead?

    "'Since silence sets thee grieving,'
            He replied,
    'And I abhor deceiving
            One so tried,
Why, Love, I'll speak, ere time us twain divide.

    "He held me, I remember,
            Just as when
    Our life was June—(September
            It was then);
And we walked on, until he spoke again:

    "'Susie, an Irish mummer,
            Loud-acclaimed
    Through the gay London summer,
            Was I; named
A master in my art, who would be famed.

" 'But lo, there beamed before me
        Lady Su ;
God's altar-vow she swore me
        When none knew,
And for her sake I bade the sock adieu.

" ' My Lord your father's pardon
        Thus I won :
He let his heart unharden
        Towards his son,
And honourably condoned what we had done ;

" ' But said—recall you, dearest ?—
        As for Su,
I'd see her—ay, though nearest
        Me unto—
Sooner entombed than in a stage purlieu!

" ' Just so.—And here he housed us,
        In this nook,
Where Love like balm has drowsed us :
        Robin, rook,
Our chief familiars, next to string and book.

" ' Our days here, peace-enshrouded,
        Followed strange
The old stage-joyance, crowded,
        Rich in range ;
But never did my soul desire a change,

" ' Till now, when far uncertain
        Lips of yore
Call, call me to the curtain,
        There once more,
But *once*, to tread the boards I trod before.

" ' A night—the last and single
        Ere I die—
To face the lights, to mingle
        As did I
Once in the game, and rivet every eye ! '

" Such was his wish.   He feared it,
        Feared it though

Rare memories so endeared it.
        I, also,
Feared it still more ; its outcome who could know ?

    " 'Alas, my Love,' said I then,
        'Since it be
A wish so mastering, why, then,
        E'en go ye !—
Despite your pledge to father and to me . . .

    "'Twas fixed ; no more was spoken
        Thereupon ;
Our silences were broken
        Only on
The petty items of his needs while gone.

    " Farewell he bade me, pleading
        That it meant
So little, thus conceding
        To his bent ;
And then, as one constrained to go, he went.

    " Thwart thoughts I let deride me,
        As, 'twere vain
To hope him back beside me
        Ever again :
Could one plunge make a waxing passion wane ?

    " I thought, ' Some wild stage-woman,
        Honour-wrecked . . .'
But no : it was inhuman
        To suspect ;
Though little cheer could my lone heart affect !

                    II

    " Yet came it, to my gladness,
        That, as vowed,
He did return.—But sadness
        Swiftly cowed
The joy with which my greeting was endowed.

"Some woe was there. Estrangement
  Marked his mind.
Each welcome-warm arrangement
  I had designed
Touched him no more than deeds of careless kind.

"'I—*failed*!' escaped him glumly.
  '—I went on
In my old part. But dumbly—
  Memory gone—
Advancing, I sank sick; my vision drawn

"'To something drear, distressing
  As the knell
Of all hopes worth possessing!'. . .
  —What befell
Seemed linked with me, but how I could not tell.

"Hours passed; till I implored him,
  As he knew
How faith and frankness toward him
  Ruled me through,
To say what ill I had done, and could undo.

"'*Faith—frankness*. Ah! Heaven save such!'
  Murmured he,
'They are wedded wealth! *I* gave such
  Liberally,
But you, Dear, not. For you suspected me.'

"I was about beseeching
  In hurt haste
More meaning, when he, reaching
  To my waist,
Led me to pace the hall as once we paced.

"'I never meant to draw you
  To own all,'
Declared he, 'But—I *saw* you—
  By the wall,
Half-hid. And that was why I failed withal!'

"'Where? when?' said I—'Why, nigh me,
  At the play.

That night.   That you should spy me,
　　Doubt my fay,
And follow, furtive, took my heart away !'

"That I had never been there,
　　But had gone
To my locked room—unseen there,
　　Curtains drawn,
Long days abiding—told I, wonder-wan.

"'Nay, 'twas your form and vesture,
　　Cloak and gown,
Your hooded features—gesture
　　Half in frown,
That faced me, pale,' he urged, 'that night in town.

"'And when, outside, I handed
　　To her chair
(As courtesy demanded
　　Of me there)
The leading lady, you peeped from the stair.

"Straight pleaded I : 'Forsooth, Love,
　　Had I gone,
I must have been in truth, Love,
　　Mad to don
Such well-known raiment.'   But he still went on

"That he was not mistaken
　　Nor misled.—
I felt like one forsaken,
　　Wished me dead,
That he could think thus of the wife he had wed !

"His going seemed to waste him
　　Like a curse,
To wreck what once had graced him ;
　　And, averse
To my approach, he mused, and moped, and worse.

"Till, what no words effected
　　Thought achieved :

It was my wraith—projected,
　　He conceived,
Thither, by my tense brain at home aggrieved.

" Thereon his credence centred
　　Till he died ;
And, no more tempted, entered
　　Sanctified,
The little vault with room for one beside."

III

Thus far the lady's story.—
　　Now she, too,
Reclines within that hoary
　　Last dark mew
In Mellstock Quire with him she loved so true.

A yellowing marble, placed there
　　Tablet-wise,
And two joined hearts enchased there
　　Meet the eyes ;
And reading their twin names we moralize :

Did she, we wonder, follow
　　Jealously ?
And were those protests hollow ?—
　　Or saw he
Some semblant dame ?　Or can wraiths really be ?

Were it she went, her honour,
　　All may hold,
Pressed truth at last upon her
　　Till she told—
(Him only—others as these lines unfold.)

Riddle death-sealed for ever,
　　Let it rest ! . . .
One's heart could blame her never
　　If one guessed
That go she did.　She knew her actor best.

UNREALIZED

Down comes the winter rain—
   Spoils my hat and bow—
Runs into the poll of me ;
   But mother won't know.

We've been out and caught a cold,
   Knee-deep in snow ;
Such a lucky thing it is
   That mother won't know !

Rosy lost herself last night—
   Couldn't tell where to go.
Yes—it rather frightened her,
   But mother didn't know.

Somebody made Willy drunk
   At the Christmas show :
O 'twas fun ! It's well for him
   That mother won't know !

Howsoever wild we are,
   Late at school or slow,
Mother won't be cross with us
   Mother won't know.

How we cried the day she died !
   Neighbours whispering low . . .
But we now do what we will—
   Mother won't know.

WAGTAIL AND BABY

A baby watched a ford, whereto
   A wagtail came for drinking ;
A blaring bull went wading through,
   The wagtail showed no shrinking.

A stallion splashed his way across,
　　The birdie nearly sinking ;
He gave his plumes a twitch and toss,
　　And held his own unblinking.

Next saw the baby round the spot
　　A mongrel slowly slinking ;
The wagtail gazed, but faltered not
　　In dip and sip and prinking.

A perfect gentleman then neared ;
　　The wagtail, in a winking,
With terror rose and disappeared ;
　　The baby fell a-thinking.

ABERDEEN

(April : 1905)

" And wisdom and knowledge shall be the stability of thy times."—
Isaiah xxxiii. 6.

I LOOKED and thought, "All is too gray and cold
To wake my place-enthusiasms of old ! "
Till a voice passed : " Behind that granite mien
Lurks the imposing beauty of a Queen."
I looked anew ; and saw the radiant form
Of Her who soothes in stress, who steers in storm,
On the grave influence of whose eyes sublime
Men count for the stability of the time.

GEORGE MEREDITH

(1828–1909)

FORTY years back, when much had place
That since has perished out of mind,
I heard that voice and saw that face.

He spoke as one afoot will wind
A morning horn ere men awake;
His note was trenchant, turning kind.

He was of those whose wit can shake
And riddle to the very core
The counterfeits that Time will break. . .

Of late, when we two met once more,
The luminous countenance and rare
Shone just as forty years before.

So that, when now all tongues declare
His shape unseen by his green hill,
I scarce believe he sits not there.

No matter.　Further and further still
Through the world's vaporous vitiate air
His words wing on—as live words will.

May 1909.

YELL'HAM-WOOD'S STORY

COOMB-FIRTREES say that Life is a moan,
　　And Clyffe-hill Clump says "Yea!"
But Yell'ham says a thing of its own:
　　　　It's not "Gray, gray
　　　　Is Life alway!"
　　　　That Yell'ham says,
　　Nor that Life is for ends unknown.

It says that Life would signify
　　A thwarted purposing:
That we come to live, and are called to die
　　　　Yes, that's the thing
　　　　In fall, in spring,
　　　　That Yell'ham says:—
　　"Life offers—to deny!"

1902.

A YOUNG MAN'S EPIGRAM ON EXISTENCE

A SENSELESS school, where we must give
Our lives that we may learn to live !
A dolt is he who memorizes
Lessons that leave no time for prizes.

16 W. P. V., 1866.

SATIRES OF CIRCUMSTANCE

LYRICS AND REVERIES

LYRICS AND REVERIES

IN FRONT OF THE LANDSCAPE

PLUNGING and labouring on in a tide of visions,
    Dolorous and dear,
Forward I pushed my way as amid waste waters
    Stretching around,
Through whose eddies there glimmered the customed landscape
    Yonder and near

Blotted to feeble mist.   And the coomb and the upland
    Coppice-crowned,
Ancient chalk-pit, milestone, rills in the grass-flat
    Stroked by the light,
Seemed but a ghost-like gauze, and no substantial
    Meadow or mound.

What were the infinite spectacles featuring foremost
    Under my sight,
Hindering me to discern my paced advancement
    Lengthening to miles ;
What were the re-creations killing the daytime
    As by the night ?

O they were speechful faces, gazing insistent,
    Some as with smiles,
Some as with slow-born tears that brinily trundled
    Over the wrecked
Cheeks that were fair in their flush-time, ash now with anguish,
    Harrowed by wiles.

285

Yes, I could see them, feel them, hear them, address them—
    Halo-bedecked—
And, alas, onwards, shaken by fierce unreason,
    Rigid in hate,
Smitten by years-long wryness born of misprision,
    Dreaded, suspect.

Then there would breast me shining sights, sweet seasons
    Further in date ;
Instruments of strings with the tenderest passion
    Vibrant, beside
Lamps long extinguished, robes, cheeks, eyes with the earth'
    crust
    Now corporate.

Also there rose a headland of hoary aspect
    Gnawed by the tide,
Frilled by the nimb of the morning as two friends stood there
    Guilelessly glad—
Wherefore they knew not—touched by the fringe of an ecstasy
    Scantly descried.

Later images too did the day unfurl me,
    Shadowed and sad,
Clay cadavers of those who had shared in the dramas,
    Laid now at ease,
Passions all spent, chiefest the one of the broad brow
    Sepulture-clad.

So did beset me scenes, miscalled of the bygone,
    Over the leaze,
Past the clump, and down to where lay the beheld ones ;
    —Yea, as the rhyme
Sung by the sea-swell, so in their pleading dumbness
    Captured me these.

For, their lost revisiting manifestations
    In their live time
Much had I slighted, caring not for their purport,
    Seeing behind
Things more coveted, reckoned the better worth calling
    Sweet, sad, sublime.

Thus do they now show hourly before the intenser
      Stare of the mind
As they were ghosts avenging their slights by my bypast
      Body-borne eyes,
Show, too, with fuller translation than rested upon them
      As living kind.

Hence wag the tongues of the passing people, saying
      In their surmise,
"Ah—whose is this dull form that perambulates, seeing nought
      Round him that looms
Whithersoever his footsteps turn in his farings,
      Save a few tombs?"

CHANNEL FIRING

THAT night your great guns, unawares,
Shook all our coffins as we lay,
And broke the chancel window-squares,
We thought it was the Judgment-day

And sat upright.   While drearisome
Arose the howl of wakened hounds:
The mouse let fall the altar-crumb,
The worms drew back into the mounds,

The glebe cow drooled.   Till God called, "No;
It's gunnery practice out at sea
Just as before you went below;
The world is as it used to be:

"All nations striving strong to make
Red war yet redder.   Mad as hatters
They do no more for Christés sake
Than you who are helpless in such matters.

"That this is not the judgment-hour
For some of them's a blessed thing,
For if it were they'd have to scour
Hell's floor for so much threatening. . . .

" Ha, ha.   It will be warmer when
I blow the trumpet (if indeed
I ever do ; for you are men,
And rest eternal sorely need)."

So down we lay again.   " I wonder,
Will the world ever saner be,"
Said one, " than when He sent us under
In our indifferent century ! "

And many a skeleton shook his head.
" Instead of preaching forty year,"
My neighbour Parson Thirdly said,
" I wish I had stuck to pipes and beer."

Again the guns disturbed the hour,
Roaring their readiness to avenge,
As far inland as Stourton Tower,
And Camelot, and starlit Stonehenge.

April 1914.

THE CONVERGENCE OF THE TWAIN

(*Lines on the loss of the " Titanic "*)

I

IN a solitude of the sea
Deep from human vanity,
And the Pride of Life that planned her, stilly couches she.

II

Steel chambers, late the pyres
Of her salamandrine fires,
Cold currents thrid, and turn to rhythmic tidal lyres.

III

Over the mirrors meant
To glass the opulent
The sea-worm crawls—grotesque, slimed, dumb, indifferent.

IV

Jewels in joy designed
To ravish the sensuous mind
Lie lightless, all their sparkles bleared and black and blind.

V

Dim moon-eyed fishes near
Gaze at the gilded gear
And query: "What does this vaingloriousness down here?" . . .

VI

Well: while was fashioning
This creature of cleaving wing,
The Immanent Will that stirs and urges everything

VII

Prepared a sinister mate
For her—so gaily great—
A Shape of Ice, for the time far and dissociate.

VIII

And as the smart ship grew
In stature, grace, and hue,
In shadowy silent distance grew the Iceberg too.

IX

Alien they seemed to be:
No mortal eye could see
The intimate welding of their later history,

X

Or sign that they were bent
By paths coincident
On being anon twin halves of one august event,

XI

Till the Spinner of the Years
Said "Now!" And each one hears,
And consummation comes, and jars two hemispheres.

THE GHOST OF THE PAST

WE two kept house, the Past and I,
    The Past and I ;
Through all my tasks it hovered nigh,
    Leaving me never alone.
It was a spectral housekeeping
    Where fell no jarring tone,
As strange, as still a housekeeping
    As ever has been known.

As daily I went up the stair
        And down the stair,
I did not mind the Bygone there—
    The Present once to me ;
Its moving meek companionship
    I wished might ever be,
There was in that companionship
    Something of ecstasy.

It dwelt with me just as it was,
        Just as it was
When first its prospects gave me pause
    In wayward wanderings,
Before the years had torn old troths
    As they tear all sweet things,
Before gaunt griefs had torn old troths
    And dulled old rapturings.

And then its form began to fade,
        Began to fade,
Its gentle echoes faintlier played
    At eves upon my ear
Than when the autumn's look embrowned
    The lonely chambers here,
When autumn's settling shades embrowned
    Nooks that it haunted near.

And so with time my vision less,
        Yea, less and less
Makes of that Past my housemistress,
    It dwindles in my eye ;

It looms a far-off skeleton
    And not a comrade nigh,
A fitful far-off skeleton
    Dimming as days draw by.

AFTER THE VISIT

(To F. E. D.)

COME again to the place
Where your presence was as a leaf that skims
Down a drouthy way whose ascent bedims
    The bloom on the farer's face.

    Come again, with the feet
That were light on the green as a thistledown ball,
And those mute ministrations to one and to all
    Beyond a man's saying sweet.

    Until then the faint scent
Of the bordering flowers swam unheeded away,
And I marked not the charm in the changes of day
    As the cloud-colours came and went.

    Through the dark corridors
Your walk was so soundless I did not know
Your form from a phantom's of long ago
    Said to pass on the ancient floors,

    Till you drew from the shade,
And I saw the large luminous living eyes
Regard me in fixed inquiring-wise
    As those of a soul that weighed,

    Scarce consciously,
The eternal question of what Life was,
And why we were there, and by whose strange laws
    That which mattered most could not be.

TO MEET, OR OTHERWISE

WHETHER to sally and see thee, girl of my dreams,
    Or whether to stay
And see thee not ! How vast the difference seems
    Of Yea from Nay
Just now. Yet this same sun will slant its beams
    At no far day
On our two mounds, and then what will the difference weigh !

Yet I will see thee, maiden dear, and make
    The most I can
Of what remains to us amid this brake
    Cimmerian
Through which we grope, and from whose thorns we ache,
    While still we scan
Round our frail faltering progress for some path or plan.

By briefest meeting something sure is won ;
    It will have been :
Nor God nor Demon can undo the done,
    Unsight the seen,
Make muted music be as unbegun,
    Though things terrene
Groan in their bondage till oblivion supervene.

So, to the one long-sweeping symphony
    From times remote
Till now, of human tenderness, shall we
    Supply one note,
Small and untraced, yet that will ever be
    Somewhere afloat
Amid the spheres, as part of sick Life's antidote.

THE DIFFERENCE

I

SINKING down by the gate I discern the thin moon,
And a blackbird tries over old airs in the pine,
But the moon is a sorry one, sad the bird's tune,
For this spot is unknown to that Heartmate of mine.

II

Did my Heartmate but haunt here at times such as now,
The song would be joyous and cheerful the moon ;
But she will see never this gate, path, or bough,
Nor I find a joy in the scene or the tune.

THE SUN ON THE BOOKCASE

(*Student's Love-song* : 1870)

ONCE more the cauldron of the sun
Smears the bookcase with winy red,
And here my page is, and there my bed,
And the apple-tree shadows travel along.
Soon their intangible track will be run,
      And dusk grow strong
      And they have fled.

Yes : now the boiling ball is gone,
And I have wasted another day. . . .
But wasted—*wasted*, do I say ?
Is it a waste to have imaged one
Beyond the hills there, who, anon,
      My great deeds done
      Will be mine alway ?

"WHEN I SET OUT FOR LYONNESSE"

(1870)

WHEN I set out for Lyonnesse,
    A hundred miles away,
    The rime was on the spray,
And starlight lit my lonesomeness
When I set out for Lyonnesse
    A hundred miles away.

What would bechance at Lyonnesse
    While I should sojourn there
    No prophet durst declare,

Nor did the wisest wizard guess
What would bechance at Lyonnesse
    While I should sojourn there.

When I came back from Lyonnesse
    With magic in my eyes,
    All marked with mute surmise
My radiance rare and fathomless,
When I came back from Lyonnesse
    With magic in my eyes!

A THUNDERSTORM IN TOWN

(A Reminiscence : 1893)

SHE wore a new "terra-cotta" dress,
And we stayed, because of the pelting storm,
Within the hansom's dry recess,
Though the horse had stopped ; yea, motionless
    We sat on, snug and warm.

Then the downpour ceased, to my sharp sad pain
And the glass that had screened our forms before
Flew up, and out she sprang to her door :
I should have kissed her if the rain
    Had lasted a minute more.

THE TORN LETTER

I

I TORE your letter into strips
    No bigger than the airy feathers
    That ducks preen out in changing weathers
Upon the shifting ripple-tips.

II

In darkness on my bed alone
    I seemed to see you in a vision,
    And hear you say : "Why this derision
Of one drawn to you, though unknown ?"

III

Yes, eve's quick mood had run its course,
 The night had cooled my hasty madness;
 I suffered a regretful sadness
Which deepened into real remorse.

IV

I thought what pensive patient days
 A soul must know of grain so tender,
 How much of good must grace the sender
Of such sweet words in such bright phrase.

V

Uprising then, as things unpriced
 I sought each fragment, patched and mended:
 The midnight whitened ere I had ended
And gathered words I had sacrificed.

VI

But some, alas, of those I threw
 Were past my search, destroyed for ever:
 They were your name and place; and never
Did I regain those clues to you.

VII

I learnt I had missed, by rash unheed,
 My track; that, so the Will decided,
 In life, death, we should be divided,
And at the sense I ached indeed.

VIII

That ache for you, born long ago,
 Throbs on: I never could outgrow it.
 What a revenge, did you but know it!
But that, thank God, you do not know.

BEYOND THE LAST LAMP

(Near Tooting Common)

I

WHILE rain, with eve in partnership,
Descended darkly, drip, drip, drip,
Beyond the last lone lamp I passed
    Walking slowly, whispering sadly,
    Two linked loiterers, wan, downcast:
Some heavy thought constrained each face,
And blinded them to time and place.

II

The pair seemed lovers, yet absorbed
In mental scenes no longer orbed
By love's young rays.   Each countenance
    As it slowly, as it sadly
    Caught the lamplight's yellow glance,
Held in suspense a misery
At things which had been or might be.

III

When I retrod that watery way
Some hours beyond the droop of day,
Still I found pacing there the twain
    Just as slowly, just as sadly,
    Heedless of the night and rain.
One could but wonder who they were,
And what wild woe detained them there.

IV

Though thirty years of blur and blot
Have slid since I beheld that spot,
And saw in curious converse there
    Moving slowly, moving sadly
    That mysterious tragic pair,
Its olden look may linger on—
All but the couple; they have gone.

v

Whither ?   Who knows, indeed. . . . And yet
To me, when nights are weird and wet,
Without those comrades there at tryst
          Creeping slowly, creeping sadly,
          That lone lane does not exist.
There they seem brooding on their pain,
And will, while such a lane remain.

THE FACE AT THE CASEMENT

          IF ever joy leave
An abiding sting of sorrow,
So befell it on the morrow
          Of that May eve. . . .

          The travelled sun dropped
To the north-west, low and lower,
The pony's trot grew slower,
          Until we stopped.

          "This cosy house just by
I must call at for a minute,
A sick man lies within it
          Who soon will die.

          "He wished to—marry me,
So I am bound, when I drive near him,
To inquire, if but to cheer him,
          How he may be."

          A message was sent in,
And wordlessly we waited,
Till some one came and stated
          The bulletin.

          And that the sufferer said,
For her call no words could thank her ;
As his angel he must rank her
          Till life's spark fled.

Slowly we drove away,
When I turned my head, although not
Called to : why I turned I know not
    Even to this day :

And lo, there in my view
Pressed against an upper lattice
Was a white face, gazing at us
    As we withdrew.

And well did I divine
It to be the man's there dying,
Who but lately had been sighing
    For her pledged mine.

Then I deigned a deed of hell ;
It was done before I knew it ;
What devil made me do it
    I cannot tell !

Yes, while he gazed above,
I put my arm about her
That he might see, nor doubt her
    My plighted Love.

The pale face vanished quick,
As if blasted, from the casement,
And my shame and self-abasement
    Began their prick.

And they prick on, ceaselessly,
For that stab in Love's fierce fashion
Which, unfired by lover's passion,
    Was foreign to me.

She smiled at my caress,
But why came the soft embowment
Of her shoulder at that moment
    She did not guess.

Long long years has he lain
In thy garth, O sad Saint Cleather :
What tears there, bared to weather,
    Will cleanse that stain !

Love is long-suffering, brave,
Sweet, prompt, precious as a jewel;
But jealousy is cruel,
    Cruel as the grave!

LOST LOVE

I PLAY my sweet old airs—
    The airs he knew
    When our love was true—
    But he does not balk
    His determined walk,
And passes up the stairs.

I sing my songs once more,
    And presently hear
    His footstep near
    As if it would stay;
    But he goes his way,
And shuts a distant door.

So I wait for another morn,
    And another night
    In this soul-sick blight;
    And I wonder much
    As I sit, why such
A woman as I was born!

"MY SPIRIT WILL NOT HAUNT THE MOUND"

My spirit will not haunt the mound
    Above my breast,
But travel, memory-possessed,
To where my tremulous being found
    Life largest, best.

My phantom-footed shape will go
    When nightfall grays

Hither and thither along the ways
I and another used to know
In backward days.

And there you'll find me, if a jot
You still should care
For me, and for my curious air;
If otherwise, then I shall not,
For you, be there.

WESSEX HEIGHTS

(1896)

THERE are some heights in Wessex, shaped as if by a kindly
    hand
For thinking, dreaming, dying on, and at crises when I stand,
Say, on Ingpen Beacon eastward, or on Wylls-Neck westwardly,
I seem where I was before my birth, and after death may be.

In the lowlands I have no comrade, not even the lone man's
    friend—
Her who suffereth long and is kind; accepts what he is too weak
    to mend:
Down there they are dubious and askance; there nobody
    thinks as I,
But mind-chains do not clank where one's next neighbour is
    the sky.

In the towns I am tracked by phantoms having weird detective
    ways—
Shadows of beings who fellowed with myself of earlier days:
They hang about at places, and they say harsh heavy things—
Men with a wintry sneer, and women with tart disparagings.

Down there I seem to be false to myself, my simple self that was,
And is not now, and I see him watching, wondering what crass
    cause
Can have merged him into such a strange continuator as this,
Who yet has something in common with himself, my chrysalis.

I cannot go to the great grey Plain ; there's a figure against the
   moon,
Nobody sees it but I, and it makes my breast beat out of tune ;
I cannot go to the tall-spired town, being barred by the forms
   now passed
For everybody but me, in whose long vision they stand there
   fast.

There's a ghost at Yell'ham Bottom chiding loud at the fall of
   the night,
There's a ghost in Froom-side Vale, thin lipped and vague, in
   a shroud of white,
There is one in the railway train whenever I do not want it near,
I see its profile against the pane, saying what I would not hear.

As for one rare fair woman, I am now but a thought of hers,
I enter her mind and another thought succeeds me that she
   prefers ;
Yet my love for her in its fulness she herself even did not know ;
Well, time cures hearts of tenderness, and now I can let her go.

So I am found on Ingpen Beacon, or on Wylls-Neck to the west,
Or else on homely Bulbarrow, or little Pilsdon Crest,
Where men have never cared to haunt, nor women have walked
   with me,
And ghosts then keep their distance ; and I know some liberty.

IN DEATH DIVIDED

I

I SHALL rot here, with those whom in their day
      You never knew,
And alien ones who, ere they chilled to clay,
      Met not my view,
Will in your distant grave-place ever neighbour you.

II

No shade of pinnacle or tree or tower,
      While earth endures,

Will fall on my mound and within the hour
    Steal on to yours ;
One robin never haunt our two green covertures.

III

Some organ may resound on Sunday noons
    By where you lie,
Some other thrill the panes with other tunes
    Where moulder I ;
No selfsame chords compose our common lullaby.

IV

The simply-cut memorial at my head
    Perhaps may take
A rustic form, and that above your bed
    A stately make ;
No linking symbol show thereon for our tale's sake.

V

And in the monotonous moils of strained, hard-run
    Humanity,
The eternal tie which binds us twain in one
    No eye will see
Stretching across the miles that sever you from me.

THE PLACE ON THE MAP

I

I LOOK upon the map that hangs by me—
Its shires and towns and rivers lined in varnished artistry—
    And I mark a jutting height
Coloured purple, with a margin of blue sea.

II

—'Twas a day of latter summer, hot and dry ;
Ay, even the waves seemed drying as we walked on, she and I,
    By this spot where, calmly quite,
She unfolded what would happen by and by.

III

This hanging map depicts the coast and place,
And re-creates therewith our unforeboded troublous case
     All distinctly to my sight,
And her tension, and the aspect of her face.

IV

Weeks and weeks we had loved beneath that blazing blue,
Which had lost the art of raining, as her eyes to-day had too,
     While she told what, as by sleight,
Shot our firmament with rays of ruddy hue.

V

For the wonder and the wormwood of the whole
Was that what in realms of reason would have joyed our double soul
     Wore a torrid tragic light
Under order-keeping's rigorous control.

VI

So, the map revives her words, the spot, the time,
And the thing we found we had to face before the next year's
     prime ;
     The charted coast stares bright,
And its episode comes back in pantomime.

THE SCHRECKHORN

(*With thoughts of Leslie Stephen*)

(June 1897)

ALOOF, as if a thing of mood and whim ;
Now that its spare and desolate figure gleams
Upon my nearing vision, less it seems
A looming Alp-height than a guise of him
Who scaled its horn with ventured life and limb,
Drawn on by vague imaginings, maybe,
Of semblance to his personality
In its quaint glooms, keen lights, and rugged trim.

At his last change, when Life's dull coils unwind,
Will he, in old love, hitherward escape,
And the eternal essence of his mind
Enter this silent adamantine shape,
And his low voicing haunt its slipping snows
When dawn that calls the climber dyes them rose?

A SINGER ASLEEP

(Algernon Charles Swinburne, 1837–1909)

I

In this fair niche above the unslumbering sea,
That sentrys up and down all night, all day,
From cove to promontory, from ness to bay,
The Fates have fitly bidden that he should be
     Pillowed eternally.

II

—It was as though a garland of red roses
Had fallen about the hood of some smug nun
When irresponsibly dropped as from the sun,
In fulth of numbers freaked with musical closes,
    Upon Victoria's formal middle time
     His leaves of rhythm and rhyme.

III

O that far morning of a summer day
When, down a terraced street whose pavements lay
Glassing the sunshine into my bent eyes,
I walked and read with a quick glad surprise
     New words, in classic guise,—

IV

The passionate pages of his earlier years,
Fraught with hot sighs, sad laughters, kisses, tears;
Fresh-fluted notes, yet from a minstrel who
Blew them not naïvely, but as one who knew
     Full well why thus he blew.

V

I still can hear the brabble and the roar
At those thy tunes, O still one, now passed through
That fitful fire of tongues then entered new!
Their power is spent like spindrift on this shore;
    Thine swells yet more and more.

VI

—His singing-mistress verily was no other
Than she the Lesbian, she the music-mother
Of all the tribe that feel in melodies;
Who leapt, love-anguished, from the Leucadian steep
Into the rambling world-encircling deep
    Which hides her where none sees.

VII

And one can hold in thought that nightly here
His phantom may draw down to the water's brim,
And hers come up to meet it, as a dim
Lone shine upon the heaving hydrosphere,
And mariners wonder as they traverse near,
    Unknowing of her and him.

VIII

One dreams him sighing to her spectral form:
"O teacher, where lies hid thy burning line;
Where are those songs, O poetess divine
Whose very orts are love incarnadine?"
And her smile back: "Disciple true and warm,
    Sufficient now are thine." . . .

IX

So here, beneath the waking constellations,
Where the waves peal their everlasting strains,
And their dull subterrene reverberations
Shake him when storms make mountains of their plains—
Him once their peer in sad improvisations,
And deft as wind to cleave their frothy manes—
I leave him, while the daylight gleam declines
    Upon the capes and chines.

BONCHURCH, 1910.

A PLAINT TO MAN

WHEN you slowly emerged from the den of Time,
And gained percipience as you grew,
And fleshed you fair out of shapeless slime,

Wherefore, O Man, did there come to you
The unhappy need of creating me—
A form like your own—for praying to?

My virtue, power, utility,
Within my maker must all abide,
Since none in myself can ever be,

One thin as a phasm on a lantern-slide
Shown forth in the dark upon some dim sheet,
And by none but its showman vivified.

"Such a forced device," you may say, "is meet
For easing a loaded heart at whiles:
Man needs to conceive of a mercy-seat

Somewhere above the gloomy aisles
Of this wailful world, or he could not bear
The irk no local hope beguiles."

—But since I was framed in your first despair
The doing without me has had no play
In the minds of men when shadows scare;

And now that I dwindle day by day
Beneath the deicide eyes of seers
In a light that will not let me stay,

And to-morrow the whole of me disappears,
The truth should be told, and the fact be faced
That had best been faced in earlier years:

The fact of life with dependence placed
On the human heart's resource alone,
In brotherhood bonded close and graced

With loving-kindness fully blown,
And visioned help unsought, unknown.

1909-10.

GOD'S FUNERAL

I

I SAW a slowly-stepping train—
Lined on the brows, scoop-eyed and bent and hoar—
Following in files across a twilit plain
A strange and mystic form the foremost bore.

II

And by contagious throbs of thought
Or latent knowledge that within me lay
And had already stirred me, I was wrought
To consciousness of sorrow even as they.

III

The fore-borne shape, to my blurred eyes,
At first seemed man-like, and anon to change
To an amorphous cloud of marvellous size,
At times endowed with wings of glorious range.

IV

And this phantasmal variousness
Ever possessed it as they drew along:
Yet throughout all it symboled none the less
Potency vast and loving-kindness strong.

V

Almost before I knew I bent
Towards the moving columns without a word;
They, growing in bulk and numbers as they went,
Struck out sick thoughts that could be overheard:—

VI

"O man-projected Figure, of late
Imaged as we, thy knell who shall survive?
Whence came it we were tempted to create
One whom we can no longer keep alive?

VII

"Framing him jealous, fierce, at first,
We gave him justice as the ages rolled,
Will to bless those by circumstance accurst,
And longsuffering, and mercies manifold.

VIII

"And, tricked by our own early dream
And need of solace, we grew self-deceived,
Our making soon our maker did we deem,
And what we had imagined we believed.

IX

"Till, in Time's stayless stealthy swing,
Uncompromising rude reality
Mangled the Monarch of our fashioning,
Who quavered, sank; and now has ceased to be.

X

"So, toward our myth's oblivion,
Darkling, and languid-lipped, we creep and grope
Sadlier than those who wept in Babylon,
Whose Zion was a still abiding hope.

XI

"How sweet it was in years far hied
To start the wheels of day with trustful prayer,
To lie down liegely at the eventide
And feel a blest assurance he was there!

XII

"And who or what shall fill his place?
Whither will wanderers turn distracted eyes
For some fixed star to stimulate their pace
Towards the goal of their enterprise?" . . .

XIII

Some in the background then I saw,
Sweet women, youths, men, all incredulous,

Who chimed : " This is a counterfeit of straw,
This requiem mockery ! Still he lives to us ! "

XIV

 I could not buoy their faith : and yet
Many I had known : with all I sympathized ;
And though struck speechless, I did not forget
That what was mourned for, I, too, long had prized.

XV

 Still, how to bear such loss I deemed
The insistent question for each animate mind,
And gazing, to my growing sight there seemed
A pale yet positive gleam low down behind,

XVI

 Whereof, to lift the general night,
A certain few who stood aloof had said,
" See you upon the horizon that small light—
Swelling somewhat ? "   Each mourner shook his head.

XVII

 And they composed a crowd of whom
Some were right good, and many nigh the best. . . .
Thus dazed and puzzled 'twixt the gleam and gloom
Mechanically I followed with the rest.

 1908-10.

SPECTRES THAT GRIEVE

" It is not death that harrows us," they lipped,
" The soundless cell is in itself relief,
For life is an unfenced flower, benumbed and nipped
At unawares, and at its best but brief."

The speakers, sundry phantoms of the gone,
Had risen like filmy flames of phosphor dye,
As if the palest of sheet lightnings shone
From the sward near me, as from a nether sky.

And much surprised was I that, spent and dead,
They should not, like the many, be at rest,
But stray as apparitions; hence I said,
"Why, having slipped life, hark you back distressed?"

"We are among the few death sets not free,
The hurt, misrepresented names, who come
At each year's brink, and cry to History
To do them justice, or go past them dumb.

"We are stript of rights; our shames lie unredressed,
Our deeds in full anatomy are not shown,
Our words in morsels merely are expressed
On the scriptured page, our motives blurred, unknown."

Then all these shaken slighted visitants sped
Into the vague, and left me musing there
On fames that well might instance what they had said,
Until the New-Year's dawn strode up the air.

"AH, ARE YOU DIGGING ON MY GRAVE?"

"AH, are you digging on my grave
        My loved one?—planting rue?"
—"No: yesterday he went to wed
One of the brightest wealth has bred.
'It cannot hurt her now,' he said,
        'That I should not be true.'"

"Then who is digging on my grave?
        My nearest dearest kin?"
—"Ah, no: they sit and think, 'What use!
What good will planting flowers produce?
No tendance of her mound can loose
        Her spirit from Death's gin.'"

"But some one digs upon my grave?
        My enemy?—prodding sly?"
—"Nay: when she heard you had passed the Gate
That shuts on all flesh soon or late,
She thought you no more worth her hate,
        And cares not where you lie."

" Then, who is digging on my grave ?
    Say—since I have not guessed ! "
—" O it is I, my mistress dear,
Your little dog, who still lives near,
And much I hope my movements here
    Have not disturbed your rest ? "

" Ah, yes !   *You* dig upon my grave . . .
    Why flashed it not on me
That one true heart was left behind !
What feeling do we ever find
To equal among human kind
    A dog's fidelity ! "

" Mistress, I dug upon your grave
    To bury a bone, in case
I should be hungry near this spot
When passing on my daily trot.
I am sorry, but I quite forgot
    It was your resting-place."

SELF-UNCONSCIOUS

ALONG the way
    He walked that day,
Watching shapes that reveries limn,
    And seldom he
    Had eyes to see
The moment that encompassed him.

Bright yellowhammers
    Made mirthful clamours,
And billed long straws with a bustling air,
    And bearing their load
    Flew up the road
That he followed, alone, without interest there.

From bank to ground
    And over and round
They sidled along the adjoining hedge ;

Sometimes to the gutter
Their yellow flutter
Would dip from the nearest slatestone ledge,

The smooth sea-line
With a metal shine,
And flashes of white, and a sail thereon,
He would also descry
With a half-wrapt eye
Between the projects he mused upon.

Yes, round him were these
Earth's artistries,
But specious plans that came to his call
Did most engage
His pilgrimage,
While himself he did not see at all.

Dead now as sherds
Are the yellow birds,
And all that mattered has passed away;
Yet God, the Elf,
Now shows him that self
As he was, and should have been shown, that day.

O it would have been good
Could he then have stood
At a clear-eyed distance, and conned the whole,
But now such vision
Is mere derision,
Nor soothes his body nor saves his soul.

Not much, some may
Incline to say,
To see therein, had it all been seen.
Nay! he is aware
A thing was there
That loomed with an immortal mien.

NEAR BOSSINEY.

THE DISCOVERY

I WANDERED to a crude coast
        Like a ghost ;
Upon the hills I saw fires—
        Funeral pyres
Seemingly—and heard breaking
Waves like distant cannonades that set the land shaking.

And so I never once guessed
        A Love-nest,
Bowered and candle-lit, lay
        In my way,
Till I found a hid hollow,
Where I burst on her my heart could not but follow

TOLERANCE

" IT is a foolish thing," said I,
" To bear with such, and pass it by ;
Yet so I do, I know not why !"

And at each cross I would surmise
That if I had willed not in that wise
I might have spared me many sighs.

But now the only happiness
In looking back that I possess—
Whose lack would leave me comfortless—

Is to remember I refrained
From masteries I might have gained,
And for my tolerance was disdained ;

For see, a tomb. And if it were
I had bent and broke, I should not dare
To linger in the shadows there.

BEFORE AND AFTER SUMMER

I

LOOKING forward to the spring
One puts up with anything.
On this February day
Though the winds leap down the street
Wintry scourgings seem but play,
And these later shafts of sleet
—Sharper pointed than the first—
And these later snows—the worst—
Are as a half-transparent blind
Riddled by rays from sun behind.

II

Shadows of the October pine
Reach into this room of mine :
On the pine there swings a bird ;
He is shadowed with the tree.
Mutely perched he bills no word ;
Blank as I am even is he.
For those happy suns are past,
Fore-discerned in winter last.
When went by their pleasure, then ?
I, alas, perceived not when.

AT DAY-CLOSE IN NOVEMBER

THE ten hours' light is abating,
    And a late bird wings across,
Where the pines, like waltzers waiting,
    Give their black heads a toss.

Beech leaves, that yellow the noon-time,
    Float past like specks in the eye ;
I set every tree in my June time,
    And now they obscure the sky.

And the children who ramble through here
    Conceive that there never has been
A time when no tall trees grew here,
    That none will in time be seen.

THE YEAR'S AWAKENING

How do you know that the pilgrim track
Along the belting zodiac
Swept by the sun in his seeming rounds
Is traced by now to the Fishes' bounds
And into the Ram, when weeks of cloud
Have wrapt the sky in a clammy shroud,
And never as yet a tint of spring
Has shown in the Earth's apparelling;
    O vespering bird, how do you know,
        How do you know?

How do you know, deep underground,
Hid in your bed from sight and sound,
Without a turn in temperature,
With weather life can scarce endure,
That light has won a fraction's strength,
And day put on some moments' length,
Whereof in merest rote will come,
Weeks hence, mild airs that do not numb,
    O crocus root, how do you know,
        How do you know?

February 1910.

UNDER THE WATERFALL

" WHENEVER I plunge my arm, like this,
In a basin of water, I never miss
The sweet sharp sense of a fugitive day
Fetched back from its thickening shroud of gray.
    Hence the only prime
    And real love-rhyme

That I know by heart,
            And that leaves no smart,
Is the purl of a little valley fall
About three spans wide and two spans tall
Over a table of solid rock,
And into a scoop of the self-same block;
The purl of a runlet that never ceases
In stir of kingdoms, in wars, in peaces;
With a hollow boiling voice it speaks
And has spoken since hills were turfless peaks."

" And why gives this the only prime
Idea to you of a real love-rhyme?
And why does plunging your arm in a bowl
Full of spring water, bring throbs to your soul?"

" Well, under the fall, in a crease of the stone,
Though where precisely none ever has known,
Jammed darkly, nothing to show how prized,
And by now with its smoothness opalized,
            Is a drinking-glass:
            For, down that pass
            My lover and I
            Walked under a sky
Of blue with a leaf-wove awning of green,
In the burn of August, to paint the scene,
And we placed our basket of fruit and wine
By the runlet's rim, where we sat to dine;
And when we had drunk from the glass together,
Arched by the oak-copse from the weather,
I held the vessel to rinse in the fall,   ·
Where it slipped, and sank, and was past recall,
Though we stooped and plumbed the little abyss
With long bared arms.   There the glass still is.
And, as said, if I thrust my arm below
Cold water in basin or bowl, a throe
From the past awakens a sense of that time,
And the glass we used, and the cascade's rhyme.
The basin seems the pool, and its edge
The hard smooth face of the brook-side ledge,
And the leafy pattern of china-ware
The hanging plants that were bathing there.

"By night, by day, when it shines or lours,
There lies intact that chalice of ours,
And its presence adds to the rhyme of love
Persistently sung by the fall above.
No lip has touched it since his and mine
In turns therefrom sipped lovers' wine."

POEMS OF 1912–13

Veteris vestigia flammae

THE GOING

WHY did you give no hint that night
That quickly after the morrow's dawn,
And calmly, as if indifferent quite,
You would close your term here, up and be gone
    Where I could not follow
    With wing of swallow
To gain one glimpse of you ever anon !

    Never to bid good-bye,
    Or lip me the softest call,
Or utter a wish for a word, while I
Saw morning harden upon the wall,
    Unmoved, unknowing
    That your great going
Had place that moment, and altered all.

Why do you make me leave the house
And think for a breath it is you I see
At the end of the alley of bending boughs
Where so often at dusk you used to be ;
    Till in darkening dankness
    The yawning blankness
Of the perspective sickens me !

    You were she who abode
    By those red-veined rocks far West,

You were the swan-necked one who rode
Along the beetling Beeny Crest,
   And, reining nigh me,
   Would muse and eye me,
While Life unrolled us its very best.

Why, then, latterly did we not speak,
Did we not think of those days long dead,
And ere your vanishing strive to seek
That time's renewal? We might have said,
   "In this bright spring weather
   We'll visit together
Those places that once we visited."

   Well, well! All's past amend,
   Unchangeable. It must go.
I seem but a dead man held on end
To sink down soon. . . . O you could not know
   That such swift fleeing
   No soul foreseeing—
Not even I—would undo me so!

   December 1912.

YOUR LAST DRIVE

HERE by the moorway you returned,
And saw the borough lights ahead
That lit your face—all undiscerned
To be in a week the face of the dead,
And you told of the charm of that haloed view
That never again would beam on you.

And on your left you passed the spot
Where eight days later you were to lie,
And be spoken of as one who was not;
Beholding it with a heedless eye
As alien from you, though under its tree
You soon would halt everlastingly.

I drove not with you. . . . Yet had I sat
At your side that eve I should not have seen

That the countenance I was glancing at
Had a last-time look in the flickering sheen,
Nor have read the writing upon your face,
"I go hence soon to my resting-place ;

"You may miss me then.   But I shall not know
How many times you visit me there,
Or what your thoughts are, or if you go
There never at all.   And I shall not care.
Should you censure me I shall take no heed,
And even your praises no more shall need."

True : never you'll know.   And you will not mind
But shall I then slight you because of such ?
Dear ghost, in the past did you ever find
The thought " What profit," move me much ?
Yet abides the fact, indeed, the same,—
You are past love, praise, indifference, blame.

December 1912.

THE WALK

You did not walk with me
Of late to the hill-top tree
    By the gated ways,
    As in earlier days ;
    You were weak and lame,
    So you never came,
And I went alone, and I did not mind,
Not thinking of you as left behind.

I walked up there to-day
Just in the former way ;
    Surveyed around
    The familiar ground
    By myself again :
    What difference, then ?
Only that underlying sense
Of the look of a room on returning thence.

RAIN ON A GRAVE

CLOUDS spout upon her
 Their waters amain
 In ruthless disdain,—
Her who but lately
 Had shivered with pain
As at touch of dishonour
If there had lit on her
So coldly, so straightly
 Such arrows of rain:

One who to shelter
 Her delicate head
Would quicken and quicken
 Each tentative tread
If drops chanced to pelt her
 That summertime spills
 In dust-paven rills
When thunder-clouds thicken
 And birds close their bills.

Would that I lay there
 And she were housed here!
Or better, together
Were folded away there
Exposed to one weather
We both,—who would stray there
When sunny the day there,
 Or evening was clear
 At the prime of the year.

Soon will be growing
 Green blades from her mound,
And daisies be showing
 Like stars on the ground,
Till she form part of them—
Ay—the sweet heart of them,
Loved beyond measure
With a child's pleasure
 All her life's round.

Jan. 31, 1913.

"I FOUND HER OUT THERE"

I FOUND her out there
On a slope few see,
That falls westwardly
To the salt-edged air,
Where the ocean breaks
On the purple strand,
And the hurricane shakes
The solid land.

I brought her here,
And have laid her to rest
In a noiseless nest
No sea beats near.
She will never be stirred
In her loamy cell
By the waves long heard
And loved so well.

So she does not sleep
By those haunted heights
The Atlantic smites
And the blind gales sweep,
Whence she often would gaze
At Dundagel's famed head,
While the dipping blaze
Dyed her face fire-red ;

And would sigh at the tale
Of sunk Lyonnesse,
As a wind-tugged tress
Flapped her cheek like a flail ;
Or listen at whiles
With a thought-bound brow
To the murmuring miles
She is far from now.

Yet her shade, maybe,
Will creep underground
Till it catch the sound
Of that western sea

As it swells and sobs
Where she once domiciled,
And joy in its throbs
With the heart of a child.

WITHOUT CEREMONY

IT was your way, my dear,
To vanish without a word
When callers, friends, or kin
Had left, and I hastened in
To rejoin you, as I inferred.

And when you'd a mind to career
Off anywhere—say to town—
You were all on a sudden gone
Before I had thought thereon,
Or noticed your trunks were down

So, now that you disappear
For ever in that swift style,
Your meaning seems to me
Just as it used to be:
" Good-bye is not worth while ! "

LAMENT

How she would have loved
A party to-day !—
Bright-hatted and gloved,
With table and tray
And chairs on the lawn
Her smiles would have shone
With welcomings. . . . But
She is shut, she is shut
    From friendship's spell
    In the jailing shell
    Of her tiny cell.

Or she would have reigned
At a dinner to-night
With ardours unfeigned,
And a generous delight:
All in her abode
She'd have freely bestowed
On her guests. . . . But alas,
She is shut under grass
     Where no cups flow,
     Powerless to know
     That it might be so.

And she would have sought
With a child's eager glance
The shy snowdrops brought
By the new year's advance,
And peered in the rime
Of Candlemas-time
For crocuses . . . chanced
It that she were not tranced
     From sights she loved best;
     Wholly possessed
     By an infinite rest!

And we are here staying
Amid these stale things,
Who care not for gaying,
And those junketings
That used so to joy her,
And never to cloy her
As us they cloy! . . . But
She is shut, she is shut
     From the cheer of them, dead
     To all done and said
     In her yew-arched bed.

THE HAUNTER

HE does not think that I haunt here nightly:
     How shall I let him know
That whither his fancy sets him wandering
     I, too, alertly go?——

Hover and hover a few feet from him
  Just as I used to do,
But cannot answer the words he lifts me—
  Only listen thereto!

When I could answer he did not say them:
  When I could let him know
How I would like to join in his journeys
  Seldom he wished to go.
Now that he goes and wants me with him
  More than he used to do,
Never he sees my faithful phantom
  Though he speaks thereto.

Yes, I companion him to places
  Only dreamers know,
Where the shy hares print long paces,
  Where the night rooks go;
Into old aisles where the past is all to him,
  Close as his shade can do,
Always lacking the power to call to him,
  Near as I reach thereto!

What a good haunter I am, O tell him!
  Quickly make him know
If he but sigh since my loss befell him
  Straight to his side I go.
Tell him a faithful one is doing
  All that love can do
Still that his path may be worth pursuing,
  And to bring peace thereto.

THE VOICE

WOMAN much missed, how you call to me, call to me,
Saying that now you are not as you were
When you had changed from the one who was all to me,
But as at first, when our day was fair.

Can it be you that I hear? Let me view you, then,
Standing as when I drew near to the town

Where you would wait for me : yes, as I knew you then,
Even to the original air-blue gown !

Or is it only the breeze, in its listlessness
Travelling across the wet mead to me here,
You being ever dissolved to wan wistlessness,
Heard no more again far or near ?

Thus I ; faltering forward,
Leaves around me falling,
Wind oozing thin through the thorn from norward,
And the woman calling.

December 1912.

HIS VISITOR

I COME across from Mellstock while the moon wastes weaker
To behold where I lived with you for twenty years and more :
I shall go in the gray, at the passing of the mail-train,
And need no setting open of the long familiar door
As before.

The change I notice in my once own quarters !
A formal-fashioned border where the daisies used to be,
The rooms new painted, and the pictures altered,
And other cups and saucers, and no cosy nook for tea
As with me.

I discern the dim faces of the sleep-wrapt servants ;
They are not those who tended me through feeble hours and stron
But strangers quite, who never knew my rule here,
Who never saw me painting, never heard my softling song
Float along.

So I don't want to linger in this re-decked dwelling,
I feel too uneasy at the contrasts I behold,
And I make again for Mellstock to return here never,
And rejoin the roomy silence, and the mute and manifold
Souls of old.

1913.

A CIRCULAR

As "legal representative"
I read a missive not my own,
On new designs the senders give
    For clothes, in tints as shown.

Here figure blouses, gowns for tea,
And presentation-trains of state,
Charming ball-dresses, millinery,
    Warranted up to date.

And this gay-pictured, spring-time shout
Of Fashion, hails what lady proud?
Her who before last year ebbed out
    Was costumed in a shroud.

A DREAM OR NO

HY go to Saint-Juliot? What's Juliot to me?
    Some strange necromancy
    But charmed me to fancy
at much of my life claims the spot as its key.

s. I have had dreams of that place in the West,
    And a maiden abiding
    Thereat as in hiding;
r-eyed and white-shouldered, broad-browed and brown-tressed.

d of how, coastward bound on a night long ago,
    There lonely I found her,
    The sea-birds around her,
d other than nigh things uncaring to know.

sweet her life there (in my thought has it seemed)
    That quickly she drew me
    To take her unto me,
d lodge her long years with me. Such have I dreamed.

But nought of that maid from Saint-Juliot I see ;
        Can she ever have been here,
        And shed her life's sheen here,
The woman I thought a long housemate with me ?

Does there even a place like Saint-Juliot exist ?
        Or a Vallency Valley
        With stream and leafed alley,
Or Beeny, or Bos with its flounce flinging mist ?

February 1913.

AFTER A JOURNEY

HERETO I come to view a voiceless ghost ;
    Whither, O whither will its whim now draw me ?
Up the cliff, down, till I'm lonely, lost,
    And the unseen waters' ejaculations awe me.
Where you will next be there's no knowing,
    Facing round about me everywhere,
        With your nut-coloured hair,
And gray eyes, and rose-flush coming and going.

Yes : I have re-entered your olden haunts at last ;
    Through the years, through the dead scenes I have track
        you ;
What have you now found to say of our past—
    Scanned across the dark space wherein I have lacked you ?
Summer gave us sweets, but autumn wrought division ?
    Things were not lastly as firstly well
        With us twain, you tell ?
But all's closed now, despite Time's derision.

I see what you are doing : you are leading me on
    To the spots we knew when we haunted here together,
The waterfall, above which the mist-bow shone
    At the then fair hour in the then fair weather,
And the cave just under, with a voice still so hollow
    That it seems to call out to me from forty years ago,
        When you were all aglow,
And not the thin ghost that I now frailly follow !

gnorant of what there is flitting here to see,
  The waked birds preen and the seals flop lazily,
Soon you will have, Dear, to vanish from me,
    For the stars close their shutters and the dawn whitens hazily.
Trust me, I mind not, though Life lours,
  The bringing me here ; nay, bring me here again !
    I am just the same as when
Our days were a joy, and our paths through flowers.

    PENTARGAN BAY.

A DEATH-DAY RECALLED

    BEENY did not quiver,
      Juliot grew not gray,
    Thin Valency's river
      Held its wonted way.
    Bos seemed not to utter
      Dimmest note of dirge,
    Targan mouth a mutter
      To its creamy surge.

    Yet though these, unheeding,
      Listless, passed the hour
    Of her spirit's speeding,
      She had, in her flower,
    Sought and loved the places—
      Much and often pined
    For their lonely faces
      When in towns confined.

    Why did not Valency
      In his purl deplore
    One whose haunts were whence he
      Drew his limpid store ?
    Why did Bos not thunder,
      Targan apprehend
    Body and Breath were sunder
      Of their former friend ?

BEENY CLIFF

March 1870—*March* 1913

I

O THE opal and the sapphire of that wandering western sea,
And the woman riding high above with bright hair flapping
free—
The woman whom I loved so, and who loyally loved me.

II

The pale mews plained below us, and the waves seemed far away
In a nether sky, engrossed in saying their ceaseless babbling say,
As we laughed light-heartedly aloft on that clear-sunned March
day.

III

A little cloud then cloaked us, and there flew an irised rain,
And the Atlantic dyed its levels with a dull misfeatured stain,
And then the sun burst out again, and purples prinked the main.

IV

—Still in all its chasmal beauty bulks old Beeny to the sky,
And shall she and I not go there once again now March is nigh,
And the sweet things said in that March say anew there by and
by?

V

What if still in chasmal beauty looms that wild weird western
shore,
The woman now is—elsewhere—whom the ambling pony bore,
And nor knows nor cares for Beeny, and will laugh there nevermore.

AT CASTLE BOTEREL

As I drive to the junction of lane and highway,
  And the drizzle bedrenches the waggonette,
I look behind at the fading byway,
  And see on its slope, now glistening wet,
    Distinctly yet

Myself and a girlish form benighted
   In dry March weather.   We climb the road
Beside a chaise.   We had just alighted
   To ease the sturdy pony's load
      When he sighed and slowed.

What we did as we climbed, and what we talked of
   Matters not much, nor to what it led,—
Something that life will not be balked of
   Without rude reason till hope is dead,
      And feeling fled.

It filled but a minute.   But was there ever
   A time of such quality, since or before,
In that hill's story?   To one mind never,
   Though it has been climbed, foot-swift, foot-sore,
      By thousands more.

Primaeval rocks form the road's steep border,
   And much have they faced there, first and last,
Of the transitory in Earth's long order;
   But what they record in colour and cast
      Is—that we two passed.

And to me, though Time's unflinching rigour,
   In mindless rote, has ruled from sight
The substance now, one phantom figure
   Remains on the slope, as when that night
      Saw us alight.

I look and see it there, shrinking, shrinking,
   I look back at it amid the rain
For the very last time; for my sand is sinking,
   And I shall traverse old love's domain
      Never again.

March 1913.

PLACES

NOBODY says: Ah, that is the place
Where chanced, in the hollow of years ago,
What none of the Three Towns cared to know—
The birth of a little girl of grace—

The sweetest the house saw, first or last;
    Yet it was so
      On that day long past.

Nobody thinks: There, there she lay
In a room by the Hoe, like the bud of a flower,
And listened, just after the bedtime hour,
To the stammering chimes that used to play
The quaint Old Hundred-and-Thirteenth tune
    In Saint Andrew's tower
      Night, morn, and noon.

Nobody calls to mind that here
Upon Boterel Hill, where the waggoners skid,
With cheeks whose airy flush outbid
Fresh fruit in bloom, and free of fear,
She cantered down, as if she must fall
    (Though she never did),
      To the charm of all.

Nay: one there is to whom these things,
That nobody else's mind calls back,
Have a savour that scenes in being lack,
And a presence more than the actual brings;
To whom to-day is beneaped and stale,
    And its urgent clack
      But a vapid tale.

PLYMOUTH, *March* 1913.

THE PHANTOM HORSEWOMAN

I

QUEER are the ways of a man I know:
    He comes and stands
    In a careworn craze,
    And looks at the sands
    And the seaward haze
    With moveless hands
    And face and gaze,
    Then turns to go . . .
And what does he see when he gazes so?

II

They say he sees as an instant thing
    More clear than to-day,
    A sweet soft scene
    That once was in play
    By that briny green ;
    Yes, notes alway
    Warm, real, and keen,
    What his back years bring—
A phantom of his own figuring.

III

Of this vision of his they might say more :
    Not only there
    Does he see this sight,
    But everywhere
    In his brain—day, night,
    As if on the air
    It were drawn rose bright—
    Yea, far from that shore
Does he carry this vision of heretofore :

IV

A ghost-girl-rider.   And though, toil-tried,
    He withers daily,
    Time touches her not,
    But she still rides gaily
    In his rapt thought
    On that shagged and shaly
    Atlantic spot,
    And as when first eyed
Draws rein and sings to the swing of the tide.

1913.

THE SPELL OF THE ROSE

" I MEAN to build a hall anon,
  And shape two turrets there,
  And a broad newelled stair,
And a cool well for crystal water ;
  Yes ; I will build a hall anon,
  Plant roses love shall feed upon,
   And apple-trees and pear."

He set to build the manor-hall,
  And shaped the turrets there,
  And the broad newelled stair,
And the cool well for crystal water ;
  He built for me that manor-hall,
  And planted many trees withal,
   But no rose anywhere.

And as he planted never a rose
  That bears the flower of love,
  Though other flowers throve
Some heart-bane moved our souls to sever
  Since he had planted never a rose ;
  And misconceits raised horrid shows,
   And agonies came thereof.

" I'll mend these miseries," then said I,
  And so, at dead of night,
  I went and, screened from sight,
That nought should keep our souls in severance,
  I set a rose-bush.   "This," said I,
  " May end divisions dire and wry,
   And long-drawn days of blight."

But I was called from earth—yea, called
  Before my rose-bush grew ;
  And would that now I knew
What feels he of the tree I planted,
  And whether, after I was called
  To be a ghost, he, as of old,
   Gave me his heart anew !

Perhaps now blooms that queen of trees
    I set but saw not grow,
    And he, beside its glow—
Eyes couched of the mis-vision that blurred me—
    Ay, there beside that queen of trees
    He sees me as I was, though sees
      Too late to tell me so !

ST. LAUNCE'S REVISITED

    SLIP back, Time !
Yet again I am nearing
Castle and keep, uprearing
    Gray, as in my prime.

    At the inn
Smiling nigh, why is it
Not as on my visit
    When hope and I were twin ?

    Groom and jade
Whom I found here, moulder ;
Strange the tavern-holder,
    Strange the tap-maid.

    Here I hired
Horse and man for bearing
Me on my wayfaring
    To the door desired.

    Evening gloomed
As I journeyed forward
To the faces shoreward,
    Till their dwelling loomed.

    If again
Towards the Atlantic sea there
I should speed, they'd be there
    Surely now as then ? . . .

Why waste thought,
When I know them vanished
Under earth ; yea, banished
Ever into nought !

WHERE THE PICNIC WAS

WHERE we made the fire
In the summer time
Of branch and briar
On the hill to the sea,
I slowly climb
Through winter mire,
And scan and trace
The forsaken place
Quite readily.

Now a cold wind blows,
And the grass is gray,
But the spot still shows
As a burnt circle—aye,
And stick-ends, charred,
Still strew the sward
Whereon I stand,
Last relic of the band
Who came that day !

Yes, I am here
Just as last year,
And the sea breathes brine
From its strange straight line
Up hither, the same
As when we four came.
—But two have wandered far
From this grassy rise
Into urban roar
Where no picnics are,
And one—has shut her eyes
For evermore.

MISCELLANEOUS PIECES

THE WISTFUL LADY

"LOVE, while you were away there came to me—
    From whence I cannot tell—
A plaintive lady pale and passionless,
Who laid her eyes upon me critically,
And weighed me with a wearing wistfulness,
    As if she knew me well."

"I saw no lady of that wistful sort
    As I came riding home.
Perhaps she was some dame the Fates constrain
By memories sadder than she can support,
Or by unhappy vacancy of brain,
    To leave her roof and roam?"

"Ah, but she knew me.   And before this time
    I have seen her, lending ear
To my light outdoor words, and pondering each,
Her frail white finger swayed in pantomime,
As if she fain would close with me in speech,
    And yet would not come near.

"And once I saw her beckoning with her hand
    As I came into sight
At an upper window.   And I at last went out;
But when I reached where she had seemed to stand,
And wandered up and down and searched about,
    I found she had vanished quite."

337

Then thought I how my dead Love used to say,
 With a small smile, when she
Was waning wan, that she would hover round
And show herself after her passing day
To any newer Love I might have found,
 But show her not to me.

THE WOMAN IN THE RYE

" Why do you stand in the dripping rye,
Cold-lipped, unconscious, wet to the knee,
When there are firesides near ? " said I.
" I told him I wished him dead," said she.

" Yea, cried it in my haste to one
Whom I had loved, whom I well loved still ;
And die he did.   And I hate the sun,
And stand here lonely, aching, chill ;

" Stand waiting, waiting under skies
That blow reproach, the while I see
The rooks sheer off to where he lies
Wrapt in a peace withheld from me ! "

THE CHEVAL-GLASS

Why do you harbour that great cheval-glass
 Filling up your narrow room ?
 You never preen or plume
Or look in a week at your full-length figure—
 Picture of bachelor gloom !

" Well, when I dwelt in ancient England,
 Renting the valley farm,
 Thoughtless of all heart-harm,
I used to gaze at the parson's daughter,
 A creature of nameless charm.

" Thither there came a lover and won her
 Carried her off from my view.

O it was then I knew
Misery of a cast undreamt of—
    More than, indeed, my due!

" Then far rumours of her ill-usage
        Came, like a chilling breath
        When a man languisheth ;
Followed by news that her mind lost balance,
        And, in a space, of her death.

" Soon sank her father ; and next was the auction—
        Everything to be sold :
        Mid things new and old
Stood this glass in her former chamber,
        Long in her use, I was told.

" Well, I awaited the sale and bought it. . . .
        There by my bed it stands,
        And as the dawn expands
Often I see her pale-faced form there
        Brushing her hair's bright bands.

" There, too, at pallid midnight moments
        Quick she will come to my call,
        Smile from the frame withal
Ponderingly, as she used to regard me
        Passing her father's wall.

" So that it was for its revelations
        I brought it oversea,
        And drag it about with me. . . .
Anon I shall break it and bury its fragments
        Where my grave is to be."

THE RE-ENACTMENT

BETWEEN the folding sea-downs,
        In the gloom
    Of a wailful wintry nightfall,
        When the boom
Of the ocean, like a hammering in a hollow tomb,

Throbbed up the copse-clothed valley
　　From the shore
To the chamber where I darkled,
　　Sunk and sore
With gray ponderings why my Loved one had not come before

To salute me in the dwelling
　　That of late
I had hired to waste a while in—
　　Dim of date,
Quaint, and remote—wherein I now expectant sate;

On the solitude, unsignalled,
　　Broke a man
Who, in air as if at home there,
　　Seemed to scan
Every fire-flecked nook of the apartment span by span.

A stranger's and no lover's
　　Eyes were these,
Eyes of a man who measures
　　What he sees
But vaguely, as if wrapt in filmy phantasies.

Yea, his bearing was so absent
　　As he stood,
It bespoke a chord so plaintive
　　In his mood,
That soon I judged he would not wrong my quietude.

"Ah—the supper is just ready!"
　　Then he said,
"And the years'-long-binned Madeira
　　Flashes red!"
(There was no wine, no food, no supper-table spread.)

"You will forgive my coming,
　　Lady fair?
I see you as at that time
　　Rising there,
The self-same curious querying in your eyes and air.

Yet no.   How so?   You wear not
        The same gown,
Your locks show woful difference,
        Are not brown :
What, is it not as when I hither came from town ?

"And the place. . . .   But you seem other—
        Can it be ?
What's this that Time is doing
        Unto me ?
You dwell here, unknown woman ? . . . Whereabouts, then,
        is she ?

"And the house-things are much shifted.—
        Put them where
They stood on this night's fellow ;
        Shift her chair :
Here was the couch : and the piano should be there."

I indulged him, verily nerve-strained
        Being alone,
And I moved the things as bidden,
        One by one,
And feigned to push the old piano where he had shown.

"Aha—now I can see her !
        Stand aside :
Don't thrust her from the table
        Where, meek-eyed,
She makes attempt with matron-manners to preside.

"She serves me : now she rises,
        Goes to ·play. . . .
But you obstruct her, fill her
        With dismay,
And all-embarrassed, scared, she vanishes away !"

And, as 'twere useless longer
        To persist,
He sighed, and sought the entry
        Ere I wist,
And retreated, disappearing soundless in the mist.

That here some mighty passion
    Once had burned,
Which still the walls enghosted,
    I discerned,
And that by its strong spell mine might be overturned.

I sat depressed ; till, later,
    My Love came ;
But something in the chamber
    Dimmed our flame,—
An emanation, making our due words fall tame,

As if the intenser drama
    Shown me there
Of what the walls had witnessed
    Filled the air,
And left no room for later passion anywhere.

So came it that our fervours
    Did quite fail
Of future consummation—
    Being made quail
By the weird witchery of the parlour's hidden tale,

Which I, as years passed, faintly
    Learnt to trace,—
One of sad love, born full-winged
    In that place
Where the predestined sorrowers first stood face to face.

And as that month of winter
    Circles round,
And the evening of the date-day
    Grows embrowned,
I am conscious of those presences, and sit spellbound.

There, often—lone, forsaken—
    Queries breed
Within me ; whether a phantom
    Had my heed
On that strange night, or was it some wrecked heart indeed ?

HER SECRET

THAT love's dull smart distressed my heart
    He shrewdly learnt to see,
But that I was in love with a dead man
    Never suspected he.

He searched for the trace of a pictured face,
    He watched each missive come,
And a sheet that seemed like a love-line
    Wrought his look lurid and numb.

He dogged my feet to the city street,
    He followed me to the sea,
But not to the nigh, still churchyard
    Did he dream of following me !

"SHE CHARGED ME"

SHE charged me with having said this and that
To another woman long years before,
In the very parlour where we sat,—

Sat on a night when the endless pour
Of rain on the roof and the road below
Bent the spring of the spirit more and more. . . .

—So charged she me ; and the Cupid's bow
Of her mouth was hard, and her eyes, and her face,
And her white forefinger lifted slow.

Had she done it gently, or shown a trace
That not too curiously would she view
A folly flown ere her reign had place,

A kiss might have closed it.   But I knew
From the fall of each word, and the pause between,
That the curtain would drop upon us two
Ere long, in our play of slave and queen.

THE NEWCOMER'S WIFE

HE paused on the sill of a door ajar
That screened a lively liquor-bar,
For the name had reached him through the door
Of her he had married the week before.

"We called her the Hack of the Parade;
But she was discreet in the games she played;
If slightly worn, she's pretty yet,
And gossips, after all, forget:

"And he knows nothing of her past;
I am glad the girl's in luck at last;
Such ones, though stale to native eyes,
Newcomers snatch at as a prize."

"Yes, being a stranger he sees her blent
Of all that's fresh and innocent,
Nor dreams how many a love-campaign
She had enjoyed before his reign!"

That night there was the splash of a fall
Over the slimy harbour-wall:
They searched, and at the deepest place
Found him with crabs upon his face.

A CONVERSATION AT DAWN

HE lay awake, with a harassed air,
And she, in her cloud of loose lank hair,
        Seemed trouble-tried
As the dawn drew in on their faces there.

The chamber looked far over the sea
From a white hotel on a white-stoned quay,
        And stepping a stride
He parted the window-drapery.

Above the level horizon spread
The sunrise, firing them foot to head
    From its smouldering lair,
And painting their pillows with dyes of red.

"What strange disquiets have stirred you, dear,
This dragging night, with starts in fear
    Of me, as it were,
Or of something evil hovering near?"

"My husband, can I have fear of you?
What should one fear from a man whom few,
    Or none, had matched
In that late long spell of delays undue!"

He watched her eyes in the heaving sun:
"Then what has kept, O reticent one,
    Those lids unlatched—
Anything promised I've not yet done?"

"O it's not a broken promise of yours
(For what quite lightly your lip assures
    The due time brings)
That has troubled my sleep, and no waking cures!" . .

"I have shaped my will; 'tis at hand," said he;
"I subscribe it to-day, that no risk there be
    In the hap of things
Of my leaving you menaced by poverty."

"That a boon provision I'm safe to get,
Signed, sealed by my lord as it were a debt,
    I cannot doubt,
Or ever this peering sun be set."

"But you flung my arms away from your side,
And faced the wall. No month-old bride
    Ere the tour be out
In an air so loth can be justified?

"Ah—had you a male friend once loved well,
Upon whose suit disaster fell
    And frustrance swift?
Honest you are, and may care to tell."

She lay impassive, and nothing broke
The stillness other than, stroke by stroke,
  The lazy lift
Of the tide below them ; till she spoke :

" I once had a friend—a Love, if you will—
Whose wife forsook him, and sank until
  She was made a thrall
In a prison-cell for a deed of ill. . . .

" He remained alone ; and we met—to love,
But barring legitimate joy thereof
  Stood a doorless wall,
Though we prized each other all else above.

" And this was why, though I'd touched my prime,
I put off suitors from time to time—
  Yourself with the rest—
Till friends, who approved you, called it crime,

" And when misgivings weighed on me
In my lover's absence, hurriedly,
  And much distrest,
I took you. . . . Ah, that such could be ! . . .

" Now, saw you when crossing from yonder shore
At yesternoon, that the packet bore
  On a white-wreathed bier
A coffined body towards the fore ?

" Well, while you stood at the other end,
The loungers talked, and I couldn't but lend
  A listening ear,
For they named the dead.   'Twas the wife of my friend.

" He was there, but did not note me, veiled,
Yet I saw that a joy, as of one unjailed,
  Now shone in his gaze ;
He knew not his hope of me just had failed !

" They had brought her home : she was born in this isle ;
And he will return to his domicile,
  And pass his days
Alone, and not as he dreamt erstwhile ! "

" —So you've lost a sprucer spouse than I !"
She held her peace, as if fain deny
        She would indeed
For his pleasure's sake, but could lip no lie.

" One far less formal and plain and slow !"
She let the laconic assertion go
        As if of need
She held the conviction that it was so.

" Regard me as his he always should,
He had said, and wed me he vowed he would
        In his prime or sere
Most verily do, if ever he could ;

" And this fulfilment is now his aim,
For a letter, addressed in my maiden name,
        Has dogged me here,
Reminding me faithfully of his claim ;

" And it started a hope like a lightning-streak
That I might go to him—say for a week—
        And afford you right
To put me away, and your vows unspeak.

" To be sure you have said, as of dim intent,
That marriage is a plain event
        Of black and white,
Without any ghost of sentiment,

" And my heart has quailed.—But deny it true
That you will never this lock undo !
        No God intends
To thwart the yearning He's father to !"

The husband hemmed, then blandly bowed
In the light of the angry morning cloud.
        " So my idyll ends,
And a drama opens !" he mused aloud ;

And his features froze.   " You may take it as true
That I will never this lock undo
        For so depraved
A passion as that which kindles you !"

Said she : " I am sorry you see it so ;
I had hoped you might have let me go,
      And thus been saved
The pain of learning there's more to know."

" More ? What may that be ? Gad, I think
You have told me enough to make me blink !
      Yet if more remain
Then own it to me. I will not shrink ! "

" Well, it is this. As we could not see
That a legal marriage would ever be,
      To end our pain
We united ourselves informally ;

" And vowed at a chancel-altar nigh,
With book and ring, a lifelong tie ;
      A contract vain
To the world, but real to Him on High."

" And you became as his wife ? "—" I did."—
He stood as stiff as a caryatid,
      And said, " Indeed ! . . .
No matter. You're mine, whatever you've hid ! "

" But is it right ! When I only gave
My hand to you in a sweat to save,
      Through desperate need
(As I thought), my fame, for I was not brave ! "

" To save your fame ? Your meaning is dim,
For nobody knew of your altar-whim ? "
      " I mean—I feared
There might be fruit of my tie with him ;

" And to cloak it by marriage I'm not the first,
Though, maybe, morally most accurst
      Through your unpeered
And strict uprightness. That's the worst !

" While yesterday his worn contours
Convinced me that love like his endures,
      And that my troth-plight
Had been his, in fact, and not truly yours."

" So, my lady, you raise the veil by degrees. . . .
I own this last is enough to freeze
    The warmest wight !
Now hear the other side, if you please :

" I did say once, though without intent,
That marriage is a plain event
    Of black and white,
Whatever may be its sentiment :

" I'll act accordingly, none the less
That you soiled the contract in time of stress,
    Thereto induced
By the feared results of your wantonness.

" But the thing is over, and no one knows,
And it's nought to the future what you disclose.
    That you'll be loosed
For such an episode, don't suppose !

" No : I'll not free you.   And if it appear
There was too good ground for your first fear
    From your amorous tricks,
I'll father the child.   Yes, by God, my dear !

" Even should you fly to his arms, I'll damn
Opinion, and fetch you ; treat as sham
    Your mutinous kicks,
And whip you home.   That's the sort I am !"

She whitened.   " Enough. . . . Since you disapprove
I'll yield in silence, and never move
    Till my last pulse ticks
A footstep from the domestic groove."

" Then swear it," he said, " and your king uncrown."
He drew her forth in her long white gown,
    And she knelt and swore.
" Good.   Now you may go and again lie down.

" Since you've played these pranks and given no sign,
You shall crave this man of yours ; pine and pine
    With sighings sore,
Till I've starved your love for him ; nailed you mine !

" I'm a practical man, and want no tears ;
You've made a fool of me, it appears ;
      That you don't again
Is a lesson I'll teach you in future years."

She answered not, lying listlessly
With her dark dry eyes on the coppery sea,
      That now and then
Flung its lazy flounce at the neighbouring quay.

    1910.

A KING'S SOLILOQUY

ON THE NIGHT OF HIS FUNERAL

FROM the slow march and muffled drum,
      And crowds distrest,
And book and bell, at length I have come
      To my full rest.

A ten years' rule beneath the sun
      Is wound up here,
And what I have done, what left undone,
      Figures out clear.

Yet in the estimate of such
      It grieves me more
That I by some was loved so much
      Than that I bore,

From others, judgment of that hue
      Which over-hope
Breeds from a theoretic view
      Of regal scope.

For kingly opportunities
      Right many have sighed ;
How best to bear its devilries
      Those learn who have tried !

I have eaten the fat and drunk the sweet,
      Lived the life out

From the first greeting glad drum-beat
    To the last shout.

What pleasure earth affords to kings
    I have enjoyed
Through its long vivid pulse-stirrings
    Even till it cloyed.

What days of drudgery, nights of stress
    Can cark a throne,
Even one maintained in peacefulness,
    I too have known.

And so, I think, could I step back
    To life again,
I should prefer the average track
    Of average men,

Since, as with them, what kingship would
    It cannot do,
Nor to first thoughts however good
    Hold itself true.

Something binds hard the royal hand,
    As all that be,
And it is That has shaped, has planned
    My acts and me.

May 1910.

THE CORONATION

At Westminster, hid from the light of day,
Many who once had shone as monarchs lay.

Edward the Pious, and two Edwards more,
The second Richard, Henrys three or four ;

That is to say, those who were called the Third,
Fifth, Seventh, and Eighth (the much self-widowered) ;

And James the Scot, and near him Charles the Second,
And, too, the second George could there be reckoned.

Of women, Mary and Queen Elizabeth,
And Anne, all silent in a musing death ;

And William's Mary, and Mary, Queen of Scots,
And consort-queens whose names oblivion blots ;

And several more whose chronicle one sees
Adorning ancient royal pedigrees.

—Now, as they drowsed on, freed from Life's old thrall,
And heedless, save of things exceptional,

Said one : " What means this throbbing thudding sound
That reaches to us here from overground ;

" A sound of chisels, augers, planes, and saws,
Infringing all ecclesiastic laws ?

" And these tons-weight of timber on us pressed,
Unfelt here since we entered into rest ?

" Surely, at least to us, being corpses royal,
A meet repose is owing by the loyal ?"

"—Perhaps a scaffold !" Mary Stuart sighed,
" If such still be.   It was that way I died."

—"Ods !   Far more like," said he the many-wived,
" That for a wedding 'tis this work's contrived.

" Ha-ha ! I never would bow down to Rimmon,
But I had a rare time with those six women !"

" Not all at once ?" gasped he who loved confession.
" Nay, nay !" said Hal.   " That would have been transgression."

"—They build a catafalque here, black and tall,
Perhaps," mused Richard, "for some funeral ?"

And Anne chimed in : " Ah, yes : it may be so !"
" Nay !" squeaked Eliza.   " Little you seem to know—

" Clearly 'tis for some crowning here in state,
As they crowned us at our long bygone date ;

" Though we'd no such a power of carpentry,
But let the ancient architecture be ;

"If I were up there where the parsons sit,
In one of my gold robes, I'd see to it!"

"But you are not," Charles chuckled.   "You are here,
And never will know the sun again, my dear!"

"Yea," whispered those whom no one had addressed;
"With slow, sad march, amid a folk distressed,
We were brought here, to take our dusty rest.

"And here, alas, in darkness laid below,
We'll wait and listen, and endure the show. . . .
Clamour dogs kingship; afterwards not so!"

    1911.

AQUAE SULIS

THE chimes called midnight, just at interlune,
And the daytime parle on the Roman investigations
Was shut to silence, save for the husky tune
The bubbling waters played near the excavations.

And a warm air came up from underground,
And a flutter, as of a filmy shape unsepulchred,
That collected itself, and waited, and looked around:
Nothing was seen, but utterances could be heard:

Those of the Goddess whose shrine was beneath the pile
Of the God with the baldachined altar overhead:
"And what did you win by raising this nave and aisle
Close on the site of the temple I tenanted?

"The notes of your organ have thrilled down out of view
To the earth-clogged wrecks of my edifice many a year,
Though stately and shining once—ay, long ere you
Had set up crucifix and candle here.

"Your priests have trampled the dust of mine without rueing,
Despising the joys of man whom I so much loved,
Though my springs boil on by your Gothic arcades and pewing,
And sculptures crude. . . . Would Jove they could be removed!"

"Repress, O lady proud, your traditional ires;
You know not by what a frail thread we equally hang;

It is said we are images both—twitched by people's desires ;
And that I, as you, fail like a song men yesterday sang ! "

" What—a Jumping-jack you, and myself but a poor Jumping-jill,
Now worm-eaten, times agone twitched at Humanity's bid ?
O I cannot endure it !—But, chance to us whatso there will,
Let us kiss and be friends !   Come, agree you ? "—None heard if
    he did. . . .

And the olden dark hid the cavities late laid bare,
And all was suspended and soundless as before,
Except for a gossamery noise fading off in the air,
And the boiling voice of the waters' medicinal pour.

BATH.

SEVENTY-FOUR AND TWENTY

HERE goes a man of seventy-four,
Who sees not what life means for him,
And here another in years a score
Who reads its very figure and trim.

The one who shall walk to-day with me
Is not the youth who gazes far,
But the breezy sire who cannot see
What Earth's ingrained conditions are.

THE ELOPEMENT

" A WOMAN never agreed to it ! " said my knowing friend to me.
" That one thing she'd refuse to do for Solomon's mines in fee :
No woman ever will make herself look older than she is."
I did not answer ; but I thought, " you err there, ancient Quiz."

It took a rare one, true, to do it ; for she was surely rare—
As rare a soul at that sweet time of her life as she was fair,
And urging heart-heaves, too, were strong, for ours was a passionate
    case,
Yea, passionate enough to lead to freaking with that young face.

I have told no one about it, should perhaps make few believe,
But I think it over now that life looms dull and years bereave,
How blank we stood at our bright wits' end, two blown barks in
  distress,
How self-regard in her was slain by her large tenderness.

I said : "The only chance for us in a crisis of this kind
Is going it thorough !"—"Yes," she calmly breathed.   "Well,
  I don't mind."
And we blanched her dark locks ruthlessly : set wrinkles on her
  brow ;
Ay—she was a right rare woman then, whatever she may be now.

That night we heard a coach drive up, and questions asked
  below.
"A gent with an elderly wife, sir," was returned from the bureau.
And the wheels went rattling on, and free at last from public ken
We washed all off in her chamber and restored her youth again.

How many years ago it was !   Some fifty can it be
Since that adventure held us, and she played old wife to me ?
But in time convention won her, as it wins all women at last,
And now she is rich and respectable, and time has buried the
  past.

"I ROSE UP AS MY CUSTOM IS"

I ROSE up as my custom is
    On the eve of All-Souls' day,
And left my grave for an hour or so
To call on those I used to know
    Before I passed away.

I visited my former Love
    As she lay by her husband's side ;
I asked her if life pleased her, now
She was rid of a poet wrung in brow,
    And crazed with the ills he eyed ;

Who used to drag her here and there
    Wherever his fancies led,
And point out pale phantasmal things,

And talk of vain vague purposings
    That she discredited.

She was quite civil, and replied,
    "Old comrade, is that you?
Well, on the whole, I like my life.—
I know I swore I'd be no wife,
    But what was I to do?

"You see, of all men for my sex
    A poet is the worst;
Women are practical, and they
Crave the wherewith to pay their way,
    And slake their social thirst.

"You were a poet—quite the ideal
    That we all love awhile:
But look at this man snoring here—
He's no romantic chanticleer,
    Yet keeps me in good style.

"He makes no quest into my thoughts,
    But a poet wants to know
What one has felt from earliest days,
Why one thought not in other ways,
    And one's Loves of long ago."

Her words benumbed my fond faint ghost;
    The nightmares neighed from their stalls,
The vampires screeched, the harpies flew,
And under the dim dawn I withdrew
    To Death's inviolate halls.

A WEEK

ON Monday night I closed my door,
And thought you were not as heretofore,
And little cared if we met no more.

I seemed on Tuesday night to trace
Something beyond mere commonplace
In your ideas, and heart, and face.

On Wednesday I did not opine
Your life would ever be one with mine,
Though if it were we should well combine.

On Thursday noon I liked you well,
And fondly felt that we must dwell
Not far apart, whatever befell.

On Friday it was with a thrill
In gazing towards your distant vill
I owned you were my dear one still.

I saw you wholly to my mind
On Saturday—even one who shrined
All that was best of womankind.

As wing-clipt sea-gull for the sea
On Sunday night I longed for thee,
Without whom life were waste to me!

HAD YOU WEPT

HAD you wept; had you but neared me with a hazed uncertain ray,
Dewy as the face of the dawn, in your large and luminous eye,
Then would have come back all the joys the tidings had slain that
    day,
And a new beginning, a fresh fair heaven, have smoothed the
    things awry.

But you were less feebly human, and no passionate need for
    clinging
Possessed your soul to overthrow reserve when I came near;
Ay, though you suffer as much as I from storms the hours are
    bringing
Upon your heart and mine, I never see you shed a tear.

The deep strong woman is weakest, the weak one is the strong;
The weapon of all weapons best for winning, you have not used;
Have you never been able, or would you not, through the evil
    times and long?
Has not the gift been given you, or such gift have you refused?

When I bade me not absolve you on that evening or the morrow,
Why did you not make war on me with those who weep like rain?
You felt too much, so gained no balm for all your torrid sorrow,
And hence our deep division, and our dark undying pain.

BEREFT, SHE THINKS SHE DREAMS

I DREAM that the dearest I ever knew
    Has died and been entombed.
I am sure it's a dream that cannot be true,
    But I am so overgloomed
By its persistence, that I would gladly
    Have quick death take me,
Rather than longer think thus sadly;
    So wake me, wake me!

It has lasted days, but minute and hour
    I expect to get aroused
And find him as usual in the bower
    Where we so happily housed.
Yet stays this nightmare too appalling,
    And like a web shakes me,
And piteously I keep on calling,
    And no one wakes me!

IN THE BRITISH MUSEUM

"WHAT do you see in that time-touched stone,
    When nothing is there
But ashen blankness, although you give it
    A rigid stare?

"You look not quite as if you saw,
    But as if you heard,
Parting your lips, and treading softly
    As mouse or bird.

"It is only the base of a pillar, they'll tell you,
    That came to us

From a far old hill men used to name
    Areopagus."

—" I know no art, and I only view
    A stone from a wall,
But I am thinking that stone has echoed
    The voice of Paul,

" Paul as he stood and preached beside it
    Facing the crowd,
A small gaunt figure with wasted features,
    Calling out loud

" Words that in all their intimate accents
    Pattered upon
That marble front, and were wide reflected,
    And then were gone.

" I'm a labouring man, and know but little,
    Or nothing at all ;
But I can't help thinking that stone once echoed
    The voice of Paul."

IN THE SERVANTS' QUARTERS

' MAN, you too, aren't you, one of these rough followers of the
    criminal ?
All hanging hereabout to gather how he's going to bear
Examination in the hall."   She flung disdainful glances on
The shabby figure standing at the fire with others there,
    Who warmed them by its flare.

' No indeed, my skipping maiden : I know nothing of the trial
    here,
Or criminal, if so he be.—I chanced to come this way,
And the fire shone out into the dawn, and morning airs are cold
    now ;
I, too, was drawn in part by charms I see before me play,
    That I see not every day."

"Ha, ha!" then laughed the constables who also stood to warm
  themselves,
The while another maiden scrutinized his features hard,
As the blaze threw into contrast every line and knot that wrinkled
  them,
Exclaiming, "Why, last night when he was brought in by the
  guard,
   You were with him in the yard!"

"Nay, nay, you teasing wench, I say! You know you speak
  mistakenly.
Cannot a tired pedestrian who has legged it long and far
Here on his way from northern parts, engrossed in humble
  marketings,
Come in and rest awhile, although judicial doings are
   Afoot by morning star?"

"O, come, come!" laughed the constables. "Why, man, you
  speak the dialect
He uses in his answers; you can hear him up the stairs.
So own it. We sha'n't hurt ye. There he's speaking now
  His syllables
Are those you sound yourself when you are talking unawares,
   As this pretty girl declares."

"And you shudder when his chain clinks!" she rejoined. "O
  yes, I noticed it.
And you winced, too, when those cuffs they gave him echoed to
  us here.
They'll soon be coming down, and you may then have to defend
  yourself
Unless you hold your tongue, or go away and keep you clear
   When he's led to judgment near!"

"No! I'll be damned in hell if I know anything about the man!
No single thing about him more than everybody knows!
Must not I even warm my hands but I am charged with
  blasphemies?" . . .
—His face convulses as the morning cock that moment crows,
   And he droops, and turns, and goes.

THE OBLITERATE TOMB

" MORE than half my life long
Did they weigh me falsely, to my bitter wrong,
But they all have shrunk away into the silence
    Like a lost song.

" And the day has dawned and come
For forgiveness, when the past may hold it dumb
On the once reverberate words of hatred uttered
    Half in delirium. . . .

" With folded lips and hands
They lie and wait what next the Will commands,
And doubtless think, if think they can : ' Let discord
    Sink with Life's sands !'

" By these late years their names,
Their virtues, their hereditary claims,
May be as near defacement at their grave-place
    As are their fames."

—Such thoughts bechanced to seize
A traveller's mind—a man of memories—
As he set foot within the western city
    Where had died these

Who in their lifetime deemed
Him their chief enemy—one whose brain had schemed
To get their dingy greatness deeplier dingied
    And disesteemed.

So, sojourning in their town,
He mused on them and on their once renown,
And said, " I'll seek their resting-place to-morrow
    Ere I lie down,

" And end, lest I forget,
Those ires of many years that I regret,
Renew their names, that men may see some liegeness
    Is left them yet."

Duly next night he went
And sought the church he had known them to frequent,
And wandered, lantern-bearing, in the precincts,
    Where they lay pent,

Till by remembrance led
He stood at length beside their slighted bed.
Above which, truly, scarce a line or letter
    Could now be read.

"Thus years obliterate
Their graven worth, their chronicle, their date!
At once I'll garnish and revive the record
    Of their past state,

"That still the sage may say
In pensive progress here where they decay,
'This stone records a luminous line whose talents
    Told in their day.'"

While dreaming thus he turned,
For a form shadowed where they lay inurned,
And he beheld a stranger in foreign vesture,
    And tropic-burned.

"Sir, I am right pleased to view
That ancestors of mine should interest you,
For I have fared of purpose here to find them. . . .
    They are time-worn, true,

"But that's a fault, at most,
Carvers can cure. On the Pacific coast
I have vowed for long that relics of my forbears
    I'd trace ere lost,

"And hitherward I come,
Before this same old Time shall strike me numb,
To carry it out."—"Strange, this is!" said the other;
    "What mind shall plumb

"Coincident design!
Though these my father's enemies were and mine,
I nourished a like purpose—to restore them
    Each letter and line."

" Such magnanimity
Is now not needed, sir ; for you will see
That since I am here, a thing like this is, plainly,
        Best done by me."

    The other bowed, and left,
Crestfallen in sentiment, as one bereft
Of some fair object he had been moved to cherish,
        By hands more deft.

    And as he slept that night
The phantoms of the ensepulchred stood upright
Before him, trembling that he had set him seeking
        Their charnel-site.

    And, as unknowing his ruth,
Asked as with terrors founded not on truth
Why he should want them. " Ha," they hollowly hackered,
        " You come, forsooth,

    " By stealth to obliterate
Our graven worth, our chronicle, our date,
That our descendant may not gild the record
        Of our past state,

    " And that no sage may say
In pensive progress near where we decay :
' This stone records a luminous line whose talents
        Told in their day.' "

    Upon the morrow he went,
And to that town and churchyard never bent
His ageing footsteps till, some twelvemonths onward,
        An accident

    Once more detained him there ;
And, stirred by hauntings, he must needs repair
To where the tomb was.   Lo, it stood still wasting
        In no man's care.

    And so the tomb remained
Untouched, untended, crumbling, weather-stained,
And though the one-time foe was fain to right it
        He still refrained.

" I'll set about it when
I am sure he'll come no more.   Best wait till then."
But so it was that never the kinsman entered
        That city again.

Till doubts grew keen
If it had chanced not that the figure seen
Shaped but in dream on that dim doubtful midnight :
        Such things had been. . . .

So, the well-meaner died
While waiting tremulously unsatisfied
That no return of the family's foreign scion
        Would still betide.

And many years slid by,
And active church-restorers cast their eye
Upon the ancient garth and hoary building
        The tomb stood nigh.

And when they had scraped each wall,
Pulled out the stately pews, and smartened all,
" It will be well," declared the spruce church-warden,
        " To overhaul

" And broaden this path where shown ;
Nothing prevents it but an old tombstone
Pertaining to a family forgotten,
        Of deeds unknown.

" Their names can scarce be read,
Depend on't, all who care for them are dead."
So went the tomb, whose shards were as path-paving
        Distributed.

Over it and about
Men's footsteps beat, and wind and waterspout,
Until the names, aforetime gnawed by weathers,
        Were quite worn out.

So that no sage can say
In pensive progress near where they decay,
" This stone records a luminous line whose talents
        Told in their day."

"REGRET NOT ME"

REGRET not me ;
Beneath the sunny tree
I lie uncaring, slumbering peacefully.

Swift as the light
I flew my faery flight ;
Ecstatically I moved, and feared no night.

I did not know
That heydays fade and go,
But deemed that what was would be always so.

I skipped at morn
Between the yellowing corn,
Thinking it good and glorious to be born.

I ran at eves
Among the piled-up sheaves,
Dreaming, "I grieve not, therefore nothing grieves."

Now soon will come
The apple, pear, and plum,
And hinds will sing, and autumn insects hum.

Again you will fare
To cider-makings rare,
And junketings ; but I shall not be there.

Yet gaily sing
Until the pewter ring
Those songs we sang when we went gipsying.

And lightly dance
Some triple-timed romance
In coupled figures, and forget mischance ;

And mourn not me
Beneath the yellowing tree ;
For I shall mind not, slumbering peacefully.

THE RECALCITRANTS

LET us off and search, and find a place
Where yours and mine can be natural lives,
Where no one comes who dissects and dives
And proclaims that ours is a curious case,
Which its touch of romance can scarcely grace

You would think it strange at first, but then
Everything has been strange in its time.
When some one said on a day of the prime
He would bow to no brazen god again
He doubtless dazed the mass of men.

None will see in us a pair whose claims
To righteous judgment we care not making ;
Who have doubted if breath be worth the taking,
And have no respect for the current fames
Whence the savour has flown while abide the names.

We have found us already shunned, disdained,
And for re-acceptance have not once striven ;
Whatever offence our course has given
The brunt thereof we have long sustained.
Well, let us away, scorned, unexplained.

STARLINGS ON THE ROOF

" No smoke spreads out of this chimney-pot,
The people who lived here have left the spot,
And others are coming who knew them not.

" If you listen anon, with an ear intent,
The voices, you'll find, will be different
From the well-known ones of those who went."

" Why did they go ? Their tones so bland
Were quite familiar to our band ;
The comers we shall not understand."

" They look for a new life, rich and strange ;
They do not know that, let them range
Wherever they may, they will get no change.

" They will drag their house-gear ever so far
In their search for a home no miseries mar ;
They will find that as they were they are,

" That every hearth has a ghost, alack,
And can be but the scene of a bivouac
Till they move their last—no care to pack ! "

THE MOON LOOKS IN

I

I have risen again,
And awhile survey
By my chilly ray
Through your window-pane
Your upturned face,
As you think, " Ah—she
Now dreams of me
In her distant place ! "

II

I pierce her blind
In her far-off home :
She fixes a comb,
And says in her mind,
" I start in an hour ;
Whom shall I meet ?
Won't the men be sweet,
And the women sour ! "

THE SWEET HUSSY

In his early days he was quite surprised
When she told him she was compromised
By meetings and lingerings at his whim,
And thinking not of herself but him ;
While she lifted orbs aggrieved and round
That scandal should so soon abound,
(As she had raised them to nine or ten
Of antecedent nice young men) :
And in remorse he thought with a sigh,
How good she is, and how bad am I !—
It was years before he understood
That she was the wicked one—he the good.

THE TELEGRAM

" O he's suffering—maybe dying—and I not there to aid,
And smooth his bed and whisper to him !   Can I nohow go ?
Only the nurse's brief twelve words thus hurriedly conveyed,
            As by stealth, to let me know.

" He was the best and brightest !—candour shone upon his bro'
And I shall never meet again a soldier such as he,
And I loved him ere I knew it, and perhaps he's sinking now,
            Far, far removed from me ! "

—The yachts ride mute at anchor and the fulling moon is fair,
And the giddy folk are strutting up and down the smooth parad'
And in her wild distraction she seems not to be aware
            That she lives no more a maid,

But has vowed and wived herself to one who blessed the grou'
            she trod
To and from his scene of ministry, and thought her history knov'
In its last particular to him—aye, almost as to God,
            And believed her quite his own.

So rapt her mind's far-off regard she droops as in a swoon,
And a movement of aversion mars her recent spousal grace,

And in silence we two sit here in our waning honeymoon
    At this idle watering-place. . . . .

What now I see before me is a long lane overhung
With lovelessness, and stretching from the present to the grave.
And I would I were away from this, with friends I knew when
       young,
    Ere a woman held me slave.

THE MOTH-SIGNAL

(*On Egdon Heath*)

"WHAT are you still, still thinking,"
    He asked in vague surmise,
"That you stare at the wick unblinking
    With those deep lost luminous eyes?"

"O, I see a poor moth burning
    In the candle flame," said she,
"Its wings and legs are turning
    To a cinder rapidly."

"Moths fly in from the heather,"
    He said, "now the days decline."
"I know," said she. "The weather,
    I hope, will at last be fine.

"I think," she added lightly,
    "I'll look out at the door.
The ring the moon wears nightly
    May be visible now no more."

She rose, and, little heeding,
    Her life-mate then went on
With his mute and museful reading
    In the annals of ages gone.

Outside the house a figure
    Came from the tumulus near,
And speedily waxed bigger,
    And clasped and called her Dear.

" I saw the pale-winged token
   You sent through the crack," sighed she.
" That moth is burnt and broken
   With which you lured out me.

" And were I as the moth is
   It might be better far
For one whose marriage troth is
   Shattered as potsherds are ! "

Then grinned the Ancient Briton
   From the tumulus treed with pine :
" So, hearts are thwartly smitten
   In these days as in mine ! "

SEEN BY THE WAITS

THROUGH snowy woods and shady
   We went to play a tune
To the lonely manor-lady
   By the light of the Christmas moon.

We violed till, upward glancing
   To where a mirror leaned,
It showed her airily dancing,
   Deeming her movements screened ;

Dancing alone in the room there,
   Thin-draped in her robe of night ;
Her postures, glassed in the gloom there,
   Were a strange phantasmal sight.

She had learnt (we heard when homing)
   That her roving spouse was dead :
Why she had danced in the gloaming
   We thought, but never said.

THE TWO SOLDIERS

JUST at the corner of the wall
    We met—yes, he and I—
Who had not faced in camp or hall
    Since we bade home good-bye,
And what once happened came back—all—
    Out of those years gone by.

And that strange woman whom we knew
    And loved—long dead and gone,
Whose poor half-perished residue,
    Tombless and trod, lay yon !
But at this moment to our view
    Rose like a phantom wan.

And in his fixed face I could see,
    Lit by a lurid shine,
The drama re-enact which she
    Had dyed incarnadine
For us, and more.   And doubtless he
    Beheld it too in mine.

A start, as at one slightly known ;
    And with an indifferent air
We passed, without a sign being shown
    That, as it real were,
A memory-acted scene had thrown
    Its tragic shadow there.

THE DEATH OF REGRET

I OPENED my shutter at sunrise,
    And looked at the hill hard by,
And I heartily grieved for the comrade
    Who wandered up there to die.

I let in the morn on the morrow,
    And failed not to think of him then,
As he trod up that rise in the twilight,
    And never came down again.

I undid the shutter a week thence,
    But not until after I'd turned
Did I call back his last departure
    By the upland there discerned.

Uncovering the casement long later,
    I bent to my toil till the gray,
When I said to myself, "Ah—what ails me,
    To forget him all the day!"

As daily I flung back the shutter
    In the same blank bald routine,
He scarcely once rose to remembrance
    Through a month of my facing the scene.

And ah, seldom now do I ponder
    At the window as heretofore
On the long valued one who died yonder,
    And wastes by the sycamore.

IN THE DAYS OF CRINOLINE

A PLAIN tilt-bonnet on her head
She took the path across the leaze.
—Her spouse the vicar, gardening, said,
"Too dowdy that, for coquetries,
    So I can hoe at ease."

But when she had passed into the heath,
And gained the wood beyond the flat,
She raised her skirts, and from beneath
Unpinned and drew as from a sheath
    An ostrich-feathered hat.

And where the hat had hung she now
Concealed and pinned the dowdy hood,
And set the hat upon her brow,
And thus emerging from the wood
    Tripped on in jaunty mood.

The sun was low and crimson-faced
As two came that way from the town,

And plunged into the wood untraced. . . .
When severally therefrom they paced
          The sun had quite gone down.

The hat and feather disappeared,
The dowdy hood again was donned,
And in the gloom the fair one neared
Her home and husband dour, who conned
          Calmly his blue-eyed blonde.

"To-day," he said, "you have shown good sense,
A dress so modest and so meek
Should always deck your goings hence
Alone."   And as a recompense
          He kissed her on the cheek.

THE ROMAN GRAVEMOUNDS

By Rome's dim relics there walks a man,
Eyes bent ; and he carries a basket and spade ;
I guess what impels him to scrape and scan ;
Yea, his dreams of that Empire long decayed.

"Vast was Rome," he must muse, "in the world's regard,
Vast it looms there still, vast it ever will be" ;
And he stoops as to dig and unmine some shard
Left by those who are held in such memory.

But no ; in his basket, see, he has brought
A little white furred thing, stiff of limb,
Whose life never won from the world a thought ;
It is this, and not Rome, that is moving him.

And to make it a grave he has come to the spot,
And he delves in the ancient dead's long home ;
Their fames, their achievements, the man knows not ;
The furred thing is all to him—nothing Rome !

"Here say you that Cæsar's warriors lie ?—
But my little white cat was my only friend !
Could she but live, might the record die
Of Cæsar, his legions, his aims, his end !"

Well, Rome's long rule here is oft and again
A theme for the sages of history,
And the small furred life was worth no one's pen;
Yet its mourner's mood has a charm for me.

November 1910.

THE WORKBOX

" SEE, here's the workbox, little wife,
    That I made of polished oak."
He was a joiner, of village life;
    She came of borough folk.

He holds the present up to her
    As with a smile she nears
And answers to the profferer,
    " 'Twill last all my sewing years!"

" I warrant it will. And longer too.
    'Tis a scantling that I got
Off poor John Wayward's coffin, who
    Died of they knew not what.

" The shingled pattern that seems to cease
    Against your box's rim
Continues right on in the piece
    That's underground with him.

" And while I worked it made me think
    Of timber's varied doom;
One inch where people eat and drink,
    The next inch in a tomb.

" But why do you look so white, my dear,
    And turn aside your face?
You knew not that good lad, I fear,
    Though he came from your native place?"

" How could I know that good young man,
    Though he came from my native town,
When he must have left far earlier than
    I was a woman grown?"

"Ah, no. I should have understood!
  It shocked you that I gave
To you one end of a piece of wood
  Whose other is in a grave?"

" Don't, dear, despise my intellect,
  Mere accidental things
Of that sort never have effect
  On my imaginings."

Yet still her lips were limp and wan,
  Her face still held aside,
As if she had known not only John,
  But known of what he died.

THE SACRILEGE

A BALLAD-TRAGEDY

(*Circa* 182-)

PART I

" I HAVE a Love I love too well
Where Dunkery frowns on Exon Moor;
I have a Love I love too well,
      To whom, ere she was mine,
' Such is my love for you,' I said,
' That you shall have to hood your head
A silken kerchief crimson-red,
      Wove finest of the fine.'

"And since this Love, for one mad moon,
On Exon Wild by Dunkery Tor,
Since this my Love for one mad moon
      Did clasp me as her king,
I snatched a silk-piece red and rare
From off a stall at Priddy Fair,
For handkerchief to hood her hair
      When we went gallanting.

" Full soon the four weeks neared their end
Where Dunkery frowns on Exon Moor;

And when the four weeks neared their end,
    And their swift sweets outwore,
I said, 'What shall I do to own
Those beauties bright as tulips blown,
And keep you here with me alone
    As mine for evermore?'

"And as she drowsed within my van
On Exon Wild by Dunkery Tor—
And as she drowsed within my van,
    And dawning turned to day,
She heavily raised her sloe-back eyes
And murmured back in softest wise,
'One more thing, and the charms you prize
    Are yours henceforth for aye.

"'And swear I will I'll never go
While Dunkery frowns on Exon Moor
To meet the Cornish Wrestler Joe
    For dance and dallyings.
If you'll to yon cathedral shrine,
And finger from the chest divine
Treasure to buy me ear-drops fine,
    And richly jewelled rings.'

"I said: 'I am one who has gathered gear
From Marlbury Downs to Dunkery Tor,
Who has gathered gear for many a year
    From mansion, mart and fair;
But at God's house I've stayed my hand,
Hearing within me some command—
Curbed by a law not of the land
    From doing damage there!'

"Whereat she pouts, this Love of mine,
As Dunkery pouts to Exon Moor,
And still she pouts, this Love of mine,
    So cityward I go.
But ere I start to do the thing,
And speed my soul's imperilling
For one who is my ravishing
    And all the joy I know,

" I come to lay this charge on thee—
On Exon Wild by Dunkery Tor—
I come to lay this charge on thee
          With solemn speech and sign :
Should things go ill, and my life pay
For botchery in this rash assay,
You are to take hers likewise—yea,
          The month the law takes mine.

" For should my rival, Wrestler Joe,
Where Dunkery frowns on Exon Moor—
My reckless rival, Wrestler Joe,
          My Love's bedwinner be,
My rafted spirit would not rest,
But wander weary and distrest
Throughout the world in wild protest :
          The thought nigh maddens me ! "

PART II

Thus did he speak—this brother of mine—
On Exon Wild by Dunkery Tor,
Born at my birth of mother of mine,
          And forthwith went his way
To dare the deed some coming night . . .
I kept the watch with shaking sight,
The moon at moments breaking bright,
          At others glooming gray.

For three full days I heard no sound
Where Dunkery frowns on Exon Moor,
I heard no sound at all around
          Whether his fay prevailed,
Or one more foul the master were,
Till some afoot did tidings bear
How that, for all his practised care,
          He had been caught and jailed.

They had heard a crash when twelve had chimed
By Mendip east of Dunkery Tor,
When twelve had chimed and moonlight climbed ;
          They watched, and he was tracked
By arch and aisle and saint and knight

Of sculptured stonework sheeted white
In the cathedral's ghostly light,
      And captured in the act.

Yes ; for this Love he loved too well
Where Dunkery sights the Severn shore,
All for this Love he loved too well
      He burst the holy bars,
Seized golden vessels from the chest
To buy her ornaments of the best,
At her ill-witchery's request
      And lure of eyes like stars. . . .

When blustering March confused the sky
In Toneborough Town by Exon Moor,
When blustering March confused the sky
      They stretched him ; and he died.
Down in the crowd where I, to see
The end of him, stood silently,
With a set face he lipped to me—
      " Remember." " Ay ! " I cried.

By night and day I shadowed her
From Toneborough Deane to Dunkery Tor,
I shadowed her asleep, astir,
      And yet I could not bear—
Till Wrestler Joe anon began
To figure as her chosen man,
And took her to his shining van—
      To doom a form so fair !

He made it handsome for her sake—
And Dunkery smiled to Exon Moor—
He made it handsome for her sake,
      Painting it out and in ;
And on the door of apple-green
A bright brass knocker soon was seen,
And window-curtains white and clean
      For her to sit within.

And all could see she clave to him
As cleaves a cloud to Dunkery Tor,
Yea, all could see she clave to him,
      And every day I said,

"A pity it seems to part those two
That hourly grow to love more true:
Yet she's the wanton woman who
          Sent one to swing till dead!"

That blew to blazing all my hate,
While Dunkery frowned on Exon Moor,
And when the river swelled, her fate
          Came to her pitilessly. . . .
I dogged her, crying: "Across that plank
They use as bridge to reach yon bank
A coat and hat lie limp and dank;
          Your goodman's, can they be?"

She paled, and went, I close behind—
And Exon frowned to Dunkery Tor,
She went, and I came up behind
          And tipped the plank that bore
Her, fleetly flitting across to eye
What such might bode.   She slid awry;
And from the current came a cry,
          A gurgle; and no more.

How that befell no mortal knew
From Marlbury Downs to Exon Moor;
No mortal knew that deed undue
          But he who schemed the crime,
Which night still covers. . . . But in dream
Those ropes of hair upon the stream
He sees, and he will hear that scream
          Until his judgment-time.

THE ABBEY MASON

INVENTOR OF THE "PERPENDICULAR" STYLE OF
GOTHIC ARCHITECTURE

(*With Memories of John Hicks, Architect*)

THE new-vamped Abbey shaped apace
In the fourteenth century of grace;

(The church which, at an after date,
Acquired cathedral rank and state.)

Panel and circumscribing wall
Of latest feature, trim and tall,

Rose roundabout the Norman core
In prouder pose than theretofore,

Encasing magically the old
With parpend ashlars manifold.

The trowels rang out, and tracery
Appeared where blanks had used to be.

Men toiled for pleasure more than pay,
And all went smoothly day by day,

Till, in due course, the transept part
Engrossed the master-mason's art.

—Home-coming thence he tossed and turned
Throughout the night till the new sun burned.

" What fearful visions have inspired
These gaingivings?" his wife inquired;

" As if your tools were in your hand
You have hammered, fitted, muttered, planned;

" You have thumped as you were working hard:
I might have found me bruised and scarred.

" What then's amiss? What eating care
Looms nigh, whereof I am unaware?"

He answered not, but churchward went,
Viewing his draughts with discontent;

And fumbled there the livelong day
Till, hollow-eyed, he came away.

—'Twas said, " The master-mason's ill!"
And all the abbey works stood still.

Quoth Abbot Wygmore: " Why, O why
Distress yourself? You'll surely die!"

The mason answered, trouble-torn,
" This long-vogued style is quite outworn!

"The upper archmould nohow serves
To meet the lower tracery curves:

"The ogees bend too far away
To give the flexures interplay.

"This it is causes my distress. . . .
So it will ever be unless

"New forms be found to supersede
The circle when occasions need.

"To carry it out I have tried and toiled,
And now perforce must own me foiled!

"Jeerers will say: 'Here was a man
Who could not end what he began!'"

—So passed that day, the next, the next;
The abbot scanned the task, perplexed;

The townsmen mustered all their wit
To fathom how to compass it,

But no raw artistries availed
Where practice in the craft had failed. . . .

—One night he tossed, all open-eyed,
And early left his helpmeet's side.

Scattering the rushes of the floor
He wandered from the chamber door

And sought the sizing pile, whereon
Struck dimly a cadaverous dawn

Through freezing rain, that drenched the board
Of diagram-lines he last had scored—

Chalked phantasies in vain begot
To knife the architectural knot—

In front of which he dully stood,
Regarding them in hopeless mood.

He closelier looked; then looked again:
The chalk-scratched draught-board faced the rain,

Whose icicled drops deformed the lines
Innumerous of his lame designs,

So that they streamed in small white threads
From the upper segments to the heads

Of arcs below, uniting them
Each by a stalactitic stem.

—At once, with eyes that struck out sparks,
He adds accessory cusping-marks,

Then laughs aloud.   The thing was done
So long assayed from sun to sun. . . .

—Now in his joy he grew aware
Of one behind him standing there,

And, turning, saw the abbot, who
The weather's whim was watching too.

Onward to Prime the abbot went,
Tacit upon the incident.

—Men now discerned as days revolved
The ogive riddle had been solved;

Templates were cut, fresh lines were chalked
Where lines had been defaced and balked,

And the work swelled and mounted higher,
Achievement distancing desire;

Here jambs with transoms fixed between,
Where never the like before had been—

There little mullions thinly sawn
Where meeting circles once were drawn.

"We knew," men said, "the thing would go
After his craft-wit got aglow,

"And, once fulfilled what he has designed,
We'll honour him and his great mind!"

When matters stood thus poised awhile,
And all surroundings shed a smile,

The master-mason on an eve
Homed to his wife and seemed to grieve. . . .

—"The abbot spoke to me to-day ;
He hangs about the works alway.

" He knows the source as well as I
Of the new style men magnify.

" He said : 'You pride yourself too much
On your creation.   Is it such ?

" ' Surely the hand of God it is
That conjured so, and only His !—

" ' Disclosing by the frost and rain
Forms your invention chased in vain ;

" ' Hence the devices deemed so great
You copied, and did not create.'

" I feel the abbot's words are just,
And that all thanks renounce I must.

" Can a man welcome praise and pelf
For hatching art that hatched itself ? . . .

" So, I shall own the deft design
Is Heaven's outshaping, and not mine."

" What !" said she.   " Praise your works ensure
To throw away, and quite obscure

" Your beaming and beneficent star ?
Better you leave things as they are !

" Why, think awhile.   Had not your zest
In your loved craft curtailed your rest—

" Had you not gone there ere the day
The sun had melted all away !"

—But, though his good wife argued so,
The mason let the people know

That not unaided sprang the thought
Whereby the glorious fane was wrought,

But that by frost when dawn was dim
The method was disclosed to him.

"Yet," said the townspeople thereat,
"'Tis your own doing, even with that!"

But he—chafed, childlike, in extremes—
The temperament of men of dreams—

Aloofly scrupled to admit
That he did aught but borrow it,

And diffidently made request
That with the abbot all should rest.

—As none could doubt the abbot's word,
Or question what the church averred,

The mason was at length believed
Of no more count than he conceived,

And soon began to lose the fame
That late had gathered round his name. . .

—Time passed, and like a living thing
The pile went on embodying,

And workmen died, and young ones grew,
And the old mason sank from view

And Abbots Wygmore and Staunton went
And Horton sped the embellishment.

But not till years had far progressed
Chanced it that, one day, much impressed,

Standing within the well-graced aisle,
He asked who first conceived the style;

And some decrepit sage detailed
How, when invention nought availed,

The cloud-cast waters in their whim
Came down, and gave the hint to him

Who struck each arc, and made each mould;
And how the abbot would not hold

As sole begetter him who applied
Forms the Almighty sent as guide;

And how the master lost renown,
And wore in death no artist's crown.

--Then Horton, who in inner thought
Had more perceptions than he taught,

Replied: "Nay; art can but transmute;
Invention is not absolute;

"Things fail to spring from nought at call,
And art-beginnings most of all.

"He did but what all artists do,
Wait upon Nature for his cue."

—"Had you been here to tell them so,
Lord Abbot, sixty years ago,

"The mason, now long underground,
Doubtless a different fate had found.

"He passed into oblivion dim,
And none knew what became of him!

"His name?   'Twas of some common kind
And now has faded out of mind."

The Abbot: "It shall not be hid!
I'll trace it." . . . . But he never did.

—When longer yet dank death had wormed
The brain wherein the style had germed

From Gloucester church it flew afar—
The style called Perpendicular.—

To Winton and to Westminster
It ranged, and grew still beautifuller:

From Solway Frith to Dover Strand
Its fascinations starred the land,

Not only on cathedral walls
But upon courts and castle halls,

Till every edifice in the isle
Was patterned to no other style,

And till, long having played its part
The curtain fell on Gothic art.

—Well: when in Wessex on your rounds,
Take a brief step beyond its bounds,

And enter Gloucester: seek the quoin
Where choir and transept interjoin,

And, gazing at the forms there flung
Against the sky by one unsung—

The ogee arches transom-topped,
The tracery-stalks by spandrels stopped,

Petrified lacework—lightly lined
On ancient massiveness behind—

Muse that some minds so modest be
As to renounce fame's fairest fee,

(Like him who crystallized on this spot
His visionings, but lies forgot,

And many a mediaeval one
Whose symmetries salute the sun)

While others boom a baseless claim,
And upon nothing rear a name.

THE JUBILEE OF A MAGAZINE

(To the Editor)

YES; your up-dated modern page—
All flower-fresh, as it appears—
Can claim a time-tried lineage,

That reaches backward fifty years
(Which, if but short for sleepy squires,
Is much in magazines' careers).

—Here, on your cover, never tires
The sower, reaper, thresher, while
As through the seasons of our sires

Each wills to work in ancient style
With seedlip, sickle, share and flail,
Though modes have since moved many a mile!

The steel-roped plough now rips the vale,
With cog and tooth the sheaves are won,
Wired wheels drum out the wheat like hail;

But if we ask, what has been done
To unify the mortal lot
Since your bright leaves first saw the sun,

Beyond mechanic furtherance—what
Advance can rightness, candour, claim?
Truth bends abashed, and answers not.

Despite your volumes' gentle aim
To straighten visions wry and wrong,
Events jar onward much the same!

—Had custom tended to prolong,
As on your golden page engrained,
Old processes of blade and prong,

And best invention been retained
For high crusades to lessen tears
Throughout the race, the world had gained! . . .
But too much, this, for fifty years.

THE SATIN SHOES

"IF ever I walk to church to wed,
          As other maidens use,
And face the gathered eyes," she said,
          "I'll go in satin shoes!"

She was as fair as early day
          Shining on meads unmown,

And her sweet syllables seemed to play
    Like flute-notes softly blown.

The time arrived when it was meet
    That she should be a bride;
The satin shoes were on her feet,
    Her father was at her side.

They stood within the dairy door,
    And gazed across the green;
The church loomed on the distant moor,
    But rain was thick between.

"The grass-path hardly can be stepped,
    The lane is like a pool!"—
Her dream is shown to be inept,
    Her wish they overrule.

"To go forth shod in satin soft
    A coach would be required!"
For thickest boots the shoes were doffed—
    Those shoes her soul desired. . . .

All day the bride, as overborne,
    Was seen to brood apart,
And that the shoes had not been worn
    Sat heavy on her heart.

From her wrecked dream, as months flew on,
    Her thought seemed not to range.
"What ails the wife," they said anon,
    "That she should be so strange?" . . .

Ah—what coach comes with furtive glide—
    A coach of closed-up kind?
It comes to fetch the last year's bride,
    Who wanders in her mind.

She strove with them, and fearfully ran
    Stairward with one low scream:
"Nay—coax her," said the madhouse man,
    "With some old household theme."

"If you will go, dear, you must fain
    Put on those shoes—the pair
Meant for your marriage, which the rain
    Forbade you then to wear."

She clapped her hands, flushed joyous hues;
    "O yes—I'll up and ride
If I am to wear my satin shoes
    And be a proper bride!"

Out then her little foot held she,
    As to depart with speed;
The madhouse man smiled pleasantly
    To see the wile succeed.

She turned to him when all was done,
    And gave him her thin hand,
Exclaiming like an enraptured one,
    "This time it will be grand!"

She mounted with a face elate,
    Shut was the carriage door;
They drove her to the madhouse gate,
    And she was seen no more. . . .

Yet she was fair as early day
    Shining on meads unmown,
And her sweet syllables seemed to play
    Like flute-notes softly blown.

EXEUNT OMNES

I

EVERYBODY else, then, going,
And I still left where the fair was? . . .
Much have I seen of neighbour loungers
    Making a lusty showing,
    Each now past all knowing.

II

There is an air of blankness
In the street and the littered spaces ;
Thoroughfare, steeple, bridge and highway
Wizen themselves to lankness ;
Kennels dribble dankness.

III

Folk all fade.   And whither,
As I wait alone where the fair was ?
Into the clammy and numbing night-fog
Whence they entered hither.
Soon one more goes thither !

June 2, 1913.

A POET

ATTENTIVE eyes, fantastic heed,
Assessing minds, he does not need,
Nor urgent writs to sup or dine,
Nor pledges in the rosy wine.

For loud acclaim he does not care
By the august or rich or fair,
Nor for smart pilgrims from afar,
Curious on where his hauntings are.

But soon or later, when you hear
That he has doffed this wrinkled gear,
Some evening, at the first star-ray,
Come to his graveside, pause and say :

" Whatever his message—glad or grim—
Two bright-souled women clave to him ";
Stand and say that while day decays ;
It will be word enough of praise.

July 1914.

SATIRES OF CIRCUMSTANCE

IN FIFTEEN GLIMPSES

(First published April 1911)

I

AT TEA

THE kettle descants in a cosy drone,
And the young wife looks in her husband's face,
And then at her guest's, and shows in her own
Her sense that she fills an envied place ;
And the visiting lady is all abloom,
And says there was never so sweet a room.

And the happy young housewife does not know
That the woman beside her was first his choice,
Till the fates ordained it could not be so. . . .
Betraying nothing in look or voice
The guest sits smiling and sips her tea,
And he throws her a stray glance yearningly.

II

IN CHURCH

"AND now to God the Father," he ends,
And his voice thrills up to the topmost tiles :
Each listener chokes as he bows and bends,
And emotion pervades the crowded aisles.

Then the preacher glides to the vestry-door,
And shuts it, and thinks he is seen no more.

The door swings softly ajar meanwhile,
And a pupil of his in the Bible class,
Who adores him as one without gloss or guile,
Sees her idol stand with a satisfied smile
And re-enact at the vestry-glass
Each pulpit gesture in deft dumb-show
That had moved the congregation so.

III

BY HER AUNT'S GRAVE

" SIXPENCE a week," says the girl to her lover,
" Aunt used to bring me, for she could confide
In me alone, she vowed. 'Twas to cover
The cost of her headstone when she died.
And that was a year ago last June ;
I've not yet fixed it. But I must soon."

" And where is the money now, my dear ? "
" O, snug in my purse . . . Aunt was so slow
In saving it—eighty weeks, or near." . . .
" Let's spend it," he hints. " For she won't know.
There's a dance to-night at the Load of Hay."
She passively nods. And they go that way.

IV

IN THE ROOM OF THE BRIDE-ELECT

" WOULD it had been the man of our wish ! "
Sighs her mother. To whom with vehemence she
In the wedding-dress—the wife to be—
" Then why were you so mollyish
As not to insist on him for me ! "
The mother, amazed : " Why, dearest one,
Because you pleaded for this or none ! "

"But Father and you should have stood out strong!
Since then, to my cost, I have lived to find
That you were right and that I was wrong;
This man is a dolt to the one declined. . . .
Ah!—here he comes with his button-hole rose.
Good God—I must marry him I suppose!"

V

AT A WATERING-PLACE

THEY sit and smoke on the esplanade,
The man and his friend, and regard the bay
Where the far chalk cliffs, to the left displayed,
Smile sallowly in the decline of day.
And saunterers pass with laugh and jest—
A handsome couple among the rest.

"That smart proud pair," says the man to his friend,
"Are to marry next week. . . . How little he thinks
That dozens of days and nights on end
I have stroked her neck, unhooked the links
Of her sleeve to get at her upper arm. . . .
Well, bliss is in ignorance: what's the harm!"

VI

IN THE CEMETERY

"YOU see those mothers squabbling there?"
Remarks the man of the cemetery.
"One says in tears, ''Tis mine lies here!'
Another, 'Nay, mine, you Pharisee!'
Another, 'How dare you move my flowers
And put your own on this grave of ours!'
But all their children were laid therein
At different times, like sprats in a tin.

"And then the main drain had to cross,
And we moved the lot some nights ago,

And packed them away in the general foss
With hundreds more. But their folks don't know,
And as well cry over a new-laid drain
As anything else, to ease your pain!"

VII

OUTSIDE THE WINDOW

"My stick!" he says, and turns in the lane
To the house just left, whence a vixen voice
Comes out with the firelight through the pane,
And he sees within that the girl of his choice
Stands rating her mother with eyes aglare
For something said while he was there.

"At last I behold her soul undraped!"
Thinks the man who had loved her more than himself;
"My God!—'tis but narrowly I have escaped.—
My precious porcelain proves it delf."
His face has reddened like one ashamed,
And he steals off, leaving his stick unclaimed.

VIII

IN THE STUDY

HE enters, and mute on the edge of a chair
Sits a thin-faced lady, a stranger there,
A type of decayed gentility;
And by some small signs he well can guess
That she comes to him almost breakfastless.

"I have called—I hope I do not err—
I am looking for a purchaser
Of some score volumes of the works
Of eminent divines I own,—
Left by my father—though it irks
My patience to offer them." And she smiles

As if necessity were unknown ;
" But the truth of it is that oftenwhiles
I have wished, as I am fond of art,
To make my rooms a little smart,
And these old books are so in the way."
And lightly still she laughs to him,
As if to sell were a mere gay whim,
And that, to be frank, Life were indeed
To her not vinegar and gall,
But fresh and honey-like ; and Need
No household skeleton at all.

IX

AT THE ALTAR-RAIL

" My bride is not coming, alas !" says the groom,
And the telegram shakes in his hand.   " I own
It was hurried !   We met at a dancing-room
When I went to the Cattle-Show alone,
And then, next night, where the Fountain leaps,
And the Street of the Quarter-Circle sweeps.

" Ay, she won me to ask her to be my wife—
'Twas foolish perhaps !—to forsake the ways
Of the flaring town for a farmer's life.
She agreed.   And we fixed it.   Now she says :
' *It's sweet of you, dear, to prepare me a nest,
But a swift, short, gay life suits me best.
What I really am you have never gleaned ;
I had eaten the apple ere you were weaned.*'"

X

IN THE NUPTIAL CHAMBER

"O THAT mastering tune ! "   And up in the bed
Like a lace-robed phantom springs the bride ;
"And why ?" asks the man she had that day wed,
With a start, as the band plays on outside.

" It's the townsfolk's cheery compliment
Because of our marriage, my Innocent."

" O but you don't know ! 'Tis the passionate air
To which my old Love waltzed with me,
And I swore as we spun that none should share
My home, my kisses, till death, save he !
And he dominates me and thrills me through,
And it's he I embrace while embracing you ! "

XI

IN THE RESTAURANT

" But hear.   If you stay, and the child be born,
It will pass as your husband's with the rest,
While, if we fly, the teeth of scorn
Will be gleaming at us from east to west ;
And the child will come as a life despised ;
I feel an elopement is ill-advised ! "

" O you realize not what it is, my dear,
To a woman !   Daily and hourly alarms
Lest the truth should out.   How can I stay here,
And nightly take him into my arms !
Come to the child no name or fame,
Let us go, and face it, and bear the shame."

XII

AT THE DRAPER'S

" I stood at the back of the shop, my dear,
      But you did not perceive me.
Well, when they deliver what you were shown
      I shall know nothing of it, believe me ! "

And he coughed and coughed as she paled and said,
      " O, I didn't see you come in there—
Why couldn't you speak ? "—" Well, I didn't.   I left
      That you should not notice I'd been there.

"You were viewing some lovely things.   '*Soon required*
    For a widow, of latest fashion';
And I knew 'twould upset you to meet the man
    Who had to be cold and ashen

"And screwed in a box before they could dress you
    '*In the last new note in mourning*,'
As they defined it. So, not to distress you,
    I left you to your adorning."

XIII

ON THE DEATH-BED

"I'LL tell—being past all praying for—
Then promptly die . . . He was out at the war,
And got some scent of the intimacy
That was under way between her and me ;
And he stole back home, and appeared like a ghost
One night, at the very time almost
That I reached her house.   Well, I shot him dead,
And secretly buried him.   Nothing was said.

"The news of the battle came next day ;
He was scheduled missing.   I hurried away,
Got out there, visited the field,
And sent home word that a search revealed
He was one of the slain ; though, lying alone
And stript, his body had not been known.

"But she suspected.   I lost her love,
Yea, my hope of earth, and of Heaven above ;
And my time's now come, and I'll pay the score,
Though it be burning for evermore."

XIV

OVER THE COFFIN

THEY stand confronting, the coffin between,
His wife of old, and his wife of late,
And the dead man whose they both had been
Seems listening aloof, as to things past date.
—"I have called," says the first.   "Do you marvel or not?"
"In truth," says the second, "I do—somewhat."

"Well, there was a word to be said by me! . . .
I divorced that man because of you—
It seemed I must do it, boundenly;
But now I am older, and tell you true,
For life is little, and dead lies he;
I would I had let alone you two!
And both of us, scorning parochial ways,
Had lived like the wives in the patriarchs' days."

XV

IN THE MOONLIGHT

"O LONELY workman, standing there
In a dream, why do you stare and stare
At her grave, as no other grave there were?

"If your great gaunt eyes so importune
Her soul by the shine of this corpse-cold moon,
Maybe you'll raise her phantom soon!"

"Why, fool, it is what I would rather see
Than all the living folk there be;
But alas, there is no such joy for me!"

"Ah—she was one you loved, no doubt,
Through good and evil, through rain and drought,
And when she passed, all your sun went out?"

"Nay: she was the woman I did not love,
Whom all the others were ranked above,
Whom during her life I thought nothing of."

MOMENTS OF VISION

AND MISCELLANEOUS VERSES

MOMENTS OF VISION

THAT mirror
Which makes of men a transparency,
Who holds that mirror
And bids us such a breast-bare spectacle see
Of you and me?

That mirror
Whose magic penetrates like a dart,
Who lifts that mirror
And throws our mind back on us, and our heart,
Until we start?

That mirror
Works well in these night hours of ache;
Why in that mirror
Are tincts we never see ourselves once take
When the world is awake?

That mirror
Can test each mortal when unaware;
Yea, that strange mirror
May catch his last thoughts, whole life foul or fair,
Glassing it—where?

THE VOICE OF THINGS

FORTY Augusts—aye, and several more—ago,
When I paced the headlands loosed from dull employ,
The waves huzza'd like a multitude below
In the sway of an all-including joy
Without cloy.

Blankly I walked there a double decade after,
    When thwarts had flung their toils in front of me,
And I heard the waters wagging in a long ironic laughter
    At the lot of men, and all the vapoury
        Things that be.

Wheeling change has set me again standing where
    Once I heard the waves huzza at Lammas-tide;
But they supplicate now—like a congregation there
    Who murmur the Confession—I outside,
        Prayer denied.

"WHY BE AT PAINS?"

(*Wooer's Song*)

WHY be at pains that I should know
    You sought not me?
Do breezes, then, make features glow
    So rosily?
Come, the lit port is at our back,
    And the tumbling sea;
Elsewhere the lampless uphill track
    To uncertainty!

O should not we two waifs join hands?
    I am alone,
You would enrich me more than lands
    By being my own.
Yet, though this facile moment flies,
    Close is your tone,
And ere to-morrow's dewfall dries
    I plough the unknown.

"WE SAT AT THE WINDOW"

(*Bournemouth*, 1875)

WE sat at the window looking out,
And the rain came down like silken strings
That Swithin's day. Each gutter and spout
Babbled unchecked in the busy way
    Of witless things:

Nothing to read, nothing to see
Seemed in that room for her and me
      On Swithin's day.

We were irked by the scene, by our own selves ; yes,
For I did not know, nor did she infer
How much there was to read and guess
By her in me, and to see and crown
      By me in her.
Wasted were two souls in their prime,
And great was the waste, that July time
      When the rain came down.

AFTERNOON SERVICE AT MELLSTOCK

(*Circa* 1850)

ON afternoons of drowsy calm
      We stood in the panelled pew,
Singing one-voiced a Tate-and-Brady psalm
      To the tune of " Cambridge New."

We watched the elms, we watched the rooks,
      The clouds upon the breeze,
Between the whiles of glancing at our books,
      And swaying like the trees.

So mindless were those outpourings !—
      Though I am not aware
That I have gained by subtle thought on things
      Since we stood psalming there.

AT THE WICKET-GATE

THERE floated the sounds of church-chiming.
      But no one was nigh,
Till there came, as a break in the loneness,
      Her father, she, I.

And we slowly moved on to the wicket,
    And downlooking stood,
Till anon people passed, and amid them
    We parted for good.

Greater, wiser, may part there than we three
    Who parted there then,
But never will Fates colder-featured
    Hold sway there again.
Of the churchgoers through the still meadows
    No single one knew
What a play was played under their eyes there
    As thence we withdrew.

IN A MUSEUM

I

HERE'S the mould of a musical bird long passed from light,
Which over the earth before man came was winging ;
There's a contralto voice I heard last night,
That lodges in me still with its sweet singing.

II

Such a dream is Time that the coo of this ancient bird
Has perished not, but is blent, or will be blending
Mid visionless wilds of space with the voice that I heard,
In the full-fugued song of the universe unending.

EXETER.

APOSTROPHE TO AN OLD PSALM TUNE

I MET you first—ah, when did I first meet you ?
When I was full of wonder, and innocent,
Standing meek-eyed with those of choric bent,
    While dimming day grew dimmer
      In the pulpit-glimmer.

Much riper in years I met you—in a temple
Where summer sunset streamed upon our shapes,

And you spread over me like a gauze that drapes,
    And flapped from floor to rafters,
      Sweet as angels' laughters.

But you had been stripped of some of your old vesture
By Monk, or another.   Now you wore no frill,
And at first you startled me.   But I knew you still,
    Though I missed the minim's waver,
      And the dotted quaver.

I grew accustomed to you thus.   And you hailed me
Through one who evoked you often.   Then at last
Your raiser was borne off, and I mourned you had passed
    From my life with your late outsetter ;
      Till I said, "'Tis better !"

But you waylaid me.   I rose and went as a ghost goes,
And said, eyes-full : " I'll never hear it again !
It is overmuch for scathed and memoried men
    When sitting among strange people
      Under their steeple."

Now, a new stirrer of tones calls you up before me
And wakes your speech, as she of Endor did
(When sought by Saul who, in disguises hid,
    Fell down on the earth to hear it)
      Samuel's spirit.

So, your quired oracles beat till they make me tremble
As I discern your mien in the old attire,
Here in these turmoiled years of belligerent fire
    Living still on—and onward, maybe,
      Till Doom's great day be !

Sunday, August 13, 1916.

AT THE WORD "FAREWELL"

SHE looked like a bird from a cloud
    On the clammy lawn,
Moving alone, bare-browed
    In the dim of dawn.

The candles alight in the room
    For my parting meal
Made all things withoutdoors loom
    Strange, ghostly, unreal.

The hour itself was a ghost,
    And it seemed to me then
As of chances the chance furthermost
    I should see her again.
I beheld not where all was so fleet
    That a Plan of the past
Which had ruled us from birthtime to meet
    Was in working at last:

No prelude did I there perceive
    To a drama at all,
Or foreshadow what fortune might weave
    From beginnings so small;
But I rose as if quicked by a spur
    I was bound to obey,
And stepped through the casement to her
    Still alone in the gray.

"I am leaving you. . . . Farewell!" I said,
    As I followed her on
By an alley bare boughs overspread;
    "I soon must be gone!"
Even then the scale might have been turned
    Against love by a feather,
——But crimson one cheek of hers burned
    When we came in together.

FIRST SIGHT OF HER AND AFTER

A DAY is drawing to its fall
    I had not dreamed to see;
The first of many to enthrall
    My spirit, will it be?
Or is this eve the end of all
    Such new delight for me?

I journey home : the pattern grows
    Of moonshades on the way :
" Soon the first quarter, I suppose,"
    Sky-glancing travellers say ;
I realize that it, for those,
    Has been a common day.

THE RIVAL

I DETERMINED to find out whose it was—
    The portrait he looked at so, and sighed ;
Bitterly have I rued my meanness
    And wept for it since he died !

I searched his desk when he was away,
    And there was the likeness—yes, my own !
Taken when I was the season's fairest,
    And time-lines all unknown.

I smiled at my image, and put it back,
    And he went on cherishing it, until
I was chafed that he loved not the me then living,
    But that past woman still.

Well, such was my jealousy at last,
    I destroyed that face of the former me ;
Could you ever have dreamed the heart of woman
    Would work so foolishly !

HEREDITY

I AM the family face ;
Flesh perishes, I live on,
Projecting trait and trace
Through time to times anon,
And leaping from place to place
Over oblivion.

The years-heired feature that can
In curve and voice and eye

Despise the human span
Of durance—that is I ;
The eternal thing in man,
That heeds no call to die.

"YOU WERE THE SORT THAT MEN FORGET"

You were the sort that men forget ;
    Though I—not yet !—
Perhaps not ever.   Your slighted weakness
    Adds to the strength of my regret !

You'd not the art—you never had
    For good or bad—
To make men see how sweet your meaning,
    Which, visible, had charmed them glad.

You would, by words inept let fall,
    Offend them all,
Even if they saw your warm devotion
    Would hold your life's blood at their call.

You lacked the eye to understand
    Those friends offhand
Whose mode was crude, though whose dim purport
    Outpriced the courtesies of the bland.

I am now the only being who
    Remembers you
It may be.   What a waste that Nature
    Grudged soul so dear the art its due !

SHE, I, AND THEY

I was sitting,
    She was knitting,
And the portraits of our fore-folk hung around ;
    When there struck on us a sigh ;
    "Ah—what is that ?" said I :
"Was it not you ?" said she.   "A sigh did sound."

I had not breathed it,
    Nor the night-wind heaved it,
And how it came to us we could not guess;
    And we looked up at each face
    Framed and glazed there in its place,
Still hearkening; but thenceforth was silentness.

        Half in dreaming,
        "Then its meaning,"
Said we, "must be surely this; that they repine
        That we should be the last
        Of stocks once unsurpassed,
And unable to keep up their sturdy line."

    1916.

NEAR LANIVET, 1872

THERE was a stunted handpost just on the crest,
    Only a few feet high:
She was tired, and we stopped in the twilight-time for her rest,
    At the crossways close thereby.

She leant back, being so weary, against its stem,
    And laid her arms on its own,
Each open palm stretched out to each end of them,
    Her sad face sideways thrown.

Her white-clothed form at this dim-lit cease of day
    Made her look as one crucified
In my gaze at her from the midst of the dusty way,
    And hurriedly "Don't," I cried.

I do not think she heard.   Loosing thence she said,
    As she stepped forth ready to go,
"I am rested now.—Something strange came into my head;
    I wish I had not leant so!"

And wordless we moved onward down from the hill
    In the west cloud's murked obscure,
And looking back we could see the handpost still
    In the solitude of the moor.

"It struck her too," I thought, for as if afraid
    She heavily breathed as we trailed ;
Till she said, " I did not think how 'twould look in the shade,
    When I leant there like one nailed."

I, lightly : " There's nothing in it. For *you*, anyhow ! "
    —" O I know there is not," said she . . .
" Yet I wonder . . . If no one is bodily crucified now,
    In spirit one may be ! "

And we dragged on and on, while we seemed to see
    In the running of Time's far glass
Her crucified, as she had wondered if she might be
    Some day.—Alas, alas !

JOYS OF MEMORY

When the spring comes round, and a certain day
Looks out from the brume by the eastern copsetrees
    And says, Remember,
I begin again, as if it were new,
A day of like date I once lived through,
Whiling it hour by hour away ;
    So shall I do till my December,
        When spring comes round.

I take my holiday then and my rest
Away from the dun life here about me,
    Old hours re-greeting
With the quiet sense that bring they must
Such throbs as at first, till I house with dust,
And in the numbness my heartsome zest
    For things that were, be past repeating
        When spring comes round.

TO THE MOON

" What have you looked at, Moon,
    In your time,
Now long past your prime ? "
" O, I have looked at, often looked at
    Sweet, sublime,

Sore things, shudderful, night and noon
  In my time."

  "What have you mused on, Moon,
   In your day,
  So aloof, so far away?"
"O, I have mused on, often mused on
   Growth, decay,
Nations alive, dead, mad, aswoon,
  In my day!"

  "Have you much wondered, Moon,
   On your rounds,
  Self-wrapt, beyond Earth's bounds?"
"Yea, I have wondered, often wondered
   At the sounds
Reaching me of the human tune
  On my rounds."

  "What do you think of it, Moon,
   As you go?
  Is Life much, or no?"
"O, I think of it, often think of it
   As a show
God ought surely to shut up soon,
  As I go."

COPYING ARCHITECTURE IN AN OLD MINSTER

(*Wimborne*)

How smartly the quarters of the hour march by
  That the jack-o'-clock never forgets;
Ding-dong; and before I have traced a cusp's eye,
Or got the true twist of the ogee over,
  A double ding-dong ricochetts.

Just so did he clang here before I came,
  And so will he clang when I'm gone
Through the Minster's cavernous hollows—the same
Tale of hours never more to be will he deliver
  To the speechless midnight and dawn!

I grow to conceive it a call to ghosts,
    Whose mould lies below and around.
Yes; the next "Come, come," draws them out from their posts,
And they gather, and one shade appears, and another,
    As the eve-damps creep from the ground.

See—a Courtenay stands by his quatre-foiled tomb,
    And a Duke and his Duchess near;
And one Sir Edmund in columned gloom,
And a Saxon king by the presbytery chamber;
    And shapes unknown in the rear.

Maybe they have met for a parle on some plan
    To better ail-stricken mankind;
I catch their cheepings, though thinner than
The overhead creak of a passager's pinion
    When leaving land behind.

Or perhaps they speak to the yet unborn,
    And caution them not to come
To a world so ancient and trouble-torn,
Of foiled intents, vain lovingkindness,
    And ardours chilled and numb.

They waste to fog as I stir and stand,
    And move from the arched recess,
And pick up the drawing that slipped from my hand,
And feel for the pencil I dropped in the cranny
    In a moment's forgetfulness.

TO SHAKESPEARE

AFTER THREE HUNDRED YEARS

BRIGHT baffling Soul, least capturable of themes,
Thou, who display'dst a life of commonplace,
Leaving no intimate word or personal trace
Of high design outside the artistry
    Of thy penned dreams,
Still shalt remain at heart unread eternally.

Through human orbits thy discourse to-day,
Despite thy formal pilgrimage, throbs on

In harmonies that cow Oblivion,
And, like the wind, with all-uncared effect
        Maintain a sway
Not fore-desired, in tracks unchosen and unchecked.

And yet, at thy last breath, with mindless note
The borough clocks but samely tongued the hour
The Avon just as always glassed the tower,
Thy age was published on thy passing-bell
        But in due rote
With other dwellers' deaths accorded a like knell.

And at the strokes some townsman (met, maybe,
And thereon queried by some squire's good dame
Driving in shopward) may have given thy name,
With, "Yes, a worthy man and well-to-do ;
        Though, as for me,
I knew him but by just a neighbour's nod, 'tis true.

"I' faith, few knew him much here, save by word,
He having elsewhere led his busier life ;
Though to be sure he left with us his wife."
—"Ah, one of the tradesmen's sons, I now recall. . . .
        Witty, I've heard. . . .
We did not know him. . . . Well, good-day.   Death comes
        to all."

So, like a strange bright bird we sometimes find
To mingle with the barn-door brood awhile,
Then vanish from their homely domicile—
Into man's poesy, we wot not whence,
        Flew thy strange mind,
Lodged there a radiant guest, and sped for ever thence.

1916.

QUID HIC AGIS?

I

WHEN I weekly knew
An ancient pew,
And murmured there
The forms of prayer

And thanks and praise
In the ancient ways,
And heard read out
During August drought
That chapter from Kings
Harvest-time brings ;
—How the prophet, broken
By griefs unspoken,
Went heavily away
To fast and to pray,
And, while waiting to die,
The Lord passed by,
And a whirlwind and fire
Drew nigher and nigher,
And a small voice anon
Bade him up and be gone,—
I did not apprehend
As I sat to the end
And watched for her smile
Across the sunned aisle,
That this tale of a seer
Which came once a year
Might, when sands were heaping,
Be like a sweat creeping,
Or in any degree
Bear on her or on me !

II

When later, by chance
Of circumstance,
It befel me to read
On a hot afternoon
At the lectern there
The selfsame words
As the lesson decreed,
To the gathered few
From the hamlets near—
Folk of flocks and herds
Sitting half aswoon,
Who listened thereto
As women and men
Not overmuch

Concerned at such—
So, like them then,
I did not see
What drought might be
With me, with her,
As the Kalendar
Moved on, and Time
Devoured our prime.

III

But now, at last,
When our glory has passed,
And there is no smile
From her in the aisle,
But where it once shone
A marble, men say,
With her name thereon
Is discerned to-day;
And spiritless
In the wilderness
I shrink from sight
And desire the night,
(Though, as in old wise,
I might still arise,
Go forth, and stand
And prophesy in the land),
I feel the shake
Of wind and earthquake,
And consuming fire
Nigher and nigher,
And the voice catch clear,
"What doest thou here?"

The Spectator: 1916.   During the War.

ON A MIDSUMMER EVE

I IDLY cut a parsley stalk,
And blew therein towards the moon;
I had not thought what ghosts would walk
With shivering footsteps to my tune.

I went, and knelt, and scooped my hand
As if to drink, into the brook,
And a faint figure seemed to stand
Above me, with the bygone look.

I lipped rough rhymes of chance, not choice,
I thought not what my words might be ;
There came into my ear a voice
That turned a tenderer verse for me.

TIMING HER

(Written to an old folk-tune)

LALAGE'S coming :
Where is she now, O ?
Turning to bow, O,
And smile, is she,
Just at parting,
Parting, parting,
As she is starting
To come to me ?

Where is she now, O,
Now, and now, O,
Shadowing a bough, O,
Of hedge or tree
As she is rushing,
Rushing, rushing,
Gossamers brushing
To come to me ?

Lalage's coming ;
Where is she now, O ;
Climbing the brow, O,
Of hills I see ?
Yes, she is nearing,
Nearing, nearing,
Weather unfearing
To come to me.

Near is she now, O,
Now, and now, O;
Milk the rich cow, O,
Forward the tea;
Shake the down bed for her,
Linen sheets spread for her,
Drape round the head for her
Coming to me.

Lalage's coming,
She's nearer now, O,
End anyhow, O,
To-day's husbandry!
Would a gilt chair were mine,
Slippers of vair were mine,
Brushes for hair were mine
Of ivory!

What will she think, O,
She who's so comely,
Viewing how homely
A sort are we!
Nothing resplendent,
No prompt attendant,
Not one dependent
Pertaining to me!

Lalage's coming;
Where is she now, O?
Fain I'd avow, O,
Full honestly
Nought here's enough for her,
All is too rough for her,
Even my love for her
Poor in degree.

She's nearer now, O,
Still nearer now, O,
She it is, I vow, O,
Passing the lea.
Rush down to meet her there,
Call out and greet her there,

Never a sweeter there
Crossed to me !

Lalage's come ; aye,
Come is she now, O ! . . .
Does Heaven allow, O,
A meeting to be ?
Yes, she is here now,
Here now, here now,
Nothing to fear now,
Here's Lalage !

BEFORE KNOWLEDGE

WHEN I walked roseless tracks and wide,
Ere dawned your date for meeting me,
O why did you not cry Halloo
Across the stretch between, and say :

" We move, while years as yet divide,
On closing lines which—though it be
You know me not nor I know you—
Will intersect and join some day ! "

Then well I had borne
Each scraping thorn ;
But the winters froze,
And grew no rose ;
No bridge bestrode
The gap at all ;
No shape you showed,
And I heard no call !

THE BLINDED BIRD

SO zestfully canst thou sing ?
And all this indignity,
With God's consent, on thee !
Blinded ere yet a-wing
By the red-hot needle thou,

I stand and wonder how
So zestfully thou canst sing !

Resenting not such wrong,
Thy grievous pain forgot,
Eternal dark thy lot,
Groping thy whole life long,
After that stab of fire ;
Enjailed in pitiless wire ;
Resenting not such wrong !

Who hath charity ?   This bird.
Who suffereth long and is kind,
Is not provoked, though blind
And alive ensepulchred ?
Who hopeth, endureth all things ?
Who thinketh no evil, but sings ?
Who is divine ?   This bird.

"THE WIND BLEW WORDS"

THE wind blew words along the skies,
    And these it blew to me
Through the wide dusk : " Lift up your eyes,
    Behold this troubled tree,
Complaining as it sways and plies ;
    It is a limb of thee.

" Yea, too, the creatures sheltering round—
    Dumb figures, wild and tame,
Yea, too, thy fellows who abound—
    Either of speech the same
Or far and strange—black, dwarfed, and browned,
    They are stuff of thy own frame."

I moved on in a surging awe
    Of inarticulateness
At the pathetic Me I saw
    In all his huge distress,
Making self-slaughter of the law
    To kill, break, or suppress.

THE FADED FACE

How was this I did not see
Such a look as here was shown
Ere its womanhood had blown
Past its first felicity?—
That I did not know you young,
        Faded Face,
            Know you young!

Why did Time so ill bestead
That I heard no voice of yours
Hail from out the curved contours
Of those lips when rosy red;
Weeted not the songs they sung,
        Faded Face,
            Songs they sung!

By these blanchings, blooms of old,
And the relics of your voice—
Leavings rare of rich and choice
From your early tone and mould—
Let me mourn,—aye, sorrow-wrung,
        Faded Face,
            Sorrow-wrung!

THE RIDDLE

I

STRETCHING eyes west
Over the sea,
Wind foul or fair,
Always stood she
Prospect-impressed;
Solely out there
Did her gaze rest,
Never elsewhere
Seemed charm to be.

II

Always eyes east
Ponders she now—
As in devotion—
Hills of blank brow
Where no waves plough.
Never the least
Room for emotion
Drawn from the ocean
Does she allow.

THE DUEL

"I AM here to time, you see;
The glade is well-screened—eh?—against alarm;
  Fit place to vindicate by my arm
  The honour of my spotless wife,
  Who scorns your libel upon her life
    In boasting intimacy!

  "'All hush-offerings you'll spurn,
My husband. Two must come; one only go,'
  She said. 'That he'll be you I know;
  To faith like ours Heaven will be just,
  And I shall abide in fullest trust
    Your speedy glad return.'"

  "Good. Here am also I;
And we'll proceed without more waste of words
  To warm your cockpit. Of the swords
  Take you your choice. I shall thereby
  Feel that on me no blame can lie,
    Whatever Fate accords."

  So stripped they there, and fought,
And the swords clicked and scraped, and the onsets sped;
  Till the husband fell; and his shirt was red
  With streams from his heart's hot cistern. Nought
  Could save him now; and the other, wrought
    Maybe to pity, said;

" Why did you urge on this ?
Your wife assured you ; and 't had better been
    That you had let things pass, serene
        In confidence of long-tried bliss,
        Holding there could be nought amiss
    In what my words might mean."

    Then, seeing nor ruth nor rage
Could move his foeman more—now Death's deaf thrall—
    He wiped his steel, and, with a call
        Like turtledove to dove, swift broke
        Into the copse, where under an oak
    His horse cropt, held by a page.

    " All's over, Sweet," he cried
To the wife, thus guised ; for the young page was she.
    "'Tis as we hoped and said 't would be.
        He never guessed. . . . We mount and ride
        To where our love can reign uneyed.
    He's clay, and we are free."

AT MAYFAIR LODGINGS

How could I be aware,
The opposite window eyeing
As I lay listless there,
That through its blinds was dying
One I had rated rare
Before I had set me sighing
For another more fair ?

Had the house-front been glass,
My vision unobscuring,
Could aught have come to pass
More happiness-insuring
To her, loved as a lass
When spouseless, all-alluring ?
I reckon not, alas !

So, the square window stood,
Steadily night-long shining
In my close neighbourhood,

Who looked forth undivining
That soon would go for good
One there in pain reclining,
Unpardoned, unadieu'd.

Silently screened from view
Her tragedy was ending
That need not have come due
Had she been less unbending.
How near, near were we two
At that last vital rending,—
And neither of us knew!

TO MY FATHER'S VIOLIN

Does he want you down there
In the Nether Glooms where
The hours may be a dragging load upon him,
As he hears the axle grind
Round and round
Of the great world, in the blind
Still profound
Of the night-time?   He might liven at the sound
Of your string, revealing you had not forgone him.

In the gallery west the nave,
But a few yards from his grave,
Did you, tucked beneath his chin, to his bowing
Guide the homely harmony
Of the quire
Who for long years strenuously—
Son and sire—
Caught the strains that at his fingering low or higher
From your four thin threads and eff-holes came outflowing.

And, too, what merry tunes
He would bow at nights or noons
That chanced to find him bent to lute a measure,
When he made you speak his heart
As in dream.

Without book or music-chart,
        On some theme
Elusive as a jack-o'-lanthorn's gleam,
And the psalm of duty shelved for trill of pleasure.

        Well, you can not, alas,
        The barrier overpass
That screens him in those Mournful Meads hereunder,
        Where no fiddling can be heard
                In the glades
                Of silentness, no bird
                Thrills the shades;
Where no viol is touched for songs or serenades,
No bowing wakes a congregation's wonder.

        He must do without you now,
        Stir you no more anyhow
To yearning concords taught you in your glory;
        While, your strings a tangled wreck,
                Once smart drawn,
                Ten worm-wounds in your neck,
                Purflings wan
With dust-hoar, here alone I sadly con
Your present dumbness, shape your olden story.

        1916.

THE STATUE OF LIBERTY

THIS statue of Liberty, busy man,
        Here erect in the city square,
I have watched while your scrubbings, this early morning,
                Strangely wistful,
                And half tristful,
        Have turned her from foul to fair;

With your bucket of water, and mop, and brush,
        Bringing her out of the grime
That has smeared her during the smokes of winter
                With such glumness
                In her dumbness,
        And aged her before her time.

You have washed her down with motherly care—
Head, shoulders, arm, and foot,
To the very hem of the robes that drape her—
  All expertly
  And alertly,
 Till a long stream, black with soot,

Flows over the pavement to the road,
 And her shape looms pure as snow :
I read you are hired by the City guardians—
  May be yearly,
  Or once merely—
 To treat the statues so ?

"Oh, I'm not hired by the Councilmen
 To cleanse the statues here.
I do this one as a self-willed duty,
  Not as paid to,
  Or at all made to,
 But because the doing is dear."

Ah, then I hail you brother and friend !
 Liberty's knight divine.
What you have done would have been my doing,
  Yea, most verily,
  Well, and thoroughly,
 Had but your courage been mine !

"Oh I care not for Liberty's mould,
 Liberty charms not me ;
What's Freedom but an idler's vision,
  Vain, pernicious,
  Often vicious,
 Of things that cannot be !

"Memory it is that brings me to this—
 Of a daughter—my one sweet own.
She grew a famous carver's model,
  One of the fairest
  And of the rarest :—
 She sat for the figure as shown.

"But alas, she died in this distant place
 Before I was warned to betake

Myself to her side! . . . And in love of my darling,
  In love of the fame of her,
  And the good name of her,
I do this for her sake."

Answer I gave not. Of that form
  The carver was I at his side;
His child, my model, held so saintly,
  Grand in feature,
  Gross in nature,
In the dens of vice had died.

THE BACKGROUND AND THE FIGURE

(Lover's Ditty)

I THINK of the slope where the rabbits fed,
  Of the periwinks' rockwork lair,
Of the fuchsias ringing their bells of red—
  And the something else seen there.

Between the blooms where the sod basked bright,
  By the bobbing fuchsia trees,
Was another and yet more eyesome sight---
  The sight that richened these.

I shall seek those beauties in the spring,
  When the days are fit and fair,
But only as foils to the one more thing
  That also will flower there!

THE CHANGE

OUT of the past there rises a week—
  Who shall read the years O!—
Out of the past there rises a week
  Enringed with a purple zone.
Out of the past there rises a week
When thoughts were strung too thick to speak,
And the magic of its lineaments remains with me alone.

In that week there was heard a singing—
   Who shall spell the years, the years!—
In that week there was heard a singing,
   And the white owl wondered why.
In that week, yea, a voice was ringing,
  And forth from the casement were candles flinging
Radiance that fell on the deodar and lit up the path thereby.

Could that song have a mocking note?—
   Who shall unroll the years O!—
Could that song have a mocking note
   To the white owl's sense as it fell?
Could that song have a mocking note
As it trilled out warm from the singer's throat,
  And who was the mocker and who the mocked when two felt all
    was well?

In a tedious trampling crowd yet later—
   Who shall bare the years, the years!—
In a tedious trampling crowd yet later,
   When silvery singings were dumb;
In a crowd uncaring what time might fate her,
  Mid murks of night I stood to await her,
And the twanging of iron wheels gave out the signal that she was
    come.

She said with a travel-tired smile—
   Who shall lift the years O!—
She said with a travel-tired smile,
   Half scared by scene so strange;
She said, outworn by mile on mile,
  The blurred lamps wanning her face the while,
"O Love, I am here; I am with you!" . . . Ah, that there should
    have come a change!

O the doom by someone spoken—
   Who shall unseal the years, the years!—
O the doom that gave no token,
   When nothing of bale saw we:
O the doom by someone spoken,
  O the heart by someone broken,
The heart whose sweet reverberances are all time leaves to me.

Jan.–Feb. 1913.

SITTING ON THE BRIDGE

(Echo of an old song)

SITTING on the bridge
  Past the barracks, town and ridge,
At once the spirit seized us
To sing a song that pleased us—
As "The Fifth" were much in rumour;
It was "Whilst I'm in the humour
    Take me, Paddy, will you now?"
  And a lancer soon drew nigh,
  And his Royal Irish eye
  Said, "Willing, faith, am I,
O, to take you anyhow, dears,
    To take you anyhow."

But, lo!—dad walking by,
  Cried, "What, you lightheels!   Fie!
Is this the way you roam
And mock the sunset gleam?"
  And he marched us straightway home,
Though we said, "We are only, daddy,
Singing, 'Will you take me, Paddy?'"
  —Well, we never saw from then,
  If we sang there anywhen,
  The soldier dear again,
Except at night in dream-time,
    Except at night in dream.

Perhaps that soldier's fighting
  In a land that's far away,
Or he may be idly plighting
  Some foreign hussy gay;
Or perhaps his bones are whiting
  In the wind to their decay! . . .
  Ah!—does he mind him how
  The girls he saw that day
On the bridge, were sitting singing
At the time of curfew-ringing,
  "Take me, Paddy; will you now, dear?
    Paddy, will you now?"

GREY'S BRIDGE.

THE YOUNG CHURCHWARDEN

WHEN he lit the candles there,
And the light fell on his hand,
And it trembled as he scanned
Her and me, his vanquished air
Hinted that his dream was done,
And I saw he had begun
    To understand.

When Love's viol was unstrung,
Sore I wished the hand that shook
Had been mine that shared her book
While that evening hymn was sung,
His the victor's, as he lit
Candles where he had bidden us sit
    With vanquished look.

Now her dust lies listless there,
His afar from tending hand,
What avails the victory scanned?
Does he smile from upper air:
"Ah, my friend, your dream is done;
And 'tis *you* who have begun
    To understand!"

"I TRAVEL AS A PHANTOM NOW"

I TRAVEL as a phantom now,
For people do not wish to see
In flesh and blood so bare a bough
    As Nature makes of me.

And thus I visit bodiless
Strange gloomy households often at odds,
And wonder if Man's consciousness
    Was a mistake of God's.

And next I meet you, and I pause,
And think that if mistake it were,
As some have said, O then it was
    One that I well can bear!

1915.

LINES

TO A MOVEMENT IN MOZART'S E-FLAT SYMPHONY

SHOW me again the time
  When in the Junetide's prime
We flew by meads and mountains northerly !—
Yea, to such freshness, fairness, fulness, fineness, freeness,
    Love lures life on.

Show me again the day
  When from the sandy bay
We looked together upon the pestered sea !—
Yea, to such surging, swaying, sighing, swelling, shrinking,
    Love lures life on.

Show me again the hour
  When by the pinnacled tower
We eyed each other and feared futurity !—
Yea, to such bodings, broodings, beatings, blanchings, blessing
    Love lures life on.

Show me again just this:
  The moment of that kiss
Away from the prancing folk, by the strawberry-tree !—
Yea, to such rashness, ratheness, rareness, ripeness, richness,
    Love lures life on.

Begun November 1898.

"IN THE SEVENTIES"

" Qui deridetur ab amico suo sicut ego." —JOB.

IN the seventies I was bearing in my breast,
    Penned tight,
Certain starry thoughts that threw a magic light
On the worktimes and the soundless hours of rest

In the seventies ; aye, I bore them in my breast
      Penned tight.

In the seventies when my neighbours—even my friend—
      Saw me pass,
Heads were shaken, and I heard the words, "Alas,
For his onward years and name unless he mend!"
In the seventies, when my neighbours and my friend
      Saw me pass.

In the seventies those who met me did not know
      Of the vision
That immuned me from the chillings of misprision
And the damps that choked my goings to and fro
In the seventies ; yea, those nodders did not know
      Of the vision.

In the seventies nought could darken or destroy it,
      Locked in me,
Though as delicate as lamp-worm's lucency ;
Neither mist nor murk could weaken or alloy it
In the seventies !—could not darken or destroy it,
      Locked in me.

THE PEDIGREE

I

I BENT in the deep of night
Over a pedigree the chronicler gave
As mine ; and as I bent there, half-unrobed,
e uncurtained panes of my window-square let in the watery
      light
      Of the moon in its old age :
d green-rheumed clouds were hurrying past where mute and
      cold it globed
Like a drifting dolphin's eye seen through a lapping wave.

II

So, scanning my sire-sown tree,
And the hieroglyphs of this spouse tied to that,
    With offspring mapped below in lineage,
      Till the tangles troubled me,

The branches seemed to twist into a seared and cynic face
   Which winked and tokened towards the window like a Mage
      Enchanting me to gaze again thereat.

III

      It was a mirror now,
   And in it a long perspective I could trace
Of my begetters, dwindling backward each past each
      All with the kindred look,
   Whose names had since been inked down in their place
      On the recorder's book,
Generation and generation of my mien, and build, and brow.

IV

      And then did I divine
   That every heave and coil and move I made
   Within my brain, and in my mood and speech,
      Was in the glass portrayed
   As long forestalled by their so making it ;
   The first of them, the primest fuglemen of my line,
Being fogged in far antiqueness past surmise and reason's reach

V

      Said I then, sunk in tone,
   " I am merest mimicker and counterfeit !—
      Though thinking, *I am I,*
   And what I do I do myself alone."
   —The cynic twist of the page thereat unknit
Back to its normal figure, having wrought its purport wry,
   The Mage's mirror left the window-square,
And the stained moon and drift retook their places there.

1916.

HIS HEART

A WOMAN'S DREAM

      At midnight, in the room where he lay dead
      Whom in his life I had never clearly read,
I thought if I could peer into that citadel
      His heart, I should at last know full and well

What hereto had been known to him alone,
Despite our long sit-out of years foreflown,
"And if," I said, "I do this for his memory's sake,
It would not wound him, even if he could wake."

So I bent over him. He seemed to smile
With a calm confidence the whole long while
That I, withdrawing his heart, held it and, bit by bit,
Perused the unguessed things found written on it.

It was inscribed like a terrestrial sphere
With quaint vermiculations close and clear—
His graving. Had I known, would I have risked the stroke
Its reading brought, and my own heart nigh broke!

Yes, there at last, eyes opened, did I see
His whole sincere symmetric history;
There were his truth, his simple singlemindedness,
Strained, maybe, by time's storms, but there no less.

There were the daily deeds from sun to sun
In blindness, but good faith, that he had done;
There were regrets, at instances wherein he swerved
(As he conceived) from cherishings I had deserved.

There were old hours all figured down as bliss—
Those spent with me—(how little had I thought this!)
There those when, at my absence, whether he slept or waked,
(Though I knew not 'twas so!) his spirit ached.

There that when we were severed, how day dulled
Till time joined us anew, was chronicled:
And arguments and battlings in defence of me
That heart recorded clearly and ruddily.

I put it back, and left him as he lay
While pierced the morning pink and then the gray
Into each dreary room and corridor around,
Where I shall wait, but his step will not sound.

WHERE THEY LIVED

DISHEVELLED leaves creep down
    Upon that bank to-day,
Some green, some yellow, and some pale brown;
    The wet bents bob and sway;
The once warm slippery turf is sodden
    Where we laughingly sat or lay.

The summerhouse is gone,
    Leaving a weedy space;
The bushes that veiled it once have grown
    Gaunt trees that interlace,
Through whose lank limbs I see too clearly
    The nakedness of the place.

And where were hills of blue,
    Blind drifts of vapour blow,
And the names of former dwellers few,
    If any, people know,
And instead of a voice that called, " Come in, Dears,"
    Time calls, " Pass below ! "

THE OCCULTATION

WHEN the cloud shut down on the morning shine,
    And darkened the sun,
I said, " So ended that joy of mine
    Years back begun."

But day continued its lustrous roll
    In upper air;
And did my late irradiate soul
    Live on somewhere ?

LIFE LAUGHS ONWARD

RAMBLING I looked for an old abode
Where, years back, one had lived I knew;
Its site a dwelling duly showed,
    But it was new.

I went where, not so long ago,
The sod had riven two breasts asunder;
Daisies throve gaily there, as though
    No grave were under.

I walked along a terrace where
Loud children gambolled in the sun:
The figure that had once sat there
    Was missed by none.

Life laughed and moved on unsubdued,
I saw that Old succumbed to Young:
'Twas well. My too regretful mood
    Died on my tongue.

THE PEACE-OFFERING

IT was but a little thing,
Yet I knew it meant to me
Ease from what had given a sting
To the very birdsinging
    Latterly.

But I would not welcome it;
And for all I then declined
O the regrettings infinite
When the night-processions flit
    Through the mind!

"SOMETHING TAPPED"

SOMETHING tapped on the pane of my room
    When there was never a trace
Of wind or rain, and I saw in the gloom
    My weary Belovéd's face.

"O I am tired of waiting," she said,
    "Night, morn, noon, afternoon;
So cold it is in my lonely bed,
    And I thought you would join me soon!"

I rose and neared the window-glass,
    But vanished thence had she:
Only a pallid moth, alas,
    Tapped at the pane for me.

August 1913.

THE WOUND

    I CLIMBED to the crest,
      And, fog-festooned,
    The sun lay west
      Like a crimson wound:

    Like that wound of mine
      Of which none knew,
    For I'd given no sign
      That it pierced me through.

A MERRYMAKING IN QUESTION

"I WILL get a new string for my fiddle,
    And call to the neighbours to come,
And partners shall dance down the middle
    Until the old pewter-wares hum:
    And we'll sip the mead, cyder, and rum!"

From the night came the oddest of answers:
  A hollow wind, like a bassoon,
And headstones all ranged up as dancers,
  And cypresses droning a croon,
  And gurgoyles that mouthed to the tune.

"I SAID AND SANG HER EXCELLENCE"

(Fickle Lover's Song)

I SAID and sang her excellence:
  They called it laud undue.
     (Have your way, my heart, O!)
Yet what was homage far above
The plain deserts of my olden Love
  Proved verity of my new.

"She moves a sylph in picture-land,
  Where nothing frosts the air:"
     (Have your way, my heart, O!)
"To all winged pipers overhead
She is known by shape and song," I said,
  Conscious of licence there.

I sang of her in a dim old hall
  Dream-built too fancifully,
     (Have your way, my heart, O!)
But lo, the ripe months chanced to lead
My feet to such a hall indeed,
  Where stood the very She.

Strange, startling, was it then to learn
  I had glanced down unborn time,
     (Have your way, my heart, O!)
And prophesied, whereby I knew
That which the years had planned to do
  In warranty of my rhyme.

BY RUSHY-POND.

A JANUARY NIGHT

(1879)

THE rain smites more and more,
The east wind snarls and sneezes;
Through the joints of the quivering door
    The water wheezes.

The tip of each ivy-shoot
Writhes on its neighbour's face;
There is some hid dread afoot
    That we cannot trace.

Is it the spirit astray
Of the man at the house below
Whose coffin they took in to-day?
    We do not know.

A KISS

BY a wall the stranger now calls his,
Was born of old a particular kiss,
Without forethought in its genesis;
Which in a trice took wing on the air.
And where that spot is nothing shows:
    There ivy calmly grows,
    And no one knows
    What a birth was there!

That kiss is gone where none can tell—
Not even those who felt its spell:
It cannot have died; that know we well.
Somewhere it pursues its flight,
One of a long procession of sounds
    Travelling aethereal rounds
    Far from earth's bounds
    In the infinite.

THE ANNOUNCEMENT

THEY came, the brothers, and took two chairs
 In their usual quiet way;
And for a time we did not think
 They had much to say.

And they began and talked awhile
 Of ordinary things,
Till spread that silence in the room
 A pent thought brings.

And then they said: "The end has come.
 Yes: it has come at last."
And we looked down, and knew that day
 A spirit had passed.

THE OXEN

CHRISTMAS EVE, and twelve of the clock.
 "Now they are all on their knees,"
An elder said as we sat in a flock
 By the embers in hearthside ease.

We pictured the meek mild creatures where
 They dwelt in their strawy pen,
Nor did it occur to one of us there
 To doubt they were kneeling then.

So fair a fancy few would weave
 In these years! Yet, I feel,
If someone said on Christmas Eve,
 "Come; see the oxen kneel,

"In the lonely barton by yonder coomb
 Our childhood used to know,"
I should go with him in the gloom,
 Hoping it might be so.

1915.

THE TRESSES

"WHEN the air was damp
It made my curls hang slack
As they kissed my neck and back
While I footed the salt-aired track
    I loved to tramp.

"When it was dry
They would roll up crisp and tight
As I went on in the light
Of the sun, which my own sprite
    Seemed to outvie.

"Now I am old;
And have not one gay curl
As I had when a girl
For dampness to unfurl
    Or sun uphold!"

THE PHOTOGRAPH

THE flame crept up the portrait line by line
As it lay on the coals in the silence of night's profound,
    And over the arm's incline,
And along the marge of the silkwork superfine,
And gnawed at the delicate bosom's defenceless round.

Then I vented a cry of hurt, and averted my eyes;
The spectacle was one that I could not bear,
    To my deep and sad surprise;
But, compelled to heed, I again looked furtivewise
Till the flame had eaten her breasts, and mouth, and hair.

"Thank God, she is out of it now!" I said at last,
In a great relief of heart when the thing was done
    That had set my soul aghast,
And nothing was left of the picture unsheathed from the past
But the ashen ghost of the card it had figured on.

She was a woman long hid amid packs of years,
She might have been living or dead; she was lost to my sight,
   And the deed that had nigh drawn tears
Was done in a casual clearance of life's arrears;
But I felt as if I had put her to death that night! . . . .

    .   .   .   .   .

—Well; she knew nothing thereof did she survive,
And suffered nothing if numbered among the dead;
   Yet—yet—if on earth alive
Did she feel a smart, and with vague strange anguish strive?
If in heaven, did she smile at me sadly and shake her head?

ON A HEATH

    I COULD hear a gown-skirt rustling
       Before I could see her shape,
    Rustling through the heather
       That wove the common's drape,
    On that evening of dark weather
       When I hearkened, lips agape.

    And the town-shine in the distance
       Did but baffle here the sight,
    And then a voice flew forward:
       "Dear, is't you? I fear the night!"
    And the herons flapped to norward
       In the firs upon my right.

    There was another looming
       Whose life we did not see;
    There was one stilly blooming
       Full nigh to where walked we;
    There was a shade entombing
       All that was bright of me.

AN ANNIVERSARY

    IT was at the very date to which we have come,
       In the month of the matching name,
   When, at a like minute, the sun had upswum,
       Its couch-time at night being the same.

And the same path stretched here that people now follow,
    And the same stile crossed their way,
And beyond the same green hillock and hollow
    The same horizon lay ;
And the same man pilgrims now hereby who pilgrimed here that
        day.

Let so much be said of the date-day's sameness ;
    But the tree that neighbours the track,
And stoops like a pedlar afflicted with lameness,
    Knew of no sogged wound or wind-crack.
And the joints of that wall were not enshrouded
    With mosses of many tones,
And the garth up afar was not overcrowded
    With a multitude of white stones,
And the man's eyes then were not so sunk that you saw the
        socket-bones.

KINGSTON-MAURWARD EWELEASE.

"BY THE RUNIC STONE"

(Two who became a story)

By the Runic Stone
    They sat, where the grass sloped down,
And chattered, he white-hatted, she in brown,
    Pink-faced, breeze-blown.

Rapt there alone
    In the transport of talking so
In such a place, there was nothing to let them know
    What hours had flown.

And the die thrown
    By them heedlessly there, the dent
It was to cut in their encompassment,
    Were, too, unknown.

It might have strown
    Their zest with qualms to see,
As in a glass, Time toss their history
    From zone to zone !

THE PINK FROCK

"O MY pretty pink frock,
I sha'n't be able to wear it !
Why is he dying just now ?
    I hardly can bear it !

" He might have contrived to live on ;
But they say there's no hope whatever :
And must I shut myself up,
    And go out never ?

" O my pretty pink frock ?
Puff-sleeved and accordion-pleated !
He might have passed in July,
    And not so cheated ! "

TRANSFORMATIONS

PORTION of this yew
Is a man my grandsire knew,
Bosomed here at its foot :
This branch may be his wife,
A ruddy human life
Now turned to a green shoot.

These grasses must be made
Of her who often prayed,
Last century, for repose ;
And the fair girl long ago
Whom I often tried to know
May be entering this rose.

So, they are not underground,
But as nerves and veins abound
In the growths of upper air,
And they feel the sun and rain,
And the energy again
That made them what they were !

IN HER PRECINCTS

HER house looked cold from the foggy lea,
And the square of each window a dull black blur
    Where showed no stir :
Yes, her gloom within at the lack of me
Seemed matching mine at the lack of her.

The black squares grew to be squares of light
As the eveshade swathed the house and lawn,
    And viols gave tone ;
There was glee within.   And I found that night
The gloom of severance mine alone.

    KINGSTON-MAURWARD PARK.

THE LAST SIGNAL

(*Oct.* 11, 1886)

A MEMORY OF WILLIAM BARNES

SILENTLY I footed by an uphill road
That led from my abode to a spot yew-boughed ;
Yellowly the sun sloped low down to westward,
    And dark was the east with cloud.

Then, amid the shadow of that livid sad east,
  Where the light was least, and a gate stood wide,
Something flashed the fire of the sun that was facing it,
    Like a brief blaze on that side.

Looking hard and harder I knew what it meant—
  The sudden shine sent from the livid east scene ;
It meant the west mirrored by the coffin of my friend there,
    Turning to the road from his green,

To take his last journey forth—he who in his prime
Trudged so many a time from that gate athwart the land !
Thus a farewell to me he signalled on his grave-way,
    As with a wave of his hand.

    WINTERBORNE-CAME PATH.

THE HOUSE OF SILENCE

" THAT is a quiet place—
That house in the trees with the shady lawn."
"—If, child, you knew what there goes on
You would not call it a quiet place.
Why, a phantom abides there, the last of its race,
  And a brain spins there till dawn."

" But I see nobody there,—
Nobody moves about the green,
Or wanders the heavy trees between."
"—Ah, that's because you do not bear
The visioning powers of souls who dare
  To pierce the material screen.

" Morning, noon, and night,
Mid those funereal shades that seem
The uncanny scenery of a dream,
Figures dance to a mind with sight,
And music and laughter like floods of light
  Make all the precincts gleam.

" It is a poet's bower,
Through which there pass, in fleet arrays,
Long teams of all the years and days,
Of joys and sorrows, of earth and heaven,
That meet mankind in its ages seven,
  An aion in an hour."

GREAT THINGS

SWEET cyder is a great thing,
 A great thing to me,
Spinning down to Weymouth town
 By Ridgway thirstily,
And maid and mistress summoning
 Who tend the hostelry :
O cyder is a great thing,
 A great thing to me !

The dance it is a great thing,
    A great thing to me,
With candles lit and partners fit
    For night-long revelry;
And going home when day-dawning
    Peeps pale upon the lea:
O dancing is a great thing,
    A great thing to me!

Love is, yea, a great thing,
    A great thing to me,
When, having drawn across the lawn
    In darkness silently,
A figure flits like one a-wing
    Out from the nearest tree:
O love is, yes, a great thing,
    A great thing to me!

Will these be always great things,
    Great things to me? . . .
Let it befall that One will call,
    " Soul, I have need of thee":
What then?   Joy-jaunts, impassioned flings,
    Love, and its ecstasy,
Will always have been great things,
    Great things to me!

THE CHIMES

THAT morning when I trod the town
The twitching chimes of long renown
    Played out to me
The sweet Sicilian sailors' tune,
And I knew not if late or soon
    My day would be:

A day of sunshine beryl-bright
And windless; yea, think as I might,
    I could not say,
Even to within years' measure, when
One would be at my side who then
    Was far away.

When hard utilitarian times
Had stilled the sweet Saint-Peter's chimes
   I learnt to see
That bale may spring where blisses are,
And one desired might be afar
     Though near to me.

THE FIGURE IN THE SCENE

It pleased her to step in front and sit
   Where the cragged slope was green,
While I stood back that I might pencil it
   With her amid the scene;
     Till it gloomed and rained;
But I kept on, despite the drifting wet
   That fell and stained
My draught, leaving for curious quizzings yet
     The blots engrained.

And thus I drew her there alone,
   Seated amid the gauze
Of moisture, hooded, only her outline shown,
   With rainfall marked across.
     —Soon passed our stay;
Yet her rainy form is the Genius still of the spot,
   Immutable, yea,
Though the place now knows her no more, and has known her no:
     Ever since that day.

From an old note.

"WHY DID I SKETCH"

Why did I sketch an upland green,
   And put the figure in
     Of one on the spot with me?—
For now that one has ceased to be seen
   The picture waxes akin
     To a wordless irony.

If you go drawing on down or cliff
    Let no soft curves intrude
    Of a woman's silhouette,
But show the escarpments stark and stiff
    As in utter solitude;
    So shall you half forget.

Let me sooner pass from sight of the sky
    Than again on a thoughtless day
    Limn, laugh, and sing, and rhyme
With a woman sitting near, whom I
    Paint in for love, and who may
    Be called hence in my time!

From an old note.

CONJECTURE

If there were in my kalendar
    No Emma, Florence, Mary,
What would be my existence now—
    A hermit's?—wanderer's weary?—
    How should I live, and how
    Near would be death, or far?

Could it have been that other eyes
    Might have uplit my highway?
That fond, sad, retrospective sight
    Would catch from this dim byway
    Prized figures different quite
    From those that now arise?

With how strange aspect would there creep
    The dawn, the night, the daytime,
If memory were not what it is
    In song-time, toil, or pray-time.—
    O were it else than this,
    I'd pass to pulseless sleep!

THE BLOW

THAT no man schemed it is my hope—
Yea, that it fell by will and scope
    Of That Which some enthrone,
And for whose meaning myriads grope.

For I would not that of my kind
There should, of his unbiassed mind,
    Have been one known
Who such a stroke could have designed;

Since it would augur works and ways
Below the lowest that man assays
    To have hurled that stone
Into the sunshine of our days!

And if it prove that no man did,
And that the Inscrutable, the Hid,
    Was cause alone
Of this foul crash our lives amid,

I'll go in due time, and forget
In some deep graveyard's oubliette
    The thing whereof I groan,
And cease from troubling; thankful yet

Time's finger should have stretched to show
No aimful author's was the blow
    That swept us prone,
But the Immanent Doer's That doth not know

Which in some age unguessed of us
May lift Its blinding incubus,
    And see, and own:
" It grieves me I did thus and thus!"

LOVE THE MONOPOLIST

(Young Lover's Reverie)

THE train draws forth from the station-yard,
    And with it carries me.
I rise, and stretch out, and regard
    The platform left, and see
An airy slim blue form there standing,
    And know that it is she.

While with strained vision I watch on,
    The figure turns round quite
To greet friends gaily ; then is gone. . . .
    The import may be slight,
But why remained she not hard gazing
    Till I was out of sight ?

"O do not chat with others there,"
    I brood.   "They are not I.
O strain your thoughts as if they were
    Gold bands between us ; eye
All neighbour scenes as so much blankness
    Till I again am by !

"A troubled soughing in the breeze
    And the sky overhead
Let yourself feel ; and shadeful trees,
    Ripe corn, and apples red,
Read as things barren and distasteful
    While we are separated !

"When I come back uncloak your gloom.
    And let in lovely day ;
Then the long dark as of the tomb
    Can well be thrust away
With sweet things I shall have to practise,
    And you will have to say !"

Begun 1871 : *finished*——

AT MIDDLE-FIELD GATE IN FEBRUARY

THE bars are thick with drops that show
      As they gather themselves from the fog
Like silver buttons ranged in a row,
And as evenly spaced as if measured, although
      They fall at the feeblest jog.

They load the leafless hedge hard by,
      And the blades of last year's grass.
While the fallow ploughland turned up nigh
In raw rolls, clammy and clogging lie—
      Too clogging for feet to pass.

How dry it was on a far-back day
      When straws hung the hedge and around,
When amid the sheaves in amorous play
In curtained bonnets and light array
      Bloomed a bevy now underground!

BOCKHAMPTON LANE.

THE YOUTH WHO CARRIED A LIGHT

I SAW him pass as the new day dawned,
      Murmuring some musical phrase;
Horses were drinking and floundering in the pond,
      And the tired stars thinned their gaze;
Yet these were not the spectacles at all that he conned,
      But an inner one, giving out rays.

Such was the thing in his eye, walking there,
      The very and visible thing,
A close light, displacing the gray of the morning air,
      And the tokens that the dark was taking wing;
And was it not the radiance of a purpose rare
      That might ripe to its accomplishing?

What became of that light?   I wonder still its fate!
      Was it quenched ere its full apogee?

Did it struggle frail and frailer to a beam emaciate?
　　Did it thrive till matured in verity?
Or did it travel on, to be a new young dreamer's freight,
　　And thence on infinitely?

　　1915.

THE HEAD ABOVE THE FOG

　　Something do I see
Above the fog that sheets the mead,
A figure like to life indeed,
Moving along with spectre-speed,
　　Seen by none but me.

　　O the vision keen!—
Tripping along to me for love
As in the flesh it used to move,
Only its hat and plume above
　　The evening fog-fleece seen.

　　In the day-fall wan,
When nighted birds break off their song,
Mere ghostly head it skims along,
Just as it did when warm and strong,
　　Body seeming gone.

　　Such it is I see
Above the fog that sheets the mead—
Yea, that which once could breathe and plead!—
Skimming along with spectre-speed
　　To a last tryst with me.

OVERLOOKING THE RIVER STOUR

The swallows flew in the curves of an eight
　　Above the river-gleam
　　In the wet June's last beam:
Like little crossbows animate
The swallows flew in the curves of an eight
　　Above the river-gleam.

Planing up shavings of crystal spray
    A moor-hen darted out
      From the bank thereabout,
And through the stream-shine ripped his way;
Planing up shavings of crystal spray
    A moor-hen darted out.

Closed were the kingcups; and the mead
    Dripped in monotonous green,
      Though the day's morning sheen
Had shown it golden and honeybee'd;
Closed were the kingcups; and the mead
    Dripped in monotonous green.

And never I turned my head, alack,
    While these things met my gaze
      Through the pane's drop-drenched glaze,
To see the more behind my back. . . .
O never I turned, but let, alack,
    These less things hold my gaze!

THE MUSICAL BOX

LIFELONG to be
Seemed the fair colour of the time;
That there was standing shadowed near
A spirit who sang to the gentle chime
Of the self-struck notes, I did not hear,
    I did not see.

    Thus did it sing
To the mindless lyre that played indoors
As she came to listen for me without:
"O value what the nonce outpours—
This best of life—that shines about
    Your welcoming!"

    I had slowed along
After the torrid hours were done,
Though still the posts and walls and road

Flung back their sense of the hot-faced sun,
And had walked by Stourside Mill, where broad
    Stream-lilies throng.

    And I descried
The dusky house that stood apart,
And her, white-muslined, waiting there
In the porch with high-expectant heart,
While still the thin mechanic air
    Went on inside.

    At whiles would flit
Swart bats, whose wings, be-webbed and tanned,
Whirred like the wheels of ancient clocks :
She laughed a hailing as she scanned
Me in the gloom, the tuneful box
    Intoning it.

    Lifelong to be
I thought it. That there watched hard by
A spirit who sang to the indoor tune,
"O make the most of what is nigh ! "
I did not hear in my dull soul-swoon—
    I did not see.

ON STURMINSTER FOOT-BRIDGE

(Onomatopœic)

RETICULATIONS creep upon the slack stream's face
    When the wind skims irritably past,
The current clucks smartly into each hollow place
That years of flood have scrabbled in the pier's sodden base ;
    The floating-lily leaves rot fast.

On a roof stand the swallows ranged in wistful waiting rows,
    Till they arrow off and drop like stones
Among the eyot-withies at whose foot the river flows :
And beneath the roof is she who in the dark world shows
    As a lattice-gleam when midnight moans.

ROYAL SPONSORS

"THE king and the queen will stand to the child;
    'Twill be handed down in song;
And it's no more than their deserving,
With my lord so faithful at Court so long,
      And so staunch and strong.

" O never before was known such a thing !
    'Twill be a grand time for all ;
And the beef will be a whole-roast bullock,
And the servants will have a feast in the hall,
      And the ladies a ball.

" While from Jordan's stream by a traveller,
    In a flagon of silver wrought,
And by caravan, stage-coach, wain, and waggon
A precious trickle has been brought,
      Clear as when caught."

The morning came.   To the park of the peer
    The royal couple bore ;
And the font was filled with the Jordan water,
And the household awaited their guests before
      The carpeted door.

But when they went to the silk-lined cot
    The child was found to have died.
" What's now to be done ?   We can disappoint not
The king and queen ! " the family cried
      With eyes spread wide.

" Even now they approach the chestnut-drive !
    The service must be read."
" Well, since we can't christen the child alive,
By God we shall have to christen him dead ! "
      The marquis said.

Thus, breath-forsaken, a corpse was taken
    To the private chapel—yea—
And the king knew not, nor the queen, God wot,
That they answered for one returned to clay
      At the font that day.

OLD FURNITURE

I KNOW not how it may be with others
    Who sit amid relics of householdry
That date from the days of their mothers' mothers,
    But well I know how it is with me
        Continually.

I see the hands of the generations
    That owned each shiny familiar thing
In play on its knobs and indentations,
    And with its ancient fashioning
        Still dallying :

Hands behind hands, growing paler and paler,
    As in a mirror a candle-flame
Shows images of itself, each frailer
    As it recedes, though the eye may frame
        Its shape the same.

On the clock's dull dial a foggy finger,
    Moving to set the minutes right
With tentative touches that lift and linger
    In the wont of a moth on a summer night,
        Creeps to my sight.

On this old viol, too, fingers are dancing—
    As whilom—just over the strings by the nut,
The tip of a bow receding, advancing
    In airy quivers, as if it would cut
        The plaintive gut.

And I see a face by that box for tinder,
    Glowing forth in fits from the dark,
And fading again, as the linten cinder
    Kindles to red at the flinty spark,
        Or goes out stark.

Well, well. It is best to be up and doing,
    The world has no use for one to-day
Who eyes things thus—no aim pursuing !
    He should not continue in this stay,
        But sink away.

A THOUGHT IN TWO MOODS

I SAW it—pink and white—revealed
    Upon the white and green ;
The white and green was a daisied field,
    The pink and white Ethleen.

And as I looked it seemed in kind
    That difference they had none ;
The two fair bodiments combined
    As varied miens of one.

A sense that, in some mouldering year,
    As one they both would lie,
Made me move quickly on to her
    To pass the pale thought by.

She laughed and said : " Out there, to me,
    You looked so weather-browned,
And brown in clothes, you seemed to be
    Made of the dusty ground ! "

THE LAST PERFORMANCE

" I AM playing my oldest tunes," declared she,
    " All the old tunes I know,—
Those I learnt ever so long ago."
    —Why she should think just then she'd play them
        Silence cloaks like snow.

When I returned from the town at nightfall
    Notes continued to pour
As when I had left two hours before :
" It's the very last time," she said in closing ;
    " From now I play no more."

A few morns onward found her fading,
    And, as her life outflew,
I thought of her playing her tunes right through ;
And I felt she had known of what was coming,
    And wondered how she knew.

        1912.

"YOU ON THE TOWER"

I

"You on the tower of my factory—
    What do you see up there?
Do you see Enjoyment with wide wings
    Advancing to reach me here?"
—"Yea; I see Enjoyment with wide wings
    Advancing to reach you here."

II

"Good. Soon I'll come and ask you
    To tell me again thereon. . . .
Well, what is he doing now? Hoi, there!"
    —"He still is flying on."
"Ah, waiting till I have full-finished.
    Good. Tell me again anon. . . .

III

Hoi, Watchman! I'm here. When comes he?
    Between my sweats I am chill."
—"Oh, you there, working still?
Why, surely he reached you a time back,
    And took you miles from your mill?
He duly came in his winging,
    And now he has passed out of view.
How can it be that you missed him?
    He brushed you by as he flew."

THE INTERLOPER

" And I saw the figure and visage of Madness seeking for a home."

There are three folk driving in a quaint old chaise,
And the cliff-side track looks green and fair:
I view them talking in quiet glee
As they drop down towards the puffins' lair
    By the roughest of ways;
But another with the three rides on, I see,
    Whom I like not to be there!

No : it's not anybody you think of.   Next
A dwelling appears by a slow sweet stream
Where two sit happy and half in the dark :
They read, helped out by a frail-wick'd gleam,
     Some rhythmic text ;
But one sits with them whom they don't mark,
     One I'm wishing could not be there.

No : not whom you knew and name.   And now
I discern gay diners in a mansion-place,
And the guests dropping wit—pert, prim, or choice,
And the hostess's tender and laughing face,
     And the host's bland brow ;
But I cannot help hearing a hollow voice,
     And I'd fain not hear it there.

No : it's not from the stranger you met once.   Ah,
Yet a goodlier scene than that succeeds ;
People on a lawn—quite a crowd of them.   Yes,
And they chatter and ramble as fancy leads ;
     And they say, " Hurrah ! "
To a blithe speech made ; save one, mirthless,
     Who ought not to be there.

Nay : it's not the pale Form your imagings raise,
That waits on us all at a destined time,
It is not the Fourth Figure the Furnace showed ;
O that it were such a shape sublime
     In these latter days !
It is that under which best lives corrode ;
     Would, would it could not be there !

LOGS ON THE HEARTH

A MEMORY OF A SISTER.

THE fire advances along the log
    Of the tree we felled,
Which bloomed and bore striped apples by the peck
    Till its last hour of bearing knelled.

The fork that first my hand would reach
      And then my foot
In climbings upward inch by inch, lies now
      Sawn, sapless, darkening with soot.

Where the bark chars is where, one year,
      It was pruned, and bled—
Then overgrew the wound.   But now, at last,
      Its growings all have stagnated.

My fellow-climber rises dim
      From her chilly grave—
Just as she was, her foot near mine on the bending limb,
      Laughing, her young brown hand awave.

        December 1915.

THE SUNSHADE

AH—it's the skeleton of a lady's sunshade,
      Here at my feet in the hard rock's chink,
      Merely a naked sheaf of wires !—
      Twenty years have gone with their livers and diers
      Since it was silked in its white or pink.

Noonshine riddles the ribs of the sunshade,
      No more a screen from the weakest ray ;
      Nothing to tell us the hue of its dyes,
      Nothing but rusty bones as it lies
      In its coffin of stone, unseen till to-day.

Where is the woman who carried that sunshade
      Up and down this seaside place ?—
      Little thumb standing against its stem,
      Thoughts perhaps bent on a love-stratagem,
      Softening yet more the already soft face !

Is the fair woman who carried that sunshade
      A skeleton just as her property is,

Laid in the chink that none may scan?
And does she regret—if regret dust can—
The vain things thought when she flourished this?

SWANAGE CLIFFS.

THE AGEING HOUSE

WHEN the walls were red
That now are seen
To be overspread
With a mouldy green,
A fresh fair head
Would often lean
From the sunny casement
And scan the scene,
While blithely spoke the wind to the little sycamore tree.

But storms have raged
Those walls about,
And the head has aged
That once looked out;
And zest is suaged
And trust grows doubt,
And slow effacement
Is rife throughout,
While fiercely girds the wind at the long-limbed sycamore tree!

THE CAGED GOLDFINCH

WITHIN a churchyard, on a recent grave,
I saw a little cage
That jailed a goldfinch. All was silence save
Its hops from stage to stage.

There was inquiry in its wistful eye,
And once it tried to sing;
Of him or her who placed it there, and why,
No one knew anything.

AT MADAME TUSSAUD'S IN VICTORIAN YEARS

" THAT same first fiddler who leads the orchéstra to-night
   Here fiddled four decades of years ago ;
He bears the same babe-like smile of self-centred delight,
Same trinket on watch-chain, same ring on the hand with the bow.

" But his face, if regarded, is woefully wanner, and drier,
   And his once dark beard has grown straggling and gray ;
Yet a blissful existence he seems to have led with his lyre,
In a trance of his own, where no wearing or tearing had sway.

" Mid these wax figures, who nothing can do, it may seem
   That to do but a little thing counts a great deal ;
To be watched by kings, councillors, queens, may be flattering
   to him—
With their glass eyes longing they too could wake notes that
   appeal."

     .   .   .

Ah, but he played staunchly—that fiddler—whoever he was,
   With the innocent heart and the soul-touching string :
May he find the Fair Haven ! For did he not smile with good
   cause ?
Yes ; gamuts that graced forty years'-flight were not a small
   thing !

THE BALLET

THEY crush together—a rustling heap of flesh—
Of more than flesh, a heap of souls ; and then
      They part, enmesh,
     And crush together again,
Like the pink petals of a too sanguine rose
   Frightened shut just when it blows.

Though all alike in their tinsel livery,
And indistinguishable at a sweeping glance,
     They muster, maybe,
    As lives wide in irrelevance ;

A world of her own has each one underneath,
　　Detached as a sword from its sheath.

Daughters, wives, mistresses ; honest or false, sold, bought ;
Hearts of all sizes ; gay, fond, gushing, or penned,
　　　　Various in thought
　　　　Of lover, rival, friend ;
Links in a one-pulsed chain, all showing one smile,
　　Yet severed so many a mile !

THE FIVE STUDENTS .

THE sparrow dips in his wheel-rut bath,
　　The sun grows passionate-eyed,
And boils the dew to smoke by the paddock-path ;
　　As strenuously we stride,—
Five of us ; dark He, fair He, dark She, fair She, I,
　　　　All beating by.

The air is shaken, the high-road hot,
　　Shadowless swoons the day,
The greens are sobered and cattle at rest ; but not
　　We on our urgent way,—
Four of us ; fair She, dark She, fair He, I, are there,
　　　　But one—elsewhere.

Autumn moulds the hard fruit mellow,
　　And forward still we press
Through moors, briar-meshed plantations, clay-pits yellow,
　　As in the spring hours—yes,
Three of us ; fair He, fair She, I, as heretofore,
　　　　But—fallen one more.

The leaf drops : earthworms draw it in
　　At night-time noiselessly,
The fingers of birch and beech are skeleton-thin,
　　And yet on the beat are we,—
Two of us ; fair She, I.　But no more left to go
　　　　The track we know.

Icicles tag the church-aisle leads,
  The flag-rope gibbers hoarse,
The home-bound foot-folk wrap their snow-flaked heads,
  Yet I still stalk the course—
One of us. . . . Dark and fair He, dark and fair She, gone
  The rest—anon.

THE WIND'S PROPHECY

I TRAVEL on by barren farms,
  And gulls glint out like silver flecks
  Against a cloud that speaks of wrecks,
And bellies down with black alarms.
I say: "Thus from my lady's arms
  I go; those arms I love the best!"
The wind replies from dip and rise,
  "Nay; toward her arms thou journeyest."

A distant verge morosely gray
  Appears, while clots of flying foam
  Break from its muddy monochrome,
And a light blinks up far away.
I sigh: "My eyes now as all day
  Behold her ebon loops of hair!"
Like bursting bonds the wind responds,
  "Nay, wait for tresses flashing fair!"

From tides the lofty coastlands screen
  Come smitings like the slam of doors,
  Or hammerings on hollow floors,
As the swell cleaves through caves unseen.
Say I: "Though broad this wild terrene,
  Her city home s matched of none!"
From the hoarse skies the wind replies:
  "Thou shouldst have said her sea-bord one."

The all-prevailing clouds exclude
  The one quick timorous transient star;
  The waves outside where breakers are
Huzza like a mad multitude.

"Where the sun ups it, mist-imbued,"
I cry, "there reigns the star for me!"
The wind outshrieks from points and peaks:
"Here, westward, where it downs, mean ye!"

Yonder the headland, vulturine,
Snores like old Skrymer in his sleep,
And every chasm and every steep
Blackens as wakes each pharos-shine.
"I roam, but one is safely mine,"
I say. "God grant she stay my own!"
Low laughs the wind as if it grinned:
"Thy Love is one thou'st not yet known."

Rewritten from an old copy.

DURING WIND AND RAIN

THEY sing their dearest songs—
He, she, all of them—yea,
Treble and tenor and bass,
    And one to play;
With the candles mooning each face. . . .
    Ah, no; the years O!
How the sick leaves reel down in throngs!

They clear the creeping moss—
Elders and juniors—aye,
Making the pathways neat
    And the garden gay;
And they build a shady seat. . . .
    Ah, no; the years, the years;
See, the white storm-birds wing across!

They are blithely breakfasting all—
Men and maidens—yea,
Under the summer tree,
    With a glimpse of the bay,
While pet fowl come to the knee. . . .
    Ah, no; the years O!
And the rotten rose is ript from the wall.

They change to a high new house,
He, she, all of them—aye,
Clocks and carpets and chairs
    On the lawn all day,
And brightest things that are theirs. . . .
    Ah, no ; the years, the years ;
Down their carved names the rain-drop ploughs.

HE PREFERS HER EARTHLY

THIS after-sunset is a sight for seeing,
Cliff-heads of craggy cloud surrounding it.
    —And dwell you in that glory-show ?
You may ; for there are strange strange things in being,
    Stranger than I know.

Yet if that chasm of splendour claim your presence
Which glows between the ash cloud and the dun,
    How changed must be your mortal mould !
Changed to a firmament-riding earthless essence
    From what you were of old :

All too unlike the fond and fragile creature
Then known to me. . . . Well, shall I say it plain ?
    I would not have you thus and there,
But still would grieve on, missing you, still feature
    You as the one you were.

THE DOLLS

"WHENEVER you dress me dolls, mammy,
    Why do you dress them so,
And make them gallant soldiers,
    When never a one I know ;
And not as gentle ladies
    With frills and frocks and curls,
As people dress the dollies
    Of other little girls ?"

Ah—why did she not answer :—
    " Because your mammy's heed
Is always gallant soldiers,
    As well may be, indeed.
One of them was your daddy,
    His name I must not tell ;
He's not the dad who lives here,
    But one I love too well,"

MOLLY GONE

No more summer for Molly and me ;
    There is snow on the tree,
And the blackbirds plump large as the rooks are, almost,
    And the water is hard
Where they used to dip bills at the dawn ere her figure was lost
    To these coasts, now my prison close-barred.

No more planting by Molly and me
    Where the beds used to be
Of sweet-william ; no training the clambering rose
    By the framework of fir
Now bowering the pathway, whereon it swings gaily and blows
    As if calling commendment from her.

No more jauntings by Molly and me
    To the town by the sea,
Or along over Whitesheet to Wynyard's green Gap,
    Catching Montacute Crest
To the right against Sedgmoor, and Corton-Hill's far-distant cap,
    And Pilsdon and Lewsdon to west.

No more singing by Molly to me
    In the evenings when she
Was in mood and in voice, and the candles were lit,
    And past the porch-quoin
The rays would spring out on the laurels ; and dumbledores hit
    On the pane, as if wishing to join.

Where, then, is Molly, who's no more with me ?
    —As I stand on this lea,

Thinking thus, there's a many-flamed star in the air,
        That tosses a sign
That her glance is regarding its face from her home, so that there
        Her eyes may have meetings with mine.

A BACKWARD SPRING

THE trees are afraid to put forth buds,
And there is timidity in the grass;
The plots lie gray where gouged by spuds,
        And whether next week will pass
Free of sly sour winds is the fret of each bush
        Of barberry waiting to bloom.

Yet the snowdrop's face betrays no gloom,
And the primrose pants in its heedless push,
Though the myrtle asks if it's worth the fight
        This year with frost and rime
        To venture one more time
On delicate leaves and buttons of white
From the selfsame bough as at last year's prime,
And never to ruminate on or remember
What happened to it in mid-December.

        April 1917.

LOOKING ACROSS

I

IT is dark in the sky,
And silence is where
Our laughs rang high;
And recall do I
That One is out there.

II

The dawn is not nigh,
And the trees are bare,

And the waterways sigh
That a year has drawn by,
And Two are out there.

III

The wind drops to die
Like the phantom of Care
Too frail for a cry,
And heart brings to eye
That Three are out there.

IV

This Life runs dry
That once ran rare
And rosy in dye,
And fleet the days fly,
And Four are out there.

V

Tired, tired am I
Of this earthly air,
And my wraith asks : Why,
Since these calm lie,
Are not Five out there ?

December 1915.

AT A SEASIDE TOWN IN 1869

(*Young Lover's Reverie*)

I WENT and stood outside myself,
    Spelled the dark sky
    And ship-lights nigh,
And grumbling winds that passed thereby.

Then next inside myself I looked,
    And there, above
    All, shone my Love,
That nothing matched the image of.

Beyond myself again I ranged ;
    And saw the free
    Life by the sea,
And folk indifferent to me.

O 'twas a charm to draw within
    Thereafter, where
    But she was ; care
For one thing only, her hid there !

But so it chanced, without myself
    I had to look,
    And then I took
More heed of what I had long forsook :

The boats, the sands, the esplanade,
    The laughing crowd ;
    Light-hearted, loud
Greetings from some not ill-endowed ;

The evening sunlit cliffs, the talk,
    Hailings and halts,
    The keen sea-salts,
The band, the Morgenblätter Waltz.

Still, when at night I drew inside
    Forward she came,
    Sad, but the same
As when I first had known her name.

Then rose a time when, as by force,
    Outwardly wooed
    By contacts crude,
Her image in abeyance stood. . . .

At last I said ; This outside life
    Shall not endure ;
    I'll seek the pure
Thought-world, and bask in her allure.

Myself again I crept within,
    Scanned with keen care
    The temple where
She'd shone, but could not find her there.

I sought and sought.   But O her soul
   Has not since thrown
   Upon my own
One beam !   Yea, she is gone, is gone.

From an old note.

THE GLIMPSE

SHE sped through the door
And, following in haste,
And stirred to the core,
I entered hot-faced ;
But I could not find her,
No sign was behind her.
" Where is she ? " I said :
—" Who ? " they asked that sat there ;
" Not a soul's come in sight."
—" A maid with red hair."
—" Ah."   They paled.   " She is dead.
People see her at night,
But you are the first
On whom she has burst
In the keen common light."

It was ages ago,
When I was quite strong :
I have waited since,—O,
I have waited so long !
—Yea, I set me to own
The house, where now lone
I dwell in void rooms
Booming hollow as tombs !
But I never come near her,
Though nightly I hear her.
And my cheek has grown thin
And my hair has grown gray
With this waiting therein ;
But she still keeps away !

THE PEDESTRIAN

AN INCIDENT OF 1883

"Sir, will you let me give you a ride?
Nox venit, and the heath is wide."
—My phaeton-lantern shone on one
    Young, fair, even fresh,
    But burdened with flesh:
A leathern satchel at his side,
His breathings short, his coat undone.

'Twas as if his corpulent figure slopped
With the shake of his walking when he stopped,
And, though the night's pinch grew acute,
    He wore but a thin
    Wind-thridded suit,
Yet well-shaped shoes for walking in,
Artistic beaver, cane gold-topped.

"Alas, my friend," he said with a smile,
"I am daily bound to foot ten mile—
Wet, dry, or dark—before I rest.
    Six months to live
    My doctors give
Me as my prospect here, at best,
Unless I vamp my sturdiest!"

His voice was that of a man refined,
A man, one well could feel, of mind,
Quite winning in its musical ease;
    But in mould maligned
    By some disease;
And I asked again.   But he shook his head:
Then, as if more were due, he said:—

"A student was I—of Schopenhauer,
Kant, Hegel,—and the fountained bower
Of the Muses, too, knew my regard:
    But ah—I fear me
    The grave gapes near me! . . .".

Would I could this gross sheath discard,
And rise an ethereal shape, unmarred!"

How I remember him!—his short breath,
His aspect, marked for early death,
As he dropped into the night for ever;
    One caught in his prime
    Of high endeavour;
From all philosophies soon to sever
Through an unconscienced trick of Time!

"WHO'S IN THE NEXT ROOM?"

"WHO'S in the next room?—who?
    I seemed to see
Somebody in the dawning passing through,
    Unknown to me."
"Nay: you saw nought. He passed invisibly."

"Who's in the next room?—who?
    I seem to hear
Somebody muttering firm in a language new
    That chills the ear."
"No: you catch not his tongue who has entered there."

"Who's in the next room?—who?
    I seem to feel
His breath like a clammy draught, as if it drew
    From the Polar Wheel."
"No: none who breathes at all does the door conceal."

"Who's in the next room?—who?
    A figure wan
With a message to one in there of something due?
    Shall I know him anon?"
"Yea he; and he brought such; and you'll know him anon."

AT A COUNTRY FAIR

AT a bygone Western country fair
I saw a giant led by a dwarf
With a red string like a long thin scarf;
How much he was the stronger there
        The giant seemed unaware.

And then I saw that the giant was blind,
And the dwarf a shrewd-eyed little thing;
The giant, mild, timid, obeyed the string
As if he had no independent mind,
        Or will of any kind.

Wherever the dwarf decided to go
At his heels the other trotted meekly,
(Perhaps—I know not—reproaching weakly)
Like one Fate bade that it must be so,
        Whether he wished or no.

Various sights in various climes
I have seen, and more I may see yet,
But that sight never shall I forget,
And have thought it the sorriest of pantomimes,
        If once, a hundred times!

THE MEMORIAL BRASS: 186–

"WHY do you weep there, O sweet lady,
Why do you weep before that brass?—
(I'm a mere student sketching the mediaeval)
Is some late death lined there, alas?—
Your father's? . . . Well, all pay the debt that paid he!"

    "Young man, O must I tell!—My husband's! And under
His name I set mine, and my *death*!—
Its date left vacant till my heirs should fill it,
    Stating me faithful till my last breath."
—"Madam, that you are a widow wakes my wonder!"

" O wait ! For last month I—remarried !
     And now I fear 'twas a deed amiss.
We've just come home.   And I am sick and saddened
     At what the new one will say to this ;
And will he think—think that I should have tarried ?

     " I may add, surely,—with no wish to harm him—
     That he's a temper—yes, I fear !
And when he comes to church next Sunday morning,
     And sees that written . . . O dear, O dear ! "
—" Madam, I swear your beauty will disarm him ! "

HER LOVE-BIRDS

WHEN I looked up at my love-birds
     That Sunday afternoon,
          There was in their tiny tune
     A dying fetch like broken words,
When I looked up at my love-birds
     That Sunday afternoon.

When he, too, scanned the love-birds
     On entering there that day,
          'Twas as if he had nought to say
     Of his long journey citywards,
When he, too, scanned the love-birds,
     On entering there that day.

And billed and billed the love-birds,
     As 'twere in fond despair
          At the stress of silence where
     Had once been tones in tenor thirds,
And billed and billed the love-birds
     As 'twere in fond despair.

O, his speech that chilled the love-birds,
     And smote like death on me,
          As I learnt what was to be,
     And knew my life was broke in sherds !
O, his speech that chilled the love-birds,
     And smote like death on me !

PAYING CALLS

I WENT by footpath and by stile
    Beyond where bustle ends,
Strayed here a mile and there a mile
    And called upon some friends.

On certain ones I had not seen
    For years past did I call,
And then on others who had been
    The oldest friends of all.

It was the time of midsummer
    When they had used to roam;
But now, though tempting was the air,
    I found them all at home.

I spoke to one and other of them
    By mound and stone and tree
Of things we had done ere days were dim
    But they spoke not to me.

THE UPPER BIRCH-LEAVES

WARM yellowy-green
In the blue serene,
How they skip and sway
On this autumn day!
They cannot know
What has happened below,—
That their boughs down there
Are already quite bare,
That their own will be
When a week has passed,—
For they jig as in glee
To this very last.

But no; there lies
At times in their tune
A note that cries
What at first I fear

I did not hear:
"O we remember
At each wind's hollo—
Though life holds yet—
We go hence soon,
For 'tis November;
—But that you follow
You may forget!"

"IT NEVER LOOKS LIKE SUMMER"

"IT never looks like summer here
      On Beeny by the sea."
But though she saw its look as drear,
      Summer it seemed to me.

It never looks like summer now
      Whatever weather's there;
But ah, it cannot anyhow,
      On Beeny or elsewhere!

BOSCASTLE.
   March 8, 1913.

EVERYTHING COMES

"THE house is bleak and cold
      Built so new for me!
All the winds upon the wold
      Search it through for me;
No screening trees abound,
And the curious eyes around,
      Keep on view for me."

"My Love, I am planting trees
      As a screen for you
Both from winds, and eyes that tease
      And peer in for you.

Only wait till they have grown,
No such bower will be known
    As I mean for you."

"Then I will bear it, Love,
    And will wait," she said.
—So, with years, there grew a grove.
    "Skill how great!" she said.
"As you wished, Dear?"—"Yes, I see!
But—I'm dying; and for me
    'Tis too late," she said.

THE MAN WITH A PAST

THERE was merry-making
    When the first dart fell
    As a heralding,—
Till grinned the fully bared thing,
    And froze like a spell—
        Like a spell.

Innocent was she,
    Innocent was I,
    Too simple we!
Before us we did not see,
    Nearing, aught wry—
        Aught wry!

I can tell it not now,
    It was long ago;
    And such things cow;
But that is why and how
    Two lives were so—
        Were so.

Yes, the years matured,
    And the blows were three
    That time ensured
On her, which she dumbly endured;
    And one on me—
        One on me.

HE FEARS HIS GOOD FORTUNE

THERE was a glorious time
At an epoch of my prime;
Mornings beryl-bespread,
And evenings golden-red;
    Nothing gray:
And in my heart I said,
"However this chanced to be,
It is too full for me,
Too rare, too rapturous, rash,
Its spell must close with a crash
    Some day!"

The radiance went on
Anon and yet anon,
And sweetness fell around
Like manna on the ground.
    "I've no claim,"
Said I, "to be thus crowned:
I am not worthy this:—
Must it not go amiss?—
Well . . . let the end foreseen
Come duly!—I am serene."
    —And it came.

HE WONDERS ABOUT HIMSELF

No use hoping, or feeling vext,
Tugged by a force above or under
Like some fantocine, much I wonder
What I shall find me doing next!

Shall I be rushing where bright eyes be?
Shall I be suffering sorrows seven?
Shall I be watching the stars of heaven,
Thinking one of them looks like thee?

Part is mine of the general Will,
Cannot my share in the sum of sources
Bend a digit the poise of forces,
And a fair desire fulfil?

Nov. 1893.

JUBILATE

" THE very last time I ever was here, " he said,
" I saw much less of the quick than I saw of the dead."
—He was a man I had met with somewhere before,
But how or when I now could recall no more.

" The hazy mazy moonlight at one in the morning
Spread out as a sea across the frozen snow,
Glazed to live sparkles like the great breastplate adorning
The priest of the Temple, with Urim and Thummim aglow.

" The yew-tree arms, glued hard to the stiff stark air,
Hung still in the village sky as theatre-scenes
When I came by the churchyard wall, and halted there
At a shut-in sound of fiddles and tambourines.

" And as I stood hearkening, dulcimers, hautboys, and shawms,
And violoncellos, and a three-stringed double-bass,
Joined in, and were intermixed with a singing of psalms ;
And I looked over at the dead men's dwelling-place.

" Through the shine of the slippery snow I now could see,
As it were through a crystal roof, a great company
Of the dead minueting in stately step underground
To the tune of the instruments I had before heard sound.

" It was ' Eden New,' and dancing they sang in a chore,
' We are out of it all !—yea, in Little-Ease cramped no more ! "
And their shrouded figures pacing with joy I could see
As you see the stage from the gallery.   And they had no heed of
    me.

" And I lifted my head quite dazed from the churchyard wall
And I doubted not that it warned I should soon have my call.
But—" . . . Then in the ashes he emptied the dregs of his cup,
And onward he went, and the darkness swallowed him up.

HE REVISITS HIS FIRST SCHOOL

I SHOULD not have shown in the flesh,
I ought to have gone as a ghost ;
It was awkward, unseemly almost,
Standing solidly there as when fresh,
  Pink, tiny, crisp-curled,
  My pinions yet furled
  From the winds of the world.

After waiting so many a year
To wait longer, and go as a sprite
From the tomb at the mid of some night
Was the right, radiant way to appear ;
  Not as one wanzing weak
  From life's roar and reek,
  His rest still to seek :

Yea, beglimpsed through the quaint quarried glass
Of green moonlight, by me greener made,
When they'd cry, perhaps, " There sits his shade
In his olden haunt—just as he was
  When in Walkingame he
  Conned the grand Rule-of-Three
  With the bent of a bee."

But to show in the afternoon sun,
With an aspect of hollow-eyed care,
When none wished to see me come there,
Was a garish thing, better undone.
  Yes ; wrong was the way ;
  But yet, let me say,
  I may right it—some day.

"I THOUGHT, MY HEART"

I THOUGHT, my Heart, that you had healed
Of those sore smartings of the past,
And that the summers had oversealed
  All mark of them at last.

But closely scanning in the night
I saw them standing crimson-bright
    Just as she made them :
    Nothing could fade them ;
    Yea, I can swear
    That there they were—
    They still were there !

Then the Vision of her who cut them came,
And looking over my shoulder said,
"I am sure you deal me all the blame
    For those sharp smarts and red ;
But meet me, dearest, to-morrow night,
In the churchyard at the moon's half-height,
    And so strange a kiss
    Shall be mine, I wis,
    That you'll cease to know
    If the wounds you show
    Be there or no !"

FRAGMENT

At last I entered a long dark gallery,
    Catacomb-lined ; and ranged at the side
    Were the bodies of men from far and wide
Who, motion past, were nevertheless not dead.

    "The sense of waiting here strikes strong ;
Everyone's waiting, waiting, it seems to me ;
    What are you waiting for so long ?—
        What is to happen ?" I said.

"O we are waiting for one called God," said they,
    "(Though by some the Will, or Force, or Laws ;
    And, vaguely, by some, the Ultimate Cause ;)
Waiting for him to see us before we are clay.
    Yes ; waiting, waiting, for God *to know it*." . . .
        "To know what ?" questioned I.
"To know how things have been going on earth and below it :
    It is clear he must know some day."
        I thereon asked them why.

" Since he made us humble pioneers
Of himself in consciousness of Life's tears,
It needs no mighty prophecy
To tell that what he could mindlessly show
His creatures, he himself will know.

" By some still close-cowled mystery
We have reached feeling faster than he,
But he will overtake us anon,
    If the world goes on."

MIDNIGHT ON THE GREAT WESTERN

IN the third-class seat sat the journeying boy,
    And the roof-lamp's oily flame
Played down on his listless form and face,
Bewrapt past knowing to what he was going,
    Or whence he came.

In the band of his hat the journeying boy
    Had a ticket stuck ; and a string
Around his neck bore the key of his box,
That twinkled gleams of the lamp's sad beams
    Like a living thing.

What past can be yours, O journeying boy
    Towards a world unknown,
Who calmly, as if incurious quite
On all at stake, can undertake
    This plunge alone ?

Knows your soul a sphere, O journeying boy,
    Our rude realms far above,
Whence with spacious vision you mark and mete
This region of sin that you find you in,
    But are not of ?

HONEYMOON TIME AT AN INN

At the shiver of morning, a little before the false dawn,
   The moon was at the window-square,
   Deedily brooding in deformed decay—
   The curve hewn off her cheek as by an adze;
At the shiver of morning a little before the false dawn
   So the moon looked in there.

Her speechless eyeing reached across the chamber,
   Where lay two souls opprest,
   One a white lady sighing, "Why am I sad!"
   To him who sighed back, "Sad, my Love, am I!"
And speechlessly the old moon conned the chamber,
   And these two reft of rest.

While their large-pupilled vision swept the scene there,
   Nought seeming imminent,
   Something fell sheer, and crashed, and from the floor
   Lay glittering at the pair with a shattered gaze,
While their large-pupilled vision swept the scene there,
   And the many-eyed thing outlent.

With a start they saw that it was an old-time pier-glass
   Which had stood on the mantel near,
   Its silvering blemished,—yes, as if worn away
   By the eyes of the countless dead who had smirked at it
Ere these two ever knew that old-time pier-glass
   And its vague and vacant leer.

As he looked, his bride like a moth skimmed forth, and kneeling
   Quick, with quivering sighs,
   Gathered the pieces under the moon's sly ray,
   Unwitting as an automaton what she did;
Till he entreated, hasting to where she was kneeling,
   "Let it stay where it lies!"

"Long years of sorrow this means!" breathed the lady
   As they retired. "Alas!"
   And she lifted one pale hand across her eyes.
   "Don't trouble, Love; it's nothing," the bridegroom said.
"Long years of sorrow for us!" murmured the lady,
   "Or ever this evil pass!"

And the Spirits Ironic laughed behind the wainscot,
　　And the Spirits of Pity sighed.
"It's good," said the Spirits Ironic, "to tickle their minds
With a portent of their wedlock's aftergrinds."
And the Spirits of Pity sighed behind the wainscot,
　　"It's a portent we cannot abide!

"More, what shall happen to prove the truth of the portent?"
　　—"Oh; in brief, they will fade till old,
And their loves grow numbed ere death, by the cark of care."
　　—"But nought see we that asks for portents there?—
'Tis the lot of all."—"Well, no less true is a portent
　　That it fits all mortal mould."

THE ROBIN

WHEN up aloft
I fly and fly,
I see in pools
The shining sky,
And a happy bird
Am I, am I!

When I descend
Towards their brink
I stand, and look,
And stoop, and drink,
And bathe my wings,
And chink and prink.

When winter frost
Makes earth as steel
I search and search
But find no meal,
And most unhappy
Then I feel.

But when it lasts,
And snows still fall,
I get to feel
No grief at all,
For I turn to a cold stiff
Feathery ball!

"I ROSE AND WENT TO ROU'TOR TOWN"

(She, alone)

I ROSE and went to Rou'tor Town
  With gaiety and good heart,
    And ardour for the start,
That morning ere the moon was down
That lit me off to Rou'tor Town
  With gaiety and good heart.

When sojourn soon at Rou'tor Town
  Wrote sorrows on my face,
    I strove that none should trace
The pale and gray, once pink and brown,
When sojourn soon at Rou'tor Town
  Wrote sorrows on my face.

The evil wrought at Rou'tor Town
  On him I'd loved so true
    I cannot tell anew:
But nought can quench, but nought can drown
The evil wrought at Rou'tor Town
  On him I'd loved so true!

THE NETTLES

THIS, then, is the grave of my son,
  Whose heart she won! And nettles grow
Upon his mound; and she lives just below.

How he upbraided me, and left,
  And our lives were cleft, because I said
She was hard, unfeeling, caring but to wed.

Well, to see this sight I have fared these miles,
  And her firelight smiles from her window there,
Whom he left his mother to cherish with tender care!

It is enough. I'll turn and go;
  Yes, nettles grow where lone lies he,
Who spurned me for seeing what he could not see.

IN A WAITING-ROOM

ON a morning sick as the day of doom
    With the drizzling gray
    Of an English May,
There were few in the railway waiting-room.
About its walls were framed and varnished
Pictures of liners, fly-blown, tarnished.
The table bore a Testament
For travellers' reading, if suchwise bent.

    I read it on and on,
And, thronging the Gospel of Saint John,
Were figures—additions, multiplications—
By some one scrawled, with sundry emendations;
    Not scoffingly designed,
    But with an absent mind,—
Plainly a bagman's counts of cost,
What he had profited, what lost;
And whilst I wondered if there could have been
    Any particle of a soul
    In that poor man at all,
    To cypher rates of wage
    Upon that printed page,
    There joined in the charmless scene
And stood over me and the scribbled book
    (To lend the hour's mean hue
    A smear of tragedy too)
A soldier and wife, with haggard look
Subdued to stone by strong endeavour;
    And then I heard
    From a casual word
They were parting as they believed for ever.

    But next there came
    Like the eastern flame
Of some high altar, children—a pair—
Who laughed at the fly-blown pictures there.
"Here are the lovely ships that we,
Mother, are by and by going to see!
When we get there it's 'most sure to be fine,
And the band will play, and the sun will shine!"

It rained on the skylight with a din
As we waited and still no train came in ;
But the words of the child in the squalid room
Had spread a glory through the gloom.

THE CLOCK-WINDER

IT is dark as a cave,
Or a vault in the nave
When the iron door
Is closed, and the floor
Of the church relaid
With trowel and spade.

But the parish-clerk
Cares not for the dark
As he winds in the tower
At a regular hour
The rheumatic clock
Whose dilatory knock
You can hear when praying
At the day's decaying,
Or at any lone while
From a pew in the aisle.

Up, up from the ground
Around and around
In the turret stair
He clambers, to where
The wheelwork is,
With its tick, click, whizz,
Reposefully measuring
Each day to its end
That mortal men spend
In sorrowing and pleasuring.
Nightly thus does he climb
To the trackway of Time.

Him I followed one night
To this place without light,
And, ere I spoke, heard

Him say, word by word,
At the end of his winding,
The darkness unminding :—

"So I wipe out one more,
My Dear, of the sore
Sad days that still be,
Like a drying Dead Sea,
Between you and me!"

Who she was no man knew:
He had long borne him blind
To all womankind;
And was ever one who
Kept his past out of view.

OLD EXCURSIONS

"WHAT'S the good of going to Ridgeway,
    Cerne, or Sydling Mill,
    Or to Yell'ham Hill,
Blithely bearing Casterbridge-way
    As we used to do?
She will no more climb up there,
Or be visible anywhere
    In those haunts we knew."

But to-night, while walking weary,
    Near me seemed her shade,
    Come as 'twere to upbraid
This my mood in deeming dreary
    Scenes that used to please;
And, if she did come to me,
Still solicitous, there may be
    Good in going to these.

So, I'll care to roam to Ridgeway,
    Cerne, or Sydling Mill,
    Or to Yell'ham Hill,
Blithely bearing Casterbridge-way
    As we used to do,

Since her phasm may flit out there,
And may greet me anywhere
    In those haunts we knew.

April 1913.

THE MASKED FACE

I FOUND me in a great surging space,
    At either end a door,
And I said : " What is this giddying place,
    With no firm-fixéd floor,
    That I knew not of before ? "
" It is Life," said a mask-clad face.

I asked : " But how do I come here,
    Who never wished to come ;
Can the light and air be made more clear,
    The floor more quietsome,
    And the doors set wide ?   They numb
Fast-locked, and fill with fear."

The mask put on a bleak smile then,
    And said, " O vassal-wight,
There once complained a goosequill pen
    To the scribe of the Infinite
    Of the words it had to write
Because they were past its ken."

IN A WHISPERING GALLERY

THAT whisper takes the voice
Of a Spirit's compassionings,
    Close, but invisible,
And throws me under a spell
At the kindling vision it brings ;
    And for a moment I rejoice,
And believe in transcendent things
    That would mould from this muddy earth
    A spot for the splendid birth

Of everlasting lives,
Whereto no night arrives;
And this gaunt gray gallery
A tabernacle of worth
On this drab-aired afternoon,
When you can barely see
Across its hazed lacune
If opposite aught there be
Of fleshed humanity
Wherewith I may commune;
Or if the voice so near
Be a soul's voice floating here.

THE SOMETHING THAT SAVED HIM

It was when
Whirls of thick waters laved me
Again and again,
That something arose and saved me;
Yea, it was then.

In that day
Unseeing the azure went I
On my way,
And to white winter bent I,
Knowing no May.

Reft of renown,
Under the night clouds beating
Up and down,
In my needfulness greeting
Cit and clown.

Long there had been
Much of a murky colour
In the scene,
Dull prospects meeting duller;
Nought between.

Last, there loomed
A closing-in blind alley,

> Though there boomed
> A feeble summons to rally
>   Where it gloomed.
>
>   The clock rang;
> The hour brought a hand to deliver;
>   I upsprang,
> And looked back at den, ditch and river,
>   And sang.

THE ENEMY'S PORTRAIT

HE saw the portrait of his enemy, offered
At auction in a street he journeyed nigh,
That enemy, now late dead, who in his lifetime
Had injured deeply him the passer-by.
"To get that picture, pleased be God, I'll try,
And utterly destroy it; and no more
Shall be inflicted on man's mortal eye
A countenance so sinister and sore!"

And so he bought the painting.   Driving homeward,
"The frame will come in useful," he declared,
"The rest is fuel."   On his arrival, weary,
Asked what he bore with him, and how he fared,
He said he had bid for a picture, though he cared
For the frame only: on the morrow he
Would burn the canvas, which could well be spared,
Seeing that it portrayed his enemy.

Next day some other duty found him busy:
The foe was laid his face against the wall;
But on the next he set himself to loosen
The straining-strips.   And then a casual call
Prevented his proceeding therewithal;
And thus the picture waited, day by day,
Its owner's pleasure, like a wretched thrall,
Until a month and more had slipped away.

And then upon a morn he found it shifted,
Hung in a corner by a servitor.

"Why did you take on you to hang that picture?
You know it was the frame I bought it for."
"It stood in the way of every visitor,
And I just hitched it there."—"Well, it must go:
I don't commemorate men whom I abhor.
Remind me 'tis to do. The frame I'll stow."

But things become forgotten. In the shadow
Of the dark corner hung it by its string,
And there it stayed—once noticed by its owner,
Who said, "Ah me—I must destroy that thing!"
But when he died, there, none remembering,
It hung, till moved to prominence, as one sees;
And comers pause and say, examining,
"I thought they were the bitterest enemies?"

IMAGININGS

SHE saw herself a lady
        With fifty frocks in wear,
And rolling wheels, and rooms the best,
        And faithful maidens' care,
And open lawns and shady
        For weathers warm or drear.

She found herself a striver,
        All liberal gifts debarred,
With days of gloom, and movements stressed,
        And early visions marred,
And got no man to wive her
        But one whose lot was hard.

Yet in the moony night-time
        She steals to stile and lea
During his heavy slumberous rest
        When homecome wearily,
And dreams of some blest bright-time
        She knows can never be.

ON THE DOORSTEP

THE rain imprinted the step's wet shine
With target-circles that quivered and crossed
As I was leaving this porch of mine;
When from within there swelled and paused
       A song's sweet note;
    And back I turned, and thought,
       "Here I'll abide."

The step shines wet beneath the rain,
Which prints its circles as heretofore:
I watch them from the porch again,
But no song-notes within the door
       Now call to me
    To shun the dripping lea;
       And forth I stride.

Jan. 1914.

SIGNS AND TOKENS

SAID the red-cloaked crone
In a whispered moan;

"The dead man was limp
When laid in his chest;
Yea, limp; and why
But to signify
That the grave will crimp
Ere next year's sun
Yet another one
Of those in that house—
It may be the best—
For its endless drowse:"

Said the brown-shawled dame
To confirm the same:

"And the slothful flies
On the rotting fruit

Have been seen to wear
While crawling there
Crape scarves, by eyes
That were quick and acute ;
As did those that had pitched
On the cows by the pails,
And with flaps of their tails
Were far away switched."

Said the third in plaid,
Each word being weighed :

"And trotting does
In the park, in the lane,
And just outside
The shuttered pane,
Have also been heard—
Quick feet as light
As the feet of a sprite—
And the wise mind knows
What things may betide
When such has occurred."

Cried the black-craped fourth,
Cold faced as the north :

" O, though giving such
Some head-room, I smile
At your falterings
When noting those things
Round your domicile !
For what, what can touch
One whom, riven of all
That makes life gay,
No hints can appal
Of more takings away !"

PATHS OF FORMER TIME

No; no;
It must not be so:
They are the ways we do not go.

Still chew
The kine, and moo
In the meadows we used to wander through;

Still purl
The rivulets and curl
Towards the weirs with a musical swirl;

Haymakers
As in former years
Rake rolls into heaps that the pitchfork rears;

Wheels crack
On the turfy track
The waggon pursues with its toppling pack.

"Why then shun—
Since summer's not done—
All this because of the lack of one?"

Had you been
Sharer of that scene
You would not ask while it bites in keen

Why it is so
We can no more go
By the summer paths we used to know!

1913.

THE CLOCK OF THE YEARS

"A spirit passed before my face; the hair of my flesh stood up."

AND the Spirit said,
"I can make the clock of the years go backward,
But am loth to stop it where you will."
And I cried, "Agreed

To that.   Proceed:
It's better than dead!"

He answered, " Peace ";
And called her up—as last before me;
Then younger, younger she freshed, to the **year**
    I first had known
    Her woman-grown,
And I cried, "Cease!—

    " Thus far is good—
It is enough—let her stay thus always!"
But alas for me—He shook his head:
    No stop was there;
    And she waned child-fair,
    And to babyhood.

    Still less in mien
To my great sorrow became she slowly,
And smalled till she was nought at all
    In his checkless griff;
    And it was as if
    She had never been.

    " Better," I plained,
" She were dead as before!   The memory of her
Had lived in me; but it cannot now!"
    And coldly his voice:
    " It was your choice
    To mar the ordained."

1916.

AT THE PIANO

A WOMAN was playing,
    A man looking on;
    And the mould of her face,
    And her neck, and her hair,
    Which the rays fell upon
    Of the two candles there,
Sent him mentally straying
    In some fancy-place
    Where pain had no trace.

A cowled Apparition
        Came pushing between ;
And her notes seemed to sigh ;
And the lights to burn pale,
As a spell numbed the scene.
But the maid saw no bale,
And the man no monition ;
        And Time laughed awry,
        And the Phantom hid nigh.

THE SHADOW ON THE STONE

I WENT by the Druid stone
That broods in the garden white and lone,
And I stopped and looked at the shifting shadows
That at some moments fall thereon
From the tree hard by with a rhythmic swing,
And they shaped in my imagining
To the shade that a well-known head and shoulders
Threw there when she was gardening.

I thought her behind my back,
Yea, her I long had learned to lack,
And I said : " I am sure you are standing behind me,
Though how do you get into this old track ? "
And there was no sound but the fall of a leaf
As a sad response ; and to keep down grief
I would not turn my head to discover
That there was nothing in my belief.

Yet I wanted to look and see
That nobody stood at the back of me ;
But I thought once more : " Nay, I'll not unvision
A shape which, somehow, there may be."
So I went on softly from the glade,
And left her behind me throwing her shade,
As she were indeed an apparition—
My head unturned lest my dream should fade.

Begun 1913 : *finished* 1916.

IN THE GARDEN

(M. H.)

WE waited for the sun
To break its cloudy prison
(For day was not yet done,
And night still unbegun)
Leaning by the dial.

After many a trial—
We all silent there—
It burst as new-arisen,
Throwing a shade to where
Time travelled at that minute.

Little saw we in it,
But this much I know,
Of lookers on that shade,
Her towards whom it made
Soonest had to go.

1915.

THE TREE AND THE LADY

I HAVE done all I could
For that lady I knew!   Through the heats I have shaded her,
Drawn to her songsters when summer has jaded her,
    Home from the heath or the wood.

    At the mirth-time of May,
When my shadow first lured her, I'd donned my new bravery
Of greenth : 'twas my all.   Now I shiver in slavery,
    Icicles grieving me gray.

    Plumed to every twig's end
I could tempt her chair under me.   Much did I treasure her
During those days she had nothing to pleasure her ;
    Mutely she used me as friend.

I'm a skeleton now,
And she's gone, craving warmth.   The rime sticks like a skin
    to me ;
Through me Arcturus peers ; Nor'lights shoot into me ;
    Gone is she, scorning my bough !

AN UPBRAIDING

Now I am dead you sing to me
    The songs we used to know,
But while I lived you had no wish
    Or care for doing so.

Now I am dead you come to me
    In the moonlight, comfortless ;
Ah, what would I have given alive
    To win such tenderness !

When you are dead, and stand to me
    Not differenced, as now,
But like again, will you be cold
    As when we lived, or how ?

THE YOUNG GLASS-STAINER

" THESE Gothic windows, how they wear me out
With cusp and foil, and nothing straight or square,
Crude colours, leaden borders roundabout,
And fitting in Peter here, and Matthew there !

" What a vocation !   Here do I draw now
The abnormal, loving the Hellenic norm ;
Martha I paint, and dream of Hera's brow,
Mary, and think of Aphrodite's form. "

    Nov. 1893.

LOOKING AT A PICTURE ON AN ANNIVERSARY

BUT don't you know it, my dear,
    Don't you know it,
That this day of the year
(What rainbow-rays embow it!)
We met, strangers confessed,
    But parted—blest?

Though at this query, my dear,
    There in your frame
Unmoved you still appear,
You must be thinking the same,
But keep that look demure
    Just to allure.

And now at length a trace
    I surely vision
Upon that wistful face
Of old-time recognition,
Smiling forth, "Yes, as you say,
    It is the day."

For this one phase of you
    Now left on earth
This great date must endue
With pulsings of rebirth?—
I see them vitalize
    Those two deep eyes!

But if this face I con
    Does not declare
Consciousness living on
Still in it, little I care
To live myself, my dear,
    Lone-labouring here!

    Spring 1913.

THE CHOIRMASTER'S BURIAL

HE often would ask us
That, when he died,
After playing so many
To their last rest,
If out of us any
Should here abide,
And it would not task us,
We would with our lutes
Play over him
By his grave-brim
The psalm he liked best—
The one whose sense suits
"Mount Ephraim"—
And perhaps we should seem
To him, in Death's dream,
Like the seraphim.

As soon as I knew
That his spirit was gone
I thought this his due,
And spoke thereupon.
"I think," said the vicar,
"A read service quicker
Than viols out-of-doors
In these frosts and hoars.
That old-fashioned way
Requires a fine day,
And it seems to me
It had better not be."

Hence, that afternoon,
Though never knew he
That his wish could not be,
To get through it faster
They buried the master
Without any tune.

But 'twas said that, when
At the dead of next night

The vicar looked out,
There struck on his ken
Thronged roundabout,
Where the frost was graying
The headstoned grass,
A band all in white
Like the saints in church-glass,
Singing and playing
The ancient stave
By the choirmaster's grave.

Such the tenor man told
When he had grown old.

THE MAN WHO FORGOT

At a lonely cross where bye-roads met
    I sat upon a gate ;
I saw the sun decline and set,
    And still was fain to wait.

A trotting boy passed up the way
    And roused me from my thought ;
I called to him, and showed where lay
    A spot I shyly sought.

"A summer-house fair stands hidden where
    You see the moonlight thrown ;
Go, tell me if within it there
    A lady sits alone.'

He half demurred, but took the track,
    And silence held the scene ;
I saw his figure rambling back ;
    I asked him if he had been.

"I went just where you said, but found
    No summer-house was there :
Beyond the slope 'tis all bare ground ;
    Nothing stands anywhere.

"A man asked what my brains were worth;
　　The house, he said, grew rotten,
And was pulled down before my birth,
　　And is almost forgotten!"

My right mind woke, and I stood dumb;
　　Forty years' frost and flower
Had fleeted since I'd used to come
　　To meet her in that bower.

WHILE DRAWING IN A CHURCHYARD

"IT is sad that so many of worth,
　　Still in the flesh," soughed the yew,
"Misjudge their lot whom kindly earth
　　Secludes from view.

"They ride their diurnal round
　　Each day-span's sum of hours
In peerless ease, without jolt or bound
　　Or ache like ours.

"If the living could but hear
　　What is heard by my roots as they creep
Round the restful flock, and the things said there
　　No one would weep."

"'Now set among the wise,'
　　They say: 'Enlarged in scope,
That no God trumpet us to rise
　　We truly hope.'"

I listened to his strange tale
　　In the mood that stillness brings,
And I grew to accept as the day wore pale
　　That show of things.

"FOR LIFE I HAD NEVER CARED GREATLY"

FOR Life I had never cared greatly,
     As worth a man's while ;
  Peradventures unsought,
  Peradventures that finished in nought,
Had kept me from youth and through manhood till lately
     Unwon by its style.

In earliest years—why I know not—
     I viewed it askance ;
  Conditions of doubt,
  Conditions that leaked slowly out,
May haply have bent me to stand and to show not
     Much zest for its dance.

With symphonies soft and sweet colour
     It courted me then,
  Till evasions seemed wrong,
  Till evasions gave in to its song,
And I warmed, until living aloofly loomed duller
     Than life among men.

Anew I found nought to set eyes on,
     When, lifting its hand,
  It uncloaked a star,
  Uncloaked it from fog-damps afar,
And showed its beams burning from pole to horizon
     As bright as a brand.

And so, the rough highway forgetting,
     I pace hill and dale
  Regarding the sky,
  Regarding the vision on high,
And thus re-illumed have no humour for letting
     My pilgrimage fail.

POEMS OF WAR AND PATRIOTISM

"MEN WHO MARCH AWAY"

(SONG OF THE SOLDIERS)

WHAT of the faith and fire within us
 Men who march away
 Ere the barn-cocks say
 Night is growing gray,
Leaving all that here can win us;
What of the faith and fire within us
 Men who march away?

Is it a purblind prank, O think you,
 Friend with the musing eye,
 Who watch us stepping by
 With doubt and dolorous sigh?
Can much pondering so hoodwink you!
Is it a purblind prank, O think you,
 Friend with the musing eye?

Nay. We well see what we are doing,
 Though some may not see—
 Dalliers as they be—
 England's need are we;
Her distress would leave us rueing:
Nay. We well see what we are doing,
 Though some may not see!

In our heart of hearts believing
 Victory crowns the just,
 And that braggarts must
 Surely bite the dust,

506

Press we to the field ungrieving,
    In our heart of hearts believing
        Victory crowns the just.

Hence the faith and fire within us
        Men who march away
        Ere the barn-cocks say
        Night is growing gray,
Leaving all that here can win us;
Hence the faith and fire within us
        Men who march away.

September 5, 1914.

HIS COUNTRY

I JOURNEYED from my native spot
    Across the south sea shine,
And found that people in hall and cot
Laboured and suffered each his lot
    Even as I did mine.

He travels southward, and looks around;

Thus noting them in meads and marts
    It did not seem to me
That my dear country with its hearts,
Minds, yearnings, worse and better parts
    Had ended with the sea.

and cannot discover the boundary

I further and further went anon,
    As such I still surveyed,
And further yet—yea, on and on,
And all the men I looked upon
    Had heart-strings fellow-made.

of his native country;

I traced the whole terrestrial round,
    Homing the other side;
Then said I, "What is there to bound
My denizenship? It seems I have found
    Its scope to be world-wide."

or where his duties to his fellow-creatures end;

nor who are
his enemies.

I asked me : " Whom have I to fight,
    And whom have I to dare,
And whom to weaken, crush, and blight?
My country seems to have kept in sight
    On my way everywhere."

1913.

ENGLAND TO GERMANY IN 1914

" O ENGLAND, may God punish thee ! "
—Is it that Teuton genius flowers
Only to breathe malignity
Upon its friend of earlier hours?
—We have eaten your bread, you have eaten ours,
We have loved your burgs, your pines' green moan,
Fair Rhine-stream, and its storied towers;
Your shining souls of deathless dowers
Have won us as they were our own :

We have nursed no dreams to shed your blood,
We have matched your might not rancorously
Save a flushed few whose blatant mood
You heard and marked as well as we
To tongue not in their country's key;
But yet you cry with face aflame,
" O England, may God punish thee ! "
And foul in onward history,
And present sight, your ancient name.

Autumn 1914.

ON THE BELGIAN EXPATRIATION

I DREAMT that people from the Land of Chimes
Arrived one autumn morning with their bells,
To hoist them on the towers and citadels
Of my own country, that the musical rhymes

Rung by them into space at meted times
Amid the market's daily stir and stress,

And the night's empty star-lit silentness,
Might solace souls of this and kindred climes.

Then I awoke ; and lo, before me stood
The visioned ones, but pale and full of fear ;
From Bruges they came, and Antwerp, and Ostend,

No carillons in their train.   Foes of mad mood
Had shattered these to shards amid the gear
Of ravaged roof, and smouldering gable-end.

October 18, 1914.

AN APPEAL TO AMERICA ON BEHALF OF THE BELGIAN DESTITUTE

SEVEN millions stand
Emaciate, in that ancient Delta-land :—
We here, full-charged with our own maimed and dead
And coiled in throbbing conflicts slow and sore,
Can poorly soothe these ails unmerited
Of souls forlorn upon the facing shore !—
Where naked, gaunt, in endless band on band
    Seven millions stand.

    No man can say
To your great country that, with scant delay,
You must, perforce, ease them in their loud need :
We know that nearer first your duty lies ;
But—is it much to ask that you let plead
Your lovingkindness with you—wooing-wise—
Albeit that aught you owe, and must repay,
    No man can say ?

December 1914.

THE PITY OF IT

I WALKED in loamy Wessex lanes, afar
From rail-track and from highway, and I heard
In field and farmstead many an ancient word
Of local lineage like " Thu bist," " Er war."

"Ich woll," "Er sholl," and by-talk similar,
Nigh as they speak who in this month's moon gird
At England's very loins, thereunto spurred
By gangs whose glory threats and slaughters are.

Then seemed a Heart crying : "Whosoever they be
At root and bottom of this, who flung this flame
Between kin folk kin tongued even as are we,

"Sinister, ugly, lurid, be their fame ;
May their familiars grow to shun their name,
And their brood perish everlastingly."

April 1915.

IN TIME OF WARS AND TUMULTS

"WOULD that I'd not drawn breath here !" some one said,
"To stalk upon this stage of evil deeds,
Where purposelessly month by month proceeds
A play so sorely shaped and blood-bespread."

Yet had his spark not quickened, but lain dead
To the gross spectacles of this our day,
And never put on the proffered cloak of clay,
He had but known not things now manifested ;

Life would have swirled the same.   Morns would have dawned
On the uprooting by the night-gun's stroke
Of what the yester noonshine brought to flower ;

Brown martial brows in dying throes have wanned
Despite his absence ; hearts no fewer been broke
By Empery's insatiate lust of power.

1915.

IN TIME OF "THE BREAKING OF NATIONS"[1]

I

ONLY a man harrowing clods
  In a slow silent walk
With an old horse that stumbles and nods
  Half asleep as they stalk.

II

Only thin smoke without flame
  From the heaps of couch-grass;
Yet this will go onward the same
  Though Dynasties pass.

III

Yonder a maid and her wight
  Come whispering by:
War's annals will fade into night
  Ere their story die.

1915.

CRY OF THE HOMELESS

AFTER THE PRUSSIAN INVASION OF BELGIUM

"INSTIGATOR of the ruin—
  Whichsoever thou mayst be
Of the masterful of Europe
  That contrived our misery—
Hear the wormwood-worded greeting
  From each city, shore, and lea
  Of thy victims:
"Conqueror, all hail to thee!"

[1] Jer. li. 20.

"Yea : 'All hail!' we grimly shout thee
    That wast author, fount, and head
Of these wounds, whoever proven
    When our times are throughly read.
'May thy loved be slighted, blighted,
    And forsaken,' be it said
        By thy victims,
    'And thy children beg their bread!'

"Nay : a richer malediction !—
    Rather let this thing befall
In time's hurling and unfurling
    On the night when comes thy call ;
That compassion dew thy pillow
    And bedrench thy senses all
        For thy victims,
    Till death dark thee with his pall."

August 1915.

BEFORE MARCHING AND AFTER

(*In Memoriam F. W. G.*)

ORION swung southward aslant
    Where the starved Egdon pine-trees had thinned,
The Pleiads aloft seemed to pant
    With the heather that twitched in the wind ;
But he looked on indifferent to sights such as these,
Unswayed by love, friendship, home joy or home sorrow,
And wondered to what he would march on the morrow.

The crazed household-clock with its whirr
    Rang midnight within as he stood,
He heard the low sighing of her
    Who had striven from his birth for his good ;
But he still only asked the spring starlight, the breeze,
What great thing or small thing his history would borrow
From that Game with Death he would play on the morrow.

When the heath wore the robe of late summer,
    And the fuchsia-bells, hot in the sun,

Hung red by the door, a quick comer
Brought tidings that marching was done
For him who had joined in that game over-seas
Where Death stood to win, though his name was to borrow
A brightness therefrom not to fade on the morrow.

September 1915.

"OFTEN WHEN WARRING"

OFTEN when warring for he wist not what,
An enemy-soldier, passing by one weak,
Has tendered water, wiped the burning cheek,
And cooled the lips so black and clammed and hot;

Then gone his way, and maybe quite forgot
The deed of grace amid the roar and reek;
Yet larger vision than loud arms bespeak
He there has reached, although he has known it not

For natural mindsight, triumphing in the act
Over the throes of artificial rage,
Has thuswise muffled victory's peal of pride,
Rended to ribands policy's specious page
That deals but with evasion, code, and pact,
And war's apology wholly stultified.

1915.

THEN AND NOW

WHEN battles were fought
With a chivalrous sense of Should and Ought,
     In spirit men said,
     "End we quick or dead,
     Honour is some reward!
Let us fight fair—for our own best or worst;
     So, Gentlemen of the Guard,
          Fire first!"

     In the open they stood,
     Man to man in his knightlihood:

VOL. I   S

They would not deign
To profit by a stain
On the honourable rules,
Knowing that practise perfidy no man durst
Who in the heroic schools
Was nurst.

But now, behold, what
Is warfare wherein honour is not !
Rama laments
Its dead innocents :
Herod breathes : " Sly slaughter
Shall rule !   Let us, by modes once called accurst,
Overhead, under water,
Stab first."

1915.

A CALL TO NATIONAL SERVICE

UP and be doing, all who have a hand
To lift, a back to bend.   It must not be
In times like these that vaguely linger we
To air our vaunts and hopes ; and leave our land

Untended as a wild of weeds and sand.
—Say, then, " I come !" and go, O women and men
Of palace, ploughshare, easel, counter, pen ;
That scareless, scathless, England still may stand.

Would years but let me stir as once I stirred
At many a dawn to take the forward track,
And with a stride plunged on to enterprize,

I now would speed like yester wind that whirred
Through yielding pines ; and serve with never a slack,
So loud for promptness all around outcries !

March 1917.

THE DEAD AND THE LIVING ONE

THE dead woman lay in her first night's grave,
And twilight fell from the clouds' concave,
And those she had asked to forgive forgave.

The woman passing came to a pause
By the heaped white shapes of wreath and cross,
And looked upon where the other was.

And as she mused there thus spoke she :
" Never your countenance did I see,
But you've been a good good friend to me ! "

Rose a plaintive voice from the sod below :
" O woman whose accents I do not know,
What is it that makes you approve me so ? "

" O dead one, ere my soldier went,
I heard him saying, with warm intent,
To his friend, when won by your blandishment :

" ' I would change for that lass here and now !
And if I return I may break my vow
To my present Love, and contrive somehow

" ' To call my own this new-found pearl,
Whose eyes have the light, whose lips the curl
I always have looked for in a girl ! '

" —And this is why that by ceasing to be—
Though never your countenance did I see—
You prove you a good good friend to me ;

" And I pray each hour for your soul's repose
In gratitude for your joining those
No lover will clasp when his campaigns close."

Away she turned, when arose to her eye
A martial phantom of gory dye,
That said, with a thin and far-off sigh :

" O sweetheart, neither shall I clasp you!
For the foe this day has pierced me through,
And sent me to where she is.   Adieu!—

" And forget not when the night-wind's whine
Calls over this turf where her limbs recline,
That it travels on to lament by mine."

There was a cry by the white-flowered mound,
There was a laugh from underground.
There was a deeper gloom around.

1915.

A NEW YEAR'S EVE IN WAR TIME

I

PHANTASMAL fears,
And the flap of the flame,
And the throb of the clock,
And a loosened slate,
And the blind night's drone,
Which tiredly the spectral pines intone!

II

And the blood in my ears
Strumming always the same.
And the gable-cock
With its fitful grate,
And myself, alone.

III

The twelfth hour nears
Hand-hid, as in shame;
I undo the lock,
And listen, and wait
For the Young Unknown.

IV

In the dark there careers—
As if Death astride came
To numb all with his knock—
A horse at mad rate
Over rut and stone.

V

No figure appears,
No call of my name,
No sound but "Tic-toc"
Without check.   Past the gate
It clatters—is gone.

VI

What rider it bears
There is none to proclaim ;
And the Old Year has struck,
And, scarce animate.
The New makes moan.

VII

Maybe that "More Tears !—
More Famine and Flame—
More Severance and Shock !"
Is the order from Fate
That the Rider speeds on
To pale Europe ; and tiredly the pines intone.

1915–1916

"I MET A MAN"

I MET a man when night was nigh,
Who said, with shining face and eye
Like Moses' after Sinai :—

"I have seen the Moulder of Monarchies,
Realms, peoples, plains and hills,

Sitting upon the sunlit seas !—
And, as He sat, soliloquies
Fell from Him like an antiphonic breeze
　　That pricks the waves to thrills.

" Meseemed that of the maimed and dead
　　Mown down upon the globe,—
Their plenteous blooms of promise shed
Ere fruiting-time—His words were said,
Sitting against the western web of red
　　Wrapt in His crimson robe.

" And I could catch them now and then :
　　—' Why let these gambling clans
Of human Cockers, pit liege men
From mart and city, dale and glen,
In death-mains, but to swell and swell again
　　Their swollen All-Empery plans,

" ' When a mere nod (if my malign
　　Compeer but passive keep)
Would mend that old mistake of mine
I made with Saul, and ever consign
All Lords of War whose sanctuaries enshrine
　　Liberticide, to sleep ?

" ' With violence the lands are spread
　　Even as in Israel's day,
And it repenteth me I bred
Chartered armipotents lust-led
To feuds. . . . Yea, grieves my heart, as then I said,
　　To see their evil way !'

　　—" The utterance grew, and flapped like flame,
　　And further speech I feared ;
But no Celestial tongued acclaim,
And no huzzas from earthlings came,
And the heavens mutely masked as 'twere in shame
　　Till daylight disappeared."

Thus ended he as night rode high-
The man of shining face and eye,
Like Moses' after Sinai.

　　1916.

"I LOOKED UP FROM MY WRITING"

I LOOKED up from my writing,
   And gave a start to see,
As if rapt in my inditing,
   The moon's full gaze on me.

Her meditative misty head
   Was spectral in its air,
And I involuntarily said,
   "What are you doing there?"

"Oh, I've been scanning pond and hole
   And waterway hereabout
For the body of one with a sunken soul
   Who has put his life-light out.

"Did you hear his frenzied tattle?
   It was sorrow for his son
Who is slain in brutish battle,
   Though he has injured none.

"And now I am curious to look
   Into the blinkered mind
Of one who wants to write a book
   In a world of such a kind."

Her temper overwrought me,
   And I edged to shun her view,
For I felt assured she thought me
   One who should drown him too.

FINALE

THE COMING OF THE END

How it came to an end!
The meeting afar from the crowd,
And the love-looks and laughters unpenned,
The parting when much was avowed,
    How it came to an end!

It came to an end;
Yes, the outgazing over the stream,
With the sun on each serpentine bend,
Or, later, the luring moon-gleam;
    It came to an end.

It came to an end,
The housebuilding, furnishing, planting,
As if there were ages to spend
In welcoming, feasting, and jaunting;
    It came to an end.

It came to an end,
That journey of one day a week:
("It always goes on," said a friend,
"Just the same in bright weathers or bleak;')
    But it came to an end.

" *How* will come to an end
This orbit so smoothly begun,
Unless some convulsion attend?"
I often said. "What will be done
    When it comes to an end?"

Well, it came to an end
Quite silently—stopped without jerk ;
Better close no prevision could lend ;
Working out as One planned it should work
Ere it came to an end.

AFTERWARDS

WHEN the Present has latched its postern behind my tremulous
    stay,
    And the May month flaps its glad green leaves like wings,
Delicate-filmed as new-spun silk, will the neighbours say,
    " He was a man who used to notice such things " ?

If it be in the dusk when, like an eyelid's soundless blink,
    The dewfall-hawk comes crossing the shades to alight
Upon the wind-warped upland thorn, a gazer may think,
    " To him this must have been a familiar sight."

If I pass during some nocturnal blackness, mothy and warm,
    When the hedgehog travels furtively over the lawn,
One may say, " He strove that such innocent creatures should
    come to no harm,
    But he could do little for them ; and now he is gone."

If, when hearing that I have been stilled at last, they stand at
    the door,
    Watching the full-starred heavens that winter sees,
Will this thought rise on those who will meet my face no more,
    " He was one who had an eye for such mysteries " ?

And will any say when my bell of quittance is heard in the gloom,
    And a crossing breeze cuts a pause in its outrollings,
Till they rise again, as they were a new bell's boom,
    " He hears it not now, but used to notice such things ? "

LATE LYRICS AND EARLIER

APOLOGY

ABOUT half the verses that follow were written quite lately. The rest are older, having been held over in MS. when past volumes were published, on considering that these would contain a sufficient number of pages to offer readers at one time, more especially during the distractions of the war. The unusually far back poems to be found here are, however, but some that were overlooked in gathering previous collections. A freshness in them, now unattainable, seemed to make up for their inexperience and to justify their inclusion. A few are dated ; the dates of others are not discoverable.

The launching of a volume of this kind in neo-Georgian days by one who began writing in mid-Victorian, and has published nothing to speak of for some years, may seem to call for a few words of excuse or explanation. Whether or no, readers may feel assured that a new book is submitted to them with great hesitation at so belated a date. Insistent practical reasons, however, among which were requests from some illustrious men of letters who are in sympathy with my productions, the accident that several of the poems have already seen the light, and that dozens of them have been lying about for years, compelled the course adopted, in spite of the natural disinclination of a writer whose works have been so frequently regarded askance by a pragmatic section here and there, to draw attention to them once more.

I do not know that it is necessary to say much on the contents of the book, even in deference to suggestions that will be mentioned presently. I believe that those readers who care for my poems at all—readers to whom no passport is required—will care for this new instalment of them, perhaps the last, as much as for any that have preceded them. Moreover, in the eyes of a less friendly class the pieces, though a very mixed collection indeed, contain, so far as I am able to see, little or nothing in technic or teaching that can be considered a Star-Chamber matter, or so much as agitating to a ladies' school ; even though, to use Wordsworth's observation in his Preface to *Lyrical Ballads*, such readers may suppose " that by the act of writing in verse an author makes a formal engagement that he will gratify certain known habits of association : that he not only thus apprises the reader that certain classes of ideas and expressions will be found in his book, but that others will be carefully excluded."

It is true, nevertheless, that some grave, positive, stark, delineations are interspersed among those of the passive, lighter, and traditional sort presumably nearer to stereotyped tastes. For—while I am quite aware that a thinker is not expected, and, indeed, is scarcely allowed, now more than heretofore, to state all that crosses his mind concerning existence in this universe, in his attempts to explain or excuse the presence of evil and the incongruity of penalizing the irresponsible—it must be obvious to open intelligences that, without denying the beauty and faithful service of certain venerable cults, such disallowance of " obstinate questionings " and " blank misgivings " tends to a paralysed intellectual stalemate. Heine observed nearly a hundred years ago that the soul has her eternal rights ; that she will not be darkened by statutes, nor lullabied by the music of bells. And what is to-day, in allusions to the present author's pages, alleged to be " pessimism " is, in truth, only such "questionings" in the exploration of reality, and is the first step towards the soul's betterment, and the body's also.

If I may be forgiven for quoting my own old words, let me repeat what I printed in this relation more than twenty years ago, and wrote much earlier, in a poem entitled " In Tenebris " :

If way to the Better there be, it exacts a full look at the Worst :

that is to say, by the exploration of reality, and its frank recognition stage by stage along the survey, with an eye to the best consummation possible : briefly, evolutionary meliorism. But it is called pessimism nevertheless ; under which word, expressed with condemnatory emphasis, it is regarded by many as some pernicious new thing (though so old as to underlie the Gospel scheme, and even to permeate the Greek drama) ; and the subject is charitably left to decent silence, as if further comment were needless.

Happily there are some who feel such Levitical passing-by to be, alas, by no means a permanent dismissal of the matter ; that comment on where the world stands is very much the reverse of needless in these disordered years of our prematurely afflicted century : that amendment and not madness lies that way. And looking down the future these few hold fast to the same : that whether the human and kindred animal races survive till the exhaustion or destruction of the globe, or whether these races perish and are succeeded by others before that conclusion comes, pain to all upon it, tongued or dumb, shall be kept down to a minimum by loving-kindness, operating through scientific knowledge, and actuated by the modicum of free will conjecturally possessed by organic life when the mighty necessitating forces—unconscious or other—that have " the balancings of the clouds," happen to be in equilibrium, which may or may not be often.

To conclude this question I may add that the argument of the so-called optimists is neatly summarized in a stern pronouncement against me by my friend Mr. Frederic Harrison in a late essay of his, in the words : " This view of life is not mine." The solemn declaration does not seem to me to be so annihilating to the said " view " (really a series of fugitive impressions which I have never tried to co-ordinate) as is complacently assumed. Surely it embodies a too human fallacy quite familiar in logic. Next, a knowing reviewer, apparently a Roman Catholic young man, speaks, with some rather gross instances of the *suggestio falsi* in his whole article, of " Mr. Hardy refusing consolation," the " dark gravity of his ideas," and so on. When a Positivist and a Romanist agree there must be something wonderful in it, which should make a poet sit up. But . . . O that 'twere possible !

I would not have alluded in this place or anywhere else to such casual personal criticisms—for casual and unreflecting they must be—but for the satisfaction of two or three friends in whose opinion a short answer was deemed desirable, on account of the continual repetition of these criticisms, or more precisely, quizzings. After all, the serious and truly literary inquiry in this connection is: Should a shaper of such stuff as dreams are made on disregard considerations of what is customary and expected, and apply himself to the real function of poetry, the application of ideas to life (in Matthew Arnold's familiar phrase)? This bears more particularly on what has been called the "philosophy" of these poems—usually reproved as "queer." Whoever the author may be that undertakes such application of ideas in this "philosophic" direction—where it is specially required—glacial judgments must inevitably fall upon him amid opinion whose arbiters largely decry individuality, to whom *ideas* are oddities to smile at, who are moved by a yearning the reverse of that of the Athenian inquirers on Mars Hill; and stiffen their features not only at sound of a new thing, but at a restatement of old things in new terms. Hence should anything of this sort in the following adumbrations seem "queer"—should any of them seem to good Panglossians to embody strange and disrespectful conceptions of this best of all possible worlds, I apologize; but cannot help it.

Such divergences, which, though piquant for the nonce, it would be affectation to say are not saddening and discouraging likewise, may, to be sure, arise sometimes from superficial aspect only, writer and reader seeing the same thing at different angles. But in palpable cases of divergence they arise, as already said, whenever a serious effort is made towards that which the authority I have cited—who would now be called old-fashioned, possibly even parochial—affirmed to be what no good critic could deny as the poet's province, the application of ideas to life. One might shrewdly guess, by the by, that in such recommendation the famous writer may have overlooked the cold-shouldering results upon an enthusiastic disciple that would be pretty certain to follow his putting the high aim in practice, and have forgotten the disconcerting experience of Gil Blas with the Archbishop.

To add a few more words to what has already taken up too many, there is a contingency liable to miscellanies of verse that I have never seen mentioned, so far as I can remember ; I mean the chance little shocks that may be caused over a book of various character like the present and its predecessors by the juxtaposition of unrelated, even discordant, effusions ; poems perhaps years apart in the making, yet facing each other. An odd result of this has been that dramatic anecdotes of a satirical and humorous intention following verse in graver voice, have been read as misfires because they raise the smile that they were intended to raise, the journalist, deaf to the sudden change of key, being unconscious that he is laughing with the author and not at him. I admit that I did not foresee such contingencies as I ought to have done, and that people might not perceive when the tone altered. But the difficulties of arranging the themes in a graduated kinship of moods would have been so great that irrelation was almost unavoidable with efforts so diverse. I must trust for right note-catching to those finely-touched spirits who can divine without half a whisper, whose intuitiveness is proof against all the accidents of inconsequence. In respect of the less alert, however, should any one's train of thought be thrown out of gear by a consecutive piping of vocal reeds in jarring tonics, without a semiquaver's rest between, and be led thereby to miss the writer's aim and meaning in one out of two contiguous compositions, I shall deeply regret it.

Having at last, I think, finished with the personal points that I was recommended to notice, I will forsake the immediate object of this Preface ; and, leaving *Late Lyrics* to whatever fate it deserves, digress for a few moments to more general considerations. The thoughts of any man of letters concerned to keep poetry alive cannot but run uncomfortably on the precarious prospects of English verse at the present day. Verily the hazards and casualties surrounding the birth and setting forth of almost every modern creation in numbers are ominously like those of one of Shelley's paper-boats on a windy lake. And a forward conjecture scarcely permits the hope of a better time, unless men's tendencies should change. So indeed of all art, literature, and "high thinking" nowadays. Whether owing to the barbarizing of taste in the younger minds by the dark madness of the late war, the unabashed cultivation of selfishness in all classes, the plethoric growth of knowledge simultaneously with the stunting of wisdom, "a degrading thirst after outrageous stimulation" (to quote Wordsworth again), or from any other cause, we seem threatened with a new Dark Age.

I formerly thought, like other much exercised writers, that so far as literature was concerned a partial cause might be impotent or mischievous criticism; the satirizing of individuality, the lack of whole-seeing in contemporary estimates of poetry and kindred work, the knowingness affected by junior reviewers, the overgrowth of meticulousness in their peerings for an opinion, as if it were a cultivated habit in them to scrutinize the tool-marks and be blind to the building, to hearken for the key-creaks and be deaf to the diapason, to judge the landscape by a nocturnal exploration with a flash-lantern. In other words, to carry on the old game of sampling the poem or drama by quoting the worst line or worst passage only, in ignorance or not of Coleridge's proof that a versification of any length neither can be nor ought to be all poetry; of reading meanings into a book that its author never dreamt of writing there. I might go on interminably.

But I do not now think any such temporary obstructions to be the cause of the hazard, for these negligences and ignorances, though they may have stifled a few true poets in the run of generations, disperse like stricken leaves before the wind of next week, and are no more heard of again in the region of letters than their writers themselves. No: we may be convinced that something of the deeper sort mentioned must be the cause.

In any event poetry, pure literature in general, religion—I include religion, in its essential and undogmatic sense, because poetry and religion touch each other, or rather modulate into each other; are, indeed, often but different names for the same

ing—these, I say, the visible signs of mental and emotional
e, must like all other things keep moving, becoming ; even
ough at present, when belief in witches of Endor is displacing
e Darwinian theory and "the truth that shall make you free,"
en's minds appear, as above noted, to be moving backwards
ther than on. I speak somewhat sweepingly, and should
xcept many thoughtful writers in verse and prose ; also men in
ertain worthy but small bodies of various denominations, and
erhaps in the homely quarter where advance might have been
e very least expected a few years back—the English Church
–if one reads it rightly as showing evidence of "removing
nose things that are shaken," in accordance with the wise
pistolary recommendation to the Hebrews. For since the
istoric and once august hierarchy of Rome some generation
go lost its chance of being the religion of the future by doing
therwise, and throwing over the little band of New Catholics
ho were making a struggle for continuity by applying the
rinciple of evolution to their own faith, joining hands with
odern science, and outflanking the hesitating English instinct
wards liturgical restatement (a flank march which I at the
me quite expected to witness, with the gathering of many
illions of waiting agnostics into its fold); since then, one may
sk, what other purely English establishment than the Church, of
ufficient dignity and footing, with such strength of old associa-
ion, such scope for transmutability, such architectural spell,
left in this country to keep the shreds of morality together ? *

It may indeed be a forlorn hope, a mere dream, that of an
lliance between religion, which must be retained unless the
vorld is to perish, and complete rationality, which must come,
nless also the world is to perish, by means of the interfusing
ffect of poetry—"the breath and finer spirit of all knowledge ;
he impassioned expression of science," as it was defined by an
nglish poet who was quite orthodox in his ideas. But if it be
rue, as Comte argued, that advance is never in a straight line,
ut in a looped orbit, we may, in the aforesaid ominous moving

* However, one must not be too sanguine in reading signs, and since the
bove was written evidence that the Church will go far in the removal of
'things that are shaken" has not been encouraging.

backward, be doing it *pour mieux sauter*, drawing back for a
spring. I repeat that I forlornly hope so, notwithstanding the
supercilious regard of hope by Schopenhauer, von Hartmann,
and other philosophers down to Einstein who have my respect.
But one dares not prophesy. Physical, chronological, and
other contingencies keep me in these days from critical studies
and literary circles

> Where once we held debate, a band
> Of youthful friends, on mind and art

(if one may quote Tennyson in this century). Hence I
cannot know how things are going so well as I used to
know them, and the aforesaid limitations must quite prevent
my knowing henceforward.

I have to thank the editors and owners of *The Times*,
Fortnightly, *Mercury*, and other periodicals in which a few of
the poems have appeared for kindly assenting to their being
reclaimed for collected publication.

T. H.

February 1922.

WEATHERS

I

THIS is the weather the cuckoo likes,
    And so do I ;
When showers betumble the chestnut spikes,
    And nestlings fly :
And the little brown nightingale bills his best,
And they sit outside at "The Travellers' Rest,"
And maids come forth sprig-muslin drest,
And citizens dream of the south and west,
    And so do I.

II

This is the weather the shepherd shuns,
    And so do I ;
When beeches drip in browns and duns,
    And thresh, and ply ;
And hill-hid tides throb, throe on throe,
And meadow rivulets overflow,
And drops on gate-bars hang in a row,
And rooks in families homeward go,
    And so do I.

THE MAID OF KEINTON MANDEVILLE

(A TRIBUTE TO SIR H. BISHOP)

I HEAR that maiden still
    Of Keinton Mandeville
Singing, in flights that played

As wind-watts through us all,
Till they made our mood a thrall
To their aery rise and fall,
    " Should he upbraid ! "

Rose-necked, in sky-gray gown,
From a stage in Stower Town
Did she sing, and singing smile
As she blent that dexterous voice
With the ditty of her choice,
And banished our annoys
        Thereawhile.

One with such song had power
To wing the heaviest hour
Of him who housed with her.
Who did I never knew
When her spoused estate ondrew,
And her warble flung its woo
        In his ear.

Ah, she's a beldame now,
Time-trenched on cheek and brow,
Whom I once heard as a maid
From Keinton Mandeville
Of matchless scope and skill
Sing, with smile and swell and trill,
    " Should he upbraid ! "

        1915 or 1916.

SUMMER SCHEMES

WHEN friendly summer calls again,
        Calls again
Her little fifers to these hills,
We'll go—we two—to that arched fane
Of leafage where they prime their bills
Before they start to flood the plain
With quavers, minims, shakes, and trills.
        " —We'll go," I sing ; but who shall say
        What may not chance before that day !

And we shall see the waters spring,
    Waters spring
From chinks the scrubby copses crown ;
And we shall trace their oncreeping
To where the cascade tumbles down
And sends the bobbing growths aswing,
And ferns not quite but almost drown.
    " —We shall," I say ; but who may sing
    Of what another moon will bring !

EPEISODIA

I

Past the hills that peep
Where the leaze is smiling,
On and on beguiling
Crisply-cropping sheep ;
Under boughs of brushwood
Linking tree and tree
In a shade of lushwood,
    There caressed we !

II

Hemmed by city walls
That outshut the sunlight,
In a foggy dun light,
Where the footstep falls
With a pit-pat wearisome
In its cadency
On the flagstones drearisome
    There pressed we !

III

Where in wild-winged crowds
Blown birds show their whiteness
Up against the lightness
Of the clammy clouds ;
By the random river
Pushing to the sea,
Under bents that quiver
    There shall rest we.

FAINTHEART IN A RAILWAY TRAIN

At nine in the morning there passed a church,
At ten there passed me by the sea,
At twelve a town of smoke and smirch,
At two a forest of oak and birch,
    And then, on a platform, she:

A radiant stranger, who saw not me.
I said, " Get out to her do I dare?"
But I kept my seat in my search for a plea,
And the wheels moved on.   O could it but be
    That I had alighted there!

AT MOONRISE AND ONWARDS

I thought you a fire
On Heath-Plantation Hill,
Dealing out mischief the most dire
To the chattels of men of hire
    There in their vill.

But by and by
You turned a yellow-green,
Like a large glow-worm in the sky;
And then I could descry
    Your mood and mien.

How well I know
Your furtive feminine shape!
As if reluctantly you show
You nude of cloud, and but by favour throw
    Aside its drape. . . . .

—How many a year
Have you kept pace with me,
Wan Woman of the waste up there,
Behind a hedge, or the bare
    Bough of a tree!

No novelty are you,
O Lady of all my time,
Veering unbid into my view
Whether I near Death's mew,
Or Life's top cyme!

THE GARDEN SEAT

Its former green is blue and thin,
And its once firm legs sink in and in ;
Soon it will break down unaware,
Soon it will break down unaware.

At night when reddest flowers are black
Those who once sat thereon come back ;
Quite a row of them sitting there,
Quite a row of them sitting there.

With them the seat does not break down,
Nor winter freeze them, nor floods drown,
For they are as light as upper air,
They are as light as upper air!

BARTHÉLÉMON AT VAUXHALL

François Hippolite Barthélémon, first-fiddler at Vauxhall Gardens, composed what was probably the most popular morning hymn-tune ever written.
was formerly sung, full-voiced, every Sunday in most churches, to Bishop
en's words, but is now seldom heard.

He said : "Awake my soul, and with the sun," . . .
And paused upon the bridge, his eyes due east,
Where was emerging like a full-robed priest
The irradiate globe that vouched the dark as done.

It lit his face—the weary face of one
Who in the adjacent gardens charged his string,
Nightly, with many a tuneful tender thing,
Till stars were weak, and dancing hours outrun.

And then were threads of matin music spun
In trial tones as he pursued his way:
"This is a morn," he murmured, "well begun:
This strain to Ken will count when I am clay!"

And count it did; till, caught by echoing lyres,
It spread to galleried naves and mighty quires.

"I SOMETIMES THINK"

(FOR F. E. H.)

I SOMETIMES think as here I sit
    Of things I have done,
Which seemed in doing not unfit
    To face the sun:
Yet never a soul has paused a whit
    On such—not one.

There was that eager strenuous press
    To sow good seed;
There was that saving from distress
    In the nick of need;
There were those words in the wilderness:
    Who cared to heed?

Yet can this be full true, or no?
    For one did care,
And, spiriting into my house, to, fro,
    Like wind on the stair,
Cares still, heeds all, and will, even though
    I may despair.

JEZREEL

ON ITS SEIZURE BY THE ENGLISH UNDER ALLENBY, SEPTEMBER 1918

DID they catch as it were in a Vision at shut of the day—
When their cavalry smote through the ancient Esdraelon Plain,
And they crossed where the Tishbite stood forth in his enemy
    way—
His gaunt mournful Shade as he bade the King haste off amain

n war-men at this end of time—even on Englishmen's eyes—
Who slay with their arms of new might in that long-ago place,
lashed he who drove furiously? . . . . Ah, did the phantom arise
f that queen, of that proud Tyrian woman who painted her
    face?

aintly marked they the words "Throw her down!" rise from
    Night eerily,
pectre-spots of the blood of her body on some rotten wall?
nd the thin note of pity that came: "A King's daughter is she,"
s they passed where she trodden was once by the chargers'
    footfall?

ould such be the hauntings of men of to-day, at the cease
f pursuit, at the dusk-hour, ere slumber their senses could seal?
nghosted seers, kings—one on horseback who asked "Is it
    peace?" . . .
ea, strange things and spectral may men have beheld in Jezreel!

September 24, 1918.

A JOG-TROT PAIR

WHO were the twain that trod this track
    So many times together
      Hither and back,
In spells of certain and uncertain weather?

Commonplace in conduct they
    Who wandered to and fro here
      Day by day:
Two that few dwellers troubled themselves to know here.

The very gravel-path was prim
    That daily they would follow:
      Borders trim:
Never a wayward sprout, or hump, or hollow.

Trite usages in tamest style
    Had tended to their plighting.
      "It's just worth while,
Perhaps," they had said. "And saves much sad good-nighting."

And petty seemed the happenings
That ministered to their joyance :
Simple things,
Onerous to satiate souls, increased their buoyance.

Who could those common people be,
Of days the plainest, barest ?
They were we ;
Yes ; happier than the cleverest, smartest, rarest.

"THE CURTAINS NOW ARE DRAWN"

(SONG)

I

THE curtains now are drawn,
And the spindrift strikes the glass,
Blown up the jaggèd pass
By the surly salt sou'-west,
And the sneering glare is gone
Behind the yonder crest,
While she sings to me :
" O the dream that thou art my Love, be it thine,
And the dream that I am thy Love, be it mine,
And death may come, but loving is divine."

II

I stand here in the rain,
With its smite upon her stone,
And the grasses that have grown
Over women, children, men,
And their texts that " Life is vain " ;
But I hear the notes as when
Once she sang to me :
" O the dream that thou art my Love, be it thine,
And the dream that I am thy Love, be it mine,
And death may come, but loving is divine."

1913.

"ACCORDING TO THE MIGHTY WORKING"

I

WHEN moiling seems at cease
    In the vague void of night-time,
    And heaven's wide roomage stormless
    Between the dusk and light-time,
    And fear at last is formless,
We call the allurement Peace.

II

Peace, this hid riot, Change,
    This revel of quick-cued mumming,
    This never truly being,
    This evermore becoming,
    This spinner's wheel onfleeing
Outside perception's range.

    1917.

"I WAS NOT HE"

(SONG)

I WAS not he—the man
Who used to pilgrim to your gate,
At whose smart step you grew elate,
    And rosed, as maidens can,
      For a brief span.

It was not I who sang
Beside the keys you touched so true
With note-bent eyes, as if with you
    It counted not whence sprang
      The voice that rang. . . .

Yet though my destiny
It was to miss your early sweet,
You still, when turned to you my feet,
    Had sweet enough to be
      A prize for me!

THE WEST-OF-WESSEX GIRL

A VERY West-of-Wessex girl,
　　As blithe as blithe could be,
　　Was once well-known to me,
And she would laud her native town,
　　And hope and hope that we
Might sometime study up and down
　　Its charms in company.

But never I squired my Wessex girl
　　In jaunts to Hoe or street
　　When hearts were high in beat,
Nor saw her in the marbled ways
　　Where market-people meet
That in her bounding early days
　　Were friendly with her feet.

Yet now my West-of-Wessex girl,
　　When midnight hammers slow
　　From Andrew's, blow by blow,
As phantom draws me by the hand
　　To the place—Plymouth Hoe—
Where side by side in life, as planned,
　　We never were to go!

Begun in Plymouth, *March* 1913.

WELCOME HOME

BACK to my native place
　　Bent upon returning,
　　Bosom all day burning
To be where my race
Well were known, 'twas keen with me
There to dwell in amity.

Folk had sought their beds,
　　But I hailed: to view me
　　Under the moon, out to me
Several pushed their heads,
And to each I told my name,
Plans, and that therefrom I came.

"Did you? . . . Ah, 'tis true
Said they, back a long time,
Here had spent his young time,
Some such man as you . . ."
Good-night." The casement closed again,
And I was left in the frosty lane.

GOING AND STAYING

I

THE moving sun-shapes on the spray,
The sparkles where the brook was flowing,
Pink faces, plightings, moonlit May,
These were the things we wished would stay;
    But they were going.

II

Seasons of blankness as of snow,
The silent bleed of a world decaying,
The moan of multitudes in woe,
These were the things we wished would go;
    But they were staying.

III

Then we looked closelier at Time,
And saw his ghostly arms revolving
To sweep off woeful things with prime,
Things sinister with things sublime
    Alike dissolving.

READ BY MOONLIGHT

I PAUSED to read a letter of hers
    By the moon's cold shine,
Eyeing it in the tenderest way,
And edging it up to catch each ray
    Upon her light-penned line.

I did not know what years would flow
   Of her life's span and mine
Ere I read another letter of hers
   By the moon's cold shine !

I chance now on the last of hers,
   By the moon's cold shine ;
It is the one remaining page
Out of the many shallow and sage
   Whereto she set her sign.
Who could foresee there were to be
   Such missives of pain and pine
Ere I should read this last of hers
   By the moon's cold shine !

AT A HOUSE IN HAMPSTEAD

SOMETIME THE DWELLING OF JOHN KEATS

O POET, come you haunting here
Where streets have stolen up all around,
And never a nightingale pours one
      Full-throated sound ?

Drawn from your drowse by the Seven famed Hills,
Thought you to find all just the same
Here shining, as in hours of old,
      If you but came ?

What will you do in your surprise
At seeing that changes wrought in Rome
Are wrought yet more on the misty slope
      One time your home ?

Will you wake wind-wafts on these stairs ?
Swing the doors open noisily ?
Show as an umbraged ghost beside
      Your ancient tree ?

Or will you, softening, the while
You further and yet further look,
Learn that a laggard few would fain
      Preserve your nook ? . . . .

—Where the Piazza steps incline,
And catch late light at eventide,
I once stood, in that Rome, and thought,
    " 'Twas here he died."

I drew to a violet-sprinkled spot,
Where day and night a pyramid keeps
Uplifted its white hand, and said,
    " 'Tis there he sleeps."

Pleasanter now it is to hold
That here, where sang he, more of him
Remains than where he, tuneless, cold,
    Passed to the dim.

   July 1920.

A WOMAN'S FANCY

"AH, Madam; you've indeed come back here?
  'Twas sad—your husband's so swift death,
And you away!   You shouldn't have left him:
    It hastened his last breath."

"Dame, I am not the lady you think me;
  I know not her, nor know her name;
I've come to lodge here—a friendless woman;
    My health my only aim."

She came; she lodged.   Wherever she rambled
  They held her as no other than
The lady named; and told how her husband
    Had died a forsaken man.

So often did they call her thuswise
  Mistakenly, by that man's name,
So much did they declare about him,
    That his past form and fame

Grew on her, till she pitied his sorrow
  As if she truly had been the cause—
Yea, his deserter; and came to wonder
    What mould of man he was.

"Tell me my history!" would exclaim she;
    " *Our* history," she said mournfully.
"But *you* know, surely, Ma'am?" they would answer,
    Much in perplexity.

Curious, she crept to his grave one evening,
    And a second time in the dusk of the morrow;
Then a third time, with crescent emotion
    Like a bereaved wife's sorrow.

No gravestone rose by the rounded hillock;
    —"I marvel why this is?" she said.
—"He had no kindred, Ma'am, but you near."
    —She set a stone at his head.

She learnt to dream of him, and told them:
    " In slumber often uprises he,
And says : ' I am joyed that, after all, Dear,
    You've not deserted me!' "

At length died too this kinless woman,
    As he had died she had grown to crave;
And at her dying she besought them
    To bury her in his grave.

Such said, she had paused; until she added:
    " Call me by his name on the stone,
As I were, first to last, his dearest,
    Not she who left him lone!"

And this they did.   And so it became there
    That, by the strength of a tender whim,
The stranger was she who bore his name tnere.
    Not she who wedded him.

HER SONG

I SANG that song on Sunday,
    To witch an idle while,
I sang that song on Monday,
    As fittest to beguile :

I sang it as the year outwore,
    And the new slid in ;
I thought not what might shape before
    Another would begin.

I sang that song in summer,
    All unforeknowingly,
To him as a new-comer
    From regions strange to me :
I sang it when in afteryears
    The shades stretched out,
And paths were faint ; and flocking fears
    Brought cup-eyed care and doubt.

Sings he that song on Sundays
    In some dim land afar,
On Saturdays, or Mondays,
    As when the evening star
Glimpsed in upon his bending face,
    And my hanging hair,
And time untouched me with a trace
    Of soul-smart or despair ?

A WET AUGUST

NINE drops of water bead the jessamine,
And nine-and-ninety smear the stones and tiles :
—'Twas not so in that August—full-rayed, fine—
When we lived out-of-doors, sang songs, strode miles.

Or **was** there then no noted radiancy
Of summer ?   Were dun clouds, a dribbling bough,
Gilt over by the light I bore in me,
And was the waste world just the same as now ?

It can have been so : yea, that threatenings
Of coming down-drip on the sunless gray,
By the then golden chances seen in things
Were wrought more bright than brightest skies to-day.

1920.

THE DISSEMBLERS

" It was not you I came to please,
    Only myself," flipped she ;
" I like this spot of phantasies,
    And thought you far from me."
But O, he was the secret spell
    That led her to the lea !

" It was not she who shaped my ways,
    Or works, or thoughts," he said.
" I scarcely marked her living days,
    Or missed her much when dead."
But O, his joyance knew its knell
    When daisies hid her head !

TO A LADY PLAYING AND SINGING IN
THE MORNING

JOYFUL lady, sing !
And I will lurk here listening,
Though nought be done, and nought begun,
And work-hours swift are scurrying.

Sing, O lady, still !
Aye, I will wait each note you trill,
Though duties due that press to do
This whole day long I unfulfil.

"—It is an evening tune ;
One not designed to waste the noon,"
You say. I know : time bids me go—
For daytide passes too, too soon !

But let indulgence be,
This once, to my rash ecstasy :
When sounds nowhere that carolled air
My idled morn may comfort me !

"A MAN WAS DRAWING NEAR TO ME"

ON that gray night of mournful drone,
Apart from aught to hear, to see,
I dreamt not that from shires unknown
   In gloom, alone,
     By Halworthy,
A man was drawing near to me.

I'd no concern at anything,
No sense of coming pull-heart play;
Yet, under the silent outspreading
   Of even's wing
     Where Otterham lay,
A man was riding up my way.

I thought of nobody—not of one,
But only of trifles—legends, ghosts—
Though, on the moorland dim and dun
   That travellers shun
     About these coasts,
The man had passed Tresparret Posts.

There was no light at all inland,
Only the seaward pharos-fire,
Nothing to let me understand
   That hard at hand
     By Hennett Byre
The man was getting nigh and nigher.

There was a rumble at the door,
A draught disturbed the drapery,
And but a minute passed before,
   With gaze that bore
     My destiny,
The man revealed himself to me.

THE STRANGE HOUSE
(MAX GATE, A.D. 2000)

"I HEAR the piano playing—
   Just as a ghost might play."
"—O, but what are you saying?
   There's no piano to-day;

Their old one was sold and broken ;
    Years past it went amiss."
" —I heard it, or shouldn't have spoken :
    A strange house, this !

" I catch some undertone here,
    From some one out of sight."
" —Impossible ; we are alone here,
    And shall be through the night."
" —The parlour-door—what stirred it ? "
    " —No one : no soul's in range."
" —But, anyhow, I heard it,
        And it seems strange !

" Seek my own room I cannot—
    A figure is on the stair ! "
" —What figure ?   Nay, I scan not
    Any one lingering there.
A bough outside is waving,
    And that's its shade by the moon."
" —Well, all is strange ! I am craving
        Strength to leave soon."

" —Ah, maybe you've some vision
    Of showings beyond our sphere ;
Some sight, sense, intuition
    Of what once happened here ?
The house is old ; they've hinted
    It once held two love-thralls,
And they may have imprinted
        Their dreams on its walls ?

" They were—I think 'twas told me—
    Queer in their works and ways ;
The teller would often hold me
    With weird tales of those days.
Some folk can not abide here,
    But we—we do not care
Who loved, laughed, wept, or died here,
        Knew joy, or despair."

"AS 'TWERE TO-NIGHT"

(SONG)

As 'twere to-night, in the brief space
    Of a far eventime,
      My spirit rang achime
At vision of a girl of grace ;
As 'twere to-night, in the brief space
    Of a far eventime.

As 'twere at noontide of to-morrow
    I airily walked and talked,
      And wondered as I walked
What it could mean, this soar from sorrow ;
As 'twere at noontide of to-morrow
    I airily walked and talked.

As 'twere at waning of this week
    Broke a new life on me ;
      Trancings of bliss to be
In some dim dear land soon to seek ;
As 'twere at waning of this week
    Broke a new life on me !

THE CONTRETEMPS

A forward rush by the lamp in the gloom,
    And we clasped, and almost kissed ;
But she was not the woman whom
I had promised to meet in the thawing brume
On that harbour-bridge ; nor was I he of her tryst.

So loosening from me swift she said :
    "O why, why feign to be
The one I had meant !—to whom I have sped
To fly with, being so sorrily wed !"
—'Twas thus and thus that she upbraided me.

My assignation had struck upon
  Some others' like it, I found.
And her lover rose on the night anon;
And then her husband entered on
The lamplit, snowflaked, sloppiness around.

  "Take her and welcome, man!" he cried:
    "I wash my hands of her.
I'll find me twice as good a bride!"
—All this to me, whom he had eyed,
Plainly, as his wife's planned deliverer.

And next the lover: "Little I knew,
    Madam, you had a third!
Kissing here in my very view!"
—Husband and lover then withdrew.
I let them; and I told them not they erred.

Why not? Well, there faced she and I—
    Two strangers who'd kissed, or near,
Chancewise. To see stand weeping by
A woman once embraced, will try
The tension of a man the most austere.

So it began; and I was young,
    She pretty, by the lamp,
As flakes came waltzing down among
The waves of her clinging hair, that hung
Heavily on her temples, dark and damp.

And there alone still stood we two;
    She one cast off for me,
Or so it seemed: while night ondrew,
Forcing a parley what should do
We twain hearts caught in one catastrophe.

In stranded souls a common strait
    Wakes latencies unknown,
Whose impulse may precipitate
A life-long leap. The hour was late,
And there was the Jersey boat with its funnel agroan.

"Is wary walking worth much pother?"
  It grunted, as still it stayed.
"One pairing is as good as another
  Where all is venture! Take each other,
And scrap the oaths that you have aforetime made." . . .

—Of the four involved there walks but one
  On earth at this late day.
And what of the chapter so begun?
In that odd complex what was done?
Well; happiness comes in full to none:
Let peace lie on lulled lips: I will not say.

  WEYMOUTH.

A GENTLEMAN'S EPITAPH ON HIMSELF AND A LADY, WHO WERE BURIED TOGETHER

I DWELT in the shade of a city,
    She far by the sea,
With folk perhaps good, gracious, witty;
    But never with me.

Her form on the ballroom's smooth flooring
    I never once met,
To guide her with accents adoring
    Through Weippert's "First Set."[1]

I spent my life's seasons with pale ones
    In Vanity Fair,
And she enjoyed hers among hale ones
    In salt-smelling air.

Maybe she had eyes of deep colour,
    Maybe they were blue,
Maybe as she aged they got duller;
    That never I knew.

[1] Quadrilles danced early in the nineteenth century.

She may have had lips like the coral,
    But I never kissed them,
Saw pouting, nor curling in quarrel,
    Nor sought for, nor missed them.

Not a word passed of love all our lifetime,
    Between us, nor thrill;
We'd never a husband-and-wife time,
    For good or for ill.

Yet as one dust, through bleak days and vernal
    Lie I and lies she,
This never-known lady, eternal
    Companion to me!

THE OLD GOWN
(SONG)

I HAVE seen her in gowns the brightest,
    Of azure, green, and red,
And in the simplest, whitest,
    Muslined from heel to head;
I have watched her walking, riding,
    Shade-flecked by a leafy tree,
Or in fixed thought abiding
    By the foam-fingered sea.

In woodlands I have known her,
    When boughs were mourning loud,
In the rain-reek she has shown her
    Wild-haired and watery-browed.
And once or twice she has cast me
    As she pomped along the street
Court-clad, ere quite she had passed me,
    A glance from her chariot-seat.

But in my memoried passion
    For evermore stands she
In the gown of fading fashion
    She wore that night when we,

Doomed long to part, assembled
    In the snug small room; yea, when
She sang with lips that trembled,
    "Shall I see his face again?"

A NIGHT IN NOVEMBER

I MARKED when the weather changed,
And the panes began to quake,
And the winds rose up and ranged,
That night, lying half-awake.

Dead leaves blew into my room,
And alighted upon my bed,
And a tree declared to the gloom
Its sorrow that they were shed.

One leaf of them touched my hand,
And I thought that it was you
There stood as you used to stand,
And saying at last you knew!

(?) 1913.

A DUETTIST TO HER PIANOFORTE

SONG OF SILENCE

(E. L. H.—H. C. H.)

SINCE every sound moves memories,
    How can I play you
Just as I might if you raised no scene,
By your ivory rows, of a form between
My vision and your time-worn sheen,
    As when each day you
Answered our fingers with ecstasy?
So it's hushed, hushed, hushed, you are for me!

And as I am doomed to counterchord
      Her notes no more
In those old things I used to know,
In a fashion, when we practised so,
" Good-night !—Good-bye ! " to your pleated show
      Of silk, now hoar,
Each nodding hammer, and pedal and key,
For dead, dead, dead, you are to me !

I fain would second her, strike to her stroke,
      As when she was by,
Aye, even from the ancient clamorous " Fall
Of Paris," or " Battle of Prague " withal,
To the " Roving Minstrels," or " Elfin Call "
      Sung soft as a sigh :
But upping ghosts press achefully,
And mute, mute, mute, you are for me !

Should I fling your polyphones, plaints, and quavers
      Afresh on the air,
Too quick would the small white shapes be here
Of the fellow twain of hands so dear ;
And a black-tressed profile, and pale smooth ear ;
      —Then how shall I bear
Such heavily-haunted harmony ?
Nay : hushed, hushed, hushed, you are for me !

"WHERE THREE ROADS JOINED"

WHERE three roads joined it was green and fair,
And over a gate was the sun-glazed sea,
And life laughed sweet when I halted there ;
Yet there I never again would be.

I am sure those branchways are brooding now,
With a wistful blankness upon their face,
While the few mute passengers notice how
Spectre-beridden is the place ;

Which nightly sighs like a laden soul,
And grieves that a pair, in bliss for a spell
Not far from thence, should have let it roll
Away from them down a plumbless well

While the phasm of him who fared starts up,
And of her who was waiting him sobs from near
As they haunt there and drink the wormwood cup
They filled for themselves when their sky was clear.

Yes, I see those roads—now rutted and bare,
While over the gate is no sun-glazed sea ;
And though life laughed when I halted there,
It is where I never again would be.

"AND THERE WAS A GREAT CALM"

(ON THE SIGNING OF THE ARMISTICE, NOV. 11, 1918)

I

THERE had been years of Passion—scorching, cold,
And much Despair, and Anger heaving high,
Care whitely watching, Sorrows manifold,
Among the young, among the weak and old,
And the pensive Spirit of Pity whispered, "Why?"

II

Men had not paused to answer. Foes distraught
Pierced the thinned peoples in a brute-like blindness,
Philosophies that sages long had taught,
And Selflessness, were as an unknown thought,
And "Hell!" and "Shell!" were yapped at Lovingkindness.

III

The feeble folk at home had grown full-used
To "dug-outs," "snipers," "Huns," from the war-adept
In the mornings heard, and at evetides perused ;
To day-dreamt men in millions, when they mused—
To nightmare-men in millions when they slept.

IV

Waking to wish existence timeless, null,
Sirius they watched above where armies fell;
He seemed to check his flapping when, in the lull
Of night a boom came thencewise, like the dull
Plunge of a stone dropped into some deep well

V

So, when old hopes that earth was bettering slowly
Were dead and damned, there sounded "War is done!"
One morrow.   Said the bereft, and meek, and lowly,
"Will men some day be given to grace? yea, wholly,
And in good sooth, as our dreams used to run?"

VI

Breathless they paused.   Out there men raised their glance
To where had stood those poplars lank and lopped,
As they had raised it through the four years' dance
Of Death in the now familiar flats of France;
And murmured, "Strange, this!   How?   All firing stopped?"

VII

Aye; all was hushed.   The about-to-fire fired not,
The aimed-at moved away in trance-lipped song.
One checkless regiment slung a clinching shot
And turned.   The Spirit of Irony smirked out, "What?
Spoil peradventures woven of Rage and Wrong?"

VIII

Thenceforth no flying fires inflamed the gray,
No hurtlings shook the dewdrop from the thorn,
No moan perplexed the mute bird on the spray;
Worn horses mused: "We are not whipped to-day";
No weft-winged engines blurred the moon's thin horn.

IX

Calm fell.   From Heaven distilled a clemency;
There was peace on earth, and silence in the sky;
Some could, some could not, shake off misery:
The Sinister Spirit sneered: "It had to be!"
And again the Spirit of Pity whispered, "Why?"

HAUNTING FINGERS

A PHANTASY IN A MUSEUM OF MUSICAL INSTRUMENTS

" ARE you awake,
    Comrades, this silent night ?
Well 'twere if all of our glossy gluey make
Lay in the damp without, and fell to fragments quite ! "

" O viol, my friend,
    I watch, though Phosphor nears,
And I fain would drowse away to its utter end
This dumb dark stowage after our loud melodious years ! "

And they felt past handlers clutch them,
    Though none was in the room,
Old players' dead fingers touch them,
        Shrunk in the tomb.

" 'Cello, good mate,
    You speak my mind as yours :
Doomed to this voiceless, crippled, corpselike state,
Who, dear to famed Amphion, trapped here, long endures ? "

" Once I could thrill
    The populace through and through,
Wake them to passioned pulsings past their will." . . .
(A contra-basso spake so, and the rest sighed anew.)

And they felt old muscles travel
    Over their tense contours,
And with long skill unravel
        Cunningest scores.

" The tender pat
    Of her aery finger-tips
Upon me daily—I rejoiced thereat ! "
(Thuswise a harpsicord, as 'twere from dampered lips.)

" My keys' white shine,
    Now sallow, met a hand
Even whiter. . . . Tones of hers fell forth with mine
In sowings of sound so sweet no lover could withstand ! "

And its clavier was filmed with fingers
    Like tapering flames—wan, cold—
Or the nebulous light that lingers
    In charnel mould.

    " Gayer than most
    Was I," reverbed a drum ;
" The regiments, marchings, throngs, hurrahs !   What a host
I stirred—even when crape mufflings gagged me well-nigh dumb !"

    Trilled an aged viol :
    " Much tune have I set free
To spur the dance, since my first timid trial
Where I had birth—far hence, in sun-swept Italy !"

And he feels apt touches on him
    From those that pressed him then ;
Who seem with their glance to con him,
        Saying, " Not again ! "

    " A holy calm,"
    Mourned a shawm's voice subdued,
" Steeped my Cecilian rhythms when hymn and psalm
Poured from devout souls met in Sabbath sanctitude."

    " I faced the sock
    Nightly," twanged a sick lyre,
" Over ranked lights !   O charm of life in mock,
O scenes that fed love, hope, wit, rapture, mirth, desire !"

Thus they, till each past player
    Stroked thinner and more thin,
And the morning sky grew grayer
    And day crawled in.

THE WOMAN I MET

A STRANGER, I threaded sunken-hearted
    A lamp-lit crowd ;
And anon there passed me a soul departed,
    Who mutely bowed.

In my far-off youthful years I had met her,
Full-pulsed ; but now, no more life's debtor,
Onward she slid
In a shroud that furs half-hid.

"Why do you trouble me, dead woman,
Trouble me ;
You whom I knew when warm and human?
—How it be
That you quitted earth and are yet upon it
Is, to any who ponder on it,
Past being read !"
"Still, it is so," she said.

"These were my haunts in my olden sprightly
Hours of breath ;
Here I went tempting frail youth nightly
To their death ;
But you deemed me chaste—me, a tinselled sinner !
How thought you one with pureness in her
Could pace this street
Eyeing some man to greet ?

"Well ; your very simplicity made me love you
Mid such town dross,
Till I set not Heaven itself above you,
Who grew my Cross ;
For you'd only nod, despite how I sighed for you ;
So you tortured me, who fain would have died for you !
—What I suffered then
Would have paid for the sins of ten !

"Thus went the days. I feared you despised me
To fling me a nod
Each time, no more : till love chastised me
As with a rod
That a fresh bland boy of no assurance
Should fire me with passion beyond endurance,
While others all
I hated, and loathed their call.

"I said : 'It is his mother's spirit
Hovering around

To shield him, maybe!'   I used to fear it,
    As still I found
My beauty left no least impression,
And remnants of pride withheld confession
    Of my true trade
  By speaking; so I delayed.

"I said: 'Perhaps with a costly flower
    He'll be beguiled.'
I held it, in passing you one late hour,
    To your face: you smiled,
Keeping step with the throng; though you did not see there
A single one that rivalled me there! . . .
    Well: it's all past.
  I died in the Lock at last."

So walked the dead and I together
    The quick among,
Elbowing our kind of every feather
    Slowly and long;
Yea, long and slowly.   That a phantom should stalk there
With me seemed nothing strange, and talk there
    That winter night
  By flaming jets of light.

She showed me Juans who feared their call-time,
    Guessing their lot;
She showed me her sort that cursed their fall-time,
    And that did not.
Till suddenly murmured she: "Now, tell me,
Why asked you never, ere death befell me,
    To have my love,
  Much as I dreamt thereof?"

I could not answer.   And she, well weeting
    All in my heart,
Said: "God your guardian kept our fleeting
    Forms apart!"
Sighing and drawing her furs around her
Over the shroud that tightly bound her,
    With wafts as from clay
  She turned and thinned away.

LONDON, 1918.

"IF IT'S EVER SPRING AGAIN"

(SONG)

IF it's ever spring again,
    Spring again,
I shall go where went I when
Down the moor-cock splashed, and hen,
Seeing me not, amid their flounder,
Standing with my arm around her;
If it's ever spring again,
    Spring again,
I shall go where went I then.

If it's ever summer-time,
    Summer-time,
With the hay crop at the prime,
And the cuckoos—two—in rhyme,
As they used to be, or seemed to,
We shall do as long we've dreamed to,
If it's ever summer-time,
    Summer-time,
With the hay, and bees achime.

THE TWO HOUSES

IN the heart of night,
    When farers were not near,
The left house said to the house on the right,
"I have marked your rise, O smart newcomer here."

Said the right, cold-eyed:
    "Newcomer here I am,
Hence haler than you with your cracked old hide,
Loose casements, wormy beams, and doors that jam.

"Modern my wood,
    My hangings fair of hue;
While my windows open as they should,
And water-pipes thread all my chambers through."

" Your gear is gray,
    Your face wears furrows untold."
"—Yours might," mourned the other, " if you held, brother
The Presences from aforetime that I hold.

" You have not known
    Men's lives, deaths, toils, and teens ;
You are but a heap of stick and stone :
A new house has no sense of the have-beens.

" Void as a drum
    You stand : I am packed with these,
Though, strangely, living dwellers who come
See not the phantoms all my substance sees !

" Visible in the morning
    Stand they, when dawn drags in ;
Visible at night ; yet hint or warning
Of these thin elbowers few of the inmates win.

" Babes new-brought-forth
    Obsess my rooms ; straight-stretched
Lank corpses, ere outborne to earth ;
Yea, throng they as when first from the Byss upfetched.

" Dancers and singers
    Throb in me now as once ;
Rich-noted throats and gossamered flingers
Of heels ; the learned in love-lore and the dunce.

" Note here within
    The bridegroom and the bride,
Who smile and greet their friends and kin,
And down my stairs depart for tracks untried.

" Where such inbe,
    A dwelling's character
Takes theirs, and a vague semblancy
To them in all its limbs, and light, and atmosphere.

" Yet the blind folk
    My tenants, who come and go
In the flesh mid these, with souls unwoke,
Of such sylph-like surrounders do not know."

"—Will the day come,"
Said the new one, awestruck, faint,
"When I shall lodge shades dim and dumb—
And with such spectral guests become acquaint?"

"—That will it, boy;
Such shades will people thee,
Each in his misery, irk, or joy,
And print on thee their presences as on me."

ON STINSFORD HILL AT MIDNIGHT

I GLIMPSED a woman's muslined form
    Sing-songing airily
Against the moon; and still she sang,
    And took no heed of me.

Another trice, and I beheld
    What first I had not scanned,
That now and then she tapped and shook
    A timbrel in her hand.

So late the hour, so white her drape,
    So strange the look it lent
To that blank hill, I could not guess
    What phantastry it meant.

Then burst I forth: "Why such from you?
    Are you so happy now?"
Her voice swam on; nor did she show
    Thought of me anyhow.

I called again: "Come nearer; much
    That kind of note I need!"
The song kept softening, loudening on,
    In placid calm unheed.

"What home is yours now?" then I said
    "You seem to have no care."
But the wild wavering tune went forth
    As if I had not been there.

"This world is dark, and where you are,"
    I said, "I cannot be!"
But still the happy one sang on,
    And had no heed of me.

NOTE.—It was said that she belonged to a body of religious enthusiasts.

THE FALLOW DEER AT THE LONELY HOUSE

ONE without looks in to-night
        Through the curtain-chink
From the sheet of glistening white;
One without looks in to-night
        As we sit and think
        By the fender-brink.

We do not discern those eyes
        Watching in the snow;
Lit by lamps of rosy dyes
We do not discern those eyes
        Wondering, aglow,
        Fourfooted, tiptoe.

THE SELFSAME SONG

A BIRD sings the selfsame song,
With never a fault in its flow,
That we listened to here those long
        Long years ago.

A pleasing marvel is how
A strain of such rapturous rote
Should have gone on thus till now
        Unchanged in a note!

——But it's not the selfsame bird.——
No: perished to dust is he. . . .
As also are those who heard
        That song with me.

THE WANDERER

THERE is nobody on the road
    But I,
And no beseeming abode
    I can try
For shelter, so abroad
    I must lie.

The stars feel not far up,
    And to be
The lights by which I sup
    Glimmeringly,
Set out in a hollow cup
    Over me.

They wag as though they were
    Panting for joy
Where they shine, above all care.
    And annoy,
And demons of despair—
    Life's alloy.

Sometimes outside the fence
    Feet swing past,
Clock-like, and then go hence,
    Till at last
There is a silence, dense,
    Deep, and vast.

A wanderer, witch-drawn
    To and fro,
To-morrow, at the dawn,
    On I go,
And where I rest anon
    Do not know!

Yet it's meet—this bed of hay
    And roofless plight;
For there's a house of clay,
    My own, quite,
To roof me soon, all day
    And all night.

A WIFE COMES BACK

THIS is the story a man told me
Of his life's one day of dreamery.

A woman came into his room
Between the dawn and the creeping day:
She was the years-wed wife from whom
He had parted, and who lived far away,
     As if strangers they.

He wondered, and as she stood
She put on youth in her look and air, ·
And more was he wonderstruck as he viewed
Her form and flesh bloom yet more fair
     While he watched her there;

Till she freshed to the pink and brown
That were hers on the night when first they met,
When she was the charm of the idle town,
And he the pick of the club-fire set. . . .
     His eyes grew wet,

And he stretched his arms: "Stay—rest!—"
He cried. "Abide with me so, my own!"
But his arms closed in on his hard bare breast;
She had vanished with all he had looked upon
     Of her beauty: gone.

He clothed, and drew downstairs,
But she was not in the house, he found;
And he passed out under the leafy pairs
Of the avenue elms, and searched around
     To the park-pale bound.

He mounted, and rode till night
To the city to which she had long withdrawn,
The vision he bore all day in his sight
Being her young self as pondered on
     In the dim of dawn.

"—The lady here long ago—
Is she now here ?—young—or such age as she is ?"
"—She is still here."—" Thank God.   Let her know ;
She'll pardon a comer so late as this
          Whom she'd fain not miss."

          She received him—an ancient dame,
Who hemmed, with features frozen and numb,
" How strange !—I'd almost forgotten your name !—
A call just now—is troublesome ;
          Why did you come ? "

A YOUNG MAN'S EXHORTATION

          CALL off your eyes from care
By some determined deftness ; put forth joys
Dear as excess without the core that cloys,
          And charm Life's lourings fair.

          Exalt and crown the hour
That girdles us, and fill it full with glee,
Blind glee, excelling aught could ever be
          Were heedfulness in power.

          Send up such touching strains
That limitless recruits from Fancy's pack
Shall rush upon your tongue, and tender back
          All that your soul contains.

          For what do we know best ?
That a fresh love-leaf crumpled soon will dry,
And that men moment after moment die,
          Of all scope dispossest.

          If I have seen one thing
It is the passing preciousness of dreams ;
That aspects are within us ; and who seems
          Most kingly is the King.

1867 : WESTBOURNE PARK VILLAS.

AT LULWORTH COVE A CENTURY BACK

HAD I but lived a hundred years ago
I might have gone, as I have gone this year,
By Warmwell Cross on to a Cove I know,
And Time have placed his finger on me there :

" *You see that man ?* "—I might have looked, and said,
" O yes : I see him.　One that boat has brought
Which dropped down Channel round Saint Alban's Head.
So commonplace a youth calls not my thought."

" *You see that man ?* "—" Why yes ; I told you ; yes :
Of an idling town-sort ; thin ; hair brown in hue ;
And as the evening light scants less and less
He looks up at a star, as many do."

" *You see that man ?* "—" Nay, leave me ! " then I plead,
" I have fifteen miles to vamp across the lea,
And it grows dark, and I am weary-kneed :
I have said the third time ; yes, that man I see ! "

" Good.　That man goes to Rome—to death, despair ;
And no one notes him now but you and I :
A hundred years, and the world will follow him there,
And bend with reverence where his ashes lie."

September 1920.

NOTE.—In September 1820 Keats, on his way to Rome, landed one da
on the Dorset coast, and composed the sonnet, " Bright star ! would I wer
steadfast as thou art."　The spot of his landing is judged to have bee
Lulworth Cove.

A BYGONE OCCASION

(SONG)

THAT night, that night,
That song, that song !
Will such again be evened quite
Through lifetimes long ?

No mirth was shown
To outer seers,
But mood to match has not been known
In modern years.

O eyes that smiled,
O lips that lured ;
That such would last was one beguiled
To think ensured !

That night, that night,
That song, that song ;
O drink to its recalled delight,
Though tears may throng !

TWO SERENADES

I

On Christmas Eve

LATE on Christmas Eve, in the street alone,
Outside a house, on the pavement-stone,
I sang to her, as we'd sung together
On former eves ere I felt her tether.—
Above the door of green by me
Was she, her casement seen by me ;
    But she would not heed
    What I melodied
    In my soul's sore need—
    She would not heed.

Cassiopeia overhead,
And the Seven of the Wain, heard what I said
As I bent me there, and voiced, and fingered
Upon the strings. . . . Long, long I lingered :
Only the curtains hid from her
One whom caprice had bid from her ;
    But she did not come,
    And my heart grew numb
    And dull my strum ;
    She did not come.

II

A Year Later

I SKIMMED the strings ; I sang quite low ;
I hoped she would not come or know
That the house next door was the one now dittied,
Not hers, as when I had played unpitied ;
—Next door, where dwelt a heart fresh stirred,
My new Love, of good will to me,
Unlike my old Love chill to me,
Who had not cared for my notes when heard :
        Yet that old Love came
        To the other's name
        As hers were the claim ;
        Yea, the old Love came.

My viol sank mute, my tongue stood still,
I tried to sing on, but vain my will :
I prayed she would guess of the later, and leave me ;
She stayed, as though, were she slain by the smart,
She would bear love's burn for a newer heart.
The tense-drawn moment wrought to bereave me
Of voice, and I turned in a dumb despair
At her finding I'd come to another there.
        Sick I withdrew
        At love's grim hue
        Ere my last Love knew ;
        Sick I withdrew.

From an old copy.

THE WEDDING MORNING

TABITHA dressed for her wedding :—
    "Tabby, why look so sad ?"
"—O I feel a great gloominess spreading, spreading,
    Instead of supremely glad ! . . .

    "I called on Carry last night,
    And he came whilst I was there,
Not knowing I'd called. So I kept out of sight,
    And I heard what he said to her :

    " '—Ah, I'd far liefer marry
      You, Dear, to-morrow!' he said,
' But that cannot be.'—O I'd give him to Carry,
    And willingly see them wed,

    " But how can I do it when
      His baby will soon be born ?
After that I hope I may die.   And then
    She can have him.   I shall not mourn ! "

END OF THE YEAR 1912

You were here at his young beginning,
    You are not here at his agèd end ;
Off he coaxed you from Life's mad spinning,
    Lest you should see his form extend
      Shivering, sighing,
      Slowly dying,
And a tear on him expend.

So it comes that we stand lonely
    In the star-lit avenue,
Dropping broken lipwords only,
    For we hear no songs from you,
      Such as flew here
      For the new year
Once, while six bells swung thereto.

THE CHIMES PLAY "LIFE'S A BUMPER!"

"Awake!   I'm off to cities far away,"
I said ; and rose, on peradventures bent.
The chimes played " Life's a Bumper ! " long that day
To the measure of my walking as I went :
Their sweetness frisked and floated on the lea,
As they played out " Life's a Bumper ! " there to me.

"Awake!" I said.   "I go to take a bride!"
—The sun arose behind me ruby-red
As I journeyed townwards from the countryside,
The chiming bells saluting near ahead.

Their sweetness swelled in tripping tings of glee
As they played out " Life's a Bumper ! " there to me.

" Again arise."　I seek a turfy slope,
And go forth slowly on an autumn noon,
And there I lay her who has been my hope,
And think, " O may I follow hither soon ! "
While on the wind the chimes come cheerily,
Playing out " Life's a Bumper ! " there to me.

　　　1913.

" I WORKED NO WILE TO MEET YOU "

(SONG)

I worked no wile to meet you,
　　My sight was set elsewhere,
I sheered about to shun you,
　　And lent your life no care.
I was unprimed to greet you
　　At such a date and place,
Constraint alone had won you
　　Vision of my strange face !

You did not seek to see me
　　Then or at all, you said,
—Meant passing when you neared me,
　　But stumbling-blocks forbade.
You even had thought to flee me,
　　By other mindings moved ;
No influent star endeared me,
　　Unknown, unrecked, unproved !

What, then, was there to tell us
　　The flux of flustering hours
Of their own tide would bring us
　　By no device of ours
To where the daysprings well us
　　Heart-hydromels that cheer,
Till Time enearth and swing us
　　Round with the turning sphere.

AT THE RAILWAY STATION, UPWAY

"THERE is not much that I can do,
  For I've no money that's quite my own!"
  Spoke up the pitying child—
A little boy with a violin
At the station before the train came in,—
" But I can play my fiddle to you,
And a nice one 'tis, and good in tone!"

  The man in the handcuffs smiled;
The constable looked, and he smiled, too,
  As the fiddle began to twang;
And the man in the handcuffs suddenly sang
          With grimful glee:
          " This life so free
          Is the thing for me!"
And the constable smiled, and said no word,
As if unconscious of what he heard;
And so they went on till the train came in—
The convict, and boy with the violin.

SIDE BY SIDE

      So there sat they,
      The estranged two,
      Thrust in one pew
      By chance that day;
      Placed so, breath-nigh,
      Each comer unwitting
      Who was to be sitting
      In touch close by.

      Thus side by side
      Blindly alighted,
      They seemed united
      As groom and bride,
      Who'd not communed
      For many years—
      Lives from twain spheres
      With hearts distuned.

Her fringes brushed
His garment's hem
As the harmonies rushed
Through each of them:
Her lips could be heard
In the creed and psalms,
And their fingers neared
At the giving of alms.

And women and men,
The matins ended,
By looks commended
Them, joined again.
Quickly said she,
"Don't undeceive them—
Better thus leave them:"
"Quite so," said he.

Slight words!—the last
Between them said,
Those two, once wed,
Who had not stood fast.
Diverse their ways
From the western door,
To meet no more
In their span of days.

DREAM OF THE CITY SHOPWOMAN

'TWERE sweet to have a comrade here,
Who'd vow to love this garreteer,
By city people's snap and sneer
          Tried oft and hard!

We'd rove a truant cock and hen
To some snug solitary glen,
And never be seen to haunt again
          This teeming yard.

Within a cot of thatch and clay
We'd list the flitting pipers play,
Our lives a twine of good and gay
      Enwreathed discreetly;

Our blithest deeds so neighbouring wise
That doves should coo in soft surprise,
"These must belong to Paradise
      Who live so sweetly."

Our clock should be the closing flowers,
Our sprinkle-bath the passing showers,
Our church the alleyed willow bowers,
      The truth our theme;

And infant shapes might soon abound:
Their shining heads would dot us round
Like mushroom balls on grassy ground. . . .
      —But all is dream!

O God, that creatures framed to feel
A yearning nature's strong appeal
Should writhe on this eternal wheel
      In rayless grime;

And vainly note, with wan regret,
Each star of early promise set;
Till Death relieves, and they forget
      Their one Life's time!

Westbourne Park Villas, 1866.

A MAIDEN'S PLEDGE

(SONG)

I do not wish to win your vow
To take me soon or late as bride,
And lift me from the nook where now
I tarry your farings to my side.

I am blissful ever to abide
In this green labyrinth—let all be,
If but, whatever may betide,
You do not leave off loving me !

Your comet-comings I will wait
With patience time shall not wear through ;
The yellowing years will not abate
My largened love and truth to you,
Nor drive me to complaint undue
Of absence, much as I may pine,
If never another 'twixt us two
Shall come, and you stand wholly mine.

THE CHILD AND THE SAGE

You say, O Sage, when weather-checked,
   " I have been favoured so
With cloudless skies, I must expect
   This dash of rain or snow."

" Since health has been my lot," you say,
   " So many months of late,
I must not chafe that one short day
   Of sickness mars my state."

You say, " Such bliss has been my share
   From Love's unbroken smile,
It is but reason I should bear
   A cross therein awhile."

And thus you do not count upon
   Continuance of joy ;
But, when at ease, expect anon
   A burden of annoy.

But, Sage—this Earth—why not a place
   Where no reprisals reign,
Where never a spell of pleasantness
   Makes reasonable a pain ?

                December 21, 1908.

MISMET

I

He was leaning by a face,
He was looking into eyes,
And he knew a trysting-place,
And he heard seductive sighs;
　　But the face,
　　And the eyes,
　　And the place,
　　And the sighs,
Were not, alas, the right ones—the ones meet for him—
Though fine and sweet the features, and the feelings all abrim.

II

She was looking at a form,
She was listening for a tread,
She could feel a waft of charm
When a certain name was said;
　　But the form,
　　And the tread,
　　And the charm,
　　And name said,
Were the wrong ones for her, and ever would be so,
While the heritor of the right it would have saved her soul to know!

AN AUTUMN RAIN-SCENE

There trudges one to a merry-making
　　With a sturdy swing,
　　On whom the rain comes down.

To fetch the saving medicament
　　Is another bent,
　　On whom the rain comes down.

One slowly drives his herd to the stall
　　Ere ill befall,
　　On whom the rain comes down.

This bears his missives of life and death
With quickening breath,
On whom the rain comes down.

One watches for signals of wreck or war
From the hill afar,
On whom the rain comes down.

No care if he gain a shelter or none,
Unhired moves one,
On whom the rain comes down.

And another knows nought of its chilling fall
Upon him at all,
On whom the rain comes down.

October 1904.

MEDITATIONS ON A HOLIDAY

(A NEW THEME TO AN OLD FOLK-MEASURE)

'Tis a May morning,
All-adorning,
No cloud warning
Of rain to-day.
Where shall I go to,
Go to, go to?—
Can I say No to
Lyonnesse-way?

Well—what reason
Now at this season
Is there for treason
To other shrines?
Tristram is not there,
Isolt forgot there,
New eras blot there
Sought-for signs!

Stratford-on-Avon—
Poesy-paven—
I'll find a haven
    There, somehow!—
Nay—I'm but caught of
Dreams long thought of,
The Swan knows nought of
    His Avon now!

What shall it be, then,
I go to see, then,
Under the plea, then,
    Of votary?
I'll go to Lakeland,
Lakeland, Lakeland,
Certainly Lakeland
    Let it be.

But—why to that place,
That place, that place,
Such a hard come-at place
    Need I fare?
When its bard cheers no more,
Loves no more, fears no more,
Sees no more, hears no more
    Anything there!

Ah, there is Scotland,
Burns's Scotland,
And Waverley's.   To what land
    Better can I hie?—
Yet—if no whit now
Feel those of it now—
Care not a bit now
    For it—why I?

I'll seek a town street,
Aye, a brick-brown street,
Quite a tumbledown street,
    Drawing no eyes.
For a Mary dwelt there,
And a Percy felt there
Heart of him melt there,
    A Claire likewise.

Why incline to *that* city,
Such a city, *that* city,
Now a mud-bespat city !—
    Care the lovers who
Now live and walk there,
Sit there and talk there,
Buy there, or hawk there.
    Or wed, or woo ?

Laughters in a volley
Greet so fond a folly
As nursing melancholy
    In this and that spot,
Which, with most endeavour,
Those can visit never,
But for ever and ever
    Will now know not !

If, on lawns Elysian,
With a broadened vision
And a faint derision
    Conscious be they,
How they might reprove me
That these fancies move me,
Think they ill behoove me,
    Smile, and say :

" What !—our hoar old houses,
Where the bygone drowses,
Nor a child nor spouse is
    Of our name at all ?
Such abodes to care for,
Inquire about and bear for,
And suffer wear and tear for—
    How weak of you and small ! "

    May 1921.

AN EXPERIENCE

WIT, weight, or wealth there was not
    In anything that was said,
    In anything that was done ;
All was of scope to cause not

A triumph, dazzle, or dread
To even the subtlest one,
   My friend,
To even the subtlest one.

But there was a new afflation—
An aura zephyring round
That care infected not:
It came as a salutation,
   And, in my sweet astound,
   I scarcely witted what
         Might pend,
   I scarcely witted what.

The hills in samewise to me
Spoke, as they grayly gazed,
   —First hills to speak so yet!
The thin-edged breezes blew me
What I, though cobwebbed, crazed.
   Was never to forget,
         My friend,
   Was never to forget!

THE BEAUTY

O DO not praise my beauty more,
   In such word-wild degree,
And say I am one all eyes adore;
   For these things harass me!

But do for ever softly say:
   "From now unto the end
Come weal, come wanzing, come what may,
   Dear, I will be your friend."

I hate my beauty in the glass:
   My beauty is not I:
I wear it: none cares whether, alas,
   Its wearer live or die!

The inner I O care for, then,
    Yea, me and what I am,
And shall be at the gray hour when
    My cheek begins to clam.

NOTE.—" The Regent Street beauty, Miss Verrey, the Swiss confectioner
daughter, whose personal attractions have been so mischievously exaggerate
died of fever on Monday evening, brought on by the annoyance she h
been for some time subject to."—London paper, October 1828.

THE COLLECTOR CLEANS HIS PICTURE

Fili hominis, ecce ego tollo a te desiderabile oculorum tuorum in plaga.
EZECH. xxiv. 16.

How I remember cleaning that strange picture ! . . .
I had been deep in duty for my sick neighbour—
His besides my own—over several Sundays,
Often, too, in the week ; so with parish pressures,
Baptisms, burials, doctorings, conjugal counsel—
All the whatnots asked of a rural parson—
Faith, I was well-nigh broken, should have been fully
Saving for one small secret relaxation,
One that in mounting manhood had grown my hobby.

This was to delve at whiles for easel-lumber,
Stowed in the backmost slums of a soon-reached city,
Merely on chance to uncloak some worthy canvas,
Panel, or plaque, blacked blind by uncouth adventure,
Yet under all concealing a precious artfeat.
Such I had found not yet.   My latest capture
Came from the rooms of a trader in ancient house-gear
Who had no scent of beauty or soul for brushcraft.
Only a tittle cost it—murked with grimefilms,
Gatherings of slow years, thick-varnished over,
Never a feature manifest of man's painting.

So, one Saturday, time ticking hard on midnight
Ere an hour subserved, I set me upon it.
Long with coiled-up sleeves I cleaned and yet cleaned,
Till a first fresh spot, a high light, looked forth,
Then another, like fair flesh, and another ;

Then a curve, a nostril, and next a finger,
Tapering, shapely, significantly pointing slantwise.
"Flemish?" I said.   "Nay, Spanish. . . . But, nay, Italian!"
—Then meseemed it the guise of the ranker Venus,
Named of some Astarte, of some Cotytto.
Down I knelt before it and kissed the panel,
Drunk with the lure of love's inhibited dreamings.

Till the dawn I rubbed, when there leered up at me
A hag, that had slowly emerged from under my hands there,
Pointing the slanted finger towards a bosom
Eaten away of a rot from the lusts of a lifetime. . .
—I could have ended myself at the lashing lesson!
Stunned I sat till roused by a clear-voiced bell-chime,
Fresh and sweet as the dew-fleece under my luthern.
It was the matin service calling to me
From the adjacent steeple.

THE WOOD FIRE

(A FRAGMENT)

"THIS is a brightsome blaze you've lit, good friend, to-night!"
"—Aye, it has been the bleakest spring I have felt for years,
And nought compares with cloven logs to keep alight:
I buy them bargain-cheap of the executioners,
As I dwell near; and they wanted the crosses out of sight
By Passover, not to affront the eyes of visitors.

"Yes, they're from the crucifixions last week-ending
At Kranion.   We can sometimes use the poles again,
But they get split by the nails, and 'tis quicker work than
    mending
To knock together new; though the uprights now and then
Serve twice when they're let stand.   But if a feast's impending,
As lately, you've to tidy up for the comers' ken.

"Though only three were impaled, you may know it didn't
    pass off
So quietly as was wont?   That Galilee carpenter's son
Who boasted he was king, incensed the rabble to scoff:

I heard the noise from my garden. This piece is the one he
    was on. . . . .
Yes, it blazes up well if lit with a few dry chips and shroff;
And it's worthless for much else, what with cuts and stains
    thereon."

SAYING GOOD-BYE

(SONG)

WE are always saying
    "Good-bye, good-bye!"
In work, in playing,
In gloom, in gaying:
    At many a stage
    Of pilgrimage
    From youth to age
We say, "Good-bye,
    Good-bye!"

We are undiscerning
    Which go to sigh,
Which will be yearning
For soon returning;
    And which no more
    Will dark our door,
    Or tread our shore,
    But go to die,
      To die.

Some come from roaming
    With joy again;
Some, who come homing
By stealth at gloaming,
    Had better have stopped
    Till death, and dropped
    By strange hands propped,
    Than come so fain,
      So fain.

So, with this saying,
    "Good-bye, good-bye,"
We speed their waying
Without betraying

Our grief, our fear
No more to hear
From them, close, clear,
Again : " Good-bye,
Good-bye ! "

ON THE TUNE CALLED THE OLD-HUNDRED-AND-FOURTH

WE never sang together
Ravenscroft's terse old tune
On Sundays or on weekdays,
In sharp or summer weather,
At night-time or at noon.

Why did we never sing it,
Why never so incline
On Sundays or on weekdays,
Even when soft wafts would wing it
From your far floor to mine ?

Shall we that tune, then, never
Stand voicing side by side
On Sundays or on weekdays ? . . .
Or shall we, when for ever
In Sheol we abide,

Sing it in desolation,
As we might long have done
On Sundays or on weekdays
With love and exultation
Before our sands had run ?

THE OPPORTUNITY

(FOR H. P.)

FORTY springs back, I recall,
We met at this phase of the Maytime :
We might have clung close through all,
But we parted when died that daytime.

We parted with smallest regret ;
　　Perhaps should have cared but slightly,
Just then, if we never had met :
　　Strange, strange that we lived so lightly !

Had we mused a little space
　　At that critical date in the Maytime,
One life had been ours, one place,
　　Perhaps, till our long cold claytime.

—This is a bitter thing
　　For thee, O man : what ails it ?
The tide of chance may bring
　　Its offer ; but nought avails it !

EVELYN G. OF CHRISTMINSTER

I CAN see the towers
　In mind quite clear
Not many hours'
　Faring from here ;
But how up and go,
　And briskly bear
Thither, and know
　That you are not there ?

Though the birds sing small,
　And apple and pear
On your trees by the wall
　Are ripe and rare,
Though none excel them,
　I have no care
To taste them or smell them
　And you not there.

Though the College stones
　Are stroked with the sun,
And the gownsmen and Dons
　Who held you as one
Of brightest brow
　Still think as they did,
Why haunt with them now
　Your candle is hid ?

Towards the river
A pealing swells :
They cost me a quiver—
Those prayerful bells !
How go to God,
Who can reprove
With so heavy a rod
As your swift remove !

The chorded keys
Wait all in a row,
And the bellows wheeze
As long ago.
And the psalter lingers,
And organist's chair ;
But where are your fingers
That once wagged there ?

Shall I then seek
That desert place
This or next week,
And those tracks trace
That fill me with cark
And cloy ; nowhere
Being movement or mark
Of you now there !

THE RIFT

(SONG : *Minor Mode*)

'TWAS just at gnat and cobweb-time,
When yellow begins to show in the leaf,
That your old gamut changed its chime
From those true tones—of span so brief !—
That met my beats of joy, of grief,
        As rhyme meets rhyme.

So sank I from my high sublime !
We faced but chancewise after that,
And never I knew or guessed my crime. . . .
Yes ; 'twas the date—or nigh thereat—
Of the yellowing leaf ; at moth and gnat
        And cobweb-time.

VOICES FROM THINGS GROWING IN A CHURCHYARD

THESE flowers are I, poor Fanny Hurd,
      Sir or Madam,
A little girl here sepultured.
Once I flit-fluttered like a bird
Above the grass, as now I wave
In daisy shapes above my grave,
      All day cheerily,
      All night eerily!

—I am one Bachelor Bowring, "Gent,"
      Sir or Madam;
In shingled oak my bones were pent;
Hence more than a hundred years I spent
In my feat of change from a coffin-thrall
To a dancer in green as leaves on a wall,
      All day cheerily,
      All night eerily!

—I, these berries of juice and gloss,
      Sir or Madam,
Am clean forgotten as Thomas Voss;
Thin-urned, I have burrowed away from the moss
That covers my sod, and have entered this yew,
And turned to clusters ruddy of view,
      All day cheerily,
      All night eerily!

—The Lady Gertrude, proud, high-bred,
      Sir or Madam,
Am I—this laurel that shades your head;
Into its veins I have stilly sped,
And made them of me; and my leaves now shine,
As did my satins superfine,
      All day cheerily,
      All night eerily!

—I, who as innocent withwind climb,
      Sir or Madam,
Am one Eve Greensleeves, in olden time
Kissed by men from many a clime,

Beneath sun, stars, in blaze, in breeze,
As now by glowworms and by bees,
    All day cheerily,
    All night eerily ! [1]

—I'm old Squire Audeley Grey, who grew,
    Sir or Madam,
Aweary of life, and in scorn withdrew ;
Till anon I clambered up anew
As ivy-green, when my ache was stayed,
And in that attire I have longtime gayed
    All day cheerily,
    All night eerily !

—And so these maskers breathe to each
    Sir or Madam
Who lingers there, and their lively speech
Affords an interpreter much to teach,
As their murmurous accents seem to come
Thence hitheraround in a radiant hum,
    All day cheerily,
    All night eerily !

ON THE WAY

THE trees fret fitfully and twist,
Shutters rattle and carpets heave,
Slime is the dust of yestereve,
    And in the streaming mist
Fishes might seem to fin a passage if they list.

    But to his feet,
    Drawing nigh and nigher
    A hidden seat,
    The fog is sweet
    And the wind a lyre.

---

[1] It was said her real name was Eve Trevillian or Trevelyan ; and that she was the handsome mother of two or three illegitimate children, *circa* 1784–95.

A vacant sameness grays the sky,
A moisture gathers on each knop
Of the bramble, rounding to a drop,
That greets the goer-by
With the cold listless lustre of a dead man's eye

But to her sight,
Drawing nigh and nigher
Its deep delight,
The fog is bright
And the wind a lyre.

"SHE DID NOT TURN"

SHE did not turn,
But passed foot-faint with averted head
In her gown of green, by the bobbing fern,
Though I leaned over the gate that led
From where we waited with table spread;
But she did not turn:
Why was she near there if love had fled?

She did not turn,
Though the gate was whence I had often sped
In the mists of morning to meet her, and learn
Her heart, when its moving moods I read
As a book—she mine, as she sometimes said;
But she did not turn,
And passed foot-faint with averted head.

GROWTH IN MAY

I ENTER a daisy-and-buttercup land,
And thence thread a jungle of grass:
Hurdles and stiles scarce visible stand
Above the lush stems as I pass.

Hedges peer over, and try to be seen,
And seem to reveal a dim sense
That amid such ambitious and elbow-high green
They make a mean show as a fence.

Elsewhere the mead is possessed of the neats,
  That range not greatly above
The rich rank thicket which brushes their teats,
  And *her* gown, as she waits for her Love.

  NEAR CHARD.

THE CHILDREN AND SIR NAMELESS

SIR NAMELESS, once of Athelhall, declared :
" These wretched children romping in my park
Trample the herbage till the soil is bared,
And yap and yell from early morn till dark !
Go keep them harnessed to their set routines :
Thank God I've none to hasten my decay ;
For green remembrance there are better means
Than offspring, who but wish their sires away."

Sir Nameless of that mansion said anon :
" To be perpetuate for my mightiness
Sculpture must image me when I am gone."
—He forthwith summoned carvers there express
To shape a figure stretching seven-odd feet
(For he was tall) in alabaster stone,
With shield, and crest, and casque, and sword complete :
When done a statelier work was never known.

Three hundred years hied ; Church-restorers came,
And, no one of his lineage being traced,
They thought an effigy so large in frame
Best fitted for the floor.   There it was placed,
Under the seats for schoolchildren.   And they
Kicked out his name, and hobnailed off his nose ;
And, as they yawn through sermon-time, they say,
" Who was this old stone man beneath our toes ?"

AT THE ROYAL ACADEMY

THESE summer landscapes—clump, and copse, and croft—
Woodland and meadowland—here hung aloft,
Gay with limp grass and leafery new and soft,

Seem caught from the immediate season's yield
I saw last noonday shining over the field,
By rapid snatch, while still are uncongealed

The saps that in their live originals climb;
Yester's quick greenage here set forth in mime
Just as it stands, now, at our breathing-time.

But these young foils so fresh upon each tree,
Soft verdures spread in sprouting novelty,
Are not this summer's though they feign to be.

Last year their May to Michaelmas term was run,
Last autumn browned and buried every one,
And no more know they sight of any sun.

HER TEMPLE

DEAR, think not that they will forget you:
    —If craftsmanly art should be mine
I will build up a temple, and set you
      Therein as its shrine.

They may say: "Why a woman such honour?"
    —Be told, "O, so sweet was her fame,
That a man heaped this splendour upon her;
      None now knows his name."

A TWO-YEARS' IDYLL

      YES; such it was;
    Just those two seasons unsought,
Sweeping like summertide wind on our ways;
      Moving, as straws,
    Hearts quick as ours in those days;
Going like wind, too, and rated as nought
    Save as the prelude to plays
    Soon to come—larger, life-fraught:
      Yes; such it was.

" Nought " it was called,
Even by ourselves—that which springs
Out of the years for all flesh, first or last,
Commonplace, scrawled
Dully on days that go past.
Yet, all the while, it upbore us like wings
Even in hours overcast :
Aye, though this best thing of things,
" Nought " it was called !

What seems it now ?
Lost : such beginning was all ;
Nothing came after : romance straight forsook
Quickly somehow
Life when we sped from our nook,
Primed for new scenes with designs smart and tall. . . .
—A preface without any book,
A trumpet uplipped, but no call ;
That seems it now.

BY HENSTRIDGE CROSS AT THE YEAR'S END

(From this centuries-old cross-road the highway leads east to London,
north to Bristol and Bath, west to Exeter and the Land's End, and south to
the Channel coast.)

WHY go the east road now ? . . .
That way a youth went on a morrow
After mirth, and he brought back sorrow
Painted upon his brow :
Why go the east road now ?

Why go the north road now ?
Torn, leaf-strewn, as if scoured by foemen,
Once edging fiefs of my forefolk yeomen,
Fallows fat to the plough :
Why go the north road now ?

Why go the west road now ?
Thence to us came she, bosom-burning,
Welcome with joyousness returning. . . .
She sleeps under the bough :
Why go the west road now ?

Why go the south road now?
That way marched they some are forgetting,
Stark to the moon left, past regretting
    Loves who have falsed their vow. . . .
    Why go the south road now?

    Why go any road now?
White stands the handpost for brisk onbearers,
"Halt!" is the word for wan-cheeked farers
    Musing on Whither, and How. . . .
    Why go any road now?

    "Yea: we want new feet now"
Answer the stones. "Want chit-chat, laughter:
Plenty of such to go hereafter
    By our tracks, we trow!
    We are for new feet now."

During the War.

PENANCE

"WHY do you sit, O pale thin man,
    At the end of the room
By that harpsichord, built on the quaint old plan?
    —It is cold as a tomb,
And there's not a spark within the grate;
    And the jingling wires
    Are as vain desires
    That have lagged too late."

"Why do I? Alas, far times ago
    A woman lyred here
In the evenfall; one who fain did so
    From year to year;
And, in loneliness bending wistfully,
    Would wake each note
    In sick sad rote,
    None to listen or see!

"I would not join. I would not stay,
    But drew away,
Though the winter fire beamed brightly. . . . **Aye!**
    I do to-day

What I would not then ; and the chill old keys,
    Like a skull's brown teeth
    Loose in their sheath,
    Freeze my touch ; yes, freeze."

"I LOOK IN HER FACE"

(SONG : *Minor*)

I LOOK in her face and say,
"Sing as you used to sing
About Love's blossoming" ;
But she hints not Yea or Nay.

"Sing, then, that Love's a pain,
If, Dear, you think it so,
Whether it be or no ;"
But dumb her lips remain.

I go to a far-off room,
A faint song ghosts my ear ;
Which song I cannot hear,
But it seems to come from a tomb.

AFTER THE WAR

LAST Post sounded
Across the mead
To where he loitered
With absent heed.
Five years before
In the evening there
Had flown that call
To him and his Dear.
"You'll never come back ;
Good-bye !" she had said ;
"Here I'll be living,
And my Love dead !"

Those closing minims
Had been as shafts darting
Through him and her pressed
In that last parting ;

They thrilled him not now,
In the selfsame place,
With the selfsame sun
On his war-seamed face.
" Lurks a god's laughter
In this ? " he said,
" That I am the living
And she the dead ! "

"IF YOU HAD KNOWN"

IF you had known
When listening with her to the far-down moan
Of the white-selvaged and empurpled sea,
And rain came on that did not hinder talk,
Or damp your flashing facile gaiety
In turning home, despite the slow wet walk
By crooked ways, and over stiles of stone :
        If you had known

You would lay roses,
Fifty years thence, on her monument, that discloses
Its graying shape upon the luxuriant green ;
Fifty years thence to an hour, by chance led there,
What might have moved you ?—yea, had you foreseen
That on the tomb of the selfsame one, gone where
The dawn of every day is as the close is,
        You would lay roses !

1920.

THE CHAPEL-ORGANIST

(A.D. 185–)

I'VE been thinking it through, as I play here to-night, to pla
    never again,
By the light of that lowering sun peering in at the window-pane,
And over the back-street roofs, throwing shades from the boys
    the chore
In the gallery, right upon me, sitting up to these keys onc
    more. . . .

How I used to hear tongues ask, as I sat here when I was new:
"Who is she playing the organ? She touches it mightily true!"
"She travels from Havenpool Town," the deacon would softly
    speak,
"The stipend can hardly cover her fare hither twice in the week."
(It fell far short of doing, indeed; but I never told,
For I have craved minstrelsy more than lovers, or beauty, or gold.)

'Twas so he answered at first, but the story grew different later:
"It cannot go on much longer, from what we hear of her now!"
At the meaning wheeze in the words the inquirer would shift
    his place
Till he could see round the curtain that screened me from
    people below.
"A handsome girl," he would murmur, upstaring (and so I am).
"But—too much sex in her build; fine eyes, but eyelids too
    heavy;
A bosom too full for her age; in her lips too voluptuous a dye."
(It may be. But who put it there? Assuredly it was not I.)

I went on playing and singing when this I had heard, and more,
Though tears half-blinded me; yes, I remained going on and on,
Just as I used me to chord and to sing at the selfsame time! . . .
For it's a contralto—my voice is; they'll hear it again here
    to-night
In the psalmody notes that I love far beyond every lower delight.

Well, the deacon, in fact, that day had learnt new tidings
    about me;
They troubled his mind not a little, for he was a worthy man.
(He trades as a chemist in High Street, and during the week he
    had sought
His fellow-deacon, who throve as a bookbinder over the way.)
"These are strange rumours," he said. "We must guard the
    good name of the chapel.
If, sooth, she's of evil report, what else can we do but dismiss her?"
"—But get such another to play here we cannot for double the
    price!"
It settled the point for the time, and I triumphed awhile in
    their strait,
And my much-beloved grand semibreves went living on, pending
    my fate.

At length in the congregation more headshakes and murmurs
    were rife,
And my dismissal was ruled, though I was not warned of it then.
But a day came when they declared it.   The news entered me
    as a sword ;
I was broken ; so pallid of face that they thought I should faint,
    they said.
I rallied.   " O, rather than go, I will play you for nothing ! "
    said I.
'Twas in much desperation I spoke it, for bring me to forfeit
    I could not
Those melodies chorded so richly for which I had laboured
    and lived.
They paused.   And for nothing I played at the chapel through
    Sundays again,
Upheld by that art which I loved more than blandishments
    lavished of men.

But it fell that murmurs anew from the flock broke the pastor's
    peace.
Some member had seen me at Havenpool, comrading close
    a sea-captain.
(O yes ; I was thereto constrained, lacking means for the fare
    to and fro.)
Yet God knows, if aught He knows ever, I loved the Old-
    Hundredth, Saint Stephen's,
Mount Zion, New Sabbath, Miles-Lane, Holy Rest, and Arabia,
    and Eaton,
Above all embraces of body by wooers who sought me and
    won ! . . . .
Next week 'twas declared I was seen coming home with a swain
    ere the sun.

The deacons insisted then, strong ; and forgiveness I did not
    implore.
I saw all was lost for me, quite, but I made a last bid in my throbs.
My bent, finding victual in lust, men's senses had libelled
    my soul,
But the soul should die game, if I knew it ! I turned to my
    masters and said :
" I yield, Gentlemen, without parlance. But—let me just hymn
    you *once* more ! "

a little thing, Sirs, that I ask ; and a passion is music
with me ! "

saw that consent would cost nothing, and show as good
grace, as knew I,

gh tremble I did, and feel sick, as I paused thereat, dumb
for their words.

gloomily nodded assent, saying, " Yes, if you care to.
Once more,

only once more, understand." To that with a bend I
agreed.

You've a fixed and a far-reaching look," spoke one who had
eyed me awhile.

e a fixed and a far-reaching plan, and my look only showed
it," I smile.

evening of Sunday is come—the last of my functioning here.
e plays as if she were possessed ! " they exclaim, glancing
upward and round.

ch harmonies I never dreamt the old instrument capable of ! "
ntime the sun lowers and goes ; shades deepen ; the lights
are turned up,

the people voice out the last singing : tune Tallis : the
Evening Hymn.

onder Dissenters sing Ken : it shows them more liberal
in spirit

iis little chapel down here than at certain new others I know.)
g as I play. Murmurs some one : " No woman's throat
richer than hers ! "

ue : in these parts," think I. " But, my man, never more
will its richness outspread."

I sing with them onward : " The grave dread as little do I
as my bed."

up my feet from the pedals ; and then, while my eyes are
still wet

n the symphonies born of my fingers, I do that whereon
I am set,

draw from my " full round bosom " (their words ; how can I
help its heave ?)

ottle blue-coloured and fluted — a vinaigrette, they may
conceive—

And before the choir measures my meaning, reads aught i*
    moves to and fro,
I drink from the phial at a draught, and they think
    pick-me-up ; so.
Then I gather my books as to leave, bend over the key
    to pray.
When they come to me motionless, stooping, quick death
    have whisked me away.

" Sure, nobody meant her to poison herself in her haste, after
The deacons will say as they carry me down and the
    shadows fall,
" Though the charges were true," they will add. " It's a
    red as scarlet withal ! "
I have never once minced it. Lived chaste I have not. He
    knows it above ! . . .
But past all the heavings of passion—it's music has been
    life-love ! . . .
That tune did go well—this last playing ! . . . I reckon t*
    bury me here.
Not a soul from the seaport my birthplace—will come, or be
    me . . . a tear.

FETCHING HER

An hour before the dawn,
        My friend,
You lit your waiting bedside-lamp,
    Your breakfast-fire anon,
And outing into the dark and damp
    You saddled, and set on.

Thuswise, before the day,
        My friend,
You sought her on her surfy shore,
    To fetch her thence away
Unto your own new-builded door
    For a staunch lifelong stay.

You said : " It seems to be,
        My friend,
That I were bringing to my place

The pure brine breeze, the sea,
The mews—all her old sky and space,
In bringing her with me!"

—But time is prompt to expugn,
                My friend,
Such magic-minted conjurings:
The brought breeze fainted soon,
And then the sense of seamews' wings,
And the shore's sibilant tune.

So, it had been more due,
                My friend,
Perhaps, had you not pulled this flower
From the craggy nook it knew,
And set it in an alien bower;
But left it where it grew!

"COULD I BUT WILL"

(SONG: *Verses 1, 3, key major; verse 2, key minor*)

    COULD I but will,
        Will to my bent,
I'd have afar ones near me still,
And music of rare ravishment,
In strains that move the toes and heels!
And when the sweethearts sat for rest
The unbetrothed should foot with zest
        Ecstatic reels.

    Could I be head,
        Head-god, "Come, now,
Dear girl," I'd say, "whose flame is fled,
Who liest with linen-banded brow,
Stirred but by shakes from Earth's deep core—"
I'd say to her: "Unshroud and meet
That Love who kissed and called thee Sweet!—
        Yea, come once more!"

Even half-god power
In spinning dooms
Had I, this frozen scene should flower,
And sand-swept plains and Arctic glooms
Should green them gay with waving leaves,
Mid which old friends and I would walk
With weightless feet and magic talk
Uncounted eves.

SHE REVISITS ALONE THE CHURCH OF HER MARRIAGE

I HAVE come to the church and chancel,
Where all's the same!
—Brighter and larger in my dreams
Truly it shaped than now, meseems,
Is its substantial frame.
But, anyhow, I made my vow,
Whether for praise or blame,
Here in this church and chancel
Where all's the same.

Where touched the check-floored chancel
My knees and his?
The step looks shyly at the sun,
And says, "'Twas here the thing was done,
For bale or else for bliss!"
Of all those there I least was ware
Would it be that or this
When touched the check-floored chancel
My knees and his!

Here in this fateful chancel
Where all's the same,
I thought the culminant crest of life
Was reached when I went forth the wife
I was not when I came.
Each commonplace one of my race,
Some say, has such an aim—
To go from a fateful chancel
As not the same.

Here, through this hoary chancel
    Where all's the same,
A thrill, a gaiety even, ranged
That morning when it seemed I changed
    My nature with my name.
Though now not fair, though gray my hair,
    He loved me, past proclaim,
Here in this hoary chancel,
      Where all's the same.

AT THE ENTERING OF THE NEW YEAR

I

(OLD STYLE)

OUR songs went up and out the chimney,
And roused the home-gone husbandmen ;
Our allemands, our heys, poussettings,
Our hands-across and back again,
Sent rhythmic throbbings through the casements
    On to the white highway,
Where nighted farers paused and muttered,
    "Keep it up well, do they !"

The contrabasso's measured booming
Sped at each bar to the parish bounds,
To shepherds at their midnight lambings,
To stealthy poachers on their rounds ;
And everybody caught full duly
    The notes of our delight,
As Time unrobed the Youth of Promise
    Hailed by our sanguine sight.

II

(NEW STYLE)

WE stand in the dusk of a pine-tree limb,
As if to give ear to the muffled peal,
Brought or withheld at the breeze's whim ;
But our truest heed is to words that steal

From the mantled ghost that looms in the gray,
And seems, so far as our sense can see,
To feature bereaved Humanity,
As it sighs to the imminent year its say :—

"O stay without, O stay without,
Calm comely Youth, untasked, untired ;
Though stars irradiate thee about
Thy entrance here is undesired.
Open the gate not, mystic one ;
Must we avow what we would close confine ?
With thee, good friend, we would have converse none,
Albeit the fault may not be thine."

December 31.   *During the War.*

THEY WOULD NOT COME

I TRAVELLED to where in her lifetime
    She'd knelt at morning prayer,
        To call her up as if there ;
But she paid no heed to my suing,
As though her old haunt could win not
        A thought from her spirit, or care.

I went where my friend had lectioned
    The prophets in high declaim,
        That my soul's ear the same
Full tones should catch as aforetime ;
But silenced by gear of the Present
        Was the voice that once there came !

Where the ocean had sprayed our banquet
    I stood, to recall it as then :
        The same eluding again !
No vision.   Shows contingent
Affrighted it further from me
        Even than from my home-den.

When I found them no responders,
      But fugitives prone to flee
    From where they had used to be,
It vouched I had been led hither
    As by night wisps in bogland,
      And bruised the heart of me!

AFTER A ROMANTIC DAY

THE railway bore him through
An earthen cutting out from a city:
    There was no scope for view,
Though the frail light shed by a slim young moon
    Fell like a friendly tune.

    Fell like a liquid ditty,
And the blank lack of any charm
    Of landscape did no harm.
The bald steep cutting, rigid, rough,
    And moon-lit, was enough
For poetry of place: its weathered face
Formed a convenient sheet whereon
The visions of his mind were drawn.

THE TWO WIVES

(SMOKER'S CLUB-STORY)

AITED at home all the while they were boating together—
    My wife and my near neighbour's wife:
Till there entered a woman I loved more than life,
1 we sat and sat on, and beheld the uprising dark weather,
    With a sense that some mischief was rife.

ings came that the boat had capsized, and that one of the ladies
    Was drowned—which of them was unknown:
    And I marvelled—my friend's wife?—or was it my own
o had gone in such wise to the land where the sun as the
    shade is?
    —We learnt it was *his* had so gone.

Then I cried in unrest : " He is free ! But no good is relea
To him as it would be to me ! "
"—But it is," said the woman I loved, quietly.
" How ? " I asked her. "—Because he has long loved me
without ceasing,
And it's just the same thing, don't you see."

"I KNEW A LADY"

(CLUB SONG)

I KNEW a lady when the days
Grew long, and evenings goldened ;
But I was not emboldened
By her prompt eyes and winning ways.

And when old Winter nipt the haws,
"Another's wife I'll be,
And then you'll care for me,"
She said, "and think how sweet I was ! "

And soon she shone as another's wife :
As such I often met her,
And sighed, " How I regret her !
My folly cuts me like a knife ! "

And then, to-day, her husband came,
And moaned, " Why did you flout her ?
Well could I do without her !
For both our burdens you are to blame ! "

A HOUSE WITH A HISTORY

THERE is a house in a city street
Some past ones made their own ;
Its floors were criss-crossed by their feet,
And their babblings beat
From ceiling to white hearth-stone.

And who are peopling its parlours now?
  Who talk across its floor?
Mere freshlings are they, blank of brow,
    Who read not how
  Its prime had passed before

Their raw equipments, scenes, and says
  Afflicted its memoried face,
That had seen every larger phase
    Of human ways
  Before these filled the place.

To them that house's tale is theirs,
  No former voices call
Aloud therein.   Its aspect bears
    Their joys and cares
  Alone, from wall to wall.

A PROCESSION OF DEAD DAYS

I SEE the ghost of a perished day;
I know his face, and the feel of his dawn:
'Twas he who took me far away
  To a spot strange and gray:
Look at me, Day, and then pass on,
But come again: yes, come anon!

Enters another into view;
His features are not cold or white,
But rosy as a vein seen through:
  Too soon he smiles adieu.
Adieu, O ghost-day of delight;
But come and grace my dying sight.

Enters the day that brought the kiss:
He brought it in his foggy hand
To where the mumbling river is,
  And the high clematis;
It lent new colour to the land,
And all the boy within me manned.

Ah, this one.   Yes, I know his name,
He is the day that wrought a shine
Even on a precinct common and tame,
    As 'twere of purposed aim.
He shows him as a rainbow sign
Of promise made to me and mine.

The next stands forth in his morning clothes,
And yet, despite their misty blue,
They mark no sombre custom-growths
    That joyous living loathes,
But a meteor act, that left in its queue
A train of sparks my lifetime through.

I almost tremble at his nod—
This next in train—who looks at me
As I were slave, and he were god
    Wielding an iron rod.
I close my eyes ; yet still is he
In front there, looking mastery.

In semblance of a face averse
The phantom of the next one comes :
I did not know what better or worse
    Chancings might bless or curse
When his original glossed the thrums
Of ivy, bringing that which numbs.

Yes ; trees were turning in their sleep
Upon their windy pillows of gray
When he stole in.   Silent his creep
    On the grassed eastern steep. . . .
I shall not soon forget that day,
And what his third hour took away !

HE FOLLOWS HIMSELF

In a heavy time I dogged myself
    Along a louring way,
Till my leading self to my following self
    Said : " Why do you hang on me
        So harassingly ? "

"I have watched you, Heart of mine," I cried,
    "So often going astray
And leaving me, that I have pursued,
    Feeling such truancy
      Ought not to be."

He said no more, and I dogged him on
    From noon to the dun of day
By prowling paths, until anew
    He begged : " Please turn and flee !—
      What do you see ?"

"Methinks I see a man," said I,
    "Dimming his hours to gray.
I will not leave him while I know
    Part of myself is he
      Who dreams such dree !"

"I go to my old friend's house," he urged,
    "So do not watch me, pray !"
"Well, I will leave you in peace," said I,
    "Though of this poignancy
      You should fight free :

"Your friend, O other me, is dead ;
    You know not what you say."
—"That do I ! And at his green-grassed door
    By night's bright galaxy
      I bend a knee."

—The yew-plumes moved like mockers' beards
    Though only boughs were they,
And I seemed to go ; yet still was there,
    And am, and there haunt we
      Thus bootlessly.

THE SINGING WOMAN

THERE was a singing woman
    Came riding across the mead
At the time of the mild May weather,
    Tameless, tireless ;
This song she sung : " I am fair, I am young !"
    And many turned to heed.

And the same singing woman
Sat crooning in her need
At the time of the winter weather ;
Friendless, fireless,
She sang this song : " Life, thou'rt too long ! "
And there was none to heed.

WITHOUT, NOT WITHIN HER

IT was what you bore with you, Woman,
Not inly were,
That throned you from all else human,
However fair !

It was that strange freshness you carried
Into a soul
Whereon no thought of yours tarried
Two moments at all.

And out from his spirit flew death,
And bale, and ban,
Like the corn-chaff under the breath
Of the winnowing-fan.

"O I WON'T LEAD A HOMELY LIFE"

(*To an old air*)

" O I WON'T lead a homely life
As father's Jack and mother's Jill,
But I will be a fiddler's wife,
With music mine at will !
Just a little tune,
Another one soon,
As I merrily fling my fill ! "

And she became a fiddler's Dear,
And merry all day she strove to be ;
And he played and played afar and near,
But never at home played he
Any little tune
Or late or soon ;
And sunk and sad was she !

IN THE SMALL HOURS

I LAY in my bed and fiddled
    With a dreamland viol and bow,
And the tunes flew back to my fingers
    I had melodied years ago.
It was two or three in the morning
    When I fancy-fiddled so
Long reels and country-dances,
    And hornpipes swift and slow.

And soon anon came crossing
    The chamber in the gray
Figures of jigging fieldfolk—
    Saviours of corn and hay—
To the air of " Haste to the Wedding,"
    As after a wedding-day ;
Yea, up and down the middle
    In windless whirls went they !

There danced the bride and bridegroom,
    And couples in a train,
Gay partners time and travail
    Had longwhiles stilled amain ! . . .
It seemed a thing for weeping
    To find, at slumber's wane
And morning's sly increeping,
    That Now, not Then, held reign.

THE LITTLE OLD TABLE

CREAK, little wood thing, creak,
When I touch you with elbow or knee ;
That is the way you speak
Of one who gave you to me !

You, little table, she brought—
Brought me with her own hand,
As she looked at me with a thought
That I did not understand.

—Whoever owns it anon,
And hears it, will never know
What a history hangs upon
This creak from long ago.

VAGG HOLLOW

Vagg Hollow is a marshy spot on the old Roman Road near Ilchest
where "things" are seen.   Merchandise was formerly fetched inland fr
the canal-boats at Load-Bridge by waggons this way.

"WHAT do you see in Vagg Hollow,
Little boy, when you go
In the morning at five on your lonely drive?"
"—I see men's souls, who follow
Till we've passed where the road lies low,
When they vanish at our creaking!

"They are like white faces speaking
Beside and behind the waggon—
One just as father's was when here.
The waggoner drinks from his flagon,
(Or he'd flinch when the Hollow is near)
But he does not give me any.

"Sometimes the faces are many;
But I walk along by the horses,
He asleep on the straw as we jog;
And I hear the loud water-courses,
And the drops from the trees in the fog,
And watch till the day is breaking,

"And the wind out by Tintinhull waking;
I hear in it father's call
As he called when I saw him dying,
And he sat by the fire last Fall,
And mother stood by sighing;
But I'm not afraid at all!"

THE DREAM IS—WHICH?

I AM laughing by the brook with her,
  Splashed in its tumbling stir ;
And then it is a blankness looms
  As if I walked not there,
Nor she, but found me in haggard rooms,
  And treading a lonely stair.

With radiant cheeks and rapid eyes
  We sit where none espies ;
Till a harsh change comes edging in
  As no such scene were there,
But winter, and I were bent and thin,
  And cinder-gray my hair.

We dance in heys around the hall,
  Weightless as thistleball ;
And then a curtain drops between,
  As if I danced not there,
But wandered through a mounded green
  To find her, I knew where.

                        March 1913.

THE COUNTRY WEDDING

(A FIDDLER'S STORY)

LITTLE fogs were gathered in every hollow,
But the purple hillocks enjoyed fine weather
As we marched with our fiddles over the heather
—How it comes back !—to their wedding that day.

Our getting there brought our neighbours and all, O !
Till, two and two, the couples stood ready.
And her father said : " Souls, for God's sake, be steady ! "
And we strung up our fiddles, and sounded out " A."

The groomsman he stared, and said, " You must follow ! "
But we'd gone to fiddle in front of the party,
(Our feelings as friends being true and hearty)
And fiddle in front we did—all the way.

Yes, from their door by Mill-tail-Shallow,
And up Styles-Lane, and by Front-Street houses,
Where stood maids, bachelors, and spouses,
Who cheered the songs that we knew how to play.

I bowed the treble before her father,
Michael the tenor in front of the lady,
The bass-viol Reub—and right well played he !—
The serpent Jim ; ay, to church and back.

I thought the bridegroom was flurried rather,
As we kept up the tune outside the chancel,
While they were swearing things none can cancel
Inside the walls to our drumstick's whack.

"Too gay !" she pleaded.   "Clouds may gather,
And sorrow come."   But she gave in, laughing,
And by supper-time when we'd got to the quaffing
Her fears were forgot, and her smiles weren't slack.

A grand wedding 'twas !   And what would follow
We never thought.   Or that we should have buried her
On the same day with the man that married her,
A day like the first, half hazy, half clear.

Yes : little fogs were in every hollow,
Though the purple hillocks enjoyed fine weather,
When we went to play 'em to church together,
And carried 'em there in an after year.

FIRST OR LAST

(SONG)

IF grief come early
Joy comes late,
If joy come early
Grief will wait ;
    Aye, my dear and tender !

Wise ones joy them early
While the cheeks are red,
Banish grief till surly
Time has dulled their dread.

And joy being ours
Ere youth has flown,
The later hours
May find us gone ;
    Aye, my dear and tender !

LONELY DAYS

LONELY her fate was,
Environed from sight
In the house where the gate was
Past finding at night.
None there to share it,
No one to tell :
Long she'd to bear it,
And bore it well.

Elsewhere just so she
Spent many a day ;
Wishing to go she
Continued to stay.
And people without
Basked warm in the air,
But none sought her out,
Or knew she was there.
Even birthdays were passed so,
Sunny and shady :
Years did it last so
For this sad lady.
Never declaring it,
No one to tell,
Still she kept bearing it—
Bore it well.

The days grew chillier,
And then she went
To a city, familiar
In years forespent,

When she walked gaily
Far to and fro,
But now, moving frailly,
Could nowhere go.

The cheerful colour
Of houses she'd known
Had died to a duller
And dingier tone.

Streets were now noisy
Where once had rolled
A few quiet coaches,
Or citizens strolled.

Through the party-wall
Of the memoried spot
They danced at a ball
Who recalled her not.

Tramlines lay crossing
Once gravelled slopes,
Metal rods clanked,
And electric ropes.

So she endured it all,
Thin, thinner wrought,
Until time cured it all,
And she knew nought.

Versified from a Diary.

"WHAT DID IT MEAN?"

WHAT did it mean that noontide, when
   You bade me pluck the flower
Within the other woman's bower,
   Whom I knew nought of then?

I thought the flower blushed deeplier—aye,
And as I drew its stalk to me
It seemed to breathe: "I am, I see,
Made use of in a human play."

And while I plucked, upstarted sheer
As phantom from the pane thereby
A corpse-like countenance, with eye
That iced me by its baleful peer—
   Silent, as from a bier. . . .

When I came back your face had changed,
    It was no face for me ;
O did it speak of hearts estranged,
    And deadly rivalry
        In times before
      I darked your door,
        To seise me of
        Mere second love,
Which still the haunting first deranged ?

AT THE DINNER-TABLE

I SAT at dinner in my prime,
And glimpsed my face in the sideboard-glass,
And started as if I had seen a crime,
And prayed the ghastly show might pass.

Wrenched wrinkled features met my sight,
Grinning back to me as my own ;
I well-nigh fainted with affright
At finding me a haggard crone.

My husband laughed.   He had slily set
A warping mirror there, in whim
To startle me.   My eyes grew wet ;
I spoke not all the eve to him.

He was sorry, he said, for what he had done,
And took away the distorting glass,
Uncovering the accustomed one ;
And so it ended ?   No, alas,

Fifty years later, when he died,
I sat me in the selfsame chair,
Thinking of him.   Till, weary-eyed,
I saw the sideboard facing there ;

And from its mirror looked the lean
Thing I'd become, each wrinkle and score
The image of me that I had seen
In jest there fifty years before.

THE MARBLE TABLET

THERE it stands, though alas, what a little of her
  Shows in its cold white look !
Not her glance, glide, or smile ; not a tittle of her
  Voice like the purl of a brook ;
    Not her thoughts, that you read like a book.

It may stand for her once in November
  When first she breathed, witless of all ;
Or in heavy years she would remember
  When circumstance held her in thrall ;
    Or at last, when she answered her call !

Nothing more.   The still marble, date-graven,
  Gives all that it can, tersely lined ;
That one has at length found the haven
  Which every one other will find ;
    With silence on what shone behind.

ST. JULIOT : *September 8, 1916.*

THE MASTER AND THE LEAVES

I

WE are budding, Master, budding,
  We of your favourite tree ;
March drought and April flooding
  Arouse us merrily,
  Our stemlets newly studding ;
    And yet you do not see !

II

We are fully woven for summer
  In stuff of limpest green,
The twitterer and the hummer
  Here rest of nights, unseen,
While like a long-roll drummer
  The nightjar thrills the treen.

III

We are turning yellow, Master,
    And next we are turning red,
And faster then and faster
    Shall seek our rooty bed,
All wasted in disaster !
    But you lift not your head.

IV

—"I mark your early going,
    And that you'll soon be clay,
I have seen your summer showing
    As in my youthful day ;
But why I seem unknowing
    Is too sunk in to say ! "

                1917.

LAST WORDS TO A DUMB FRIEND

PET was never mourned as you,
Purrer of the spotless hue,
Plumy tail, and wistful gaze
While you humoured our queer ways,
Or outshrilled your morning call
Up the stairs and through the hall—
Foot suspended in its fall—
While, expectant, you would stand
Arched, to meet the stroking hand ;
Till your way you chose to wend
Yonder, to your tragic end.

Never another pet for me !
Let your place all vacant be ;
Better blankness day by day
Than companion torn away.
Better bid his memory fade,
Better blot each mark he made,
Selfishly escape distress
By contrived forgetfulness,
Than preserve his prints to make
Every morn and eve an ache.

From the chair whereon he sat
Sweep his fur, nor wince thereat ;
Rake his little pathways out
Mid the bushes roundabout ;
Smooth away his talons' mark
From the claw-worn pine-tree bark,
Where he climbed as dusk embrowned,
Waiting us who loitered round.

Strange it is this speechless thing,
Subject to our mastering,
Subject for his life and food
To our gift, and time, and mood ;
Timid pensioner of us Powers,
His existence ruled by ours,
Should—by crossing at a breath
Into safe and shielded death,
By the merely taking hence
Of his insignificance—
Loom as largened to the sense,
Shape as part, above man's will,
Of the Imperturbable.

As a prisoner, flight debarred,
Exercising in a yard,
Still retain I, troubled, shaken,
Mean estate, by him forsaken ;
And this home, which scarcely took
Impress from his little look,
By his faring to the Dim
Grows all eloquent of him.

Housemate, I can think you still
Bounding to the window-sill,
Over which I vaguely see
Your small mound beneath the tree,
Showing in the autumn shade
That you moulder where you played.

                    October 2, 1904.

A DRIZZLING EASTER MORNING

AND he is risen ?   Well, be it so. . . .
And still the pensive lands complain,
And dead men wait as long ago,
As if, much doubting, they would know
What they are ransomed from, before
They pass again their sheltering door.

I stand amid them in the rain,
While blusters vex the yew and vane ;
And on the road the weary wain
Plods forward, laden heavily ;
And toilers with their aches are fain
For endless rest—though risen is he.

ON ONE WHO LIVED AND DIED WHERE
HE WAS BORN

WHEN a night in November
    Blew forth its bleared airs
An infant descended
    His birth-chamber stairs
    For the very first time,
    At the still, midnight chime ;
All unapprehended
    His mission, his aim.—
Thus, first, one November,
An infant descended
        The stairs.

On a night in November
    Of wearíful cares,
A frail aged figure
    Ascended those stairs
    For the very last time :
    All gone his life's prime,
All vanished his vigour,
    And fine, forceful frame :
Thus, last, one November
Ascended that figure
        Upstairs.

On those nights in November—
Apart eighty years—
The babe and the bent one
Who traversed those stairs
From the early first time
To the last feeble climb—
That fresh and that spent one—
Were even the same :
Yea, who passed in November
As infant, as bent one,
　　Those stairs.

Wise child of November !
　From birth to blanched hairs
Descending, ascending,
　Wealth-wantless, those stairs ;
Who saw quick in time
As a vain pantomime
Life's tending, its ending,
　The worth of its fame.
Wise child of November,
Descending, ascending
　　Those stairs !

THE SECOND NIGHT

(BALLAD)

I MISSED one night, but the next I went ;
　It was gusty above, and clear ;
She was there, with the look of one ill-content,
　And said : " Do not come near ! "

—" I am sorry last night to have failed you here,
　And now I have travelled all day ;
And it's long rowing back to the West-Hoe Pier,
　So brief must be my stay."

—" O man of mystery, why not say
　Out plain to me all you mean ?
Why you missed last night, and must now away
　Is—another has come between ! "

—"O woman so mocking in mood and mien,
  So be it!" I replied:
"And if I am due at a differing scene
  Before the dark has died,

"'Tis that, unresting, to wander wide
  Has ever been my plight,
And at least I have met you at Cremyll side
  If not last eve, to-night."

—"You get small rest—that read I quite;
  And so do I, maybe;
Though there's a rest hid safe from sight
  Elsewhere awaiting me!"

A mad star crossed the sky to the sea,
  Wasting in sparks as it streamed,
And when I looked back at her wistfully
  She had changed, much changed, it seemed.

The sparks of the star in her pupils gleamed,
  She was vague as a vapour now,
And ere of its meaning I had dreamed
  She'd vanished—I knew not how.

I stood on, long; each cliff-top bough,
  Like a cynic nodding there,
Moved up and down, though no man's brow
  But mine met the wayward air.

Still stood I, wholly unaware
  Of what had come to pass,
Or had brought the secret of my new Fair
  To my old Love, alas!

I went down then by crag and grass
  To the boat wherein I had come.
Said the man with the oars: "This news of the lass
  Of Edgcumbe, is sharp for some!

"Yes: found this daybreak, stiff and numb
  On the shore here, whither she'd sped
To meet her lover last night in the glum,
  And he came not, 'tis said."

"And she leapt down, heart-hit.   Pity she's dead:
        So much for the faithful-bent!" . . .
I looked, and again a star overhead
        Shot through the firmament.

SHE WHO SAW NOT

"DID you see something within the house
That made me call you before the red sunsetting?
Something that all this common scene endows
With a richened impress there can be no forgetting?"

"—I have found nothing to see therein,
O Sage, that should have made you urge me to enter,
Nothing to fire the soul, or the sense to win:
I rate you as a rare misrepresenter!"

"—Go anew, Lady,—in by the right. . . ,
Well: why does your face not shine like the face of Moses?"
"—I found no moving thing there save the light
And shadow flung on the wall by the outside roses."

"—Go yet once more, pray.   Look on a seat."
"—I go. . . .   O Sage, it's only a man that sits there
With eyes on the sun.   Mute,—average head to feet."
"—No more?"—"No more.   Just one the place befits there,

"As the rays reach in through the open door,
And he looks at his hand, and the sun glows through his fingers,
While he's thinking thoughts whose tenour is no more
To me than the swaying rose-tree shade that lingers."

No more.   And years drew on and on
Till no sun came, dank fogs the house enfolding;
And she saw inside, when the form in the flesh had gone,
As a vision what she had missed when the real beholding.

THE OLD WORKMAN

"WHY are you so bent down before your time,
Old mason?   Many have not left their prime
So far behind at your age, and can still
        Stand full upright at will."

He pointed to the mansion-front hard by,
And to the stones of the quoin against the sky ;
" Those upper blocks," he said, " that there you see,
    It was that ruined me."

There stood in the air up to the parapet
Crowning the corner height, the stones as set
By him—ashlar whereon the gales might drum
    For centuries to come.

" I carried them up," he said, " by a ladder there ;
The last was as big a load as I could bear ;
But on I heaved ; and something in my back
    Moved, as 'twere with a crack.

" So I got crookt.   I never lost that sprain ;
And those who live there, walled from wind and rain
By freestone that I lifted, do not know
    That my life's ache came so.

" They don't know me, or even know my name,
But good I think it, somehow, all the same
To have kept 'em safe from harm, and right and tight,
    Though it has broke me quite.

' Yes ; that I fixed it firm up there I am proud,
Facing the hail and snow and sun and cloud,
And to stand storms for ages, beating round
    When I lie underground."

THE SAILOR'S MOTHER

" O WHENCE do you come,
Figure in the night-fog that chills me numb ? "

" I come to you across from my house up there,
And I don't mind the brine-mist clinging to me
    That blows from the quay,
For I heard him in my chamber, and thought you unaware.

" But what did you hear,
That brought you blindly knocking in this middle-watch so drear ? "

"My sailor son's voice as 'twere calling at your door,
And I don't mind my bare feet clammy on the stones,
    And the blight to my bones,
For he only knows of *this* house I lived in before."

    "Nobody's nigh,
Woman like a skeleton, with socket-sunk eye."

"Ah—nobody's nigh! And my life is drearisome,
And this is the old home we loved in many a day
    Before he went away;
And the salt fog mops me. And nobody's come!"

    From "To Please his Wife."

OUTSIDE THE CASEMENT

(A REMINISCENCE OF THE WAR)

    WE sat in the room
    And praised her whom
We saw in the portico-shade outside:
    She could not hear
    What was said of her,
But smiled, for its purport we did not hide.

    Then in was brought
    That message, fraught
With evil fortune for her out there,
    Whom we loved that day
    More than any could say,
And would fain have fenced from a waft of care.

    And the question pressed
    Like lead on each breast,
Should we cloak the tidings, or call her and tell?
    It was too intense
    A choice for our sense,
As we pondered and watched her we loved so well.

Yea, spirit failed us
At what assailed us;
How long, while seeing what soon must come,
Should we counterfeit
No knowledge of it,
And stay the stroke that would blanch and numb?

And thus, before
For evermore
Joy left her, we practised to beguile
Her innocence when
She now and again
Looked in, and smiled us another smile.

THE PASSER-BY

(L. H. RECALLS HER ROMANCE)

HE used to pass, well-trimmed and brushed,
    My window every day,
And when I smiled on him he blushed,
That youth, quite as a girl might; aye,
    In the shyest way.

Thus often did he pass hereby,
    That youth of bounding gait,
Until the one who blushed was I,
And he became, as here I sate,
    My joy, my fate.

And now he passes by no more,
    That youth I loved too true!
I grieve should he, as here of yore,
Pass elsewhere, seated in his view,
    Some maiden new!

If such should be, alas for her!
    He'll make her feel him dear,
Become her daily comforter,
Then tire him of her beauteous gear,
    And disappear!

"I WAS THE MIDMOST"

I WAS the midmost of my world
    When first I frisked me free,
For though within its circuit gleamed
    But a small company,
And I was immature, they seemed
    To bend their looks on me.

She was the midmost of my world
    When I went further forth,
And hence it was that, whether I turned
    To south, east, west, or north,
Beams of an all-day Polestar burned
    From that new axe of earth.

Where now is midmost in my world?
    I trace it not at all:
No midmost shows it here, or there,
    When wistful voices call
"We are fain!   We are fain!" from everywhere
    On Earth's bewildering ball!

A SOUND IN THE NIGHT

(WOODSFORD CASTLE : 17—)

"WHAT do I catch upon the night-wind, husband?—
What is it sounds in this house so eerily?
It seems to be a woman's voice: each little while I hear it,
    And it much troubles me!"

"'Tis but the eaves dripping down upon the plinth-slopes:
Letting fancies worry thee!—sure 'tis a foolish thing,
When we were on'y coupled half an hour before the noontide,
    And now it's but evening."

"Yet seems it still a woman's voice outside the castle, husband,
And 'tis cold to-night, and rain beats, and this is a lonely place.
Didst thou fathom much of womankind in travel or adventure
    Ere ever thou sawest my face?"

It may be a tree, bride, that rubs his arms acrosswise,
 it is not the eaves-drip upon the lower slopes,
r the river at the bend, where it whirls about the hatches
      Like a creature that sighs and mopes."

Yet it still seems to me like the crying of a woman,
nd it saddens me much that so piteous a sound
n this my bridal night when I would get agone from sorrow
      Should so ghost-like wander round ! "

To satisfy thee, Love, I will strike the flint-and-steel, then,
nd set the rush-candle up, and undo the door,
nd take the new horn-lantern that we bought upon our journey,
      And throw the light over the moor."

e struck a light, and breeched and booted in the further chamber,
nd lit the new horn-lantern and went from her sight,
nd vanished down the turret ; and she heard him pass the
      postern,
      And go out into the night.

he listened as she lay, till she heard his step returning,
nd his voice as he unclothed him : " 'Twas nothing, as I said,
ut the nor'-west wind a-blowing from the moor ath'art the river,
      And the tree that taps the gurgoyle-head."

Nay, husband, you perplex me ; for if the noise I heard here,
waking me from sleep so, were but as you avow,
he rain-fall, and the wind, and the tree-bough, and the river,
      Why is it silent now ?

And why is thy hand and thy clasping arm so shaking,
nd thy sleeve and tags of hair so muddy and so wet,
nd why feel I thy heart a-thumping every time thou kissest me,
      And thy breath as if hard to get ? "

e lay there in silence for a while, still quickly breathing,
hen started up and walked about the room resentfully :
O woman, witch, whom I, in sooth, against my will have wedded,
      Why castedst thou thy spells on me ?

"There was one I loved once : the cry you heard was her cry :
She came to me to-night, and her plight was passing sore,
As no woman. . . . Yea, and it was e'en the cry you heard, wife,
    But she will cry no more !

"And now I can't abide thee : this place, it hath a curse on't,
This farmstead once a castle : I'll get me straight away !"
He dressed this time in darkness, unspeaking, as she listened,
    And went ere the dawn turned day.

They found a woman's body at a spot called Rocky Shallow,
Where the Froom stream curves amid the moorland, washed
    aground,
And they searched about for him, the yeoman, who had darkly
    known her,
    But he could not be found.

And the bride left for good-and-all the farmstead once a castle,
And in a county far away lives, mourns, and sleeps alone,
And thinks in windy weather that she hears a woman crying,
    And sometimes an infant's moan.

ON A DISCOVERED CURL OF HAIR

    WHEN your soft welcomings were said,
    This curl was waving on your head,
    And when we walked where breakers dinned
    It sported in the sun and wind,
    And when I had won your words of grace
    It brushed and clung about my face.
    Then, to abate the misery
    Of absentness, you gave it me.

    Where are its fellows now ? Ah, they
    For brightest brown have donned a gray,
    And gone into a caverned ark,
    Ever unopened, always dark !

Yet this one curl, untouched of time,
Beams with live brown as in its prime,
So that it seems I even could now
Restore it to the living brow
By bearing down the western road
Till I had reached your old abode.

February 1913.

AN OLD LIKENESS

(RECALLING R. T.)

WHO would have thought
That, not having missed her
Talks, tears, laughter
In absence, or sought
To recall for so long
Her gamut of song;
Or ever to waft her
Signal of aught
That she, fancy-fanned,
Would well understand,
I should have kissed her
Picture when scanned
Yawning years after!

Yet, seeing her poor
Dim-outlined form
Chancewise at night-time,
Some old allure
Came on me, warm,
Fresh, pleadful, pure,
As in that bright time
At a far season
Of love and unreason,
And took me by storm
Here in this blight-time!

And thus it arose
That, yawning years after
Our early flows
Of wit and laughter,

And framing of rhymes
   At idle times,
At sight of her painting,
   Though she lies cold
   In churchyard mould,
I took its feinting
   As real, and kissed it,
   As if I had wist it
Herself of old.

HER APOTHEOSIS

" Secretum meum mihi "

(FADED WOMAN'S SONG)

THERE were years vague of measure
   Needless the asking when ;
No honours, praises, pleasure
   Reached common maids from men.

And hence no lures bewitched them,
   No hand was stretched to raise,
No gracious gifts enriched them,
   No voices sang their praise.

Yet an iris at that season
   Amid the accustomed slight
From denseness, dull unreason,
   Ringed me with living light.

"SACRED TO THE MEMORY"

(MARY H.)

THAT " Sacred to the Memory "
Is clearly carven there I own,
And all may think that on the stone
The words have been inscribed by me
In bare conventionality.

They know not and will never know
That my full script is not confined
To that stone space, but stands deep lined
Upon the landscape high and low
Wherein she made such worthy show.

TO A WELL-NAMED DWELLING

GLAD old house of lichened stonework,
What I owed you in my lone work,
  Noon and night !
Whensoever faint or ailing,
Letting go my grasp and failing,
  You lent light.

How by that fair title came you ?
Did some forward eye so name you
  Knowing that one,
Stumbling down his century blindly,
Would remark your sound, so kindly,
  And be won ?

Smile in sunlight, sleep in moonlight,
Bask in April, May, and June-light,
  Zephyr-fanned ;
Let your chambers show no sorrow,
Blanching day, or stuporing morrow,
  While they stand.

THE WHIPPER-IN

" MY father was the whipper-in,—
  Is still—if I'm not misled ?
And now I see, where the hedge is thin,
  A little spot of red ;
   Surely it is my father
   Going to the kennel-shed !

" I cursed and fought my father—aye,
        And sailed to a foreign land ;
And feeling sorry, I'm back, to stay,
        Please God, as his helping hand.
            Surely it is my father
            Near where the kennels stand ? "

" —True.   Whipper-in he used to be
        For twenty years or more ;
And you did go away to sea
        As youths have done before.
            Yes, oddly enough that red there
            Is the very coat he wore.

" But he—he's dead ; was thrown somehow,
        And gave his back a crick,
And though that is his coat, 'tis now
        The scarecrow of a rick ;
            You'll see when you get nearer—
            'Tis spread out on a stick.

" You see, when all had settled down
        Your mother's things were sold,
And she went back to her own town,
        And the coat, ate out with mould,
            Is now used by the farmer
            For scaring, as 'tis old."

A MILITARY APPOINTMENT

(SCHERZANDO)

" So back you have come from the town, Nan, dear !
And have you seen him there, or near—
        That soldier of mine—
Who long since promised to meet me here ? "

" —O yes, Nell : from the town I come,
And have seen your lover on sick-leave home—
        That soldier of yours—
Who swore to meet you, or Strike-him-dumb ;

" But has kept himself of late away :
Yet,—in short, he's coming, I heard him say—
    That lover of yours—
To this very spot on this very day."

" —Then I'll wait, I'll wait, through wet or dry !
I'll give him a goblet brimming high—
    This lover of mine—
And not of complaint one word or sigh ! "

" —Nell, him I have chanced so much to see,
That—he has grown the lover of me !—
    That lover of yours—
And it's here our meeting is planned to be."

THE MILESTONE BY THE RABBIT-BURROW

(ON YELL'HAM HILL)

In my loamy nook
As I dig my hole
I observe men look
At a stone, and sigh
As they pass it by
To some far goal.

Something it says
To their glancing eyes
That must distress
The frail and lame,
And the strong of frame
Gladden or surprise.

Do signs on its face
Declare how far
Feet have to trace
Before they gain
Some blest champaign
Where no gins are ?

THE LAMENT OF THE LOOKING-GLASS

WORDS from the mirror softly pass
To the curtains with a sigh :
" Why should I trouble again to glass
These smileless things hard by,
Since she I pleasured once, alas,
Is now no longer nigh ! "

" I've imaged shadows of coursing cloud,
And of the plying limb
On the pensive pine when the air is loud
With its aerial hymn ;
But never do they make me proud
To catch them within my rim !

" I flash back phantoms of the night
That sometimes flit by me,
I echo roses red and white—
The loveliest blooms that be—
But now I never hold to sight
So sweet a flower as she."

CROSS-CURRENTS

THEY parted—a pallid, trembling pair,
And rushing down the lane
He left her lonely near me there ;
—I asked her of their pain.

" It is for ever," at length she said,
" His friends have schemed it so,
That the long-purposed day to wed
Never shall we two know."

" In such a cruel case," said I,
" Love will contrive a course ? "
" —Well, no . . . A thing may underlie,
Which robs that of its force ;

"A thing I could not tell him of,
   Though all the year I have tried ;
This : never could I have given him love,
   Even had I been his bride.

"So, when his kinsfolk stop the way
   Point-blank, there could not be
A happening in the world to-day
   More opportune for me !

"Yet hear—no doubt to your surprise—
   I am grieving, for his sake,
That I have escaped the sacrifice
   I was distressed to make ! "

THE OLD NEIGHBOUR AND THE NEW

'TWAS to greet the new rector I called here,
   But in the arm-chair I see
My old friend, for long years installed here,
   Who palely nods to me.

The new man explains what he's planning
   In a smart and cheerful tone,
And I listen, the while that I'm scanning
   The figure behind his own.

The newcomer urges things on me ;
   I return a vague smile thereto,
The olden face gazing upon me
   Just as it used to do !

And on leaving I scarcely remember
   Which neighbour to-day I have seen,
The one carried out in September,
   Or him who but entered yestreen.

THE CHOSEN

"Ἄτινά ἐστιν ἀλληγορούμενα

"A WOMAN for whom great gods might strive!"
    I said, and kissed her there:
And then I thought of the other five,
    And of how charms outwear.

I thought of the first with her eating eyes,
And I thought of the second with hers, green-gray,
And I thought of the third, experienced, wise,
And I thought of the fourth who sang all day.

And I thought of the fifth, whom I'd called a jade,
    And I thought of them all, tear-fraught;
And that each had shown her a passable maid,
    Yet not of the favour sought.

So I traced these words on the bark of a beech,
Just at the falling of the mast:
"After scanning five; yes, each and each,
I've found the woman desired—at last!"

"—I feel a strange benumbing spell,
    As one ill-wished!" said she.
And soon it seemed that something fell
    Was starving her love for me.

"I feel some curse. O, *five* were there?"
And wanly she swerved, and went away.
I followed sick: night numbed the air,
And dark the mournful moorland lay.

I cried: "O darling, turn your head!"
    But never her face I viewed;
"O turn, O turn!" again I said,
    And miserably pursued.

At length I came to a Christ-cross stone
Which she had passed without discern;
And I knelt upon the leaves there strown,
And prayed aloud that she might turn.

I rose, and looked ; and turn she did ;
I cried, " My heart revives ! "
" Look more," she said. I looked as bid ;
Her face was all the five's.

All the five women, clear come back,
I saw in her—with her made one,
The while she drooped upon the track,
And her frail term seemed well-nigh run.

She'd half forgot me in her change ;
" Who are you ?   Won't you say
Who you may be, you man so strange,
Following since yesterday ? "

I took the composite form she was,
And carried her to an arbour small,
Not passion-moved, but even because
In one I could atone to all.

And there she lies, and there I tend,
Till my life's threads unwind,
A various womanhood in blend—
Not one, but all combined.

THE INSCRIPTION

(A TALE)

SIR JOHN was entombed, and the crypt was closed, and she,
Like a soul that could meet no more the sight of the sun,
Inclined her in weepings and prayings continually,
As his widowed one.

And to pleasure her in her sorrow, and fix his name
As a memory Time's fierce frost should never kill,
She caused to be richly chased a brass to his fame,
Which should link them still ;

For she bonded her name with his own on the brazen page,
As if dead and interred there with him, and cold, and numb,
(Omitting the day of her dying and year of her age
Till her end should come ;)

And implored good people to pray " 𝔒𝔣 𝔱𝔥𝔢𝔦𝔯 𝔆𝔥𝔞𝔯𝔶𝔱𝔦𝔢
𝔉𝔬𝔯 𝔱𝔥𝔢𝔰𝔢 𝔱𝔴𝔞𝔦𝔫𝔢 𝔖𝔬𝔲𝔩𝔢𝔰,"—yea, she who did last remain
Forgoing Heaven's bliss if ever with spouse should she
      Again have lain.

Even there, as it first was set, you may see it now,
Writ in quaint Church-text, with the date of her death left bare,
In the aged Estminster aisle, where the folk yet bow
      Themselves in prayer.

Thereafter some years slid, till there came a day
When it slowly began to be marked of the standers-by
That she would regard the brass, and would bend away
      With a drooping sigh.

Now the lady was fair as any the eye might scan
Through a summer day of roving—a type at whose lip
Despite her maturing seasons, no meet man
      Would be loth to sip.

And her heart was stirred with a lightning love to its pith
For a newcomer who, while less in years, was one
Full eager and able to make her his own forthwith,
      Restrained of none.

But she answered Nay, death-white ; and still as he urged
She adversely spake, overmuch as she loved the while,
Till he pressed for why, and she led with the face of one scourged
      To the neighbouring aisle,

And showed him the words, ever gleaming upon her pew,
Memorizing her there as the knight's eternal wife,
Or falsing such, debarred inheritance due
      Of celestial life.

He blenched, and reproached her that one yet undeceased
Should bury her future—that future which none can spell ;
And she wept, and purposed anon to inquire of the priest
      If the price were hell

Of her wedding in face of the record.   Her lover agreed,
And they parted before the brass with a shudderful kiss,
For it seemed to flash out on their impulse of passionate need,
      " Mock ye not this ! "

Well, the priest, whom more perceptions moved than one,
Said she erred at the first to have written as if she were dead
Her name and adjuration ; but since it was done
      Nought could be said

Save that she must abide by the pledge, for the peace of her soul,
And so, by her life, maintain the apostrophe good,
If she wished anon to reach the coveted goal
      Of beatitude.

To erase from the consecrate text her prayer as there prayed
Would aver that, since earth's joys most drew her, past doubt,
Friends' prayers for her joy above by Jesu's aid
      Could be done without.

Moreover she thought of the laughter, the shrug, the jibe
That would rise at her back in the nave when she should pass
As another's avowed by the words she had chosen to inscribe
      On the changeless brass.

And so for months she replied to her Love : " No, no " ;
While sorrow was gnawing her beauties ever and more,
Till he, long-suffering and weary, grew to show
      Less warmth than before.

And, after an absence, wrote words absolute :
That he gave her till Midsummer morn to make her mind clear ;
And that if, by then, she had not said Yea to his suit,
      He should wed elsewhere.

Thence on, at unwonted times through the lengthening days
She was seen in the church—at dawn, or when the sun dipt
And the moon rose, standing with hands joined, blank of gaze,
      Before the script.

She thinned as he came not ; shrank like a creature that cowers
As summer drew nearer ; but yet had not promised to wed,
When, just at the zenith of June, in the still night hours,
      She was missed from her bed.

" The church ! " they whispered with qualms ; " where often she
    sits."
They found her : facing the brass there, else seeing none,
But feeling the words with her finger, gibbering in fits ;
      And she knew them not one.

And so she remained, in her handmaids' charge ; late, soon,
Tracing words in the air with her finger, as seen that night—
Those incised on the brass—till at length unwatched one noon,
    She vanished from sight.

And, as talebearers tell, thence on to her last-taken breath
Was unseen, save as wraith that in front of the brass made moan
So that ever the way of her life and the time of her death
    Remained unknown.

And hence, as indited above, you may read even now
The quaint Church-text, with the date of her death left bare,
In the aged Estminster aisle, where folk yet bow
    Themselves in prayer.

    October 30, 1907.

THE MARBLE-STREETED TOWN

I REACH the marble-streeted town,
    Whose "Sound" outbreathes its air
      Of sharp sea-salts ;
I see the movement up and down
    As when she was there.
Ships of all countries come and go,
    The bandsmen boom in the sun
      A throbbing waltz ;
The schoolgirls laugh along the Hoe
    As when she was one.

I move away as the music rolls :
    The place seems not to mind
      That she—of old
The brightest of its native souls—
    Left it behind !
Over this green aforedays she
    On light treads went and came,
      Yea, times untold ;
Yet none here knows her history—
    Has heard her name.

    PLYMOUTH (1914?).

A WOMAN DRIVING

How she held up the horses' heads,
 Firm-lipped, with steady rein,
Down that grim steep the coastguard treads,
 Till all was safe again!

With form erect and keen contour
 She passed against the sea,
And, dipping into the chine's obscure,
 Was seen no more by me.

To others she appeared anew
 At times of dusky light,
But always, so they told, withdrew
 From close and curious sight.

Some said her silent wheels would roll
 Rutless on softest loam,
And even that her steeds' footfall
 Sank not upon the foam.

Where drives she now? It may be where
 No mortal horses are,
But in a chariot of the air
 Towards some radiant star.

A WOMAN'S TRUST

If he should live a thousand years
 He'd find it not again
 That scorn of him by men
Could less disturb a woman's trust
In him as a steadfast star which must
Rise scathless from the nether spheres:
If he should live a thousand years
 He'd find it not again.

She waited like a little child,
    Unchilled by damps of doubt,
    While from her eyes looked out
A confidence sublime as Spring's
When stressed by Winter's loiterings.
Thus, howsoever the wicked wiled,
She waited like a little child
    Unchilled by damps of doubt.

Through cruel years and crueller
    Thus she believed in him
    And his aurore, so dim ;
That, after fenweeds, flowers would blow ;
And above all things did she show
Her faith in his good faith with her ;
Through cruel years and crueller
    Thus she believed in him !

BEST TIMES

WE went a day's excursion to the stream,
Basked by the bank, and bent to the ripple-gleam,
    And I did not know
    That life would show,
However it might flower, no finer glow.

I walked in the Sunday sunshine by the road
That wound towards the wicket of your abode,
    And I did not think
    That life would shrink
To nothing ere it shed a rosier pink.

Unlooked for I arrived on a rainy night,
And you hailed me at the door by the swaying light.
    And I full forgot
    That life might not
Again be touching that ecstatic height.

And that calm eve when you walked up the stair,
After a gaiety prolonged and rare,
          No thought soever
          That you might never
Walk down again, struck me as I stood there.

> Rewritten from an old draft.

THE CASUAL ACQUAINTANCE

WHILE he was here with breath and bone,
          To speak to and to see,
Would I had known—more clearly known—
          What that man did for me

When the wind scraped a minor lay,
          And the spent west from white
To gray turned tiredly, and from gray
          To broadest bands of night!

But I saw not, and he saw not
          What shining life-tides flowed
To me-ward from his casual jot
          Of service on that road.

He would have said: "'Twas nothing new;
          We all do what we can;
'Twas only what one man would do
          For any other man."

Now that I gauge his goodliness
          He's slipped from human eyes;
And when he passed there's none can guess,
          Or point out where he lies.

INTRA SEPULCHRUM

WHAT curious things we said,
          What curious things we did
Up there in the world we walked till dead,
          Our kith and kin amid!

How we played at love,
And its wildness, weakness, woe ;
Yes, played thereat far more than enough
As it turned out, I trow !

Played at believing in gods
And observing the ordinances,
I for your sake in impossible codes
Right ready to acquiesce.

Thinking our lives unique,
Quite quainter than usual kinds,
We held that we could not abide a week
The tether of typic minds.

—Yet people who day by day
Pass by and look at us
From over the wall in a casual way
Are of this unconscious.

And feel, if anything,
That none can be buried here
Removed from commonest fashioning,
Or lending note to a bier :

No twain who in heart-heaves proved
Themselves at all adept,
Who more than many laughed and loved
Who more than many wept,

Or were as sprites or elves
Into blind matter hurled,
Or ever could have been to themselves
The centre of the world.

THE WHITEWASHED WALL

WHY does she turn in that shy soft way
Whenever she stirs the fire,
And kiss to the chimney-corner wall,
As if entranced to admire

Its whitewashed bareness more than the sight
    Of a rose in richest green?
I have known her long, but this raptured rite
    I never before have seen.

—Well, once when her son cast his shadow there,
    A friend took a pencil and drew him
Upon that flame-lit wall. And the lines
    Had a lifelike semblance to him.
And there long stayed his familiar look;
    But one day, ere she knew,
The whitener came to cleanse the nook,
    And covered the face from view.

"Yes," he said: "My brush goes on with a rush,
    And the draught is buried under;
When you have to whiten old cots and brighten,
    What else can you do, I wonder?"
But she knows he's there. And when she yearns
    For him, deep in the labouring night,
She sees him as close at hand, and turns
    To him under his sheet of white.

JUST THE SAME

I SAT. It all was past;
    Hope never would hail again;
Fair days had ceased at a blast,
    The world was a darkened den.

The beauty and dream were gone,
    And the halo in which I had hied
So gaily gallantly on
    Had suffered blot and died!

I went forth, heedless whither,
    In a cloud too black for name:
—People frisked hither and thither;
    The world was just the same.

THE LAST TIME

THE kiss had been given and taken,
    And gathered to many past :
It never could reawaken ;
    But I heard none say : " It's the last !"

The clock showed the hour and the minute
    But I did not turn and look :
I read no finis in it,
    As at closing of a book.

But I read it all too rightly
    When, at a time anon,
A figure lay stretched out whitely,
    And I stood looking thereon.

THE SEVEN TIMES

THE dark was thick.   A boy he seemed at that time
    Who trotted by me with uncertain air ;
" I'll tell my tale," he murmured, "for I fancy
    A friend goes there ? . . ."

Then thus he told.   " I reached—'twas for the first time—
    A dwelling.   Life was clogged in me with care ;
thought not I should meet an eyesome maiden,
    But found one there.

" I entered on the precincts for the second time—
    'Twas an adventure fit and fresh and fair—
I slackened in my footsteps at the porchway,
    And found her there.

" I rose and travelled thither for the third time,
    The hope-hues growing gayer and yet gayer
As I hastened round the boscage of the outskirts,
    And found her there.

" I journeyed to the place again the fourth time
  (The best and rarest visit of the rare,
As it seemed to me, engrossed about these goings),
        And found her there.

" When I bent me to my pilgrimage the fifth time
  (Soft-thinking as I journeyed I would dare
A certain word at token of good auspice),
        I found her there.

" That landscape did I traverse for the sixth time,
  And dreamed on what we purposed to prepare ;
I reached a tryst before my journey's end came,
        And found her there.

" I went again—long after—aye, the seventh time ;
  The look of things was sinister and bare
As I caught no customed signal, heard no voice call,
        Nor found her there.

" And now I gad the globe—day, night, and any time,
  To light upon her hiding unaware,
And, maybe, I shall nigh me to some nymph-niche,
        And find her there ! "

" But how," said I, " has your so little lifetime
  Given roomage for such loving, loss, despair ?
A boy so young !"   Forthwith I turned my lantern
        Upon him there.

His head was white.   His small form, fine aforetime,
  Was shrunken with old age and battering wear,
An eighty-years long plodder saw I pacing
        Beside me there.

E SUN'S LAST LOOK ON THE COUNTRY GIRL

(M. H.)

THE sun threw down a radiant spot
    On the face in the winding-sheet—
The face it had lit when a babe's in its cot ;
And the sun knew not, and the face knew not
    That soon they would no more meet.

Now that the grave has shut its door,
  And lets not in one ray,
Do they wonder that they meet no more—
That face and its beaming visitor—
  That met so many a day?

    December 1915.

IN A LONDON FLAT

I

"YOU look like a widower," she said
Through the folding-doors with a laugh from the bed,
As he sat by the fire in the outer room,
Reading late on a night of gloom,
And a cab-hack's wheeze, and the clap of its feet
In its breathless pace on the smooth wet street,
Were all that came to them now and then. . . .
"You really do!" she quizzed again.

II

And the Spirits behind the curtains heard,
And also laughed, amused at her word,
And at her light-hearted view of him.
"Let's get him made so—just for a whim!"
Said the Phantom Ironic.   "'Twould serve her right
If we coaxed the Will to do it some night."
"O pray not!" pleaded the younger one,
The Sprite of the Pities.   "She said it in fun!"

III

But so it befell, whatever the cause,
That what she had called him he next year was;
And on such a night, when she lay elsewhere,
He, watched by those Phantoms, again sat there,
And gazed, as if gazing on far faint shores,
At the empty bed through the folding-doors
As he remembered her words; and wept
That she had forgotten them where she slept.

DRAWING DETAILS IN AN OLD CHURCH

I HEAR the bell-rope sawing,
And the oil-less axle grind,
As I sit alone here drawing
What some Gothic brain designed;
And I catch the toll that follows
    From the lagging bell,
Ere it spreads to hills and hollows
    Where people dwell.

I ask not whom it tolls for,
Incurious who he be;
So, some morrow, when those knolls for
One unguessed, sound out for me,
A stranger, loitering under
    In nave or choir,
May think, too, "Whose, I wonder?"
    But not inquire.

RAKE-HELL MUSES

YES; since she knows not need,
    Nor walks in blindness,
I may without unkindness
    This true thing tell:

Which would be truth, indeed,
    Though worse in speaking,
Were her poor footsteps seeking
    A pauper's cell.

I judge, then, better far
    She now have sorrow,
Than gladness that to-morrow
    Might know its knell.—

It may be men there are
    Could make of union
A lifelong sweet communion
    Or passioned spell;

But *I*, to save her name
     And bring salvation
By altar-affirmation
     And bridal bell;

I, by whose rash unshame
     These tears come to her :—
My faith would more undo her
     Than my farewell!

Chained to me, year by year
     My moody madness
Would make her olden gladness
     An intermell.

She'll take the ill that's near,
     And bear the blaming.
'Twill pass.   Full soon her shaming
     They'll cease to yell.

Our unborn, first her moan,
     Will grow her guerdon,
Until from blot and burden
     A joyance swell;

In that therein she'll own
     My good part wholly,
My evil staining solely
     My own vile fell.

Of the disgrace, may be
     " He shunned to share it,
Being false," they'll say.   I'll bear it;
     Time will dispel

The calumny, and prove
     This much about me,
That she lives best without me
     Who would live well.

That, this once, not self-love
     But good intention
Pleads that against convention
     We two rebel.

For, is one moonlight dance,
    One midnight passion,
A rock whereon to fashion
    Life's citadel?

Prove they their power to prance
    Life's miles together
From upper slope to nether
    Who trip an ell?

—Years hence, or now apace,
    May tongues be calling
News of my further falling
    Sinward pell-mell:

Then this great good will grace
    Our lives' division,
She's saved from more misprision
    Though I plumb hell.

189–

THE COLOUR

*(The following lines are partly original, partly
remembered from a Wessex folk-rhyme)*

" WHAT shall I bring you?
Please will white do
Best for your wearing
    The long day through?"
"—White is for weddings,
Weddings, weddings,
White is for weddings,
    And that won't do."

" What shall I bring you?
Please will red do
Best for your wearing
    The long day through?"
"—Red is for soldiers,
Soldiers, soldiers,
Red is for soldiers,
    And that won't do."

"What shall I bring you?
Please will blue do
Best for your wearing
 The long day through?"
"—Blue is for sailors,
Sailors, sailors,
Blue is for sailors,
 And that won't do."

"What shall I bring you?
Please will green do
Best for your wearing
 The long day through?"
"—Green is for mayings,
Mayings, mayings,
Green is for mayings,
 And that won't do."

"What shall I bring you
Then? Will black do
Best for your wearing
 The long day through?"
"—Black is for mourning,
Mourning, mourning,
Black is for mourning,
 And black will do."

MURMURS IN THE GLOOM

(NOCTURNE)

I WAYFARED at the nadir of the sun
Where populations meet, though seen of none;
 And millions seemed to sigh around
 As though their haunts were nigh around,
 And unknown throngs to cry around
  Of things late done.

"O Seers, who well might high ensample show"
(Came throbbing past in plainsong small and slow),

" Leaders who lead us aimlessly,
   Teachers who train us shamelessly,
   Why let ye smoulder flamelessly
        The truths ye trow ?

" Ye scribes, that urge the old medicament,
Whose fusty vials have long dried impotent,
   Why prop ye meretricious things,
   Denounce the sane as vicious things,
   And call outworn factitious things
        Expedient ?

" O Dynasties that sway and shake us so,
Why rank your magnanimities so low
   That grace can smooth no waters yet,
   But breathing threats and slaughters yet
   Ye grieve Earth's sons and daughters yet
        As long ago ?

" Live there no heedful ones of searching sight,
Whose accents might be oracles that smite
   To hinder those who frowardly
   Conduct us, and untowardly ;
   To lead the nations vawardly
        From gloom to light ? "

September 22, 1899.

EPITAPH

I NEVER cared for Life : Life cared for me,
And hence I owed it some fidelity.
It now says, " Cease ; at length thou hast learnt to grind
Sufficient toll for an unwilling mind,
And I dismiss thee—not without regard
That thou didst ask no ill-advised reward,
Nor sought in me much more than thou couldst find."

AN ANCIENT TO ANCIENTS

WHERE once we danced, where once we sang,
   Gentlemen,
The floors are sunken, cobwebs hang,
And cracks creep ; worms have fed upon
The doors. Yea, sprightlier times were then
Than now, with harps and tabrets gone,
   Gentlemen !

Where once we rowed, where once we sailed,
   Gentlemen,
And damsels took the tiller, veiled
Against too strong a stare (God wot
Their fancy, then or anywhen !)
Upon that shore we are clean forgot,
   Gentlemen !

We have lost somewhat, afar and near,
   Gentlemen,
The thinning of our ranks each year
Affords a hint we are nigh undone,
That we shall not be ever again
The marked of many, loved of one,
   Gentlemen.

In dance the polka hit our wish,
   Gentlemen,
The paced quadrille, the spry schottische,
" Sir Roger."—And in opera spheres
The " Girl " (the famed " Bohemian "),
And " Trovatore," held the ears,
   Gentlemen.

This season's paintings do not please,
   Gentlemen,
Like Etty, Mulready, Maclise ;
Throbbing romance has waned and wanned ;
No wizard wields the witching pen
Of Bulwer, Scott, Dumas, and Sand,
   Gentlemen.

The bower we shrined to Tennyson,
> Gentlemen,
Is roof-wrecked ; damps there drip upon
Sagged seats, the creeper-nails are rust,
The spider is sole denizen ;
Even she who voiced those rhymes is dust,
> Gentlemen !

We who met sunrise sanguine-souled,
> Gentlemen,
Are wearing weary.   We are old ;
These younger press ; we feel our rout
Is imminent to Aïdes' den,—
That evening shades are stretching out,
> Gentlemen !

And yet, though ours be failing frames,
> Gentlemen,
So were some others' history names,
Who trode their track light-limbed and fast
As these youth, and not alien
From enterprise, to their long last,
> Gentlemen.

Sophocles, Plato, Socrates,
> Gentlemen,
Pythagoras, Thucydides,
Herodotus, and Homer,—yea,
Clement, Augustin, Origen,
Burnt brightlier towards their setting-day,
> Gentlemen.

And ye, red-lipped and smooth-browed ; list,
> Gentlemen ;
Much is there waits you we have missed ;
Much lore we leave you worth the knowing,
Much, much has lain outside our ken :
Nay, rush not : time serves : we are going,
> Gentlemen.

AFTER READING PSALMS XXXIX., XL., ETC.

SIMPLE was I and was young ;
Kept no gallant tryst, I ;
Even from good words held my tongue,
Quoniam Tu fecisti !

Through my youth I stirred me not,
High adventure missed I,
Left the shining shrines unsought ;
Yet—*me deduxisti !*

At my start by Helicon
Love-lore little wist I,
Worldly less ; but footed on ;
Why ? *Me suscepisti !*

When I failed at fervid rhymes,
"Shall," I said, "persist I ?"
"*Dies*" (I would add at times)
"*Meos posuisti !*"

So I have fared through many suns ;
Sadly little grist I
Bring my mill, or any one's,
Domine, Tu scisti !

And at dead of night I call :
"Though to prophets list I,
Which hath understood at all ?
Yea : *Quem elegisti ?*"
187–

SURVIEW

" Cogitavi vias meas "

A CRY from the green-grained sticks of the fire
Made me gaze where it seemed to be :
'Twas my own voice talking therefrom to me
On how I had walked when my sun was higher—
My heart in its arrogancy.

"You held not to whatsoever was true,"
    Said my own voice talking to me :
" Whatsoever was just you were slack to see ;
Kept not things lovely and pure in view,"
    Said my own voice talking to me.

" You slighted her that endureth all,"
    Said my own voice talking to me ;
" Vaunteth not, trusteth hopefully ;
That suffereth long and is kind withal,"
    Said my own voice talking to me.

" You taught not that which you set about,"
    Said my own voice talking to me ;
" That the greatest of things is Charity. . . ."
—And the sticks burnt low, and the fire went out,
    And my voice ceased talking to me.

HUMAN SHOWS

FAR PHANTASIES

WAITING BOTH

A STAR looks down at me,
And says: "Here I and you
Stand, each in our degree:
What do you mean to do,—
     Mean to do?"

I say: "For all I know,
Wait, and let Time go by,
Till my change come,"—"Just so,"
The star says: "So mean I:—
     So mean I."

A BIRD-SCENE AT A RURAL DWELLING

WHEN the inmate stirs, the birds retire discreetly
From the window-ledge, whereon they whistled sweetly
    And on the step of the door,
    In the misty morning hoar;
But now the dweller is up they flee
To the crooked neighbouring codlin-tree;
And when he comes fully forth they seek the garden,
And call from the lofty costard, as pleading pardon
    For shouting so near before
    In their joy at being alive:—
Meanwhile the hammering clock within goes five.

I know a domicile of brown and green,
Where for a hundred summers there have been
Just such enactments, just such daybreaks seen.

"ANY LITTLE OLD SONG"

ANY little old song
        Will do for me,
Tell it of joys gone long,
        Or joys to be,
Or friendly faces best
        Loved to see.

Newest themes I want not
        On subtle strings,
And for thrillings pant not
        That new song brings:
I only need the homeliest
        Of heartstirrings.

IN A FORMER RESORT AFTER MANY YEARS

Do I know these, slack-shaped and wan,
Whose substance, one time fresh and furrowless,
Is now a rag drawn over a skeleton,
        As in El Greco's canvases?—
Whose cheeks have slipped down, lips become indrawn,
        And statures shrunk to dwarfishness?

Do they know me, whose former mind
Was like an open plain where no foot falls,
But now is as a gallery portrait-lined,
        And scored with necrologic scrawls,
Where feeble voices rise, once full-defined,
        From underground in curious calls?

A CATHEDRAL FAÇADE AT MIDNIGHT

ALONG the sculptures of the western wall
        I watched the moonlight creeping:
It moved as if it hardly moved at all,
        Inch by inch thinly peeping

Round on the pious figures of freestone, brought
And poised there when the Universe was wrought
To serve its centre, Earth, in mankind's thought.

The lunar look skimmed scantly toe, breast, arm,
    Then edged on slowly, slightly,
To shoulder, hand, face; till each austere form
    Was blanched its whole length brightly
Of prophet, king, queen, cardinal in state,
That dead men's tools had striven to simulate;
And the stiff images stood irradiate.

A frail moan from the martyred saints there set
    Mid others of the erection
Against the breeze, seemed sighings of regret
    At the ancient faith's rejection
Under the sure, unhasting, steady stress
Of Reason's movement, making meaningless
The coded creeds of old-time godliness.

THE TURNIP-HOER

Of tides that toss the souls of men
Some are foreseen, and weathered warefully;
More burst at flood, none witting why or when,
    And are called Destiny.

—Years past there was a turnip-hoer,
Who loved his wife and child, and worked amain
In the turnip-time from dawn till day outwore
    And night bedimmed the plain.

The thronging plants of blueish green
Would fall in lanes before his skilful blade,
Which, as by sleight, would deftly slip between
    Those spared and those low-laid.

'Twas afternoon: he hoed his best
Unlifting head or eye, when, through the fence,
He heard a gallop dropping from the crest
    Of the hill above him, whence,

    Descending at a crashing pace,
An open carriage came, horsed by a pair:
A lady sat therein, with lilywhite face
    And wildly windblown hair.

    The man sprang over, and horse and horse
Faced in the highway as the pair ondrew;
Like Terminus stood he there, and barred their course,
    And almost ere he knew

    The lady was limp within his arms
And, half-unconscious, clutched his hair and beard;
And so he held her, till from neighbouring farms
    Came hinds, and soon appeared

    Footman and coachman on the way:—
The steeds were guided back, now breath-bespent,
And the hoer was rewarded with good pay:—
    So passed the accident.

    "She was the Duchess of Southernshire,
They tell me," said the second hoe, next day:
"She's come a-visiting not far from here;
    This week will end her stay."

    The hoer's wife that evening set
Her hand to a crusted stew in the three-legged pot,
And he sat looking on in silence; yet
    The cooking saw he not,

    But a woman, with her arms around him,
Glove-handed, clasping his neck and clutching his blouse,
And ere he went to bed that night he found him,
    Outside a manor-house.

A page there smoking answered him:
"Her Grace's room is where you see that light;
By now she's up there slipping off her trim:
    The Dook's is on the right."

She was, indeed, just saying through the door,
"That dauntless fellow saved me from collapse:
I'd not much with me, or 'd have given him more:
    'Twas not enough, perhaps!"

Up till she left, before he slept,
He walked, though tired, to where her window shined,
And mused till it went dark; but close he kept
    All that was in his mind.

"What is it, Ike?" inquired his wife;
"You are not so nice now as you used to be.
What have I done? You seem quite tired of life!"
    "Nothing at all," said he.

In the next shire this lady of rank,
So 'twas made known, would open a bazaar:
He took his money from the savings-bank
    To go there, for 'twas far.

And reached her stall, and sighted, clad
In her ripe beauty and the goodliest guise,
His Vision of late. He straight spent all he had,
    But not once caught her eyes.

Next week he heard, with heart of clay,
That London held her for three months or so:
Fearing to tell his wife he went for a day,
    Pawning his watch to go;

And scanned the Square of her abode,
And timed her moves, as well as he could guess,
That he might glimpse her; till afoot by road
    He came home penniless. . . .

—The Duke of Wessex once again,
Glanced at the Wessex paper, where he read
Of a man, late taken to drink, killed by a train
     At a crossing, so it said.

"Why—he who saved your life, I think?"
—"O no," said she.   "It cannot be the same:
He was sweet-breath'd, without a taint of drink;
     Yet it is like his name."

THE CARRIER

"THERE'S a seat, I see, still empty?"
     Cried the hailer from the road;
"No there is not!" said the carrier,
     Quickening his horse and load.

"—They say you are in the grave, Jane;
     But still you ride with me!"
And he looked towards the vacant space
     He had kept beside his knee.

And the passengers murmured: " 'Tis where his wife
     In journeys to and fro
Used always to sit; but nobody does
     Since those long years ago."

Rumble-mumble went the van
     Past Sidwell Church and wall,
Till Exon Towers were out of scan,
     And night lay over all.

LOVER TO MISTRESS
(SONG)

BECKON to me to come
With handkerchief or hand,
Or finger mere or thumb;
Let forecasts be but rough,

Parents more bleak than bland,
'Twill be enough,
Maid mine,
'Twill be enough!

Two fields, a wood, a tree,
Nothing now more malign
Lies between you and me;
But were they bysm, or bluff,
Or snarling sea, one sign
Would be enough,
Maid mine,
Would be enough!

From an old copy.

THE MONUMENT-MAKER

I chiselled her monument
To my mind's content,
Took it to the church by night,
When her planet was at its height,
And set it where I had figured the place in the daytime.
Having niched it there
I stepped back, cheered, and thought its outlines fair.
And its marbles rare.

Then laughed she over my shoulder as in our Maytime:
"It spells not me!" she said:
"Tells nothing about my beauty, wit, or gay time
With all those, quick and dead,
Of high or lowlihead,
That hovered near,
Including you, who carve there your devotion;
But you felt none, my dear!"

And then she vanished. Checkless sprang my emotion,
And forced a tear

At seeing I'd not been truly known by her,
And never prized!—that my memorial here,
    To consecrate her sepulchre,
       Was scorned, almost,
       By her sweet ghost:
Yet I hoped not quite, in her very innermost!

1916.

CIRCUS–RIDER TO RINGMASTER

WHEN I am riding round the ring no longer,
      Tell a tale of me;
Say, no steed-borne woman's nerve was stronger
      Than used mine to be.
    Let your whole soul say it; do:
      O it will be true!

Should I soon no more be mistress found in
      Feats I've made my own,
Trace the tan-laid track you'd whip me round in
      On the cantering roan:
    There may cross your eyes again
      My lithe look as then.

Show how I, when clay became my cover,
      Took the high-hoop leap
Into your arms, who coaxed and grew my lover,—
      Ah, to make me weep
    Since those claspings cared for so
      Ever so long ago!

Though not now as when you freshly knew me,
      But a fading form,
Shape the kiss you'd briskly blow up to me
      While our love was warm,
    And my cheek unstained by tears,
      As in these last years!

LAST WEEK IN OCTOBER

THE trees are undressing, and fling in many places—
On the gray road, the roof, the window-sill—
Their radiant robes and ribbons and yellow laces;
A leaf each second so is flung at will,
Here, there, another and another, still and still.

A spider's web has caught one while downcoming,
That stays there dangling when the rest pass on;
Like a suspended criminal hangs he, mumming
In golden garb, while one yet green, high yon,
Trembles, as fearing such a fate for himself anon.

COME NOT; YET COME!

(SONG)

IN my sage moments I can say,
    Come not near,
But far in foreign regions stay,
    So that here
A mind may grow again serene and clear.

But the thought withers. Why should I
    Have fear to earn me
Fame from your nearness, though thereby
    Old fires new burn me,
And lastly, maybe, tear and overturn me!

So I say, Come: deign again shine
    Upon this place,
Even if unslackened smart be mine
    From that sweet face,
And I faint to a phantom past all trace.

THE LATER AUTUMN

GONE are the lovers, under the bush
      Stretched at their ease;
      Gone the bees,
Tangling themselves in your hair as they rush
      On the line of your track,
      Leg-laden, back
      With a dip to their hive
      In a prepossessed dive.

Toadsmeat is mangy, frosted, and sere;
      Apples in grass
      Crunch as we pass,
And rot ere the men who make cyder appear.
      Couch-fires abound
      On fallows around,
      And shades far extend
      Like lives soon to end.

Spinning leaves join the remains shrunk and brown
      Of last year's display
      That lie wasting away,
On whose corpses they earlier as scorners gazed down
      From their aery green height:
      Now in the same plight
      They huddle; while yon
      A robin looks on.

"LET ME"

(SONG)

LET me believe it, dearest,
      Let it be
As just a dream—the merest—
      Haunting me,

That a frank full-souled sweetness
    Warmed your smile
And voice, to indiscreetness
    Once, awhile!

And I will fondly ponder
    Till I lie
Earthed up with others yonder
    Past a sigh,
That you may name at stray times
    With regret
One whom through green and gray times
    You forget!

AT A FASHIONABLE DINNER

WE sat with the banqueting-party
    By the table-end—
Unmarked,—no diners out
    Were we: scarce a friend
    Of our own mind's trend
Was there, though the welcome was hearty.
    Then we noticed a shade extend
    By a distant screen,
And I said: "What to you does it seem to mean,
        Lavine?"

"—It is like my own body lying
    Beyond the door
Where the servants glide in and about
    The carpeted floor;
    And it means my death hour!—"
"—What a fancy! Who feels like dying
    While these smart sallies pour,
    With laughter between!
To me it is more like satin sheen,
        Lavine."

"—That means your new bride, when you win her:
>   Yes, so it must be!
It's her satin dress, no doubt—
>   That shine you see—
>   My own corpse to me!"
And a gloom came over the dinner,
>   Where almost strangers were we,
>   As the spirit of the scene
Forsook her—the fairest of the whole thirteen—
>   Lavine!

GREEN SLATES

(PENPETHY)

IT happened once, before the duller
>   Loomings of life defined them,
I searched for slates of greenish colour
>   A quarry where men mined them;

And saw, the while I peered around there,
>   In the quarry standing
A form against the slate background there,
>   Of fairness eye-commanding.

And now, though fifty years have flown me,
>   With all their dreams and duties,
And strange-pipped dice my hand has thrown me
>   And dust are all her beauties,

Green slates—seen high on roofs, or lower
>   In waggon, truck, or lorry—
Cry out: "Our home was where you saw her
>   Standing in the quarry!"

AN EAST-END CURATE

A SMALL blind street off East Commercial Road;
>   Window, door; window, door;
>   Every house like the one before,

Is where the curate, Mr. Dowle, has found a pinched abode.
Spectacled, pale, moustache straw-coloured, and with a long
    thin face,
Day or dark his lodgings' narrow doorstep does he pace.

A bleached pianoforte, with its drawn silk plaitings faded,
Stands in his room, its keys much yellowed, cyphering, and
    abraded,
"Novello's Anthems" lie at hand, and also a few glees,
And "Laws of Heaven for Earth" in a frame upon the wall
    one sees.

He goes through his neighbours' houses as his own, and none
    regards,
And opens their back-doors off-hand, to look for them in their
    yards:
A man is threatening his wife on the other side of the wall,
But the curate lets it pass as knowing the history of it all.

Freely within his hearing the children skip and laugh and say:
    "There's Mister Dow-well! There's Mister Dow-well!"
        in their play;
    And the long, pallid, devoted face notes not,
But stoops along abstractedly, for good, or in vain, God wot!

AT RUSHY-POND

    On the frigid face of the heath-hemmed pond
        There shaped the half-grown moon:
    Winged whiffs from the north with a husky croon
        Blew over and beyond.

    And the wind flapped the moon in its float on the pool,
        And stretched it to oval form;
    Then corkscrewed it like a wriggling worm:
        Then wanned it weariful.

And I cared not for conning the sky above
    Where hung the substant thing,
For my thought was earthward sojourning
    On the scene I had vision of.

Since there it was once, in a secret year,
    I had called a woman to me
From across this water, ardently—
    And practised to keep her near;

Till the last weak love-words had been said,
    And ended was her time,
And blurred the bloomage of her prime,
    And white the earlier red.

And the troubled orb in the pond's sad shine
    Was her very wraith, as scanned
When she withdrew thence, mirrored, and
    Her days dropped out of mine.

FOUR IN THE MORNING

At four this day of June I rise:
The dawn-light strengthens steadily;
Earth is a cerule mystery,
As if not far from Paradise
    At four o'clock,

Or else in the Great Nebula,
Or where the Pleiads blink and smile:
(For though we see with eyes of guile
The grisly grin of things by day,
    At four o'clock

They show their best.) . . . In this vale's space
I am up the first, I think. Yet, no,
A whistling? and the to-and-fro
Wheezed whettings of a scythe apace
    At four o'clock? . . .

—Though pleasure spurred, I rose with irk:
Here is one at compulsion's whip
Taking his life's stern stewardship
With blithe uncare, and hard at work
      At four o'clock!

BOCKHAMPTON.

ON THE ESPLANADE

MIDSUMMER: 10 P.M.

THE broad bald moon edged up where the sea was wide,
    Mild, mellow-faced;
Beneath, a tumbling twinkle of shines, like dyed,
    A trackway traced
To the shore, as of petals fallen from a rose to waste,
    In its overblow,
And fluttering afloat on inward heaves of the tide:—
All this, so plain; yet the rest I did not know.

The horizon gets lost in a mist new-wrought by the night:
    The lamps of the Bay
That reach from behind me round to the left and right
    On the sea-wall way
For a constant mile of curve, make a long display
    As a pearl-strung row,
Under which in the waves they bore their gimlets of light:—
All this was plain; but there was a thing not so.

Inside a window, open, with undrawn blind,
    There plays and sings
A lady unseen a melody undefined:
    And where the moon flings
Its shimmer a vessel crosses, whereon to the strings
    Plucked sweetly and low
Of a harp, they dance. Yea, such did I mark. That, behind,
My Fate's masked face crept near me I did not know!

IN ST. PAUL'S A WHILE AGO

SUMMER and winter close commune
On this July afternoon
As I enter chilly Paul's,
With its chasmal classic walls.
—Drifts of gray illumination
From the lofty fenestration
Slant them down in bristling spines that spread
Fan-like upon the vast dust-moted shade.

Moveless here, no whit allied
To the daemonian din outside,
Statues stand, cadaverous, wan,
Round the loiterers looking on
Under the yawning dome and nave,
Pondering whatnot, giddy or grave.
Here a verger moves a chair,
Or a red rope fixes there:—
A brimming Hebe, rapt in her adorning,
Brushes an Artemisia craped in mourning;

Beatrice Benedick piques, coquetting;
All unknowing or forgetting
That strange Jew, Damascus-bound,
Whose name, thereafter travelling round
To this precinct of the world,
Spread here like a flag unfurled:
Anon inspiring architectural sages
To frame this pile, writ his throughout the ages:
Whence also the encircling mart
Assumed his name, of him no part,
And to his vision-seeing mind
Charmless, blank in every kind;
And whose displays, even had they called his eye,
No gold or silver had been his to buy;

Whose haunters, had they seen him stand
On his own steps here, lift his hand
In stress of eager, stammering speech,
And his meaning chanced to reach,
Would have proclaimed him as they passed
An epilept enthusiast.

COMING UP OXFORD STREET: EVENING

THE sun from the west glares back,
And the sun from the watered track,
And the sun from the sheets of glass,
And the sun from each window-brass;
Sun-mirrorings, too, brighten
From show-cases beneath
The laughing eyes and teeth
Of ladies who rouge and whiten.
And the same warm god explores
Panels and chinks of doors;
Problems with chymists' bottles
Profound as Aristotle's
He solves, and with good cause,
Having been ere man was.

Also he dazzles the pupils of one who walks west,
A city-clerk, with eyesight not of the best,
Who sees no escape to the very verge of his days
From the rut of Oxford Street into open ways;
And he goes along with head and eyes flagging forlorn,
Empty of interest in things, and wondering why he was born.

As seen July 4, 1872.

A LAST JOURNEY

'FATHER, you seem to have been sleeping fair?"
The child uncovered the dimity-curtained window-square
And looked out at the dawn,

And back at the dying man nigh gone,
    And propped up in his chair,
Whose breathing a robin's "chink" took up in antiphon.

    The open fireplace spread
    Like a vast weary yawn above his head,
Its thin blue blower waved against his whitening crown,
    For he could not lie down:
He raised him on his arms so emaciated:—

"Yes; I've slept long, my child.   But as for rest,
    Well, that I cannot say.
The whole night have I footed field and turnpike-way—
    A regular pilgrimage—as at my best
    And very briskest day!

" 'Twas first to Weatherb'ry, to see them there,
    And thence to King's-Stag, where
I joined in a jolly trip to Weydon-Priors Fair:
    I shot for nuts, bought gingerbreads, cream-cheese;
    And, not content with these,
I went to London: heard the watchmen cry the hours.

"I soon was off again, and found me in the bowers
    Of father's apple-trees,
And he shook the apples down: they fell in showers,
Whereon he turned, smiled strange at me, as ill at ease;
    And then you pulled the curtain; and, ah me,
I found me back where I wished not to be!"

'Twas told the child next day: "Your father's dead."
    And, struck, she questioned, "O,
That journey, then, did father really go?—
Buy nuts, and cakes, and travel at night till dawn was red,
    And tire himself with journeying, as he said,
    To see those old friends that he cared for so?"

SINGING LOVERS

I ROWED: the dimpled tide was at the turn,
And mirth and moonlight spread upon the bay:
There were two singing lovers in the stern;
    But mine had gone away,—
    Whither, I shunned to say!

The houses stood confronting us afar,
A livid line against the evening glare;
The small lamps livened; then out-stole a star;
    But my Love was not there,—
    Vanished, I sorrowed where!

His arm was round her, both full facing me
With no reserve.   Theirs was not love to hide;
He held one tiller-rope, the other she;
    I pulled—the merest glide,—
    Looked on at them, and sighed.

The moon's glassed glory heaved as we lay swinging
Upon the undulations. Shoreward, slow,
The plash of pebbles joined the lovers' singing,
    But she of a bygone vow
    Joined in the song not now!

    WEYMOUTH.

THE MONTH'S CALENDAR

    TEAR off the calendar
    Of this month past,
    And all its weeks, that are
    Flown, to be cast
    To oblivion fast!

Darken that day
On which we met,
With its words of gay
Half-felt regret
That you'll forget!

The second day, too;
The noon I nursed
Well—thoughts; yes, through
To the thirty-first;
That was the worst.

For then it was
You let me see
There was good cause
Why you could not be
Aught ever to me!

A SPELLBOUND PALACE

(HAMPTON COURT)

ON this kindly yellow day of mild low-travelling winter sun
    The stirless depths of the yews
    Are vague with misty blues:
Across the spacious pathways stretching spires of shadow run,
And the wind-gnawed walls of ancient brick are fired vermilion

    Two or three early sanguine finches tune
   Some tentative strains, to be enlarged by May or June:
    From a thrush or blackbird
    Comes now and then a word,
While an enfeebled fountain somewhere within is heard.

    Our footsteps wait awhile,
    Then draw beneath the pile,
    When an inner court outspreads
    As 'twere History's own aisle,

Where the now-visioned fountain its attenuate crystal sheds
In passive lapse that seems to ignore the yon world's clamorous
    clutch,
And lays an insistent stillness on the place, like a cold hand's
    touch.

And there swaggers the Shade of a straddling King, plumed,
    sworded, with sensual face,
And lo, too, that of his Minister, at a bold self-centred pace:
Sheer in the sun they pass; and thereupon all is still,
Save the mindless fountain tinkling on with thin enfeebled will.

WHEN DEAD

TO ——

IT will be much better when
    I am under the bough;
I shall be more myself, Dear, then,
    Than I am now.

No sign of querulousness
    To wear you out
Shall I show there: strivings and stress
    Be quite without.

This fleeting life-brief blight
    Will have gone past
When I resume my old and right
    Place in the Vast.

And when you come to me
    To show you true,
Doubt not I shall infallibly
    Be waiting you.

SINE PROLE

(MEDIAEVAL LATIN SEQUENCE METRE)

FORTH from ages thick in mystery,
Through the morn and noon of history,
    To the moment where I stand
As my line wound; I the last one—
Outcome of each spectral past one
    Of that file, so many-manned!

Nothing in its time-trail marred it:
As one long life I regard it
    Throughout all the years till now,
When it fain—the close seen coming—
After annals past all plumbing—
    Makes to Being its parting bow.

Unlike Jahveh's ancient nation,
Little in their line's cessation
    Moderns see for surge of sighs:
They have been schooled by lengthier vision,
View Life's lottery with misprision,
    And its dice that fling no prize!

TEN YEARS SINCE

'TIS ten years since
I saw her on the stairs,
    Heard her in house-affairs,
    And listened to her cares;
And the trees are ten feet taller,
And the sunny spaces smaller
Whose bloomage would enthrall her;
And the piano wires are rustier,
The smell of bindings mustier,
And lofts and lumber dustier

Than when, with casual look
And ear, light note I took
Of what shut like a book
    Those ten years since!

November, 1922.

EVERY ARTEMISIA

"YOUR eye-light wanes with an ail of care,
Frets freeze gray your face and hair."

    "I was the woman who met him,
        Then cool and keen,
            Whiling away
Time, with its restless scene on scene
            Every day."

"Your features fashion as in a dream
Of things that were, or used to seem."

    "I was the woman who won him:
        Steadfast and fond
            Was he, while I
Tepidly took what he gave, nor conned
        Wherefore or why."

"Your house looks blistered by a curse,
As if a wraith ruled there, or worse."

    "I was the woman who slighted him:
        Far from my town
            Into the night
He went. . . . My hair, then auburn-brown,
        Pangs have wanned white."

"Your ways reflect a monstrous gloom;
Your voice speaks from within a tomb."

"I was the woman who buried him:
  My misery
  God laughed to scorn:
The people said: ' 'Twere well if she
    Had not been born!' "

"You plod to pile a monument
So madly that your breath is spent."

  "I am the woman who god him:
    I build, to ease
    My scalding fires,
A temple topping the Deities'
    Fanes of my sires."

THE BEST SHE COULD

  NINE leaves a minute
  Swim down shakily;
  Each one fain would spin it
  Straight to earth; but, see,
  How the sharp airs win it
Slantwise away!—Hear it say,
"Now we have finished our summer show
Of what we knew the way to do:
Alas, not much!   But, as things go,
As fair as any.   And night-time calls,
    And the curtain falls!"

  Sunlight goes on shining
  As if no frost were here,
  Blackbirds seem designing
  Where to build next year;
  Yet is warmth declining:

And still the day seems to say,
"Saw you how Dame Summer drest?
Of all God taught her she bethought her!
Alas, not much! And yet the best
She could, within the too short time
        Granted her prime."

November, 1923.

THE GRAVEYARD OF DEAD CREEDS

I LIT upon the graveyard of dead creeds
In wistful wanderings through old wastes of thought,
Where bristled fennish fungi, fruiting nought,
Amid the sepulchres begirt with weeds,

Which stone by stone recorded sanct, deceased
Catholicons that had, in centuries flown,
Physicked created man through his long groan,
Ere they went under, all their potence ceased.

When in a breath-while, lo, their spectres rose
Like wakened winds that autumn summons up:—
"Out of us cometh an heir, that shall disclose
New promise!" cried they.   "And the caustic cup

We ignorantly upheld to men, be filled
With draughts more pure than those we ever distilled,
That shall make tolerable to sentient seers
The melancholy marching of the years."

"THERE SEEMED A STRANGENESS"

A PHANTASY

THERE seemed a strangeness in the air,
Vermilion light on the land's lean face;
I heard a Voice from I knew not where:—
"The Great Adjustment is taking place!

"I set thick darkness over you,
And fogged you all your years therein;
    At last I uncloud your view,
Which I am weary of holding in.

"Men have not heard, men have not seen
Since the beginning of the world
        What earth and heaven mean;
But now their curtains shall be furled,

"And they shall see what is, ere long,
Not through a glass, but face to face;
And Right shall disestablish Wrong:
The Great Adjustment is taking place."

A NIGHT OF QUESTIONINGS

On the eve of All-Souls' Day
I heard the dead men say
Who lie by the tottering tower,
To the dark and doubling wind
At the midnight's turning hour,
When other speech had thinned:
        "What of the world now?"
The wind whiffed back: "Men still
Who are born, do good, do ill
Here, just as in your time:
Till their years the locust hath eaten,
Leaving them bare, downbeaten;
Somewhiles in springtide rime,
Somewhiles in summer glow,
Somewhiles in winter snow:—
        No more I know."

The same eve I caught cry
To the selfsame wind, those dry
As dust beneath the aisles
Of old cathedral piles,

Walled up in vaulted biers
Through many Christian years:
   "What of the world now?"
Sighed back the circuiteer:
"Men since your time, shrined here
By deserved ordinance,
Their own craft, or by chance,
Which follows men from birth
Even until under earth,
But little difference show
When ranged in sculptured row,
Different as dyes although:—
     No more I know."

On the selfsame eve, too, said
Those swayed in the sunk sea-bed
To the selfsame wind as it played
With the tide in the starless shade
From Comorin to Horn,
And round by Wrath forlorn:
   "What of the world now?"
And the wind for a second ceased,
Then whirred: "Men west and east,
As each sun soars and dips,
Go down to the sea in ships
As you went—hither and thither;
See the wonders of the deep,
As you did, ere they sleep;
But few at home care whither
They wander to and fro;
Themselves care little also!—
     No more I know."

Said, too, on the selfsame eve
The troubled skulls that heave
And fust in the flats of France,
To the wind wayfaring over
Listlessly as in trance

From the Ardennes to Dover,
 "What of the world now?"
And the farer moaned: "As when
You mauled these fields, do men
Set them with dark-drawn breaths
To knave their neighbours' deaths
In periodic spasms!
Yea, fooled by foul phantasms,
In a strange cyclic throe
Backward to type they go:—
 No more I know."

That night, too, men whose crimes
Had cut them off betimes,
Who lay within the pales
Of town and county jails
With the rope-groove on them yet,
Said to the same wind's fret
 "What of the world now?"
And the blast in its brooding tone
Returned: "Men have not shown,
Since you were stretched that morning,
A white cap your adorning,
More lovely deeds or true
Through thus neck-knotting you;
Or that they purer grow,
Or ever will, I trow!—
 No more I know."

XENOPHANES, THE MONIST OF COLOPHON

ANN: AET: SUAE XCII.—A: C: CCCCLXXX

"ARE You groping Your way?
Do You do it unknowing?—
Or mark Your wind blowing?

Night tell You from day,
O Mover?   Come, say!"
    Cried Xenophanes.

"I mean, querying so,
Do You do it aware,
Or by rote, like a player,
Or in ignorance, nor care
Whether doing or no?"
    Pressed Xenophanes.

"Thus strive I to plumb
Your depths, O Great Dumb!—
Not a god, but the All
(As I read); yet a thrall
To a blind ritual,"
    Sighed Xenophanes.

"If I only could bring
You to own it, close Thing,
I would write it again
With a still stronger pen
To my once neighbour-men!"
    Said Xenophanes.

—Quoth the listening Years:
"You ask It in vain;
You waste sighs and tears
On these callings inane,
Which It grasps not nor hears,
    O Xenophanes!"

"When you penned what you thought
You were cast out, and sought
A retreat over sea
From aroused enmity:
So it always will be,
    Yea, Xenophanes!

"In the lone of the nights
At Elea unseen,
Where the swinging wave smites
Of the restless Tyrrhene,
You may muse thus, serene,
    Safe, Xenophanes.

"But write it not back
To your dear Colophon;
Brows still will be black
At your words, 'All is One,'
From disputers thereon,
    Know, Xenophanes.

"Three thousand years hence,
Men who hazard a clue
To this riddle immense,
And still treat it as new,
Will be scowled at, like you,
    O Xenophanes!

"'*Some day I may tell,
When I've broken My spell*,'
It snores in Its sleep
If you listen long, deep
At Its closely-sealed cell,
    Wronged Xenophanes!

"Yea, on, near the end,
Its doings may mend;
Aye, when you're forgotten,
And old cults are rotten,
And bulky codes shotten,
    Xenophanes!"

1921.

LIFE AND DEATH AT SUNRISE

(NEAR DOGBURY GATE, 1867)

THE hills uncap their tops
Of woodland, pasture, copse,
And look on the layers of mist
At their foot that still persist:
They are like awakened sleepers on one elbow lifted,
Who gaze around to learn if things during night have shifted.

A waggon creaks up from the fog
With a laboured leisurely jog;
Then a horseman from off the hill-tip
Comes clapping down into the dip;
While woodlarks, finches, sparrows, try to entune at one time,
And cocks and hens and cows and bulls take up the chime.

With a shouldered basket and flagon
A man meets the one with the waggon,
And both the men halt of long use.
"Well," the waggoner says, "what's the news?"
—'Tis a boy this time. You've just met the doctor trotting
back.
he's doing very well. And we think we shall call him 'Jack.'

"And what have you got covered there?"
He nods to the waggon and mare.
"Oh, a coffin for old John Thinn:
We are just going to put him in."
—So he's gone at last. He always had a good constitution."
—He was ninety-odd. He could call up the French Revolution."

NIGHT-TIME IN MID-FALL

IT is a storm-strid night, winds footing swift
Through the blind profound;
I know the happenings from their sound;

Leaves totter down still green, and spin and drift;
The tree-trunks rock to their roots, which wrench and lif
The loam where they run onward underground.

The streams are muddy and swollen; eels migrate
    To a new abode;
  Even cross, 'tis said, the turnpike-road;
(Men's feet have felt their crawl, home-coming late):
The westward fronts of towers are saturate,
Church-timbers crack, and witches ride abroad.

A SHEEP FAIR

The day arrives of the autumn fair,
    And torrents fall,
Though sheep in throngs are gathered there,
    Ten thousand all,
Sodden, with hurdles round them reared:
And, lot by lot, the pens are cleared,
And the auctioneer wrings out his beard,
And wipes his book, bedrenched and smeared,
And rakes the rain from his face with the edge of his hand,
    As torrents fall.

The wool of the ewes is like a sponge
    With the daylong rain:
Jammed tight, to turn, or lie, or lunge,
    They strive in vain.
Their horns are soft as finger-nails,
Their shepherds reek against the rails,
The tied dogs soak with tucked-in tails,
The buyers' hat-brims fill like pails,
Which spill small cascades when they shift their stand
    In the daylong rain.

POSTSCRIPT

Time has trailed lengthily since met
    At Pummery Fair
Those panting thousands in their wet
    And woolly wear:
And every flock long since has bled,
And all the dripping buyers have sped,
And the hoarse auctioneer is dead,
Who "Going—going!" so often said,
As he consigned to doom each meek, mewed band
    At Pummery Fair.

SNOW IN THE SUBURBS

EVERY branch big with it,
    Bent every twig with it;
Every fork like a white web-foot;
Every street and pavement mute:
Some flakes have lost their way, and grope back upward, when
Meeting those meandering down they turn and descend again.
    The palings are glued together like a wall,
    And there is no waft of wind with the fleecy fall.

    A sparrow enters the tree,
    Whereon immediately
A snow-lump thrice his own slight size
Descends on him and showers his head and eyes,
    And overturns him,
    And near inurns him,
And lights on a nether twig, when its brush
Starts off a volley of other lodging lumps with a rush.

    The steps are a blanched slope,
    Up which, with feeble hope,
A black cat comes, wide-eyed and thin;
    And we take him in.

A LIGHT SNOW-FALL AFTER FROST

On the flat road a man at last appears:
    How much his whitening hairs
Owe to the settling snow's mute anchorage,
And how much to a life's rough pilgrimage,
      One cannot certify.

    The frost is on the wane,
And cobwebs hanging close outside the pane
Pose as festoons of thick white worsted there,
Of their pale presence no eye being aware
      Till the rime made them plain.

    A second man comes by;
His ruddy beard brings fire to the pallid scene:
    His coat is faded green;
    Hence seems it that his mien
    Wears something of the dye
Of the berried holm-trees that he passes nigh.

The snow-feathers so gently swoop that though
    But half an hour ago
The road was brown, and now is starkly white,
A watcher would have failed defining quite
    When it transformed it so.

NEAR SURBITON.

WINTER NIGHT IN WOODLAND

(OLD TIME)

The bark of a fox rings, sonorous and long:—
Three barks, and then silentness; "wong, wong, wong!"
In quality horn-like, yet melancholy,
    As from teachings of years; for an old one is he.
The hand of all men is against him, he knows; and yet, why?
That he knows not,—will never know, down to his death-halloo
    cry.

With clap-nets and lanterns off start the bird-baiters.
In trim to make raids on the roosts in the copse,
Where they beat the boughs artfully, while their awaiters
Grow heavy at home over divers warm drops.
The poachers, with swingels, and matches of brimstone, outcreep
To steal upon pheasants and drowse them a-perch and asleep.

Out there, on the verge, where a path wavers through,
Dark figures, filed singly, thrid quickly the view,
Yet heavily laden: land-carriers are they
In the hire of the smugglers from some nearest bay.
Each bears his two "tubs," slung across, one in front, one behind,
To a further snug hiding, which none but themselves are to find.

And then, when the night has turned twelve the air brings
From dim distance, a rhythm of voices and strings:
'Tis the quire, just afoot on their long yearly rounds,
To rouse by worn carols each house in their bounds;
Robert Penny, the Deweys, Mail, Voss, and the rest; till anon
Tired and thirsty, but cheerful, they home to their beds in the
        dawn.

ICE ON THE HIGHWAY

SEVEN buxom women abreast, and arm in arm,
        Trudge down the hill, tip-toed,
                And breathing warm;
They must perforce trudge thus, to keep upright
        On the glassy ice-bound road,
And they must get to market whether or no,
        Provisions running low
        With the nearing Saturday night,
While the lumbering van wherein they mostly ride
                Can nowise go:
Yet loud their laughter as they stagger and slide!

        YELL'HAM HILL.

MUSIC IN A SNOWY STREET

THE weather is sharp,
But the girls are unmoved:
One wakes from a harp,
The next from a viol
A strain that I loved
When life was no trial.

The tripletime beat
Bounds forth on the snow,
But the spry springing feet
Of a century ago,
And the arms that enlaced
As the couples embraced,
Are silent old bones
Under graying gravestones.

The snow-feathers sail
Across the harp-strings,
Whose throbbing threads wail
Like love-satiate things.
Each lyre's grimy mien,
With its rout-raising tune,
Against the new white
Of the flake-laden noon,
Is incongruous to sight,
Hinting years they have seen
Of revel at night
Ere these damsels became
Possessed of their frame.

O bygone whirls, heys,
Crotchets, quavers, the same
That were danced in the days
Of grim Bonaparte's fame,
Or even by the toes
Of the fair Antoinette,—

Yea, old notes like those
Here are living on yet!—
But of their fame and fashion
How little these know
Who strum without passion
For pence, in the snow!

THE FROZEN GREENHOUSE

(ST. JULIOT)

"THERE was a frost
Last night!" she said,
"And the stove was forgot
When we went to bed,
And the greenhouse plants
Are frozen dead!"

By the breakfast blaze
Blank-faced spoke she,
Her scared young look
Seeming to be
The very symbol
Of tragedy.

The frost is fiercer
Than then to-day,
As I pass the place
Of her once dismay,
But the greenhouse stands
Warm, tight, and gay,

While she who grieved
At the sad lot
Of her pretty plants—
Cold, iced, forgot—
Herself is colder,
And knows it not.

TWO LIPS

I KISSED them in fancy as I came
  Away in the morning glow:
I kissed them through the glass of her picture-frame:
  She did not know.

I kissed them in love, in troth, in laughter
  When she knew all; long so!
That I should kiss them in a shroud thereafter
  She did not know.

NO BUYERS

A STREET SCENE

A LOAD of brushes and baskets and cradles and chairs
  Labours along the street in the rain:
With it a man, a woman, a pony with whiteybrown hairs.—
  The man foots in front of the horse with a shambling sway
    At a slower tread than a funeral train,
  While to a dirge-like tune he chants his wares,
  Swinging a Turk's-head brush (in a drum-major's way
    When the bandsmen march and play).

A yard from the back of the man is the whiteybrown pony'
    nose:
He mirrors his master in every item of pace and pose:
  He stops when the man stops, without being told,
  And seems to be eased by a pause; too plainly he's old,
    Indeed, not strength enough shows
    To steer the disjointed waggon straight,
  Which wriggles left and right in a rambling line,
  Deflected thus by its own warp and weight,
  And pushing the pony with it in each incline.

The woman walks on the pavement verge,
　　Parallel to the man:
She wears an apron white and wide in span,
And carries a like Turk's-head, but more in nursing-wise:
　　Now and then she joins in his dirge,
　　But as if her thoughts were on distant things.
　　The rain clams her apron till it clings.—
So, step by step, they move with their merchandize,
　　And nobody buys.

ONE WHO MARRIED ABOVE HIM

" 'Tis you, I think? Back from your week's work, Steve?"
"It is I. Back from work this Christmas Eve."
"But you seem off again?—in this night-rime?"
"I am off again, and thoroughly off this time."
　　"What does that mean?"
　　"More than may first be seen . . .

"Half an hour ago I footed homeward here,
No wife found I, nor child, nor maid, indoors or near.
She has, as always, gone with them to her mother's at the
　　farm,
Where they fare better far than here, and, maybe, meet less
　　harm,
She's left no fire, no light, has cooked me nothing to eat,
Though she had fuel, and money to get some Christmas meat.
Christmas with them is grand, she knows, and brings good
　　victual,
Other than how it is here, where it's but lean and little.
　　But though not much, and rough,
　　If managed neat there's enough.
　　She and hers are too highmade for me;
　　But she's whimmed her once too often, she'll see!

Farmer Bollen's daughter should never have married a man
    that's poor;
And I can stand it no longer; I'm leaving; you'll see me no
    more, be sure."

"But nonsense: you'll be back again ere bedtime, and lighting a
    fire,
And sizzling your supper, and vexing not that her views of
    supper are higher."

"Never for me."

"Well, we shall see

The sceptical neighbour and Stephen then followed their fore-
    designed ways,
And their steps dimmed into white silence upon the slippery
    glaze;
And the trees went on with their spitting amid the icicled
    haze.

The evening whiled, and the wife with the babies came
    home,
But he was not there, nor all Christmas Day did he come.
Christmastide went, and likewise went the New Year.
    But no husband's footfall revived,
And month after month lapsed, graytime to green and to sere,
    And other new years arrived,
And the children grew up: one husbanded and one wived.—
    She wept and repented,
    But Stephen never relented.
And there stands the house, and the sycamore-tree and all,
With its roots forming steps for the passers who care to call,
And there are the mullioned windows, and Ham-Hill door,
Through which Steve's wife was brought out, but which Steve
    re-entered no more.

THE NEW TOY

She cannot leave it alone,
    The new toy;
She pats it, smooths it, rights it, to show it's her own,
As the other train-passengers muse on its temper and tone,
    Till she draws from it cries of annoy:—
She feigns to appear as if thinking it nothing so rare
    Or worthy of pride, to achieve
This wonder a child, though with reason the rest of them there
    May so be inclined to believe.

QUEEN CAROLINE TO HER GUESTS

Dear friends, stay!
Lamplit wafts of wit keep sorrow
In the purlieus of to-morrow:
    Dear friends, stay!

Haste not away!
Even now may Time be weaving
Tricks of ravage, wrack, bereaving,
    Haste not away!

Through the pane,
Lurking along the street, there may be
Heartwrings, keeping hid till day be,
    Through the pane.

Check their reign:
Since while here we are the masters,
And can barricade dim disasters:
    Check their reign!

Give no ear
To those ghosts withoutside mumming,
Mouthing, threatening, "We are coming!"
Give no ear!

Sheltered here
Care we not that next day bring us
Pains, perversions! No racks wring us
Sheltered here.

Homeward gone,
Sleep will slay this merrymaking;
No resuming it at waking,
Homeward gone.

After dawn
Something sad may be befalling;
Mood like ours there's no recalling
After dawn!

Morrow-day
Present joy that moments strengthen
May be past our power to lengthen,
Morrow-day!

Dear friends, stay!
Lamplit wafts of wit keep sorrow
In the limbo of to-morrow;
Dear friends, stay!

PLENA TIMORIS

THE lovers looked over the parapet-stone:
The moon in its southing directly blent
Its silver with their environment.
Her ear-rings twinkled; her teeth, too, shone
As, his arm around her, they laughed and leant.

PLENA TIMORIS

A man came up to them; then one more.
"There's a woman in the canal below,"
They said; climbed over; slid down; let go,
And a splashing was heard, till an arm upbore,
And a dripping body began to show.

"Drowned herself for love of a man,
Who at one time used to meet her here,
Until he grew tired. But she'd wait him near,
And hope, till hopeless despair began.
So much for love in this mortal sphere!"

The girl's heart shuddered; it seemed as to freeze her
That here, at their tryst for so many a day,
Another woman's tragedy lay.
Dim dreads of the future grew slowly to seize her,
And her arm dropt from his as they wandered away.

THE WEARY WALKER

A plain in front of me,
    And there's the road
Upon it. Wide country,
    And, too, the road!

Past the first ridge another,
    And still the road
Creeps on. Perhaps no other
    Ridge for the road?

Ah! Past that ridge a third,
    Which still the road
Has to climb furtherward—
    The thin white road!

Sky seems to end its track;
    But no. The road
Trails down the hill at the back.
    Ever the road!

LAST LOVE–WORD

(SONG)

THIS is the last; the very, very last!
  Anon, and all is dead and dumb,
  Only a pale shroud over the past,
    That cannot be
    Of value small or vast,
      Love, then to me!

I can say no more: I have even said too much.
  I did not mean that this should come:
  I did not know 'twould swell to such—
    Nor, perhaps, you—
    When that first look and touch,
      Love, doomed us two!

                189–.

NOBODY COMES

TREE-LEAVES labour up and down,
  And through them the fainting light
  Succumbs to the crawl of night.
Outside in the road the telegraph wire
  To the town from the darkening land
Intones to travellers like a spectral lyre
  Swept by a spectral hand.

A car comes up, with lamps full-glare,
  That flash upon a tree:
  It has nothing to do with me,
And whangs along in a world of its own,
  Leaving a blacker air;
And mute by the gate I stand again alone,
  And nobody pulls up there.

  October 9, 1924.

IN THE STREET

(SONG)

ONLY acquaintances
Seem do we,
Each of whom, meeting, says
Civilly
"Good morning."—Yes: thus we appear to be!

But far, near, left and right,
Here or there,
By day or dingiest night,
Everywhere
I see you: one incomparably fair!

So do we wend our ways,
Beautiful girl,
Along our parallel days;
While unfurl
Our futures, and what there may whelm and whirl.

THE LAST LEAF

"THE leaves throng thick above:—
Well, I'll come back, dear Love,
When they all are down!"

She watched that August tree,
(None now scorned summer as she),
Till it broidered it brown.

And then October came blowing,
And the leaves showed signs they were going,
And she saw up through them.

O how she counted them then!
—November left her but ten,
And started to strew them.

"Ah, when they all are gone,
And the skeleton-time comes on,
   Whom shall I see!"

—When the fifteenth spread its sky
That month, her upturned eye
   Could count but three.

And at the close of the week
A flush flapped over her cheek:
   The last one fell.

But—he did not come. And, at length,
Her hope of him lost all strength,
   And it was as a knell. . . .

When he did come again,
Years later, a husband then,
   Heavy somewhat,

With a smile she reminded him:
And he cried: "Ah, that vow of our whim!—
   Which I forgot,

"As one does!—And was that the tree?
So it was!—Dear me, dear me:
   Yes: I forgot."

AT WYNYARD'S GAP

SHE (*on horseback*)

THE hounds pass here?

HE (*on horseback*)

        They did an hour ago,
Just in full cry, and went down-wind, I saw,
Towards Pen Wood, where they may kill, and draw
A second time, and bear towards the Yeo.

She

How vexing! And I've crept along unthinking.

He

Ah!—lost in dreams. Fancy to fancy linking!

She (*more softly*)

Not that, quite. . . . Now, to settle what I'll do.

He

Go home again. But have you seen the view
From the top there? Not? It's really worth your while.—
You must dismount, because there is a stile.

*They dismount, hitch their horses, and climb a few-score yards
from the road.*

There you see half South Wessex,—combe, and glen,
And down, to Lewsdon Hill and Pilsdon Pen.

She

Yes. It is fine. And I, though living out there
By Crewkerne, never knew it. (*She turns her head*) Well, I
declare,
Look at the horses!—How shall I catch my mare?

The horses have got loose and scampered off.

Now that's your fault, through leading me up here!
You must have known 'twould happen—

He
No, my dear!

She

I'm not your dear.

He (*blandly*)
But you can't help being so,
If it comes to that. The fairest girl I've seen
Is of course dear—by her own fault, I mean.

SHE (*quickly*)

What house is that we see just down below?

HE

Oh—that's the inn called "Wynyard's Gap."—I'll go
While you wait here, and catch those brutes. Don't stir.

He goes. She waits.

SHE

What a handsome man. Not local, I'll aver.

He comes back.

HE

I met a farmer's labourer some way on;
He says he'll bring them to us here anon,
If possible before the day is dim.
Come down to the inn: there we can wait for him.

They descend slowly in that direction.

SHE

What a lonely inn. Why is there such a one?

HE

For us to wait at. Thus 'tis things are done.

SHE

Thus things are done? Well—what things do you mean?

HE

Romantic things. Meetings unknown, unseen.

SHE

But ours is accident, and needn't have been,
And isn't what I'd plan with a stranger, quite,
Particularly at this time—nearly night.

HE

or I. But still, the tavern's loneliness
favourable for lovers in distress,
hen they've eloped, for instance, and are in fear
f being pursued. No one would find them here.

He goes to speak to the labourer approaching; and returns.

e says the horses long have passed the combe,
nd cannot be overtaken. They'll go home.

SHE

nd what's to be done? And it's beginning to rain.
`is always so. One trouble brings a train!

HE

seems to me that here we'd better stay
nd rest us till some vehicle comes this way:
a fact, we might put up here till the morning:
he floods are high, and night-farers have warning.

SHE

ut up? Do you think so!

HE

I incline to such.
y *dear* (do you mind?)

SHE

Yes.—Well (*more softly*), I don't much,
I seem like it. But I ought to tell you
ne thing. I'm married. Being so, it's well you—

HE

h, so am I. (*A silence, he regarding her*) I note a charming
    thing—
ou stand so stock-still that your ear-ring shakes
t each pulsation which the vein there makes.

SHE

Does it? Perhaps because it's flustering
To be caught thus! (*In a murmur*) Why did we chance to meet
  here?

HE

God knows! Perhaps to taste a bitter-sweet here.—
Still, let us enter. Shelter we must get:
The night is darkening and is growing wet.
So, anyhow, you can treat me as a lover
Just for this once. To-morrow 'twill be over!

  They reach the inn. The door is locked, and they discern a
  board marked "To Let." While they stand stultified a van
  is seen drawing near with passengers.

SHE

Ah, here's an end of it! The Crewkerne carrier.

HE

So cynic circumstance erects its barrier!

SHE (*mischievously*)

To your love-making, which would have grown stronger,
No doubt, if we had stayed on here much longer?

  The carrier comes up. Her companion reluctantly hails him.

HE

Yes. . . . And in which you might have shown some ruth
Had but the inn been open!—Well, forsooth,
I'm sorry it's not. Are you? Now, dear, the truth!

SHE (*with gentle evasiveness*)

I am—almost. But best 'tis thus to be.
For—dear one—there I've said it!—you can see
That both at one inn (though roomed separately,
Of course)—so lone, too—might have been unfit,
Perfect as 'tis for lovers, I admit.

HE (*after a sigh*)

Carrier! A lift for my wife, pleas⸺

SHE (*in quick undertones*)

Wife? But nay⸺

HE (*continuing*)

Her horse has thrown her and has gone astray:
See she gets safe to Crewkerne. I've to stay.

CARRIER

I will, sir! I'm for Crookhorn straight away.

HE (*to her, aloud*)

Right now, dear. I shall soon be home. Adieu! (*Kisses her*).

SHE (*whispering confusedly*)

You shouldn't! Pretending you are my husband, too!
I now must act the part of wife to you!

HE (*whispering*)

Yes, since I've kissed you, dear. You see it's done
To silence tongues as we're found here alone
At night, by gossipers, and seem as shown
Staying together!

SHE (*whispering*)

Then must I, too, kiss?

HE

Yes; a mere matter of form you know,
To check all scandal. People will talk so!

SHE

'd no idea it would reach to this!

(*Kisses him*)

What makes it worse is, I'm ashamed to say,
've a young baby waiting me at home!

He

Ah—there you beat me!—But, my dearest, play
The wife to the end, and don't give me away,
Despite the baby, since we've got so far,
And what we've acted feel we almost are!

She (*sighing*)

Yes. 'Tis so! And my conscience has gone dumb!

(*Aloud*)

'Bye, dear, awhile! I'll sit up till you come.

(*In a whisper*)

Which means Good-bye for ever, truly heard!
Upon to-night be silent!

He

Never a word,
Till Pilsdon Pen by Marshwood wind is stirred!
He hands her up. Exeunt omnes.

AT SHAG'S HEATH, 1685

(TRADITIONAL)

I GRIEVE and grieve for what I have done,
And nothing now is left to me
But straight to drown; yea, I have slain
The rarest soul the world shall see!
—My husband said: "Now thou art wed
Thou must beware! And should a man
Cajole, mind, he means ill to thee,
Depend on't: fool him if ye can!"
   But 'twas King Monmouth, he!

As truth I took what was not true:
Till darked my door just such a one.
He asked me but the way to go,
Though looking all so down and done.
And as he stood he said, unsued,
"The prettiest wife I've eyed to-day!"
And then he kissed me tenderly
Before he footed fast away
    Did dear King Monmouth, he!

Builded was he so beautiful!—
Why did I pout a pettish word
For what he'd done?—Then whisking off—
For his pursuers' feet were heard—
"Dear one, keep faith!" he turns and saith,
And next he vanished in the copse
Before I knew what such might be,
And how great fears and how great hopes
    Had rare King Monmouth—he!

Up rode the soldiers. "Where's this man?—
He is the rebel Duke," say they.
"And calls himself King Monmouth, sure!"
Then I believed my husband; aye,
Though he'd spoke lies in jealous-wise!
—To Shag's nigh copse beyond the road
I moved my finger mercilessly;
And there lay hidden where I showed:
    My dear King Monmouth, he!

The soldiers brought him by my door,
His elbows bound behind him, fast;
Passing, he me-ward cast his eyes—
What eyes of beauty did he cast!
Grieved was his glance at me askance:
"I wished all weal might thee attend,
But this is what th'st done to me,
O heartless woman, held my friend!"
    Said sweet King Monmouth, he!

O then I saw he was no hind,
But a great lord of loftihood,
Come here to claim his rule and rights,
Who'd wished me, as he'd said, but good.—
With tug and jolt, then, out to Holt,
To Justice Ettricke, he was led,
And thence to London speedily,
Where under yester's headsman bled
     The rare King Monmouth, he!

Last night, the while my husband slept,
He rose up at the window there,
All blood and blear, and hacked about,
With heavy eyes, and rumpled hair;
And said: "My Love, 'twas cruel of
A Fair like thee to use me so!
But now it's nought: from foes I'm free!
Sooner or later all must go,"
     Said dear King Monmouth, he!

"Yes, lovely cruel one!" he said
In through the mullioned pane, shroud-pale,
"I love you still, would kiss you now,
But blood would stain your nighty-rail!"
—That's all. And so to drown I go:
O wear no weeds, my friends, for me . . .
When comes the waterman, he'll say,
"Who's done her thuswise?"—'Twill be, yea,
     Sweet, slain King Monmouth—he!

A SECOND ATTEMPT

THIRTY years after
I began again
An old-time passion:
And it seemed as fresh as when
The first day ventured on:

When mutely I would waft her
In Love's past fashion
Dreams much dwelt upon,
Dreams I wished she knew.

I went the course through,
From Love's fresh-found sensation—
Remembered still so well—
To worn words charged anew,
That left no more to tell:
Thence to hot hopes and fears,
And thence to consummation,
And thence to sober years,
Markless, and mellow-hued.

Firm the whole fabric stood,
Or seemed to stand, and sound
As it had stood before.
But nothing backward climbs,
And when I looked around
As at the former times,
There was Life—pale and hoar:
And slow it said to me,
"Twice-over cannot be!"

"FREED THE FRET OF THINKING"

FREED the fret of thinking,
    Light of lot were we,
Song with service linking
    Like to bird or bee:
Chancing bale unblinking,
Freed the fret of thinking
    On mortality!

Had not thought-endowment
    Beings ever known,
What Life once or now meant

None had wanted shown—
Measuring but the moment—
Had not thought-endowment
Caught Creation's groan!

Loosed from wrings of reason,
    We might blow like flowers,
Sense of Time-wrought treason
    Would not then be ours
In and out of season;
Loosed from wrings of reason
    We should laud the Powers!

THE ABSOLUTE EXPLAINS

I

"O NO," said It; "her lifedoings
    Time's touch hath not destroyed:
They lie their length, with the throbbing things
    Akin them, down the Void,
        Live, unalloyed.

II

"Know, Time is toothless, seen all through;
    The Present, that men but see,
Is phasmal: since in a sane purview
    All things are shaped to be
        Eternally.

III

"Your 'Now' is just a gleam, a glide
    Across your gazing sense:
With me, 'Past,' 'Future,' ever abide:
    They come not, go not, whence
        They are never hence.

IV

"As one upon a dark highway,
　　Plodding by lantern-light,
Finds but the reach of its frail ray
　　Uncovered to his sight,
　　　　Though mid the night.

V

"The road lies all its length the same,
　　Forwardly as at rear,
So, outside what you 'Present' name,
　　Future and Past stand sheer
　　　　Cognate and clear "

VI

—Thus It: who straightway opened then
　　The vista called the Past,
Wherein were seen, as fair as when
　　They seemed they could not last,
　　　　Small things and vast.

VII

There were those songs, a score times sung,
　　With all their tripping tunes,
There were the laughters once that rung,
　　There those unmatched full moons,
　　　　Those idle noons!

VIII

There fadeless, fixed, were dust-dead flowers
　　Remaining still in blow;
Elsewhere, wild love-makings in bowers;
　　Hard by, that irised bow
　　　　Of years ago.

IX

There were my ever memorable
　　Glad days of pilgrimage,
Coiled like a precious parchment fell,
　　Illumined page by page.
　　　　Unhurt by age.

X

"—Here you see spread those mortal ails
　　So powerless to restrain
Your young life's eager hot assails,
　　With hazards then not plain
　　　　Till past their pain.

XI

"Here you see her who, by these laws
　　You learn of, still shines on,
As pleasing-pure as erst she was,
　　Though you think she lies yon,
　　　　Graved, glow all gone.

XII

"Here are those others you used to prize.—
　　But why go further we?
The Future?—Well, I would advise
　　You let the future be,
　　　　Unshown by me!

XIII

"'Twould harrow you to see undraped
　　The scenes in ripe array
That wait your globe—all worked and shaped;
　　And I'll not, as I say,
　　　　Bare them to-day.

XIV

"In fine, Time is a mock,—yea, such!—
    As he might well confess:
Yet hath he been believed in much,
    Though lately, under stress
        Of science, less.

XV

"And hence, of her you asked about
    At your first speaking: she
Hath, I assure you, not passed out
    Of continuity,
        But is in me.

XVI

"So thus doth Being's length transcend
    Time's ancient regal claim
To see all lengths begin and end.
    'The Fourth Dimension' fame
        Bruits as its name."

New Year's Eve, 1922.

"SO, TIME"

(The same thought resumed)

    So, Time,
        Royal, sublime;
Heretofore held to be
Master and enemy,
Thief of my Love's adornings,
Despoiling her to scornings:—
The sound philosopher
Now sets him to aver
    You are nought
    But a thought
Without reality.

Young, old
Passioned, cold,
All the loved-lost thus
Are beings continuous,
In dateless dure abiding,
Over the present striding
With placid permanence
That knows not transience:
Firm in the Vast,
First, last;
Afar, yet close to us.

AN INQUIRY

A PHANTASY

Circumdederunt me dolores mortis.—Ps. xviii.

I SAID to It: "We grasp not what you meant,
(Dwelling down here, so narrowly pinched and pent)
By crowning Death the King of the Firmament:
—The query I admit to be
One of unwonted size,
But it is put you sorrowingly,
And not in idle-wise."

"Sooth, since you ask me gravely," It replied,
"Though too incisive questions I have decried,
This shows some thought, and may be justified.
I'll gauge its value as I go
Across the Universe,
And bear me back in a moment or so
And say, for better or worse."

Many years later, when It came again,
"That matter an instant back which brought you pain,"
It said, "and you besought me to explain:

Well, my forethoughtless modes to you
        May seem a shameless thing,
But—I'd no meaning, that I knew,
        In crowning Death as King!"

THE FAITHFUL SWALLOW

WHEN summer shone
        Its sweetest on
        An August day,
        "Here evermore,"
I said, "I'll stay;
        Not go away
        To another shore
As fickle they!"

December came:
        'Twas not the same!
I did not know
        Fidelity
Would serve me so.
        Frost, hunger, snow;
And now, ah me,
        Too late to go!

IN SHERBORNE ABBEY

(17—)

THE moon has passed to the panes of the south-aisle wall,
And brought the mullioned shades and shines to fall
On the cheeks of a woman and man in a pew there, pressed
Together as they pant, and recline for rest.

Forms round them loom, recumbent like their own,
    Yet differing; for they are chiselled in frigid stone;
In doublets are some; some mailed, as whilom ahorse they leapt;
And stately husbands and wives, side by side as they anciently
        slept.

"We are not like those," she murmurs. "For ever here set!"
"True, Love," he replies. "We two are not marble yet."
    "And, worse," said she; "not husband and wife!"
    "But we soon shall be" (from him) "if we've life!"
A silence. A trotting of horses is heard without.
The lovers scarce breathe till its echo has quite died out.

    "It was they! They have passed, anyhow!"
    "Our horse, slily hid by the conduit,
    They've missed, or they'd rushed to impound it!"
    "And they'll not discover us now."
    "Will not, until 'tis too late,
    And we can outface them straight!"

"Why did you make me ride in your front?" says she.
"To outwit the law. That was my strategy.
    As I was borne off on the pillion behind you,
    Th'abductor was you, Dearest, let me remind you;
And seizure of me by an heiress is no felony,
Whatever to do it with me as the seizer may be."

Another silence falls. And a cloud comes over the moon:
The print of the panes upon them enfeebles, as fallen in a swoon,
    Until they are left in darkness unbroke and profound,
As likewise are left their chill and chiselled neighbours around.

    A family tradition.

THE PAIR HE SAW PASS

O SAD man, now a long dead man,
    To whom it was so real,
I picture, as 'twere yesterday,
    How you would tell the tale!

Just wived were you, you sad dead man,
　　And "settling down," you'd say,
And had rigged the house you had reared for yourself
　　And the mate now yours alway.

You had eyed and tried each door and lock,
　　And cupboard, and bell, and glass,
When you glanced across to the road without,
　　And saw a carriage pass.

It bowled along from the old town-gate;
　　Two forms its freight, and those
Were a just-joined pair, as you discerned
　　By the favours and the bows.

And one of the pair you saw was a Fair
　　Whom you had wooed awhile,
And the other you saw, with a creeping awe,
　　Was yourself, in bridegroom style.

"And there we rode as man and wife
　　In the broad blaze of the sun,"
Would you aver; yea, you with her
　　You had left for another one.

"The morning," you said, my friend long dead,
　　"Was ordinary and fine;
And yet there gleamed, it somehow seemed,
　　At moments, a strange shine."

You hailed a boy from your garden-plot,
　　And sent him along the way
To the parish church; whence word was brought
　　No marriage had been that day.

You mused, you said; till you heard anon
　　That at that hour she died
Whom once, instead of your living wife,
　　You had meant to make your bride. . . .

You, dead man, dwelt in your new-built house
   With no great spirit or will,
And after your soon decease your spouse
   Re-mated: she lives there still.

Which should be blamed, if either can,
   The teller does not know
For your mismatch, O weird-wed man,
   Or what you thought was so.

From an old draft.

THE MOCK WIFE

It's a dark drama, this, and yet I know the house, and date;
That is to say, the where and when John Channing met his fate.
The house was one in High Street, seen of burghers still alive.
The year was some two centuries bygone; seventeen-hundred
   and five.

And dying was Channing the grocer. All the clocks had struck
   eleven,
And the watchers saw that ere the dawn his soul would be in
   Heaven;
When he said on a sudden; "I should *like* to kiss her before
   I go,—
For one last time!" They looked at each other and murmured,
   "Even so."

She'd just been haled to prison, his wife; yea, charged with
   shaping his death:
By poison, 'twas told; and now he was nearing the moment of
   his last breath:
He, witless that his young housemate was suspect of such a
   crime,
Lay thinking that his pangs were but a malady of the time.

Outside the room they pondered gloomily, wondering what to do,
As still he craved her kiss—the dying man who nothing knew:
"Guilty she may not be," they said; "so why should we torture him
In these his last few minutes of life? Yet how indulge his whim?"

And as he begged there piteously for what could not be done,
And the murder-charge had flown about the town to every one,
The friends around him in their trouble thought of a hasty plan,
And straightway set about it. Let denounce them all who can.

"O will you do a kindly deed—it may be a soul to save;
At least, great misery to a man with one foot in the grave?"
Thus they to the buxom woman not unlike his prisoned wife;
"The difference he's past seeing; it will soothe his sinking life."

Well, the friendly neighbour did it; and he kissed her; held her fast;
Kissed her again and yet again. "I—knew she'd—come at last!—
Where have you been?—Ah, kept away!—I'm sorry—overtried—
God bless you!" And he loosed her, fell back tiredly, and died.

His wife stood six months after on the scaffold before the crowd,
Ten thousand of them gathered there; fixed, silent, and hard-browed,
To see her strangled and burnt to dust, as was the verdict then
On women truly judged, or false, of doing to death their men.

Some of them said as they watched her burn: "I am glad he never knew,
Since a few hold her as innocent—think such she could not do!
Glad, too, that (as they tell) he thought she kissed him ere he died."
And they seemed to make no question that the cheat was justified.

THE FIGHT ON DURNOVER MOOR

(183—)

WE'D loved, we two, some while,
And that had come which comes when men too much beguile;
 And without more ado
My lady said: "O shame! Get home, and hide!" But he was
 true.

Yes: he was true to me,
And helped me some miles homealong; and vowing to come
 Before the weeks were three,
And do in church a deed should strike all scandal dumb.

And when we had traipsed to Grey's great Bridge, and pitched
 my box
 On its cope, to breathe us there,
He cried: "What wrangle's that in yonder moor? Those knocks,
 Gad, seem not to be fair!"

"And a woman on her knees! . . . I'll go. . . . There's surely
 something wrong!"
I said: "You are tired and spent
With carrying my heavy things so far and long!"
 But he would go, and went.

And there I stood, steadying my box, and screened from none,
 Upon the crown of the bridge,
Ashamed o' my shape, as lower and lower slipped the sun
 Down behind Pummery Ridge. . . .

"O you may long wait so!
Your young man's done—aye, dead!" they by and by ran and
 cried.
 "You shouldn't have let him go
And join that whorage, but have kept him at your side!

"It was another wench,
Biggening as you, that he championed: yes, he came on straight
    With a warmth no words could quench
For her helpless face, as soon as ever he eyed her state,

"And fought her fancy-lad, who had used her far from well,
    So soon to make her moan,
Aye, closed with him in fight, till at a blow yours fell,
    His skull against a stone.

"She'd followed him there, this man who'd won her, and over-
      won,
    So, when he set to twit her
Yours couldn't abide him—him all other fighters shun,
    For he's a practised hitter.

"Your man moved not, and the constables came for the other;
      so he,
    He'll never make her his wife
Any more than yours will you; for they say that at least 'twill be
    Across the water for life."

    "O what has she brought about!"
I groaned: "this woman met here in my selfsame plight;
She's put another yielding heart's poor candle out
    By dogging her man to-night!

    "He might never have done her his due
Of amends! But mine had bidden the banns for marrying me!
Why did we rest on this bridge; why rush to a quarrel did he
    With which he had nothing to do!"

    But vain were bursts of blame:
We twain stood like and like, though strangers till that hour,
Foredoomed to tread our paths beneath like gaze and glower,
    Bear a like blushful name,

    Almost the selfsame day
It fell that her time and mine came on,—a lad and a lass:
The father o' mine was where the worms waggle under the grass,
    Of hers, at Botany Bay.

LAST LOOK ROUND ST. MARTIN'S FAIR

THE sun is like an open furnace door,
Whose round revealed retort contains the roar
    Of fires beyond terrene;
The moon presents the lustre-lacking face
Of a brass dial gone green,
    Whose hours no eye can trace.

The unsold heathcroppers are driven home
To the shades of the Great Forest whence they come
By men with long cord-waistcoats in brown monochrome.
The stars break out, and flicker in the breeze,
    It seems, that twitches the trees.—
    From its hot idol soon
The fickle unresting earth has turned to a fresh patroon—
    The cold, now brighter, moon.

The woman in red, at the nut-stall with the gun,
    Lights up, and still goes on:
She's redder in the flare-lamp than the sun
    Showed it ere it was gone.
Her hands are black with loading all the day,
And yet she treats her labour as 'twere play,
Tosses her ear-rings, and talks ribaldry
To the young men around as natural gaiety,
    And not a weary work she'd readily stay
And never again nut-shooting see,
    Though crying, "Fire away!"

THE CARICATURE

OF the Lady Lu there were stories told,
For she was a woman of comely mould,
    In heart-experience old.

Too many a man for her whimful sake
Had borne with patience chill and ache,
    And nightly lain awake!

This epicure in pangs, in her tooth
For more of the sweet, with a calm unruth
    Cast eyes on a painter-youth.

Her junior he; and the bait of bliss
Which she knew to throw—not he to miss—
    She threw, till he dreamed her his.

To her arts not blind, he yet sued long,
As a songster jailed by a deed of wrong
    Will shower the doer with song;

Till tried by tones now smart, now suave,
He would flee in ire, to return a slave
    Who willingly forgave.

When no! One day he left her door,
"I'll ease mine agony!" he swore,
    "And bear this thing no more!

"I'll practise a plan!" Thereon he took
Her portrait from his sketching-book,
    And, though his pencil shook,

He moulded on the real its mock;
Of beauteous brow, lip, eye, and lock
    Composed a laughingstock.

Amazed at this satire of his long lure,
Whenever he scanned it he'd scarce endure
    His laughter. 'Twas his cure.

And, even when he woke in the night,
And chanced to think of the comic sight,
    He laughed till exhausted quite.

"Why do you laugh?" she said one day
As he gazed at her in a curious way.
    "Oh—for nothing," said he. "Mere play."

—A gulf of years then severed the twain;
Till he heard—a painter of high attain—
    She was dying on her domain.

"And," dryly added the friend who told,
"You may know or not that, in semblance cold,
    She loved once, loved whole-souled;

"And that you were the man? Did you break your vow?
Well, well; she is good as gone by now . . .
    But you hit her, all allow!"

Ah, the blow past bearing that he received!
In his bachelor quiet he grieved and grieved;
    How cruel; how self-deceived!

Did she ever know? . . . Men pitied his state
As the curse of his own contrivance ate
    Like canker into his fate.

For ever that thing of his evil craft
Uprose on his grief—his mocking draught—
    Till, racked, he insanely laughed.

Thence onward folk would muse in doubt
What gloomed him so as he walked about,
    But few, or none, found out.

A LEADER OF FASHION

NEVER has she known
The way a robin will skip and come,
With an eye half bold, half timorsome,
To the table's edge for a breakfast crumb:

    Nor has she seen
A streak of roseate gently drawn
Across the east, that means the dawn,
When, up and out, she foots it on:

        Nor has she heard
The rustle of the sparrow's tread
To roost in roof-holes near her head
When dusk bids her, too, seek her bed:

        Nor has she watched
Amid a stormy eve's turmoil
The pipkin slowly come to boil,
In readiness for one at toil:

        Nor has she hearkened
Through the long night-time, lone and numb,
For sounds of sent-for help to come
Ere the swift-sinking life succumb:

        Nor has she ever
Held the loved-lost one on her arm,
Attired with care his straightened form,
As if he were alive and warm:

        Yea, never has she
Known, seen, heard, felt, such things as these,
Haps of so many in their degrees
Throughout their count of calvaries!

MIDNIGHT ON BEECHEN, 187–

ON Beechen Cliff self-commune I
This night of mid-June, mute and dry;
When darkness never rises higher
Than Bath's dim concave, towers, and spire,
Last eveglow loitering in the sky

To feel the dawn, close lurking by,
The while the lamps as glow-worms lie
In a glade, myself their lonely eyer
        On Beechen Cliff:

The city sleeps below. I sigh,
For there dwells one, all testify,
To match the maddest dream's desire:
What swain with her would not aspire
To walk the world, yea, sit but nigh
        On Beechen Cliff!

THE AËROLITE

I THOUGHT a germ of Consciousness
Escaped on an aërolite
      Aions ago
From some far globe, where no distress
Had means to mar supreme delight;

But only things abode that made
The power to feel a gift uncloyed
      Of gladsome glow,
And life unendingly displayed
Emotions loved, desired, enjoyed.

And that this stray, exotic germ
Fell wanderingly upon our sphere,
      After its wingings,
Quickened, and showed to us the worm
That gnaws vitalities native here,

And operated to unblind
Earth's old-established innocence
      Of stains and stingings,
Which grin no griefs while not opined
But cruelly tax intelligence.

"How shall we," then the seers said,
"Oust this awareness, this disease
      Called sense, here sown,
Though good, no doubt, where it was bred,
And wherein all things work to please?"

Others cried: "Nay, we rather would,
Since this untoward gift is sent
            For ends unknown,
Limit its registerings to good,
And hide from it all anguishment."

I left them pondering. This was how
(Or so I dreamed) was waked on earth
            The mortal moan
Begot of sentience. Maybe now
Normal unawareness waits rebirth.

THE PROSPECT

THE twigs of the birch imprint the December sky
      Like branching veins upon a thin old hand;
I think of summer-time, yes, of last July,
      When she was beneath them, greeting a gathered band
            Of the urban and bland.

Iced airs wheeze through the skeletoned hedge from the north,
      With steady snores, and a numbing that threatens snow,
And skaters pass; and merry boys go forth
      To look for slides. But well, well do I know
            Whither I would go!

December 1912.

GENITRIX LAESA

(MEASURE OF A SARUM SEQUENCE)

NATURE, through these generations
You have nursed us with a patience
Cruelly crossed by malversations,
      Marring mother-ministry

To your multitudes, so blended
By your processes, long-tended,
And the painstaking expended
    On their chording tunefully.

But this stuff of slowest moulding,
In your fancy ever enfolding
Life that rhythmic chime is holding:
    (Yes; so deem it you, Ladye—
This "concordia discors"!)—truly,
Rather, as if some imp unruly
Twitched your artist-arm when newly
    Shaping forth your scenery!

Aye.   Yet seem you not to know it.
Hence your world-work needs must show it
Good in dream, in deed below it:
    (Lady, yes: so sight it we!)
Thus, then, go on fondly thinking:
Why should man your purblind blinking
Crave to cure, when all is sinking
    To dissolubility.

THE FADING ROSE

I saw a rose, in bloom, but sad,
Shedding the petals that still it had,
And I heard it say: "O where is she
Who used to come and muse on me?

"The pruner says she comes no more
Because she loves another flower,
The weeder says she's tired of me
Because I droop so suddenly.

"Because of a sweetheart she comes not,
Declares the man with the watering-pot;

'She does not come,' says he with the rake,
'Because all women are fickle in make.'

"He with the spade and humorous leer
Says: 'Know, I delve elsewhere than here,
Mid text-writ stones and grassy heaps,
Round which a curious silence creeps.

"'She must get to you underground
If any way at all be found,
For, clad in her beauty, marble's kin,
'Tis there I have laid her and trod her in.'"

WHEN OATS WERE REAPED

THAT day when oats were reaped, and wheat was ripe, and
barley ripening,
   The road-dust hot, and the bleaching grasses dry,
     I walked along and said,
While looking just ahead to where some silent people lie:

"I wounded one who's there, and now know well I wounded her;
   But, ah, she does not know that she wounded me!"
     And not an air stirred,
Nor a bill of any bird; and no response accorded she.

August 1913.

LOUIE

I AM forgetting Louie the buoyant;
  Why not raise her phantom, too,
    Here in daylight
    With the elect one's?
She will never thrust the foremost figure out of view!

Mid this heat, in gauzy muslin
  See I Louie's life-lit brow
    Here in daylight
  By the elect one's.—
Long two strangers they and far apart; such neighbours now.

    July 1913.

"SHE OPENED THE DOOR"

SHE opened the door of the West to me,
  With its loud sea-lashings,
    And cliff-side clashings
Of waters rife with revelry.

She opened the door of Romance to me,
  The door from a cell
    I had known too well,
Too long, till then, and was fain to flee.

She opened the door of a Love to me,
  That passed the wry
    World-welters by
As far as the arching blue the lea.

She opens the door of the Past to me,
  Its magic lights,
    Its heavenly heights,
When forward little is to see!

  1913.

"WHAT'S THERE TO TELL?"

(SONG)

WHAT's there to tell of the world
  More than is told?
  Into its vortex hurled,

Out of it rolled,
Can we yet more of the world
Find to be told?
Lalla-la, lu!

If some could last alive
Much might be told;
Yes, gladness might survive;
But they go cold—
Each and each late alive—
All their tale told.
Lalla-la, lu!

There's little more of the world,
Then, to be told;
Had ever life unfurled
Joys manifold
There had been more of the world
Left to be told.
Lalla-la, lalla-la, lalla-la, lu!

190-.

THE HARBOUR BRIDGE

From here, the quay, one looks above to mark
The bridge across the harbour, hanging dark
Against the day's-end sky, fair-green in glow
Over and under the middle archway's bow:
It draws its skeleton where the sun has set,
Yea, clear from cutwater to parapet;
On which mild glow, too, lines of rope and spar
Trace themselves black as char.

Down here in shade we hear the painters shift
Against the bollards with a drowsy lift,
As moved by the incoming stealthy tide.
High up across the bridge the burghers glide

As cut black-paper portraits hastening on
In conversation none knows what upon:
Their sharp-edged lips move quickly word by word
    To speech that is not heard.

There trails the dreamful girl, who leans and stops,
There presses the practical woman to the shops,
There is a sailor, meeting his wife with a start,
And we, drawn nearer, judge they are keeping apart.
Both pause. She says: "I've looked for you. I thought
We'd make it up." Then no words can be caught.
At last: "Won't you come home?" She moves still nigher:
    "'Tis comfortable, with a fire."

"No," he says gloomily. "And, anyhow,
I can't give up the other woman now:
You should have talked like that in former days,
When I was last home." They go different ways.
And the west dims, and yellow lamplights shine:
And soon above, like lamps more opaline,
White stars ghost forth, that care not for men's wives,
    Or any other lives.

WEYMOUTH.

VAGRANT'S SONG

(WITH AN OLD WESSEX REFRAIN)

I

WHEN a dark-eyed dawn
    Crawls forth, cloud-drawn,
And starlings doubt the night-time's close;
    And "three months yet,"
    They seem to fret,
"Before we cease us slaves of snows,

And sun returns
To loose the burns,
And this wild woe called Winter goes!"—
O a hollow tree
Is as good for me
As a house where the back-brand glows!
Che-hane, mother; che-hane, mother,
As a house where the back-brand glows!

II

When autumn brings
A whirr of wings
Among the evergreens around,
And sundry thrills
About their quills
Awe rooks, and misgivings abound,
And the joyless pines
In leaning lines
Protect from gales the lower ground,
O a hollow tree
Is as good for me
As a house of a thousand pound!
Che-hane, mother; che-hane, mother,
As a house of a thousand pound!

NOTE — "Back-brand" (line 12), the log which used to be laid at the back of a wood fire.

FARMER DUNMAN'S FUNERAL

"BURY me on a Sunday,"
He said; "so as to see
Poor folk there. 'Tis their one day
To spare for following me."

And mindful of that Sunday,
    He wrote, while he was well,
On ten rum-bottles one day,
    "*Drink for my funeral.*"

They buried him on a Sunday,
    That folk should not be balked
His wish, as 'twas their one day:
    And forty couple walked.

They said: "To have it Sunday
    Was always his concern;
His meaning being that one day
    He'd do us a good turn.

"We must, had it been Monday,
    Have got it over soon,
But now we gain, being Sunday,
    A jolly afternoon."

THE SEXTON AT LONGPUDDLE

HE passes down the churchyard track
    On his way to toll the bell;
And stops, and looks at the graves around,
And notes each finished and greening mound
        Complacently,
      As their shaper he,
    And one who can do it well.
And, with a prosperous sense of his doing,
    Thinks he'll not lack
Plenty such work in the long ensuing
        Futurity.
    For people will always die,
    And he will always be nigh
      To shape their cell.

THE HARVEST-SUPPER

(*Circa* 1850)

NELL and the other maids danced their best
    With the Scotch-Greys in the barn;
These had been asked to the harvest-feast;
    Red shapes amid the corn.

Nell and the other maids sat in a row
    Within the benched barn-nook;
Nell led the songs of long ago
    She'd learnt from never a book.

She sang of the false Sir John of old,
    The lover who witched to win,
And the parrot, and cage of glittering gold;
    And the other maids joined in.

Then whispered to her a gallant Grey,
    "Dear, sing that ballet again!
For a bonnier mouth in a bonnier way
    Has sung not anywhen!"

As she loosed her lips anew there sighed
    To Nell through the dark barn-door
The voice of her Love from the night outside,
    Who was buried the month before:

"O Nell, can you sing ballets there,
    And I out here in the clay,
Of lovers false of yore, nor care
    What you vowed to me one day!

"O can you dance with soldiers bold,
    Who kiss when dancing's done,
Your little waist within their hold,
    As ancient troth were none!"

She cried: "My heart is pierced with a wound!
        There's something outside the wall
That calls me forth to a greening mound:
        I can sing no more at all!

"My old Love rises from the worms,
        Just as he used to be,
And I must let gay gallants' arms
        No more encircle me!"

They bore her home from the merry-making;
        Bad dreams disturbed her bed:
"Nevermore will I dance and sing,"
        Mourned Nell; "and never wed!"

AT A PAUSE IN A COUNTRY DANCE

(MIDDLE OF LAST CENTURY)

THEY stood at the foot of the figure,
And panted: they'd danced it down through—
That "Dashing White Serjeant" they loved so:—
A window, uncurtained, was nigh them
That end of the room. Thence in view

Outside it a valley updrew,
Where the frozen moon lit frozen snow:
At the furthermost reach of the valley
A light from a window shone low.
"They are inside that window," said she,

As she looked. "They sit up there for me;
And baby is sleeping there, too."
He glanced. "Yes," he said. "Never mind,"
Let's foot our way up again; do!
And dance down the line as before.

"What's the world to us, meeting once more!"
"—Not much, when your husband full trusts you,
And thinks the child his that I bore!"
He was silent. The fiddlers six-eighted
With even more passionate vigour.

The pair swept again up the figure,
The child's cuckoo-father and she,
And the next couples threaded below,
And the twain wove their way to the top
Of "The Dashing White Serjeant" they loved so,
Restarting: right, left, to and fro.

—From the homestead, seen yon, the small glow
Still adventured forth over the white,
Where the child slept, unknowing who sired it,
In the cradle of wicker tucked tight,
And its grandparents, nodding, admired it
In elbow-chairs through the slow night.

ON THE PORTRAIT OF A WOMAN
ABOUT TO BE HANGED

COMELY and capable one of our race,
Posing there in your gown of grace,
        Plain, yet becoming;
            Could subtlest breast
            Ever have guessed
What was behind that innocent face,
        Drumming, drumming!

Would that your Causer, ere knoll your knell
For this riot of passion, might deign to tell
        Why, since It made you
            Sound in the germ,
            It sent a worm
To madden Its handiwork, when It might well
        Not have assayed you,

Not have implanted, to your deep rue,
The Clytaemnestra spirit in you,
And with purblind vision
Sowed a tare
In a field so fair,
And a thing of symmetry, seemly to view,
Brought to derision!

January 6, 1923.

THE CHURCH AND THE WEDDING

"I'LL restore this old church for our marriage:
I've ordered the plans:
Style of wedding your choice—foot or carriage—
By license, or banns."

He restored it, as though built newly:
The bishop was won
To preach, who pronounced it truly
A thing well done.

But the wedding waits; long, long has waited;
And guesswork is dumb
Why those who were there to have mated
Do not come.

And when the nights moan like the wailings
Of souls sore-tried,
The folk say who pass the church-palings
They hear inside

Strange sounds as of anger and sadness
That cut the heart's core,
And shaken words bitter to madness;
And then no more.

THE SHIVER

FIVE long clangs from the house-clock nigh,
  And I woke with a sigh:
Stars wore west like a slow tide flowing,
And my lover had told yesternight of his going,—
That at this gray hour he'd be hasting by,

Starting betimes on a journey afar:—
  So, casement ajar,
I eyed in the upland pasture his figure,
A dim dumb speck, growing darker and bigger,
Then smalling to nought where the nut-trees are.

He could not bend his track to my window, he'd said,
  Being hurried ahead:
But I wished he had tried to!—and then felt a shiver,
Corpse-cold, as he sank toward the town by the river;
And back I went sadly and slowly to bed.

What meant my shiver while seeing him pass
  As a dot on the grass
I surmised not then. But later I knew it
When came again he; and my words outdrew it,
As said he: "It's hard for your bearing, alas!

"But I've seen, I have clasped, where the smart ships plough,
  One of far brighter brow.
A sea-goddess. Shiver not. One far rarer
In gifts than I find thee; yea, warmer and fairer:—
I seek her again; and I love you not now."

"NOT ONLY I"

NOT only I
  Am doomed awhile to lie
In this close bin with earthen sides;
But the things I thought, and the songs I sang,
And the hopes I had, and the passioned pang

For people I knew
Who passed before me,
Whose memory barely abides;
And the visions I drew
That daily upbore me!

And the joyous springs and summers,
And the jaunts with blithe newcomers,
And my plans and appearances; drives and rides
That fanned my fare to a lively red;
And the grays and blues
Of the far-off views,
That nobody else discerned outspread;
And little achievements for blame or praise;
Things left undone; things left unsaid;
In brief, my days!

Compressed here in six feet by two,
In secrecy
To lie with me
Till the Call shall be,
Are all these things I knew,
Which cannot be handed on;
Strange happenings quite unrecorded,
Lost to the world and disregarded,
That only thinks: "Here moulders till
Doom's-dawn
A woman's skeleton."

SHE SAW HIM, SHE SAID

"Why, I saw you with the sexton, outside the church-door,
So I did not hurry me home,
Thinking you'd not be come,
Having something to him to say.—
Yes: 'twas you, Dear, though you seemed sad, heart-sore:
How fast you've got therefrom!"

"I've not been out. I've watched the moon through the birch,
        And heard the bell toll. Yes,
            Like a passing soul in distress!"
            "—But no bell's tolled to-day?" . . .
His face looked strange, like the face of him seen by the church,
        And she sank to musefulness

ONCE AT SWANAGE

    THE spray sprang up across the cusps of the moon,
        And all its light loomed green
        As a witch-flame's weirdsome sheen
    At the minute of an incantation scene;
    And it greened our gaze—that night at demilune.

    Roaring high and roaring low was the sea
        Behind the headland shores:
        It symboled the slamming of doors,
    Or a regiment hurrying over hollow floors. . . .
    And there we two stood, hands clasped; I and she!

THE FLOWER'S TRAGEDY

    IN the bedchamber window, near the glass,
    Stood the little flower in the little vase,
            Unnoticed quite
            For a whole fortnight,
    And withered for lack of watering
    To a skeleton mere—a mummied thing.

    But it was not much, mid a world of teen,
    That a flower should waste in a nook unseen!

One needed no thought to ascertain
How it happened; that when she went in the rain
    To return here not,
    She was mindless what
She had left here to perish.—Ah, well: for an hour
I wished I had not found the flower!

Yet it was not much. And she never had known
Of the flower's fate; nor it of her own.

AT THE AQUATIC SPORTS

WITH their backs to the sea two fiddlers stand
Facing the concourse on the strand,
    And a third man who sings.
The sports proceed; there are crab-catchings;
The people laugh as levity spreads;
Yet these three do not turn their heads
    To see whence the merriment springs.

They cease their music, but even then
They stand as before, do those three men
    Though pausing, nought to do:
They never face to the seaward view
To enjoy the contests, add their cheer,
So wholly is their being here
    A business they pursue.

A WATCHER'S REGRET

J. E.'S STORY

I SLEPT across the front of the clock,
    Close to the long case-door;
The hours were brought by their brazen knock
    To my ear as the slow nights wore.

Thus did I, she being sick to death,
    That each hour as it belled
Should wake me to rise, and learn by her breath
    Whether her strength still held.

Yet though throughout life's midnights all
    I would have watched till spent
For her dear sake, I missed the call
    Of the hour in which she went.

HORSES ABOARD

HORSES in horseclothes stand in a row
On board the huge ship, that at last lets go:
Whither are they sailing? They do not know,
Nor what for, nor how.—
             They are horses of war,
And are going to where there is fighting afar;
But they gaze through their eye-holes unwitting they are,
And that in some wilderness, gaunt and ghast,
Their bones will bleach ere a year has passed,
And the item be as "war-waste" classed.—
And when the band booms, and the folk say "Good-bye!"
And the shore slides astern, they appear wrenched awry
From the scheme Nature planned for them,—wondering why.

THE HISTORY OF AN HOUR

VAIN is the wish to try rhyming it, writing it!
Pen cannot weld into words what it was;
Time will be squandered in toil at inditing it;
        Clear is the cause!

Yea, 'twas too satiate with soul, too ethereal;
June-morning scents of a rose-bush in flower
Catch in a clap-net of hempen material;
        So catch that hour!

THE MISSED TRAIN

How I was caught
Hieing home, after days of allure,
And forced to an inn—small, obscure—
    At the junction, gloom-fraught.

How civil my face
To get them to chamber me there—
A roof I had scorned, scarce aware
    That it stood at the place.

And how all the night
I had dreams of the unwitting cause
Of my lodgment. How lonely I was
    How consoled by her sprite!

Thus onetime to me . . .
Dim wastes of dead years bar away
Then from now. But such happenings to-day
    Fall to lovers, may be!

Years, years as shoaled seas,
Truly, stretch now between! Less and less
Shrink the visions then vast in me.—Yes,
    Then in me: Now in these.

UNDER HIGH–STOY HILL

Four climbed High-Stoy from Ivelwards,
Where hedge meets hedge, and cart-ruts wind,
    Chattering like birds,
And knowing not what lay behind.

We laughed beneath the moonlight blink,
Said supper would be to our mind,
    And did not think
Of Time, and what might lie behind. . . .

The moon still meets that tree-tipped height,
The road—as then—still trails inclined;
  But since that night
We have well learnt what lay behind!

For all of the four then climbing here
But one are ghosts, and he brow-lined;
  With him they fare,
Yet speak not of what lies behind.

AT THE MILL

O MILLER KNOX, whom we knew well,
  And the mill, and the floury floors,
And the corn,—and those two women,
  And infants—yours!

The sun was shining when you rode
  To market on that day:
The sun was set when home-along
  You ambled in the gray,
And gathered what had taken place
  While you were away.

O Miller Knox, 'twas grief to see
  Your good wife hanging there
By her own rash and passionate hand,
  In a throe of despair;

And those two children, one by her,
  And one by the waiting-maid,
Borne the same hour, and you afar,
  And she past aid.

And though sometimes you walk of nights,
  Sleepless, to Yalbury Brow,
And glance the graveyard way, and grunt,
  " 'Twas not much, anyhow:
She shouldn't ha' minded!" nought it helps
  To say that now.

And the water dribbles down your wheel,
   Your mead blooms green and gold,
And birds twit in your apple-boughs
   Just as of old.

ALIKE AND UNLIKE

(GREAT-ORME'S HEAD)

WE watched the selfsame scene on that long drive,
Saw the magnificent purples, as one eye,
Of those near mountains; saw the storm arrive;
Laid up the sight in memory, you and I,
As if for joint recallings by and by.

But our eye-records, like in hue and line,
Had superimposed on them, that very day,
Gravings on your side deep, but slight on mine!—
Tending to sever us thenceforth alway;
Mine commonplace; yours tragic, gruesome, gray.

THE THING UNPLANNED

THE white winter sun struck its stroke on the bridge,
   The meadow-rills rippled and gleamed
As I left the thatched post-office, just by the ridge,
And dropped in my pocket her long tender letter,
With: "This must be snapped! it is more than it seemed;
   And now is the opportune time!"

But against what I willed worked the surging sublime
   Of the thing that I did—the thing better!

THE SHEEP BOY

A YAWNING, sunned concave
Of purple, spread as an ocean wave
Entroughed on a morning of swell and sway

After a night when wind-fiends have been heard to rave:
  Thus was the Heath called "Draäts", on an August day.

   Suddenly there intunes a hum:
   This side, that side, it seems to come.
   From the purple in myriads rise the bees
With consternation mid their rapt employ.
So headstrongly each speeds him past, and flees,
   As to strike the face of the shepherd-boy.
Awhile he waits, and wonders what they mean:
Till none is left upon the shagged demesne.

   To learn what ails, the sheep-boy looks around;
      Behind him, out of the sea in swirls
   Flexuous and solid, clammy vapour-curls
Are rolling over Pokeswell Hills to the inland ground.
         In to the heath they sail,
         And travel up the vale
Like the moving pillar of cloud raised by the Israelite:—
In a trice the lonely sheep-boy seen so late ago,
         Draäts'-Hollow in gorgeous blow,
         And Kite-Hill's regal glow,
Are viewless—folded into those creeping scrolls of white.

On Rainbarrows.

RETTY'S PHASES

I

RETTY used to shake her head,
      Look with wicked eye;
Say, "I'd tease you, simplehead,
      If I cared to try!"
Then she'd hot-up scarlet red,
      Stilly step away,
Much afraid that what she'd said
      Sounded bold to say.

II

Retty used to think she loved
　　(Just a little) me
Not untruly, as it proved
　　Afterwards to be.
For, when weakness forced her rest
　　If we walked a mile,
She would whisper she was blest
　　By my clasp awhile.

III

Retty used at last to say
　　When she neared the Vale,
"Mind that you, Dear, on that day
　　Ring my wedding peal!"
And we all, with pulsing pride,
　　Vigorous sounding gave
Those six bells, the while outside
　　John filled in her grave.

IV

Retty used to draw me down
　　To the turfy heaps,
Where, with yeoman, squire, and clown
　　Noticeless she sleeps.
Now her silent slumber-place
　　Seldom do I know,
For when last I saw her face
　　Was so long ago!

From an old draft of 1868.

Note.—In many villages it was customary after the funeral of an
unmarried young woman to ring a peal as for her wedding while the
grave was being filled in, as if Death were not to be allowed to balk
her of bridal honours.   Young unmarried men were always her bearers.

A POOR MAN AND A LADY

WE knew it was not a valid thing,
And only sanct in the sight of God
(To use your phrase), as with fervent nod
You swore your assent when I placed the ring
On your pale slim hand. Our whispering
Was soft as the fan of a turtledove
That round our heads might have seemed to wing;
So solemn were we; so sincere our love.

We could do no better; and thus it stood
Through a time of timorous secret bliss,
Till we were divided, and never a kiss
Of mine could touch you, or likelihood
Illumed our sky that we might, or should
Be each to each in the world's wide eye
What we were unviewed; and our vows make good
In the presence of parents and standers by.

I was a striver with deeds to do,
And little enough to do them with,
And a comely woman of noble kith,
With a courtly match to make, were you;
And we both were young; and though sterling-true
You had proved to our pledge under previous strains,
Our "union," as we called it, grew
Less grave to your eyes in your town campaigns.

Well: the woeful neared, you needn't be told:
The current news-sheets clarioned soon
That you would be wived on a summer noon
By a man of illustrious line and old:
Nor better nor worse than the manifold
Of marriages made, had there not been
Our faith-swearing when fervent-souled,
Which, to me, seemed a breachless bar between.

We met in a Mayfair church, alone:
(The request was mine, which you yielded to.)
"But we were not married at all!" urged you:
"Why, of course we were!" I said. Your tone,
I noted, was world-wise. You went on:
" 'Twas sweet while it lasted. But you well know
That law is law. He'll be, anon,
My husband *really*. You, Dear, weren't so."

"I wished—but to learn if——" faltered I,
And stopped. "But I'll sting you not. Farewell!"
And we parted.—Do you recall the bell
That tolled by chance as we said good-bye? . . .
I saw you no more. The track of a high,
Sweet, liberal lady you've doubtless trod.
—All's past! No heart was burst thereby,
And no one knew, unless it was God.

NOTE.—The foregoing was intended to preserve an episode in the
story of "The Poor Man and the Lady," written in 1868, and, like these
lines, in the first person: but never printed, and ultimately destroyed.

AN EXPOSTULATION

WHY want to go afar
    Where pitfalls are,
When all we swains adore
    Your featness more and more
As heroine of our artless masquings here,
And count few Wessex' daughters half so dear?

Why paint your appealing face,
    When its born grace
Is such no skill can match
    With powder, puff, or patch,
Whose every touch defames your bloomfulness,
And with each stain increases our distress?

Yea, is it not enough
    That (rare or rough
Your lines here) all uphold you,
And as with wings enfold you,
But you must needs desert the kine-cropt vale
Wherein your foredames gaily filled the pail?

TO A SEA–CLIFF

(DURLSTON HEAD)

LEND me an ear
    While I read you here
A page from your history,
    Old cliff—not known
    To your solid stone,
Yet yours inseparably.

    Near to your crown
    There once sat down
A silent listless pair;
    And the sunset ended,
    And dark descended,
And still the twain sat there.

    Past your jutting head
    Then a line-ship sped,
Lit brightly as a city;
    And she sobbed: "There goes
    A man who knows
I am his, beyond God's pity!"

    He slid apart
    Who had thought her heart
His own, and not aboard
    A bark, sea-bound. . . .
    That night they found
Between them lay a sword.

THE ECHO ELF ANSWERS

How much shall I love her?
For life, or not long?
    "Not long."

Alas! When forget her?
In years, or by June?
    "By June."

And whom woo I after?
No one, or a throng?
    "A throng."

Of these shall I wed one
Long hence, or quite soon?
    "Quite soon."

And which will my bride be?
The right or the wrong?
    "The wrong."

And my remedy—what kind?
Wealth-wove, or earth-hewn?
    "Earth-hewn."

CYNIC'S EPITAPH

A RACE with the sun as he downed
    I ran at evetide,
Intent who should first gain the ground
    And there hide.

He beat me by some minutes then,
    But I triumphed anon,
For when he'd to rise up again
    I stayed on.

A BEAUTY'S SOLILOQUY
DURING HER HONEYMOON

Too late, too late! I did not know my fairness
    Would catch the world's keen eyes so!
How the men look at me! My radiant rareness
    I deemed not they would prize so!

That I was a peach for any man's possession
    Why did not some one say
Before I leased myself in an hour's obsession
    To this dull mate for aye!

His days are mine. I am one who cannot steal her
    Ahead of his plodding pace:
As he is, so am I. One doomed to feel her
    A wasted form and face!

I was so blind! It did sometimes just strike me
    All girls were not as I,
But, dwelling much alone, how few were like me
    I could not well descry;

Till, at this Grand Hotel, all looks bend on me
    In homage as I pass
To take my seat at breakfast, dinner,—con me
    As poorly spoused, alas!

I was too young. I dwelt too much on duty:
    If I had guessed my powers
Where might have sailed this cargo of choice beauty
    In its unanchored hours!

Well, husband, poor plain man; I've lost life's battle!—
    Come—let them look at me.
O damn, don't show in your looks that I'm your chattel
    Quite so emphatically!

In a London Hotel, 1892.

DONAGHADEE

(SONG)

I'VE never gone to Donaghadee,
That vague far townlet by the sea;
In Donaghadee I shall never be:
Then why do I sing of Donaghadee,
That I know not in a faint degree? . .
—Well, once a woman wrote to me
With a tender pen from Donaghadee.

"Susan," I've sung, "Pride of Kildare,"
Because I'd heard of a Susan there,
The "Irish Washerwoman's" capers
I've shared for hours to midnight tapers,
And "Kitty O'Linch" has made me spin
Till dust rose high, and day broke in:
That other "Kitty, of Coleraine,"
Too, set me aching in heart and brain:
While "Kathleen Mavourneen," of course, would ring
When that girl learnt to make me sing.

Then there was "Irish Molly O"
I tuned as "the fairest one I know,"
And "Nancy Dawson," if I remember,
Rhymed sweet in moonlight one September.

But the damsel who once wrote so free
And tender toned from Donaghadee,
Is a woman who has no name for me—
Moving sylph-like, mysteriously,
(For doubtless, of that sort is she)
In the pathways of her destiny;
But that is where I never shall be;—
And yet I sing of Donaghadee!

HE INADVERTENTLY CURES HIS LOVE-PAINS

(SONG)

I SAID: "O let me sing the praise
Of her who sweetly racks my days,—
    Her I adore;
Her lips, her eyes, her moods, her ways!"

In miseries of pulse and pang
I strung my harp, and straightway sang
    As none before:—
To wondrous words my quavers rang!

Thus I let heartaches lilt my verse,
Which suaged and soothed, and made disperse
    The smarts I bore
To quiet like a sepulchre's.

But, eased, the days that thrilled ere then
Lost value; and I ask, O when,
    And how, restore
Those old sweet agonies again!

THE PEACE PEAL

(AFTER FOUR YEARS OF SILENCE)

SAID a wistful daw in Saint Peter's tower,
High above Casterbridge slates and tiles,
Why do the walls of my Gothic bower
Shiver, and shrill out sounds for miles?

This gray old rubble
Has scorned such din
Since I knew trouble
And joy herein.
How still did abide them
These bells now swung,
While our nest beside them
Securely clung! . . .
It means some snare
For our feet or wings;
But I'll beware
Of such baleful things!"
And forth he flew from his louvred niche
To take up life in a damp dark ditch.
—So mortal motives are misread,
And false designs attributed,
In upper spheres of straws and sticks,
Or lower, of pens and politics.

At the end of the War.

LADY VI

THERE goes the Lady Vi. How well,
How well I know the spectacle
     The earth presents
     And its events
     To her sweet sight
     Each day and night!

"Life is a wheeling show, with *me*
As its pivot of interest constantly.
Below in the hollows of towns is sin,
Like a blue brimstone mist therein,
Which makes men lively who plunge amid it,
But wrongfully, and wives forbid it.

London is a place for prancing
Along the Row and, later, dancing,
Till dawn, with tightening arm-elbowments
As hours warm up to tender moments.

"Travel is piquant, and most thrilling
If, further, joined to big-game killing:
At home, too, hunting, hounds full cry,
When Reynard nears his time to die,
'Tis glee to mark his figure flag,
And how his brush begins to drag,
Till, his earth reached by many a wend,
He finds it *stopped*, and meets his end.

"Religion is good for all who are meek;
It stays in the Bible through the week,
And floats about the house on Sundays,
But does not linger on till Mondays.
The Ten Commandments in one's prime
Are matter for another time,
While griefs and graves and things allied
In well-bred talk one keeps outside."

A POPULAR PERSONAGE AT HOME

"I LIVE here: 'Wessex' is my name:
I am a dog known rather well:
I guard the house; but how that came
To be my whim I cannot tell.

"With a leap and a heart elate I go
At the end of an hour's expectancy
To take a walk of a mile or so
With the folk I let live here with me.

"Along the path, amid the grass
I sniff, and find out rarest smells
For rolling over as I pass
The open fields towards the dells.

"No doubt I shall always cross this sill,
And turn the corner, and stand steady,
Gazing back for my mistress till
She reaches where I have run already,

"And that this meadow with its brook,
And bulrush, even as it appears
As I plunge by with hasty look,
Will stay the same a thousand years."

Thus "Wessex." But a dubious ray
At times informs his steadfast eye,
Just for a trice, as though to say,
"Yet, will this pass, and pass shall I?"

1924.

INSCRIPTIONS FOR A PEAL OF
EIGHT BELLS

AFTER A RESTORATION

I. THOMAS TREMBLE new-made me
   Eighteen hundred and fifty-three·
   Why he did I fail to see.

II. I was well-toned by William Brine,
   Seventeen hundred and twenty-nine;
   Now, recast, I weakly whine!

III. Fifteen hundred used to be
   My date, but since they melted me
   'Tis only eighteen fifty-three.

IV. Henry Hopkins got me made,
And I summon folk as bade;
Not to much purpose, I'm afraid!

V. I likewise; for I bang and bid
In commoner metal than I did,
Some of me being stolen and hid.

VI. I, too, since in a mould they flung me,
Drained my silver, and rehung me,
So that in tin-like tones I tongue me.

VII. In nineteen hundred, so 'tis said,
They cut my canon off my head,
And made me look scalped, scraped, and dead.

VIII. I'm the peal's tenor still, but rue it!
Once it took two to swing me through it:
Now I'm rehung, one dolt can do it.

A REFUSAL

SAID the grave Dean of Westminster:
Mine is the best minster
Seen in Great Britain,
As many have written:
So therefore I cannot
Rule here if I ban not
Such liberty-taking
As movements for making
Its greyness environ
The memory of Byron,
Which some are demanding
Who think them of standing,
But in my own viewing
Require some subduing

For tendering suggestions
On Abbey-wall questions
That must interfere here
With my proper sphere here,
And bring to disaster
This fane and its master,
Whose dict is but Christian
Though nicknamed Philistian.

A lax Christian charity—
No mental clarity
Ruling its movements
For fabric improvements—
Demands admonition
And strict supervision
When bent on enshrining
Rapscallions, and signing
Their names on God's stonework,
As if like His own work
Were their lucubrations:
And passed is my patience
That such a creed-scorner
(Not mentioning horner)
Should claim Poet's Corner.

'Tis urged that some sinners
Are here for worms' dinners
Already in person;
That he could not worsen
The walls by a name mere
With men of such fame here.
Yet nay; they but leaven
The others in heaven
In just true proportion,
While more mean distortion.

'Twill next be expected
That I get erected

To Shelley a tablet
In some niche or gablet.
Then—what makes my skin burn,
Yea, forehead to chin burn—
That I ensconce Swinburne!

August 1924.

EPITAPH ON A PESSIMIST

I'M Smith of Stoke, aged sixty-odd,
      I've lived without a dame
From youth-time on; and would to God
      My dad had done the same.

From the French.

THE PROTEAN MAIDEN

(SONG)

THIS single girl is two girls:
      How strange such things should be!
One noon eclipsed by few girls,
      The next no beauty she.

And daily cries the lover,
      In voice and feature vext:
"My last impression of her
      Is never to be the next!

"She's plain: I will forget her!
      She's turned to fair. Ah no,
Forget?—not I! I'll pet her
      With kisses swift and slow."

A WATERING–PLACE LADY
INVENTORIED

A SWEETNESS of temper unsurpassed and unforgettable,
A mole on the cheek whose absence would have been regrettable,
A ripple of pleasant converse full of modulation,
A bearing of inconveniences without vexation,
Till a cynic would find her amiability provoking,
Tempting him to indulge in mean and wicked joking.

Flawlessly oval of face, especially cheek and chin,
With a glance of a quality that beckoned for a glance akin,
A habit of swift assent to any intelligence broken,
Before the fact to be conveyed was fully spoken
And she could know to what her colloquist would win her,—
This from a too alive impulsion to sympathy in her,—
All with a sense of the ridiculous, keen yet charitable;
In brief, a rich profuse attractiveness unnarratable.

I should have added her hints that her husband prized her but
    slenderly,
And that (with a sigh) 'twas a pity she'd no one to treat her
    tenderly.

THE SEA FIGHT

31 *May*: 1916

IN MEMORIAM CAPTAIN PROWSE

DOWN went the grand "Queen Mary,"
"Queen Mary's" captain, and her crew;
The brunt of battle bare he,
    And he died;
And he died, as heroes do.

More really now we view him,
More really lives he, moves with men,
    Than while on earth we knew him
        As our fellow,
        As our fellow-denizen.

Maybe amid the changes
Of ocean's caverned dim profound,
    Gaily his spirit ranges
        With his comrades,
        With his comrades all around.

1916.

PARADOX

(M. H.)

THOUGH out of sight now, and as 'twere not the least to us;
Comes she in sorrows, as one bringing peace to us?
Lost to each meadow, each hill-top, each tree around,
Yet the whole truth may her largened sight see around?
        Always away from us
        She may not stray from us!
Can she, then, know how men's fatings befall?
Yea indeed, may know well; even know thereof all.

THE ROVER COME HOME

HE's journeyed through America
    From Canso Cape to Horn,
And from East Indian Comorin
    To Behring's Strait forlorn;
He's felled trees in the backwoods,
    In swamps has gasped for breath;
In Tropic heats, in Polar ice,
    Has often prayed for death.

He has fought and bled in civil wars
        Of no concern to him,
Has shot his fellows—beasts and men—
        At risk of life and limb.
He has suffered fluxes, fevers,
        Agues, and ills allied,
And now he's home. You look at him
        As he talks by your fireside.

And what is written in his glance
        Stressed by such foreign wear,
After such alien circumstance
        What does his face declare?
His mother's; she who saw him not
        After his starting year,
Who never left her native spot,
        And lies in the churchyard near.

"KNOWN HAD I"

(SONG)

KNOWN had I what I knew not
        When we met eye to eye,
That thenceforth I should view not
        Again beneath the sky
So truefooted a farer
        As you who faced me then,
My path had been a rarer
        Than it figures among men!

I would have trod beside you
        To guard your feet all day,
And borne at night to guide you
        A lantern on your way:
Would not have left you lonely
        With wringing doubt, to cow
Old hope, if I could only
        Have known what I know now.

THE PAT OF BUTTER

ONCE, at the Agricultural Show,
    We tasted—all so yellow—
    Those butter-pats, cool and mellow!
Each taste I still remember, though
    It was so long ago.

This spoke of the grass of Netherhay,
    And this of Kingcomb Hill,
    And this of Coker Rill:
Which was the prime I could not say
    Of all those tried that day,

Till she, the fair and wicked-eyed,
    Held out a pat to me:
    Then felt I all Yeo-Lea
Was by her sample sheer outvied;
    And, "This is the best," I cried.

BAGS OF MEAT

"HERE's a fine bag of meat,"
Says the master-auctioneer,
As the timid, quivering steer,
Starting a couple of feet
At the prod of a drover's stick,
And trotting lightly and quick,
A ticket stuck on his rump,
Enters with a bewildered jump.

    "Where he's lived lately, friends,
I'd live till lifetime ends:
They've a whole life everyday
Down there in the Vale, have they!

He'd be worth the money to kill
And give away Christmas for good-will."

"Now here's a heifer — worth more
    Than bid, were she bone-poor;
    Yet she's round as a barrel of beer";
"She's a plum," said the second auctioneer.

"Now this young bull—for thirty pound?
    Worth that to manure your ground!"
    "Or to stand," chimed the second one,
    "And have his picter done!"
The beast was rapped on the horns and snout
    To make him turn about.
"Well," cried a buyer, "another crown—
Since I've dragged here from Taunton Town!"

"That calf, she sucked three cows,
    Which is not matched for bouse
    In the nurseries of high life
By the first-born of a nobleman's wife!"
The stick falls, meaning, "A true tale's told,"
On the buttock of the creature sold,
    And the buyer leans over and snips
His mark on one of the animal's hips.

Each beast, when driven in,
Looks round at the ring of bidders there
With a much-amazed reproachful stare,
    As at unnatural kin,
For bringing him to a sinister scene
So strange, unhomelike, hungry, mean;
His fate the while suspended between
    A butcher, to kill out of hand,
    And a farmer, to keep on the land;
One can fancy a tear runs down his face
When the butcher wins, and he's driven from the place.

THE SUNDIAL ON A WET DAY

I DRIP, drip here
In Atlantic rain,
Falling like handfuls
Of winnowed grain,
Which, tear-like, down
My gnomon drain,
And dim my numerals
With their stain,—
Till I feel useless,
And wrought in vain!

And then I think
In my despair
That, though unseen,
He is still up there,
And may gaze out
Anywhen, anywhere;
Not to help clockmen
Quiz and compare,
But in kindness to let me
My trade declare.

St. Juliot.

HER HAUNTING—GROUND

Can it be so?   It must be so,
That visions have not ceased to be
In this the chiefest sanctuary
Of her whose form we used to know.
—Nay, but her dust is far away,
And "where her dust is, shapes her shade,
If spirit clings to flesh," they say:
Yet here her life-parts most were played!

Her voice explored this atmosphere,
Her foot impressed this turf around,
Her shadow swept this slope and mound,
Her fingers fondled blossoms here;
And so, I ask, why, why should she
Haunt elsewhere, by a slighted tomb,
When here she flourished sorrow-free,
And, save for others, knew no gloom?

A PARTING SCENE

THE two pale women cried,
But the man seemed to suffer more,
Which he strove hard to hide.
They stayed in the waiting-room, behind the door,
Till startled by the entering engine-roar,
As if they could not bear to have unfurled
Their misery to the eyes of all the world.

A soldier and his young wife
Were the couple; his mother the third,
Who had seen the seams of life.
He was sailing for the East I later heard.
—They kissed long, but they did not speak a word;
Then, strained, he went.   To the elder the wife in tears
"Too long; too long!" burst out.   ('Twas for five years.)

SHORTENING DAYS AT THE HOMESTEAD

THE first fire since the summer is lit, and is smoking into the
    room:
  The sun-rays thread it through, like woof-lines in a loom.
Sparrows spurt from the hedge, whom misgivings appal
That winter did not leave last year for ever, after all.
    Like shock-headed urchins, spiny-haired,
    Stand pollard willows, their twigs just bared.

Who is this coming with pondering pace,
Black and ruddy, with white embossed,
His eyes being black, and ruddy his face,
And the marge of his hair like morning frost?
    It's the cider-maker,
    And appletree-shaker,
And behind him on wheels, in readiness,
His mill, and tubs, and vat, and press.

DAYS TO RECOLLECT

    Do you recall
    That day in Fall
When we walked towards Saint Alban's Head,
Over thistledown that summer had shed,
    Or must I remind you?
Winged thistle-seeds which hitherto
Had lain as none were there, or few,
But rose at the brush of your petticoat-seam
(As ghosts might rise of the recent dead),
And sailed on the breeze in a nebulous stream
    Like a comet's tail behind you:
    You don't recall
    That day in Fall?

    Then do you remember
    That sad November
When you left me never to see me more,
And looked quite other than theretofore,
    As if it could not *be* you?
And lay by the window whence you had gazed
So many times when blamed or praised,
Morning or noon, through years and years,
Accepting the gifts that Fortune bore,
Sharing, enduring, joys, hopes, fears!
    Well: I never more did see you.—
    Say you remember
    That sad November!

TO C. F. H.

ON HER CHRISTENING-DAY

FAIR Caroline, I wonder what
You think of earth as a dwelling-spot,
And if you'd rather have come, or not?

To-day has laid on you a name
That, though unasked for, you will claim
Lifelong, for love or praise or blame.

May chance and change impose on you
No heavier burthen than this new
Care-chosen one your future through!

Dear stranger here, the prayer is mine
That your experience may combine
Good things with glad. . . . Yes, Caroline!

THE HIGH–SCHOOL LAWN

GRAY prinked with rose,
White tipped with blue,
Shoes with gay hose,
Sleeves of chrome hue;
Fluffed frills of white,
Dark bordered light;
Such shimmerings through
Trees of emerald green are eyed
This afternoon, from the road outside.

They whirl around:
Many laughters run
With a cascade's sound;
Then a mere one.

A bell: they flee:
Silence then:—
So it will be
Some day again
With them,—with me.

THE FORBIDDEN BANNS

A BALLAD OF THE EIGHTEEN-THIRTIES

I

"O WHAT's the gain, my worthy Sir,
    In stopping the banns to-day!
Your son declares he'll marry her
    If a thousand folk say Nay."

"I'll do't; I'll do't; whether or no!
    And, if I drop down dead,
To church this morning I will go,
    And say they shall not wed!"

That day the parson clear outspoke
    The maid's name and the man's:
His father, mid the assembled folk
    Said, "I forbid the banns!"

Then, white in face, lips pale and cold,
    He turned him to sit down,
When he fell forward; and behold,
    They found his life had flown.

II

'Twas night-time, towards the middle part,
    When low her husband said,
"I would from the bottom of my heart
    That father was not dead!"

She turned from one to the other side,
    And a sad woman was she
As he went on: "He'd not have died
    Had it not been for me!"

She brought him soon an idiot child,
    And then she brought another:
His face waned wan, his manner wild
    With hatred of their mother.

"Hearken to me, my son.   No: no:
    There's madness in her blood!"
Those were his father's words; and lo,
    Now, now he understood.

What noise is that?   One noise, and two
    Resound from a near gun.
Two corpses found: and neighbours knew
    By whom the deed was done.

THE PAPHIAN BALL

ANOTHER CHRISTMAS EXPERIENCE OF THE MELLSTOCK QUIRE

WE went our Christmas rounds once more,
With quire and viols as theretofore.

Our path was near by Rushy-Pond,
Where Egdon-Heath outstretched beyond.

There stood a figure against the moon,
Tall, spare, and humming a weirdsome tune.

"You tire of Christian carols," he said:
"Come and lute at a ball instead.

"'Tis to your gain, for it ensures
That many guineas will be yours.

"A slight condition hangs on't, true,
But you will scarce say nay thereto:

"That you go blindfold; that anon
The place may not be gossiped on."

They stood and argued with each other:
"Why sing from one house to another

"These ancient hymns in the freezing night,
And all for nought? 'Tis foolish, quite!"

"—'Tis serving God, and shunning evil:
Might not elsedoing serve the devil?"

"But grand pay!" . . . They were lured by his call,
Agreeing to go blindfold all.

They walked, he guiding, some new track,
Doubting to find the pathway back.

In a strange hall they found them when
They were unblinded all again.

Gilded alcoves, great chandeliers,
Voluptuous paintings ranged in tiers.

In brief, a mansion large and rare,
With rows of dancers waiting there.

They tuned and played; the couples danced;
Half-naked women tripped, advanced,

With handsome partners footing fast,
Who swore strange oaths, and whirled them past.

And thus and thus the slow hours wore them:
While shone their guineas heaped before them.

Drowsy at length, in lieu of the dance
"*While Shepherds watched* . . ." they bowed by chance;

And in a moment, at a blink,
There flashed a change; ere they could think

The ball-room vanished and all its crew:
Only the well-known heath they view—

The spot of their crossing overnight,
When wheedled by the stranger's sleight.

There, east, the Christmas dawn hung red,
And dark Rainbarrow with its dead

Bulged like a supine negress' breast
Against Clyffe-Clump's faint far-off crest.

Yea; the rare mansion, gorgeous, bright,
The ladies, gallants, gone were quite.

The heaped-up guineas, too, were gone
With the gold table they were on.

"Why did not grasp we what was owed!"
Cried some, as homeward, shamed, they strode.

Now comes the marvel and the warning:
When they had dragged to church next morning,

With downcast heads and scarce a word,
They were astound at what they heard.

Praises from all came forth in showers
For how they'd cheered the midnight hours.

"We've heard you many times," friends said,
"But like *that* never have you played!"

"*Rejoice ye tenants of the earth,*
And celebrate your Saviour's birth,

"Never so thrilled the darkness through,
Or more inspired us so to do!" . . .

—The man who used to tell this tale
Was the tenor-viol, Michael Mail;

Yes; Mail the tenor, now but earth!—
I give it for what it may be worth.

ON MARTOCK MOOR

I

My deep-dyed husband trusts me,
    He feels his mastery sure,
Although I leave his evening hearth
    To walk upon the moor.

II

—I had what wealth I needed,
    And of gay gowns a score,
And yet I left my husband's house
    To muse upon the moor.

III

O how I loved a dear one
    Who, save in soul, was poor!
O how I loved the man who met
    Me nightly on the moor.

IV

I'd feather-beds and couches,
    And carpets for the floor,
Yet brighter to me was, at eves,
    The bareness of the moor.

V

There was a dogging figure,
    There was a hiss of "Whore!"
There was a flounce at Weir-water
    One night upon the moor. . . .

VI

Yet do I haunt there, knowing
    By rote each rill's low pour,
But only a fitful phantom now
    Meets me upon the moor.

THAT MOMENT

THE tragedy of that moment
    Was deeper than the sea,
When I came in that moment
    And heard you speak to me!

What I could not help seeing
    Covered life as a blot;
Yes, that which I was seeing,
    And knew that you were not!

PREMONITIONS

"THE bell went heavy to-day
At afternoon service, they say,
And a screech-owl cried in the boughs,
And a raven flew over the house,
And Betty's old clock with one hand,
That's worn out, as I understand,
And never goes now, never will,
Struck twelve when the night was dead still,
Just as when my last loss came to me. . . .
Ah! I wonder who next it will be!

THIS SUMMER AND LAST

UNHAPPY summer you,
    Who do not see
What your yester-summer saw!
Never, never will you be
     Its match to me,
   Never, never draw
   Smiles your forerunner drew,
     Know what it knew!

   Divine things done and said
     Illumined it,
Whose rays crept into corn-brown curls,
Whose breezes heard a humorous wit
     Of fancy flit.—
   Still the alert brook purls,
   Though feet that there would tread
     Elsewhere have sped.

   So, bran-new summer, you
     Will never see
All that yester-summer saw!
Never, never will you be
     In memory
   Its rival, never draw
   Smiles your forerunner drew,
     Know what it knew!

1913?

'NOTHING MATTERS MUCH"

(B. F. L.)

"NOTHING matters much," he said
Of something just befallen unduly;
He, then active, but now dead,
     Truly, truly!

He knew the letter of the law
As voiced by those of wig and gown,
Whose slightest syllogistic flaw
    He hammered down.

And often would he shape in word
That nothing needed much lamenting;
And she who sat there smiled and heard,
    Sadly assenting.

Facing the North Sea now he lies,
Toward the red altar of the East,
The Flamborough roar his psalmodies,
    The wind his priest.

And while I think of his bleak bed,
Of Time that builds, of Time that shatters,
Lost to all thought is he, who said
    "Nothing much matters."

IN THE EVENING

IN MEMORIAM FREDERICI TREVES, 1853–1923

In the evening, when the world knew he was dead,
    He lay amid the dust and hoar
Of ages; and to a spirit attending said:
      "This chalky bed?—
I surely seem to have been here before?"

"O yes. You have been here. You knew the place,
    Substanced as you, long ere your call:
And if you cared to do so you might trace
      In this gray space
Your being, and the being of men all."

Thereto said he: "Then why was I called away?
   I knew no trouble or discontent:
Why did I not prolong my ancient stay
      Herein for aye?"
The spirit shook its head. "None knows: you went.

"And though, perhaps, Time did not sign to you
   The need to go, dream-vision sees
How Aesculapius' phantom hither flew,
      With Galen's, too,
And his of Cos—plague-proof Hippocrates,

"And beckoned you forth, whose skill had read as theirs
   Maybe, had Science chanced to spell
In their day, modern modes to stem despairs
      That mankind bears! . . .
Enough. You have returned. And all is well."

Dorchester Cemetery, January, 2, 1924

THE SIX BOARDS

      SIX boards belong to me:
   I do not know where they may be;
   If growing green, or lying dry
      In a cockloft nigh.

      Some morning I shall claim them,
   And who may then possess will aim them
   To bring to me those boards I need
      With thoughtful speed.

      But though they hurry so
   To yield me mine, I shall not know
   How well my want they'll have supplied
      When notified.

Those boards and I—how much
In common we, of feel and touch
Shall share thence on,—earth's far core-quakings,
Hill-shocks, tide-shakings—

Yea, hid where none will note,
The once live tree and man, remote
From mundane hurt as if on Venus, Mars,
Or furthest stars.

BEFORE MY FRIEND ARRIVED

I SAT on the eve-lit weir,
Which gurgled in sobs and sighs;
I looked across the meadows near
To the towered church on the rise.
Overmuch cause had my look!
I pulled out pencil and book,
And drew a white chalk mound,
Outthrown on the sepulchred ground.

Why did I pencil that chalk?
It was fetched from the waiting grave,
And would return there soon,
Of one who had stilled his walk
And sought oblivion's cave.
He was to come on the morrow noon
And take a good rest in the bed so hewn.

He came, and there he is now, although
This was a wondrous while ago.
And the sun still dons a ruddy dye;
The weir still gurgles nigh;
The tower is dark on the sky,

COMPASSION

AN ODE

IN CELEBRATION OF THE CENTENARY OF THE ROYAL SOCIETY FOR THE PREVENTION OF CRUELTY TO ANIMALS

I

BACKWARD among the dusky years
    A lonesome lamp is seen arise,
Lit by a few fain pioneers
    Before incredulous eyes.—
We read the legend that it lights:
"Wherefore beholds this land of historied rights
Mild creatures, despot-doomed, bewildered, plead
Their often hunger, thirst, pangs, prisonment.
    In deep dumb gaze more eloquent
        Than tongues of widest heed?"

II

What was faint-written, read in a breath
In that year—ten times ten away—
    A larger louder conscience saith
        More sturdily to-day.—
But still those innocents are thralls
To throbless hearts, near, far, that hear no calls
Of honour towards their too-dependent frail,
And from Columbia Cape to Ind we see
    How helplessness breeds tyranny
        In power above assail.

III

Cries still are heard in secret nooks,
    Till hushed with gag or slit or thud;
And hideous dens whereon none looks
    Are sprayed with needless blood.

But here, in battlings, patient, slow,
Much has been won—more, maybe, than we know—
And on we labour hopeful.   "Ailinon!"
A mighty voice calls: "But may the good prevail!"
And "Blessed are the merciful!"
   Calls a yet mightier one.

January 22, 1924.

"WHY SHE MOVED HOUSE"

(THE DOG MUSES)

WHY she moved house, without a word,
  I cannot understand;
She'd mirrors, flowers, she'd book and bird,
  And callers in a band.

And where she is she gets no sun,
  No flowers, no book, no glass;
Of callers I am the only one,
  And I but pause and pass.

TRAGEDIAN TO TRAGEDIENNE

SHALL I leave you behind me
  When I play
In earnest what we've played in mock to-day?

Why, yes; most surely shall I
  Leave you behind
In yet full orbit, when my years unwind.

I may creep off in the night-time,
  And none know
Till comes the morning, bringing news 'tis so.

Will you then turn for a moment
  White or red,
Recall those spells of ours; things done, things said?

Aye, those adventurous doings
    And those days
Of stress, when I'd the blame and you the praise?

Still you will meet adventure—
    None knows what—
Still you will go on changing: I shall not.

Still take a call at the mummings
    Daily or nightly,
Yielding to custom, calmly, gloomily, brightly.

Last, you will flag, and finish
    Your masquings too:
Yes: end them: I not there to succour you.

THE LADY OF FOREBODINGS

"WHAT do you so regard, my lady,
    Sitting beside me here?
    Are there not days as clear
As this to come—ev'n shaped less shady?"
"O no," said she. "Come what delight
    To you, by voice or pen,
To me will fall such day, such night,
    Not, not again!"

The lamps above and round were fair,
    The tables were aglee,
    As if 'twould ever be
That we should smile and sit on there,
But yet she said, as though she must,
    "Yes: it will soon be gone,
And all its dearness leave but dust
    To muse upon."

THE BIRD-CATCHER'S BOY

"FATHER, I fear your trade:
　　Surely it's wrong!
Little birds limed and made
　　Captive life-long.

"Larks bruise and bleed in jail,
　　Trying to rise;
Every caged nightingale
　　Soon pines and dies."

"Don't be a dolt, my boy!
　　Birds must be caught;
My lot is such employ,
　　Yours to be taught.

"Soft shallow stuff as that
　　Out from your head!
Just learn your lessons pat,
　　Then off to bed."

Lightless, without a word
　　Bedwise he fares;
Groping his way is heard
　　Seek the dark stairs

Through the long passage, where
　　Hang the caged choirs:
Harp-like his fingers there
　　Sweep on the wires.

Next day, at dye of dawn,
　　Freddy was missed:
Whither the boy had gone
　　Nobody wist.

That week, the next one, whiled:
    No news of him:
Weeks up to months were piled:
    Hope dwindled dim.

Yet not a single night
    Locked they the door,
Waiting, heart-sick, to sight
    Freddy once more.

Hopping there long anon
    Still the birds hung:
Like those in Babylon
    Captive, they sung.

One wintry Christmastide
    Both lay awake;
All cheer within them dried,
    Each hour an ache.

Then some one seemed to flit
    Soft in below;
"Freddy's come!" Up they sit
    Faces aglow.

Thereat a groping touch
    Dragged on the wires
Lightly and softly—much
    As they were lyres;

"Just as it used to be
    When he came in,
Feeling in darkness the
    Stairway to win!"

Waiting a trice or two
    Yet, in the gloom,
Both parents pressed into
    Freddy's old room.

There on the empty bed
   White the moon shone,
As ever since they'd said,
   "Freddy is gone!"

That night at Durdle-Door *
   Foundered a hoy,
And the tide washed ashore
   One sailor boy.

NOTE. — * "Durdle-Door", a rock on the south coast.

November 21, 1912.

A HURRIED MEETING

IT is August moonlight in the tall plantation,
Whose elms, by aged squirrels' footsteps worn,
   Outscreen the noon, and eve, and morn.
On the facing slope a faint irradiation
   From a mansion's marble front is borne,
     Mute in its woodland wreathing.
   Up here the night-jar whirrs forlorn,
And the trees seem to withhold their softest breathing.

To the moonshade slips a woman in muslin vesture:
Her naked neck the gossamer-web besmears,
   And she sweeps it away with a hasty gesture.
Again it touches her forehead, her neck, her ears,
   Her fingers, the backs of her hands.
     She sweeps it away again
     Impatiently, and then
She takes no notice; and listens, and sighs, and stands.

The night-hawk stops. A man shows in the obscure:
     They meet, and passively kiss,
And he says: "Well, I've come quickly. About this—
     Is it really so? You are sure?"

"I am sure.   In February it will be.
That such a thing should come to me!
We should have known.   We should have left off meeting.
Love is a terrible thing: a sweet allure
      That ends in heart-outeating!"

    "But what shall we do, my Love, and how?"
    "You need not call me by that name now."
Then he more coldly: "What is your suggestion?"
"I've told my mother, and she sees a way,
Since of our marriage there can be no question.
We are crossing South—near about New Year's Day
      The event will happen there.
It is the only thing that we can dare
      To keep them unaware!"
      "Well, you can marry me."
She shook her head.   "No: that can never be.

"'Twill be brought home as hers.   She's forty-one,
When many a woman's bearing is not done,
      And well might have a son.—
We should have left off specious self-deceiving:
      I feared that such might come,
      And knowledge struck me numb.
Love is a terrible thing: witching when first begun,
      To end in grieving, grieving!"

And with one kiss again the couple parted:
Inferior clearly he; she haughty-hearted.
He watched her down the slope to return to her place,
The marble mansion of her ancient race,
And saw her brush the gossamers from her face
As she emerged from shade to the moonlight ray.

    And when she had gone away
    The night-jar seemed to imp, and say,
      "You should have taken warning:
Love is a terrible thing: sweet for a space,
      And then all mourning, mourning!"

DISCOURAGEMENT

To see the Mother, naturing Nature, stand
All racked and wrung by her unfaithful lord,
Her hopes dismayed by his defiling hand,
Her passioned plans for bloom and beauty marred.

Where she would mint a perfect mould, an ill;
Where she would don divinest hues, a stain,
Over her purposed genial hour a chill,
Upon her charm of flawless flesh a blain:

Her loves dependent on a feature's trim,
A whole life's circumstance on hap of birth,
A soul's direction on a body's whim,
Eternal Heaven upon a day of Earth,
Is frost to flower of heroism and worth,
And fosterer of visions ghast and grim.

WESTBOURNE PARK VILLAS, 1863–7.
(From an old MS.)

A LEAVING

KNOWING what it bore
I watched the rain-smitten back of the car—
(Brown-curtained, such as the old ones were)—
When it started forth for a journey afar
Into the sullen November air,
And passed the glistening laurels and round the bend.

I have seen many gayer vehicles turn that bend
In autumn, winter, and summer air,
Bearing for journeys near or afar
Many who now are not, but were,
But I don't forget that rain-smitten car,
Knowing what it bore!

SONG TO AN OLD BURDEN

THE feet have left the wormholed flooring,
    That danced to the ancient air,
    The fiddler, all-ignoring,
Sleeps by the gray-grassed 'cello player:
Shall I then foot around around around,
    As once I footed there!

The voice is heard in the room no longer
    That trilled, none sweetlier,
    To gentle stops or stronger,
Where now the dust-draped cobwebs stir:
Shall I then sing again again again,
    As once I sang with her!

The eyes that beamed out rapid brightness
    Have longtime found their close,
    The cheeks have wanned to whiteness
That used to sort with summer rose:
Shall I then joy anew anew anew,
    As once I joyed in those!

O what's to me this tedious Maying,
    What's to me this June?
    O why should viols be playing
To catch and reel and rigadoon?
Shall I sing, dance around around around,
    When phantoms call the tune!

"WHY DO I?"

WHY do I go on doing these things?
    Why not cease?
Is it that you are yet in this world of welterings
    And unease,
And that, while so, mechanic repetitions please?

When shall I leave off doing these things?—
    When I hear
You have dropped your dusty cloak and taken you wondrous
    wings
        To another sphere,
Where no pain is: Then shall I hush this dinning gear.

INDEX TO FIRST LINES

(See also Supplementary Index on page 815)

	PAGE
A baby watched a ford, whereto	278
A bird sings the selfsame song	566
A cry from the green-grained sticks of the fire	660
A day is drawing to its fall	406
A dream of mine flew over the mead	130
A forward rush by the lamp in the gloom	551
A plain tilt-bonnet on her head	372
A senseless school, where we must give	281
A shaded lamp and a waving blind	134
A spirit seems to pass	96
A stranger, I threaded sunken-hearted	560
A time there was—as one may guess	260
A very West-of-Wessex girl	542
"A woman for whom great gods might strive"	640
"A woman never agreed to it !" said my knowing friend to me	354
A woman was playing	497
"Ah, are you digging on my grave	310
Ah, child, thou art but half thy darling mother's	58
Ah—it's the skeleton of a lady's sunshade	460
"Ah, Madam ; you've indeed come back here ?	545
"Alive ?"—And I leapt in my wonder	45
Along the way	311
Aloof, as if a thing of mood and whim	303
An hour before the dawn	602
And are ye one of Hermitage	224
And he is risen ? Well, be it so	623
"And now to God the Father," he ends	391
And the Spirit said	496
"Are you awake	559
Around the house the flakes fly faster	135
As evening shaped I found me on a moor	51
As I drive to the junction of lane and highway	330
As I lay awake at night-time	177
As "legal representative"	327
As newer comers crowd the fore	133
As some bland soul, to whom a debtor says	218
As 'twere to-night, in the brief space	551

801

	PAGE
At a bygone Western country fair	474
At a lonely cross where bye-roads met	503
At last I entered a long dark gallery	482
At last I put off love	220
At last! In sight of home again	87
At midnight, in the room where he lay dead	432
At nine in the morning there passed a church	536
At the shiver of morning, a little before the false dawn	484
At Westminster, hid from the light of day	351
Attentive eyes, fantastic heed	390
"Awake! I'm off to cities far away"	573
Beeny did not quiver	329
Before we part to alien thoughts and aims	71
Beneath a knap where flown	13
Beside the Mead of Memories	240
Between the folding sea-downs	339
Between us now and here	124
Black'on frowns east on Maidon	224
Breathe not, hid Heart: cease silently	116
Bright baffling Soul, least capturable of themes	412
Brother Bulleys, let us sing	111
But don't you know it, my dear	501
"But hear. If you stay, and the child be born	396
By a wall the stranger now calls his	438
By Rome's dim relics there walks a man	373
By the Runic Stone	442
Call off your eyes from care	569
"Can anything avail	232
Change and chancefulness in my flowering youthtime	5
Child, were I king, I'd yield my royal rule	167
Christmas Eve, and twelve of the clock	439
Close up the casement, draw the blind	201
Clouds spout upon her	321
Come again to the place	291
Con the dead page as 'twere live love: press on	123
Coomb-Firtrees say that Life is a moan	280
Could I but will	603
Creak, little wood thing, creak	613
Dead shalt thou lie; and nought	166
Dear Lizbie Browne	118
"Dear! Shall I see thy face," she said	141
Dear, think not that they will forget you	594
Did he who drew her in the years ago—	218
Did they catch as it were in a Vision at shut of the day—	538
"Did you see something within the house	626
Dishevelled leaves creep down	434
Does he want you down there	423
Down comes the winter rain—	278
Down Wessex way, when spring's a-shine	228

Everybody else, then, going 389

For Life I had never cared greatly 505
For long the cruel wish I knew 126
Forty Augusts—aye, and several more—ago . . . 401
Forty springs back, I recall 587
Forty years back, when much had place . . . 279
From the slow march and muffled drum . . . 350
From Wynyard's Gap the livelong day . . . 182

Gilbert had sailed to India's shore . . . 249
Glad old house of lichened stonework . . . 635
Good Father ! . . . It was eve in middle June . . 26
Gruffly growled the wind on Toller downland broad and bare . 234

"Had he and I but met 269
Had I but lived a hundred years ago . . . 570
Had you wept ; had you but neared me with a hazed uncertain ray . 357
He bends his travel-tarnished feet . . . 162
He does not think that I haunt here nightly . . 324
He enters, and mute on the edge of a chair . . 394
He lay awake, with a harassed air . . . 344
He often would ask us 502
He paused on the sill of a door ajar . . . 344
He said : "Awake, my soul, and with the sun . . 537
He saw the portrait of his enemy, offered . . 492
He sees the world as a boisterous place . . 193
He used to pass, well-trimmed and brushed . . 629
He was leaning by a face 579
Her house looked cold from the foggy lea . . 444
Here alone by the logs in my chamber . . 195
Here are the tracks upon the sand . . . 209
Here by the baring bough 200
Here by the moorway you returned . . . 319
Here goes a man of seventy-four . . . 354
Here is the ancient floor 152
Here is your parents' dwelling with its curtained windows telling . 214
Here's one in whom Nature feared—faint at such vying— . 168
Here's the mould of a musical bird long passed from sight . 404
Here we broached the Christmas barrel . . 192
Here, where Vespasian's legions struck the sands . 78
Hereto I come to view a voiceless ghost . . 328
How could I be aware 422
How do you know that the pilgrim track . . 315
How great my grief, my joys how few . . 125
How I remember cleaning that strange picture ! . . . 584
How it came to an end ! 520
How she held up the horses' heads . . . 645
How she would have loved 323
How smartly the quarters of the hour march by . 411
How was this I did not see 420

PAGE
"I am here to time, you see 421
I am laughing by the brook with her . . . 615
"I am playing my oldest tunes," declared she . . 457
I am the family face 407
I asked the Lord : "Sire, is this true . . . 245
I bent in the deep of night 431
I bore a daughter flower-fair 188
I busied myself to find a sure 216
I can see the towers 588
I climbed to the crest 436
I come across from Mellstock while the moon wastes weaker . 326
I could hear a gown-skirt rustling . . . 441
I determined to find out whose it was— . . 407
I do not see the hills around 252
I do not wish to win your vow 577
I dream that the dearest I ever knew . . . 358
I dreamt that people from the Land of Chimes . . 508
I drew the letter out, while gleamed . . . 215
I dwelt in the shade of a city 553
I enter a daisy-and-buttercup land . . . 592
I found her out there 322
I found me in a great surging space . . . 490
I glimpsed a woman's muslined form . . . 565
"I have a Love I love too well 375
I have come to the church and chancel . . . 604
I have done all I could 499
"I have finished another year," said God . . 260
I have lived with Shades so long . . . 169
I have risen again 367
I have seen her in gowns the brightest . . . 554
I hear that maiden still 533
I hear the bell-rope sawing 653
"I hear the piano playing— 549
I heard a small sad sound 131
I idly cut a parsley stalk 415
I journeyed from my native spot 597
I knew a lady when the days 608
I know not how it may be with others . . . 456
I lay in my bed and fiddled 613
I leant upon a coppice gate 137
I lingered through the night to break of day . . 204
"I'll tell—being past all praying for— . . 397
I longed to love a full-boughed beech . . . 50
I look in her face and say 597
I look into my glass 72
I look upon the map that hangs by me— . . 302
I looked and thought, "All is too gray and cold . 279
I looked up from my writing 519
I mark the months in liveries dank and dry . . 43
I marked her ruined hues 6
I marked when the weather changed . . . 555
"I mean to build a hall anon 334

PAGE

I met a man when night was nigh 517
I met her, as we had privily planned 207
I met you first—ah, when did I first meet you ? . . 404
I missed one night, but the next I went . . . 624
I need not go 125
I never cared for Life : Life cared for me . . . 657
I opened my shutter at sunrise 371
I pace along, the rain-shafts riddling me . . . 259
I passed the lodge and avenue 128
I paused to read a letter of hers 543
I pitched my day's leazings in Crimmercrock Lane . . 227
I play my sweet old airs 299
I plodded to Fairmile Hill-top, where . . . 257
I reach the marble-streeted town 644
I read your name when you were strange to me . . 219
I rose and went to Rou'tor Town 486
I rose at night, and visited 268
I rose up as my custom is 355
I said and sang her excellence 437
I said to Love 103
I sang that song on Sunday 546
I sat at dinner in my prime 619
I sat in the Muses' Hall at the mid of the day . . 94
I sat.   It all was past 649
I saw a dead man's finer part 130
I saw a slowly-stepping train— 307
I saw him pass as the new day dawned . . . 451
I saw him steal the light away 261
I saw it—pink and white—revealed . . . 457
I say, " I'll seek her side 207
I say, " She was as good as fair !" 123
I scanned her picture, dreaming 167
I see the ghost of a perished day 609
I shall rot here, with those whom in their day . . 301
I should not have shown in the flesh . . . 481
I skimmed the strings ; I sang quite low . . . 572
I sometimes think as here I sit 538
" I stood at the back of the shop, my dear . . . 396
I think of the slope where the rabbits fed . . . 426
I thought and thought of thy crass clanging town . . 217
I thought, my Heart, that you had healed . . . 481
I thought they'd be strangers aroun' me . . . 194
I thought a fire 536
I told her when I left one day 212
I tore your letter into strips 294
I towered far, and lo ! I stood within . . . 112
I traced the Circus whose gray stones incline . . 92
I travel as a phantom now 429
I travel on by barren farms 464
I travelled to where in her life-time . . . 606
I traversed a dominion 115
I've been thinking it through, as I play here to-night, to play never again 598

PAGE

I waited at home all the while they were boating together . 607
I walked in loamy Wessex lanes, afar . . . 509
I wandered to a crude coast 31
I wanted to marry, but father said, "No— . . 228
I was not he—the man 543
I was sitting 408
I was the midmost of my world . . . 630
I wayfared at the nadir of the sun . . . 656
I went and stood outside myself . . . 469
I went by footpath and by stile . . . 476
I went by star and planet shine . . . 121
I went by the Druid stone 498
I will be faithful to thee ; aye, I will . . . 12
"I will get a new string for my fiddle . . . 436
I worked no wile to meet you . . . 574
I would that folk forgot me quite . . . 161
If but some vengeful god would call to me . . 7
"If ever I walk to church to wed . . . 387
If ever joy leave 297
If grief come early 616
If he should live a thousand years . . . 645
If hours be years the twain are blest . . . 130
If it's ever spring again 563
If seasons all were summers 199
If there were in my kalendar . . . 448
If you had known 598
In a ferny byway 30
In a heavy time I dogged myself . . . 610
In a solitude of the sea 288
In Casterbridge there stood a noble pile . . 140
In days when men found joy in war . . . 88
In five-score summers ! All new eyes . . 204
In his early days he was quite surprised . . 368
In my loamy nook 637
In the black winter morning 192
In the heart of night 563
In the middle of the night 254
In the seventies I was bearing in my breast . . 430
In the third-class seat sat the journeying boy . . 483
In the vaulted way, where the passage turned . 210
In this fair niche above the unslumbering sea . 304
In vision I roamed the flashing Firmament . . 7
In years defaced and lost 127
Indulge no more may we 211
"Instigator of the ruin— 511
Is it worth while, dear, now 128
It bends far over Yell'ham Plain . . . 138
"It is a foolish thing," said I 313
It is dark as a cave 488
It is dark in the sky 468
"It is not death that harrows us," they lipped . 309
"It is sad that so many of worth . . . 504

PAGE

It never looks like summer here 477
pleased her to step in front and sit . . . 447
was a wet wan hour in spring 148
was at the very date to which we have come . . 441
was but a little thing 435
It was not you I came to please 548
was what you bore with you, Woman . . . 612
was when 491
was your way, my dear 323
s former green is blue and thin . . . 537
s roots are bristling in the air 149

oyful lady, sing ! 548
ust at the corner of the wall 371

night, a true sister-love 167

alage's coming 416
ast Post sounded 597
ast year I called this world of gaingivings . . 82
ate on Christmas Eve, in the street alone . . 571
et me enjoy the earth no less . . . 222
et us off and search, and find a place . . . 366
ifelong to be 453
ittle fogs were gathered in every hollow . . 615
ittle head against my shoulder . . . 211
onely her fate was 617
ong have I framed weak phantasies of Thee . . 171
ooking forward to the spring . . . 314
Love, while you were away there came to me— . 337

Man, you too, aren't you, one of these rough followers of the criminal ? 359
Men know but little more than we . . . 134
More than half my life long 361
uch wonder I—here long low-laid— . . . 113
y ardours for emprize nigh lost . . . 99
My bride is not coming, alas !" says the groom . 395
My father was the whipper-in . . . 635
y spirit will not haunt the mound . . . 299
My stick !" he says, and turns in the lane . . 394

ever a careworn wife but shows . . . 132
ine drops of water bead the jessamine . . 547
o more summer for Molly and me . . . 467
o ; no 496
No—not where I shall make my own . . . 151
No smoke spreads out of this chimney-pot . . 366
o use hoping, or feeling vext . . . 479
obody says : Ah, that is the place . . . 331
obody took any notice of her as she stood on the causey kerb . 224
ot a line of her writing have I . . . 55
ot far from Mellstock—so tradition saith— . . 246

  PAG

Now I am dead you sing to me   .   .   .   5c
Now that my page is exiled,—doomed, maybe   .   .   5

O do not praise my beauty more   .   .   . 58
"O England, may God punish thee!"   .   .   . 50
O epic-famed, god-haunted Central Sea   .   .   9
"O he's suffering—maybe dying—and I not there to aid   . 36
"O, I won't lead a homely life   .   .   . 61
O it was sad enough, weak enough, mad enough—   .   .   8
O Life with the sad seared face   .   .   . 10
"O lonely workman, standing there   .   .   . 10
"O Lord, why grievest Thou?—   .   .   . 39
"O 'Melia, my dear this does everything crown! .   . 11
"O Memory, where is now my youth   .   .   . 14
"O my pretty pink frock   .   .   . 17
O my trade it is the rarest one   .   .   . 44
"O Passenger, pray list and catch   .   .   .   1
O Poet, come you haunting here   .   .   . 14
O sweet sincerity!—   .   .   . 54
O sweet To-morrow!—   .   .   . 26
"O that mastering tune!"   And up in the bed   .   . 12
O the opal and the sapphire of that wandering western sea . 39
"O Time, whence comes the Mother's moody look amid her labours . 33
"O whence do you come   .   .   . 10
Often when warring for he wist not what   .   . 62
"Old Norbert with the flat blue cap— .   .   . 51
On a morning sick as the day of doom .   .   .   2
On afternoons of drowsy calm   .   .   . 48
On Monday night I closed my door   .   .   . 40
On that gray night of mournful drone .   .   . 35
Once more the cauldron of the sun   .   .   . 54
One mile more is   .   .   . 29
One without looks in to-night   .   .   . 23
Only a man harrowing clods.   .   .   . 56
Orion swung southward aslant   .   .   . 51
Our songs went up and out the chimney .   .   . 51
Out of the past there rises a week—   .   .   . 60

Pale beech and pine so blue.   .   .   . 42

Past the hills that peep   .   .   .   5
Perhaps, long hence, when I have passed away   .   . 53
Pet was never mourned as you   .   .   .   1
Phantasmal fears   .   .   . 62
Plunging and labouring on in a tide of visions   .   . 51
"Poor wanderer," said the leaden sky .   .   . 28
Portion of this yew.   .   .   . 11

Queer are the ways of a man I know.   .   .   . 44

Rain on the windows, creaking doors   .   . 33

Rambling I looked for an old abode.   .   .   . 20
Regret not me.   .   .   . 43
Reticulations creep upon the slack stream's face .   . 36
                                                               45

PAGE

said the red-cloaked crone 494
' See, here's the workbox, little wife . . . 374
Seven millions stand 509
Shall we conceal the Case, or tell it . . . 109
She charged me with having said this and that . 343
She did not turn 592
She looked like a bird from a cloud . . . 405
She saw herself a lady 493
She sits in the tawny vapour 83
She sought the Studios, beckoning to her side . 67
She sped through the door 471
She told how they used to form for the country dances 257
She turned in the high pew, until her sight . 236
She wore a new " terra cotta " dress . . . 294
Show me again the time 430
Show thee as I thought thee 54
Silently I footed by an uphill road . . . 444
Simple was I and was young 660
Since every sound moves memories . . . 555
Since Reverend Doctors now declare . . . 146
Sing, Ballad-singer, raise a hearty tune . . 223
Sing ; how 'a would sing ! 229
Sinking down by the gate I discern the thin moon . 292
Sir John was entombed, and the crypt was closed, and she 641
Sir Nameless, once of Athelhall, declared . . 593
" Sir, will you let me give you a ride ? . . 472
Sirmio, thou dearest dear of strands . . . 166
Sitting on the bridge 428
" Sixpence a week," says the girl to her lover . 392
Slip back, Time ! 335
Snow-bound in woodland, a mournful word . . 8
" So back you have come from the town, Nan, dear ! 636
So there sat they 575
So zestfully canst thou sing ? 418
Some say the spot is banned : that the pillar Cross-and-Hand . 158
Something do I see 452
Something tapped on the pane of my room . . 436
Somewhere afield here something lies . . . 92
South of the Line, inland from far Durban . . 82
Stretching eyes west 420
Sunned in the South, and here to-day . . 117
Sweet cyder is a great thing 445

Tabitha dressed for her wedding . . . 572
" That is a quiet place— 445
That love's dull smart distressed my heart . . 343
That mirror 401
That morning when I trod the town . . . 446
That night, that night 570
That night your great guns, unawares . . . 287
That no man schemed it is my hope . . . 449
That " Sacred to the Memory " 634

PAGE

"That same first fiddler who leads the orchéstra to-night . . 462
That was once her casement 210
That whisper takes the voice 490
That with this bright believing band 59
The bars are thick with drops that show . . . 451
The chimes called midnight, just at interlune . . . 353
The church flings forth a battled shade . . . 156
The cold moon hangs to the sky by its horn . . . 215
The curtains now are drawn 540
The dark was thick. A boy he seemed at that time . . 650
The day is turning ghost 104
The dead woman lay in her first night's grave . . 515
The dubious daylight ended 185
The fiddler knows what's brewing 231
The fire advances along the log 459
The flame crept up the portrait line by line . . 440
The grey gaunt days dividing us in twain . . . 219
"The house is bleak and cold 477
The kettle descants in a cozy drone 391
"The king and the queen will stand to the child . . 455
The kiss had been given and taken 650
The mightiest moments pass uncalendared . . . 77
The moving sun-shapes on the spray . . . 543
The new-vamped Abbey shaped apace . . . 379
"The quay recedes. Hurrah! Ahead we go! . . 79
The railway bore him through 607
The rain imprinted the step's wet shine . . . 494
The rain smites more and more 438
The Roman Road runs straight and bare . . . 248
The singers are gone from the Cornmarket-place . . 226
The sparrow dips in his wheel-rut bath . . . 463
The summons was urgent: and forth I went . . 34
The sun had wheeled from Grey's to Dammer's crest . 20
The sun said, watching my watering-pot . . . 147
The sun threw down a radiant spot . . . 651
The swallows flew in the curves of an eight . . 452
The ten hours' light is abating 314
The thick lids of Night closed upon me . . . 84
The train draws forth from the station-yard . . 450
The trees are afraid to put forth buds . . . 468
The trees fret fitfully and twist 591
The two were silent in a sunless church . . . 10
"The very last time that I ever was here," he said . . 480
The wind blew words along the skies . . . 419
The years have gathered grayly 62
There are some heights in Wessex, shaped as if by a kindly hand . 300
There are three folk driving in a quaint old chaise . . 458
There dwells a mighty pair 108
There floated the sounds of church-chiming . . 403
There had been years of Passion—scorching, cold . . 557
There have been times when I well might have passed and the ending
        have come 155

PAGE

There is a house in a city street 608
There is a house with ivied walls 147
There is nobody on the road 567
" There is not much that I can do " 575
There it stands, though alas, what a little of her . . . 620
There's no more to be done, or feared, or hoped . . . 253
There trudges one to a merry-making 579
There was a glorious time 479
There was a singing woman 611
There was a stunted handpost just on the crest . . . 409
There was a time in former years 258
There was merry-making 478
There were years vague of measure 634
There were two youths of equal age 68
These flowers are I, poor Fanny Hurd 590
" These Gothic windows, how they wear me out . . 500
These market-dames, mid-aged, with lips thin-drawn . . 223
These people have not heard your name 206
These summer landscapes—clump, and copse, and croft . . 593
These umbered cliffs and gnarls of masonry . . . 93
They are not those who used to feed us . . . 135
They bear him to his resting-place 10
They came, the brothers, and took two chairs . . . 439
They crush together—a rustling heap of flesh— . . . 462
They had long met o' Zundays—her true love and she— . . 63
They hail me as one living 202
They parted—a pallid, trembling pair 638
They sing their dearest songs— 465
They sit and smoke on the esplanade 393
They stand confronting, the coffin between . . . 398
They throw in Drummer Hodge, to rest 83
Thirty-two years since, up against the sun . . . 96
This after-sunset is a sight for seeing 466
" This is a brightsome blaze you've lit, good friend, to-night ! " . 585
This is the story a man told me 568
This is the weather the cuckoo likes 533
This love puts all humanity from me 13
This statue of Liberty, busy man 424
This, then, is the grave of my son 486
Though I waste watches framing words to fetter . . 11
Three captains went to Indian wars 42
Through snowy woods and shady 370
Through vaults of pain 139
Throughout the field I find no grain 136
" Thy husband—poor, poor Heart !—is dead— . . . 61
Thy shadow, Earth, from Pole to Central Sea . . . 105
'Tis a May morning 580
To Jenny came a gentle youth 38
To my native place 542
'Twas just at gnat and cobweb-time 589
'Twas to greet the new rector I called here . . . 639
'Twere sweet to have a comrade here 576

	PAGE
Under a daisied bank	143
Up and be doing, all who have a hand	514
Upon a noon I pilgrimed through	48
Upon a poet's page I wrote	10
"War ends, and he's returning	246
Warm yellowy-green	476
We are always saying	586
We are budding, Master, budding	620
We Christmas-carolled down the Vale, and up the Vale, and round the Vale	236
We kissed at the barrier ; and passing through	205
"We moved with pensive faces	272
We never sang together	587
We passed where flag and flower	55
We sat at the window looking out	402
We sat in the room	628
We shall see her no more	199
We stand in the dusk of a pine-tree limb	605
We stood by a pond that winter day	9
We trenched, we trumpeted and drummed	15
We two kept house, the Past and I	290
We waited for the sun	499
We walked where Victor Jove was shrined awhile	93
We went a day's excursion to the stream	646
We work here together	255
"What are you still, still thinking"	369
What curious things we said	647
What did it mean that noontide, when	618
"What do I catch upon the night-wind, husband?—	630
"What do you see in that time-touched stone	358
"What do you see in Vagg Hollow	614
"What have you looked at, Moon	410
"What's the good of going to Ridgeway	489
What of the faith and fire within us	506
"What shall I bring you?	655
When a night in November	623
When battles were fought	513
When friendly summer calls again	534
When he lit the candles there	429
When I am in hell or some such place	271
When I look forth at dawning, pool	58
When I looked up at my love-birds	475
When I set out for Lyonnesse	293
When I walked roseless tracks and wide	418
When I weekly knew	413
When Lawyers strive to heal a breach	15
When mid-autumn's moan shook the night-time	101
When moiling seems at cease	541
When night was lifting	208
When of tender mind and body	97
When, soul in soul reflected	51

PAGE

"When the air was damp 440
When the cloud shut down on the morning shine . . 434
When the clouds' swoln bosoms echo back the shouts of the many and
strong 154
When the hamlet hailed a birth 138
When the Present has latched its postern behind my tremulous stay . 521
When the spring comes round, and a certain day . . 410
When the thorn on the down 216
When the walls were red 461
When the wasting embers redden the chimney-breast . . 253
When up aloft 485
When we as strangers sought 60
When wilt thou wake, O Mother, wake and see— . . 110
When you paced forth, to await maternity . . . 8
When you shall see me in the toils of Time . . . 11
When you slowly emerged from the den of Time . . 306
When your soft welcomings were said . . . 632
Whence comes Solace?—Not from seeing . . . 118
"Whenever I plunge my arm, like this . . . 315
"Whenever you dress me dolls, mammy . . . 466
Where Blackmoor was, the road that led . . . 270
Where once we danced, where once we sang . . 658
Where three roads joined it was green and fair . . 556
Where we made the fire 336
Whether to sally and see thee, girl of my dreams . . 292
While he was here with breath and bone . . . 647
While I watch the Christmas blaze . . . 252
While rain, with eve in partnership . . . 296
While the far farewell music thins and fails . . . 78
"Who's in the next room?—who? 473
Who now remembers Almack's balls 201
Who, then, was Cestius 95
Who were the twain that trod this track . . . 539
Who would have thought 633
Whose child is this they bring 244
"Why are you so bent down before your time . . 626
Why be at pains that I should know 402
Why did I sketch an upland green . . . 447
Why did you give no hint that night . . . 318
Why didn't you say you was promised, Rose-Ann? . . 233
Why do you harbour that great cheval-glass . . . 338
"Why do you sit, O pale thin man . . . 596
"Why do you stand in the dripping rye . . . 338
"Why do you weep there, O sweet lady . . . 474
Why does she turn in that shy soft way . . . 648
Why go the east road now? 595
Why go to Saint-Juliot? What's Juliot to me? . . 327
"Why, Sergeant, stray on the Ivel Way . . . 17
Why should this flower delay so long . . . 136
Will's at the dance in the Club-room below . . . 225
William Dewy, Tranter Reuben, Farmer Ledlow late at plough . 52
Winter is white on turf and tree 143

PAGE

Wintertime nighs 153
Wit, weight, or wealth there was not 582
Within a churchyard, on a recent grave 461
Woman much missed, how you call to me, call to me . . 325
Words from the mirror softly pass 638
" Would it had been the man of our wish ! " . . . 392
" Would that I'd not drawn breath here ! " some one said . . 510

Yea, as I sit here, crutched, and cricked, and bent . . 262
Yes ; since she knows not need 653
Yes ; such it was 594
Yes, we'll wed, my little fay 213
Yes ; your up-dated modern page 386
You did not come 124
You did not walk with me 320
" You look like a widower," she said 652
" You on the tower of my factory— 458
You say, O Sage, when weather-checked 578
" You see those mothers squabbling there ? " . . . 393
You turn your back, you turn your back 227
You were here at his young beginning 573
You were the sort that men forget 408
Your troubles shrink not, though I feel them less . . 9

(See Supplementary Index on following page)

SUPPLEMENTARY INDEX

	PAGE
A load of brushes and baskets and cradles and chairs	702
A plain in front of me	707
A race with the sun as he downed	762
A small blind street off East Commercial Road	676
A star looks down at me	665
A sweetness of temper unsurpassed and unforgettable	772
A yawning, sunned concave	756
Along the sculptures of the western wall	666
Any little old song	666
Are you groping your way?	692
At four this day of June I rise	678
Backward among the dusky years	791
Beckon to me to come	670
"Bury me on a Sunday"	743
Can it be so? It must be so	777
Comely and capable one of our race	747
Dear friends, stay	705
Do I know these, slack-shaped and wan	666
Do you recall	779
Down went the grand "Queen Mary"	772
Every branch big with it	697
Fair Caroline, I wonder what	780
"Father, I fear your trade"	794
"Father, you seem to have been sleeping fair?"	681
Five long clangs from the house-clock nigh	749
Forth from ages thick in mystery	686
Four climbed High-Stoy from Ivelwards	754
Freed the fret of thinking	719
From here, the quay, one looks above to mark	741
Gone are the lovers, under the bush	674
Gray prinked with rose	780
He passes down the churchyard track	744
He's journeyed through America	773
"Here's a fine bag of meat"	775
Horses in horsecloths stand in a row	753
How I was caught	754
How much shall I love her?	762

PAGE

I am forgetting Louie the buoyant 739
I chiselled her monument 671
I drip, drip here 777
I grieve and grieve for what I have done . . . 716
I kissed them in fancy as I came 702
"I'll restore this old church for our marriage" . . . 748
I lit upon the graveyard of dead creeds . . . 689
"I live here: 'Wessex' is my name" 767
I'm Smith of Stoke, aged sixty-odd 771
I rowed: the dimpled tide was at the turn . . . 683
I said: "O let me sing the praise" 765
I said to it: "We grasp not what you meant" . . . 724
I sat on the eve-lit weir 790
I saw a rose, in bloom, but sad 738
I slept across the front of the clock 752
I thought a germ of consciousness 736
I've never gone to Donaghadee 764
In my sage moments I can say 673
In the bedchamber window, near the glass . . . 751
In the evening, when the world knew he was dead . . 788
It happened once, before the duller 676
It is a storm-strid night, winds footing swift . . . 695
It is August moonlight in the tall plantation . . . 796
It's a dark drama, this, and yet I know the house, and date . 728
It will be much better when 685
Knowing what it bore 798
Known had I what I knew not 774
Lend me an ear 761
Let me believe it, dearest 674
My deep-dyed husband trusts me 785
Nature, through these generations 737
Nell and the other maids danced their best . . . 745
Never has she known 734
Nine leaves a minute 688
Not only I 749
"Nothing matters much," he said 787
O Miller Knox, whom we know well 755
"O no," said it; "her lifedoings" 720
O sad man, now a long dead man 726
"O what's the gain, my worthy Sir" 781
Of the Lady Lu there were stories told 732
Of tides that toss the souls of men 667
On Beechen Cliff self-commune I 735
On the eve of All-Souls' Day 690
On the flat road a man at last appears 608
On the frigid face of the heath-hemmed pond . . . 677
On this kindly yellow day of mild low-travelling winter sun . 684
Once at the Agricultural Show 775
Only acquaintances 709
Retty used to shake her head 757

SUPPLEMENTARY INDEX

PAGE

Said a wistful daw in Saint Peter's tower . . . 765
Said the grave Dean of Westminster . . . 769
Seven buxom women abreast, and arm in arm . . 699
Shall I leave you behind me 792
She cannot leave it alone 705
She opened the door of the West to me . . . 740
Six boards belong to me 789
So, Time 723
Summer and winter close commune . . . 680
Tear off the calendar 683
That day when oats were reaped, and wheat was ripe, and barley ripen-
    ing 739
The bark of a fox rings, sonorous and long . . 698
"The bell went heavy to-day" 786
The broad bald mooon edged up where the sea was wide . 679
The day arrives of the autumn-fair . . . 696
The feet have left the wormholed flooring . . 799
The first fire since the summer is lit . . . 778
The hills uncap their tops 695
The hounds pass here? 710
"The leaves throng thick above" . . . 709
The lovers looked over the parapet-stone . . 706
The moon has passed to the panes of the south-aisle wall . 725
The spray sprang up across the cusps of the moon . 751
The sun from the west glares back . . . 681
The sun is like an open furnace door . . . 732
The tragedy of that moment 786
The trees are undressing, and fling in many places . 673
The twigs of the birch imprint the December sky . 737
The two pale women cried 778
The weather is sharp 700
The white winter sun struck its stroke on the bridge . 756
There goes the Lady Vi. How well . . . 766
"There's a seat, I see, still empty?" . . . 670
There seemed a strangeness in the air . . . 689
"There was a frost" 701
They stood at the foot of the figure . . . 746
Thirty years after 718
This is the last; the very, very last! . . . 708
This single girl is two girls 771
Thomas Tremble new-made me 768
Though out of sight now, and as 'twere not the least of us . 773
'Tis ten years since 686
" 'Tis you, I think? Back from your week's work, Steve?" . 703
To see the Mother, naturing Nature, stand . . 798
Too late, too late! I did not know my fairness . 763
Tree-leaves labour up and down . . . 708
Unhappy summer you 787
Vain is the wish to try rhyming it, writing it! . . 753
We'd loved, we two, some while . . . 730

                                                                  PAGE
We knew it was not a valid thing   759
We sat with the banqueting-party   675
We watched the selfsame scene on that long drive   .   .   .   756
We went over Christmas rounds once more   782
"What do you so regard, my lady"   793
What's there to tell of the world   740
When a dark-eyed dawn   742
When I am riding round the ring no longer   672
When summer shone   725
When the inmate stirs, the birds retire discreetly .   .   .   665
Why do I go on doing these things?   799
"Why, I saw you with the sexton"   750
Why she moved house, without a word   792
Why want to go afar?   760
With their backs to the sea two fiddlers stand   .   .   .   752
"Your eye-light wanes with an ail of care"   687